T0304791

PRICING THE PRICELESS

While large literatures have separately examined the history of the environmental movement, government planning, and modern economics, *Pricing the Priceless* triangulates on all three. Offering the first book-length study of the history of modern environmental economics, it uncovers the unlikely role economists played in developing tools and instruments in support of environmental preservation. While economists were, and still are, seen as scientists who argue in favour of extracting natural resources, H. Spencer Banzhaf shows how some economists by the 1960s turned tools and theories used in defense of development into arguments in defense of the environment. Engaging with widely recognized names, such as John Muir, and major environmental disasters such as the Exxon Valdez oil spill, he offers a detailed examination of the environment and explains how economics came to enter the field in a new way that made it possible to be "on the side" of the environment.

H. Spencer Banzhaf is Professor of Agricultural and Resource Economics at North Carolina State University (NCSU) and the director of the Center for Environmental and Resource Economic Policy. In addition to his role at NCSU, he is a fellow at the National Bureau of Economic Research (NBER) and the Property and Environment Research Center. He also serves as an editor of the *Review of Environmental Economics and Policy* and on the advisory board of the Environmental Defense Fund. He is the author of over seventy books and articles.

HISTORICAL PERSPECTIVES ON MODERN ECONOMICS

Series Editor: Professor Harro Maas, *Walras-Pareto Centre for the History of Economic and Political Thought, University of Lausanne*

This series contains original works that challenge and enlighten historians of economics. For the profession as a whole, it promotes better understanding of the origin and content of modern economics

Other books in the series:

TILL DÜPPE, *The Closed World of East German Economists: Hopes and Defeats of a Generation (2023)*

ERWIN DEKKER, *Jan Tinbergen (1903–1994) and the Rise of Economic Expertise (2021)*

JEFF E. BIDDLE, *Progression through Regression (2020)*

ERWIN DEKKER, *The Viennese Students of Civilization (2016)*

STEVEN G. MEDEMA, ANTHONY M.C. WATERMAN (eds.), *Paul Samuelson on the History of Economic Analysis: Selected Essays (2014)*

FLORIS HEUKELOM, *Behavioral Economics: A History (2014)*

ROGER E. BACKHOUSE, MAURO BOIANOVSKY, *Transforming Modern Macroeconomics: Exploring Disequilibrium Microfoundations, 1956–2003 (2013)*

SUSAN HOWSON, *Lionel Robbins (2012)*

ROBERT VAN HORN, PHILIP MIROWSKI, THOMAS A. STAPLEFORD (eds.), *Building Chicago Economics: New Perspectives on the History of America's Most Powerful Economics Program (2012)*

ARIE ARNON, *Monetary Theory and Policy from Hume and Smith to Wicksell: Money, Credit, and the Economy (2011)*

MALCOLM RUTHERFORD, *The Institutionalist Movement in American Economics, 1918–1947: Science and Social Control (2011)*

SAMUEL HOLLANDER, *Friedrich Engels and Marxian Political Economy (2011)*

ROBERT LEONARD, *Von Neumann, Morgenstern, and the Creation of Game Theory: From Chess to Social Science, 1900–1960 (2010)*

SIMON J. COOK, *The Intellectual Foundations of Alfred Marshall's Economic Science: A Rounded Globe of Knowledge (2009)*

SAMUEL HOLLANDER, *The Economics of Karl Marx: Analysis and Applications (2008)*

DONALD MOGGRIDGE, *Harry Johnson: A Life in Economics (2008)*

FILIPPO CESARANO, *Monetary Theory and Bretton Woods: The Construction of an International Monetary Order (2006)*

TIMOTHY DAVIS, *Ricardo's Macroeconomics: Money, Trade Cycles, and Growth (2005)*

Series list continues after index

Pricing the Priceless

A History of Environmental Economics

H. SPENCER BANZHAF

North Carolina State University

Shaftesbury Road, Cambridge CB2 8EA, United Kingdom

One Liberty Plaza, 20th Floor, New York, NY 10006, USA

477 Williamstown Road, Port Melbourne, VIC 3207, Australia

314–321, 3rd Floor, Plot 3, Splendor Forum, Jasola District Centre, New Delhi – 110025, India

103 Penang Road, #05–06/07, Visioncrest Commercial, Singapore 238467

Cambridge University Press is part of Cambridge University Press & Assessment, a department of the University of Cambridge.

We share the University's mission to contribute to society through the pursuit of education, learning and research at the highest international levels of excellence.

www.cambridge.org
Information on this title: www.cambridge.org/9781108491006

DOI: 10.1017/9781108867184

First published 2024

A catalogue record for this publication is available from the British Library

A Cataloging-in-Publication data record for this book is available from the Library of Congress

ISBN 978-1-108-49100-6 Hardback
ISBN 978-1-108-79206-6 Paperback

For Neil

Contents

Figures

Acknowledgments

This book has taken longer to write than I care to admit. It really began over twenty years ago, when I was a graduate student. From that time to today, my university mentors have been a continued inspiration to me. Neil De Marchi, to whom this book is dedicated, first inspired me to a career in scholarship. Through many conversations over the years, he helped steer me on the course that led to this book. Kerry Smith has read and reread the material in this book numerous times and provided priceless feedback. Together, I could not have asked for a better combination of mentorship in history and environmental economics.

The book draws on previously published work, although substantially revised and reconfigured. Portions of Chapters 2, 3, and 6 draw on "The Environmental Turn in Natural Resource Economics: John Krutilla and 'Conservation Reconsidered'," *Journal of the History of Economic Thought* 44(1), 2019, pp. 27–46. Chapters 3 and 4 draw on "Consumer Surplus with Apology: A Historical Perspective on Non-Market Valuation and Recreation Demand," *Annual Review of Resource Economics* 2, 2010, pp. 183–207. Chapter 7 draws on "The Cold War Origins of the Value of Statistical Life (VSL)," *Journal of Economic Perspectives* 28(4), 2014, pp. 213–26. Chapter 8 draws on "Objective or Multi-objective? Two Historically Competing Visions for Benefit-Cost Analysis," *Land Economics* 85(1), 2009, pp. 1–23. Finally, Chapter 9 draws on "Constructing Markets: Environmental Economics and the Contingent Valuation Controversy," in *The Age of the Applied Economist: The Transformation of Economics since the 1970s*, ed. by R. Backhouse and B. Cherrier, *History of Political Economy* 49(s), Durham, NC: Duke University Press, 2017, pp. 213–39. I thank these publishers for permission to republish from these works.

Along the way, I received help from many people. I'm especially grateful for comments and suggestions from Roger Backhouse, Nathalie Berta,

Elodie Bertrand, Dan Bromley, Béatrice Cherrier, Charlie Cicchetti, Robert Dimand, Maxime Desmarais-Tremblay, Michael Hanemann, Bob Haveman, Reginald Hebert, Robert Ekelund, Jack Knetsch, Kerry Krutilla, Harro Maas, David Major, Steve Medema, Philip Mirowski, Theodore Porter, Malcolm Rutherford, Thomas Schelling, Tom Stapleford, Chris Weber, Roy Weintraub, and two anonymous reviewers from Cambridge University Press.

This research has been supported with generous grants from the National Science Foundation (grant #0750610), the Alliance for Market Solutions, and Georgia State University. I thank them for their support. I also thank the Property and Environment Research Center for generous hospitality over the various summers in which I worked on this manuscript. For access to their special collections, I thank the libraries and their staff at the American Heritage Center, the RAND Corporation, the Rockefeller Archive Center, SUNY Stony Brook, the US Army Corps of Engineers Office of History, and the US National Archives. For help with the manuscript and seeing it to the finish, I thank the staff at CUP, including Phil Good and Sable Gravesandy, and the series editor, Harro Maas.

Last but not least, this book was written only with the constant patience of my family, Melissa, Lizzy, and John. I'm so grateful to them.

Acronyms

Organizations and Government Agencies

BAE	Bureau of Agricultural Economics
BLM	Bureau of Land Management
BOB	Bureau of the Budget
BOR	Bureau of Reclamation
DOI	Department of the Interior
EPA	Environmental Protection Agency
FIARBC	Federal Inter-Agency River Basin Committee
FPC	Federal Power Commission
FWS	Fish and Wildlife Service
NOAA	National Oceanic and Atmospheric Administration
NPS	National Park Service
NRPB	National Resources Planning Board
NSRB	National Security Resources Board
OIRA	Office of Information and Regulatory Affairs
OMB	Office of Management and Budget
ORRRC	Outdoor Recreation Resources Review Commission
RFF	Resources for the Future
TVA	Tennessee Valley Authority
USACE	US Army Corps of Engineers
USAF	US Air Force
USDA	US Department of Agriculture
WRC	Water Resources Council

Economic and Policy Concepts

CV(M)	Contingent Valuation (Method)
NDP	Net Domestic Product

NRDA — Natural Resource Damage Assessment
OR — Operations Research
PPB — Planning-Programming-Budgeting
WTA — Willingness to Accept
WTP — Willingness to Pay

Archives

AMP — Arthur Maass Papers, Army Corps of Engineers Office of History, Fort Belvoir, VA. Box numbers given.
EDF — Environmental Defense Fund Collection, Special Collections, Stony Brook University Libraries. Record group, series group, series, and box numbers given.
MMR — Mark M. Regan Papers, American Heritage Center, Laramie, WY. Box numbers given.
NA — US National Archives, College Park, MD. Record group, entry number, and box number given.
RA — RAND Corporation archives
RAC — Rockefeller Archive Center, Sleepy Hollow, NY (location of Ford Foundation archives). Record group, series, box number, and folder number given.
RCP — Reginald C. Price Papers, American Heritage Center, Laramie, WY. Box numbers given.

Prologue

Already growing as a small community for a quarter century, the field of environmental economics announced itself to the world on January 23, 1979.

On that day, the so-called God Committee met to decide the fate of the Snail Darter, a small perch that was the first big test of the 1973 US Endangered Species Act. The fish had only just been identified in three Tennessee rivers and quickly listed as endangered. That move eventually halted construction of the Tellico Dam, which threatened the snail darter's habitat. "The case was depicted as an irrational obstruction of a valuable project, a quixotic conflict between a trivial fish of no known value and a huge hydroelectric dam." Reacting to this turn of events, the US Congress had amended the Endangered Species Act, creating the God Committee to review projects and bring "common sense" to the act's enforcement. The committee's charge was to grant an exemption from the act and allow a development project to go forward if the benefits of doing so outweighed the costs.[1]

Staff economists for the committee, which comprised environmental economists like Robert Davis (chair) and Reed Johnson, had found that the net economic benefits of the dam were dubious, at best. Without quantifying monetary values for the fish, their report essentially suggested that if one were to give any credit to that fish at all, it would tip the scales against the dam. After the summary of the staff's economic report, there was an awkward pause before the God Committee began its deliberations. Participants describe a tension in the room, with the outcome uncertain. Who would break the silence first?

Charles Schultze, head of Carter's White House Council of Economic Advisors, signals his willingness to start. A gasp comes from the environmental lobby. Uh oh. Schultze had been placed on the committee at the

[1] On the politics of the Tellico Dam, see Platter (2013). Quotation from p. 2.

insistence of pro-development Sen. Howard Baker in lieu of the White House environmental advisor. Somebody from an environmental lobby groaned, "oh no, not the economist."[2] But Schultze's comment surprised them. He said,

> It seems to me the examination of the staff report, which I thought was excellently done, would indicate that … it would be very difficult … to say there are no reasonable and prudent alternatives to the project. The interesting phenomenon is that here is a project that is 95 percent complete, and if one takes just the cost of finishing it against the benefits and does it properly, it doesn't pay, which says something about the original design![3]

Schultze then moved to deny the exemption, and the motion was approved unanimously.

On that day, if not for the first time, at least in a very public way, the environmental movement saw that economics could be on "their side" of the debate. This book is the story of how that happened – and why it was so surprising.

[2] Plater (2013 p. 287); personal conversation with F. Reed Johnson.
[3] *Proceedings* (1979 p. 26).

1

Introduction

Environmental Economics in Context

I looked around the store and there was nothing but healthy people, educated-class naturalists.... They were evidently well informed about their outdoor gear options, judging by their boots, packs, and shopping bags. Moreover, as they sat there reading Aldo Leopold's *A Sand County Almanac* ..., they radiated environment concern. Here was a community of good stewards, people who were protecting the earth and themselves. Nature used to mean wildness, abandon, Dionysian lustfulness. But here was a set of people who went out into nature carefully, who didn't want to upset the delicate balance, who studied their options, prepared and trained.

–David Brooks, *Bobos in Paradise* (2000)

Inevitably, humanity conceives its relationship with the natural environment by holding together two contradictory ideas. We delight in the wilderness as we encounter it, beautiful and sublime, and we bend it to our will, making it tame and useful.

Economists too have wrestled with that tension. Consider their efforts to quantify nature. Over the course of the twentieth century, these efforts evolved along with other efforts to measure an ever wider range of objects in monetary terms. For example, economists began to measure abstract indices like Gross Domestic Product and inflation as well as the benefits and costs of public investments. When they similarly turned to quantifying natural resources and the environment, economists realized that if they limited themselves to those resources traded in markets, which come with a readily observed market price, they would omit much of what society holds dear. On the other hand, to quantify the value of untraded nature would seem to focus attention on its tame and useful aspects, or even, in some sense, to tame it.

This book is a history of how economists have thought about this dilemma. Far from being a comprehensive review of everything that could be classified as environmental economics, it is limited in time, space, and subject matter. First, it focuses on the twentieth century, especially the postwar period up to the 1980s.[1] This limitation fits the modern environmental movement. Indeed, as Hays (1982) and other historians have emphasized, merely to use the modifier "environmental" is already to restrict oneself to the postwar period, when the environmental movement emerged through the realignment of two earlier movements, one grounded in the rational planning and conservation of material resources, the other emphasizing the beautiful and the sublime. In the United States, these earlier movements had been represented by Gifford Pinchot and John Muir, respectively, but similar tendencies existed globally. With the concept of "environmental" being new, the term "environmental economics" was not used until the late 1960s, becoming common usage around 1970.[2]

Second, though European influences certainly play a role, the book primarily focuses on applied economics in the United States. This focus is reasonable as well, as US economists had enormous influence on the profession worldwide in the postwar period. Too, they were among the first to conduct large-scale benefit–cost analyses of natural resource projects and environmental regulations. Nevertheless, this limitation leaves much ground uncovered.[3]

Finally, the book also focuses on economists' efforts to understand and quantify the value of scarce environmental resources and amenities, particularly by institutional and neoclassical economists of various strands. This emphasis thus leaves for others to explore additional aspects of the history of environmental economics, including property rights and institutional

[1] Previous books on the history of environmental economics include Kula (1998), de Steiguer (2006), and Wolloch (2017). De Steiguer (2006) considers the history of modern environmental thought through a series of episodes, many of them intersecting economics. Kula (1998) and Wolloch (2017) consider a broader sweep of the history of environmental economic thought.

[2] The term first appears in JSTOR (an electronic database of publications) in 1966, with the announcement of a new Environmental Economics Branch, in the new Natural Resources Division of the USDA's Economic Research Service. The branch was to be "concerned with recreation and natural beauty; resource conservation and multiple use; quality of the environment, including air and water pollution; and urbanization of rural areas" (*Journal of Farm Economics* 1966 p. 177).

[3] In recent years, several authors have considered international aspects to the history of environmental economics. Fourcade (2011) makes interesting comparisons between US and French approaches to valuing nature. Franco (2018), Franco and Missemer (2023), and Røpke (2004) consider the international history of a more heterodox ecological economics. Leonard (2019) considers the small-is-beautiful approach of German-British economist E. F. Schumacher.

factors; causal studies of the effects of environmental quality on human health and economic productivity; and modern heterodox approaches such as ecological economics, which tends to emphasize the biophysical constraints on economic activity.[4]

Following this introduction, Chapters 2 and 3 discuss the prewar historical context inherited by environmental economics. Rational planners like Pinchot and romantics like Muir had been at an impasse, holding incommensurable values. One wanted to tame wilderness and bend it to human wants, the other accepted it for what it was. In the following decades, economists and others trying to measure the economic value of wilderness concluded it could not be done. In their view, because economics was a study of material wealth, whereas wilderness involved decidedly immaterial and intangible experiences, economics simply could not address it. Thus, at the mid-century mark, there appeared to be little future for anything like an environment economics.

As discussed in the remainder of the book, that inauspicious beginning was overcome, slowly in the late 1950s, then swiftly in the 1960s. By about 1970, one could recognize the existence of a new and successful research program in environmental economics. This success was attended by three key moves. One was to approach the problem of valuing the environment through the lens of the consumer enjoying environmental amenities, rather than through the lens of a producer using natural resources as a material input. For example, Chapter 4 tells the story of efforts to incorporate outdoor recreation into benefit–cost analysis, by modeling individuals as consumer "purchasing" a recreation trip when selecting where to travel.

Indeed, economists during this period were considering increasingly abstract measures of consumer welfare for ever more intangible objects. Whereas, in the 1940s, they viewed outdoor recreation as too immaterial to value, by the 1970s, it was on the more material and concrete side of the spectrum of things they were attempting to value. As told in Chapter 9, economists then were extending measures of environmental values from uses such as recreation to so-called "non-uses:" values for simply enjoying the existence of wilderness.

A second move was to accompany the broader economics profession as it redefined itself as the study of tradeoffs and opportunity costs, rather

4 Franco (2018), Franco and Missemer (2023), Missemer (2017, 2018), and Røpke (2004) consider the history of ecological economics. The bio-physical approach has led to some very different suggestions for pricing the environment from the neoclassical approaches discussed in this book (e.g., Costanza, Farber, and Maxwell 1989).

than as the study of material welfare. As discussed in Chapter 5, the economist John Krutilla pointed out that there is always a tradeoff between developing a natural resource or preserving it. The price we pay for developing a resource is the opportunity cost of enjoying the natural amenities (and vice versa). As discussed in Chapter 7, Thomas Schelling and others similarly considered how to value health and mortality risks. They argued that, while, from one point of view, an individual life may be infinitely precious, from another individuals are constantly making tradeoffs between small *risks* and other goods.

A third move was to draw on the large body of thought by land economists and others on property rights. For example, Chapter 6 discusses work by Allen Kneese and others on how to use pollution fees to incentivize pollution abatement. This work drew on the American experience with designing new institutions to govern common property resources, ones that create a different set of incentives than private property. Whereas when property is held privately people have an interest in caring for it, when it is held in common their private interests push them toward over depletion. Thus, farmers may have an incentive to exhaust the fertility of a commonly owned farm or to overuse water from a commonly held source, fishers may have an incentive to overfish the seas, and so forth. Experience with these problems informed the work of applied economists in the 1960s as they began to think about the degradation of commonly held environmental resources.

Although focused on postwar pricing of the environment, the story told in this book obviously fits into a wider historical context. The remainder of this introductory chapter reviews six topics in the history of economics that serve as essential background. These include: (i) the long history of thinking about humanity's relationship to the natural environment, (ii) the increasing role given to the consumer in the twentieth century, (iii) ideas about pricing and incentives as found in the public finance literature during the period, (iv) the creation of separate schools of agricultural economics in the early twentieth century, (v) developments in postwar neoclassical economics, and (vi) the spread of economists into government and think tanks.

1.1 The Economy of Nature

Almost axiomatically, human thought about the natural environment is as old as our interaction with it. While a book on postwar environmental pricing is no place to attempt a thorough survey of such vast ground, it will be useful to establish some of the enduring questions and themes that thinkers have wrestled with.[5]

In the opening chapters of Genesis, we read that God created the world, and all that lives in it, and declared it to be good. After creating humanity, He gave to us all good things to eat and commanded us to name the animals and to till the garden. Taking this as an origin story about the history of thought about our natural environment, we find already three dialectics that remain in tension over time. First, according to this account, we are placed into a natural world that is outside us and exists independently of us. Yet in this, we are no different than the plants and animals, so if they are part of "nature" then so too are we, and presumably so too is our relationship with them. Second, insofar as we use it to meet our own need for food and other material needs, we receive nature passively, as a gift, yet we also inherit it to actively manage, as a gardener. Third, taken in isolation, this parable of a gardener and a garden invites an anthropocentric thinking that situates the worth of nature in its instrumental use. Yet it is nested within a broader story, in which the inherent worthiness of nature is antecedent to humanity.

In his posthumously published essay *On Nature* (1874), John Stuart Mill (1806–1873) made a sharp distinction between two senses of the word. He wrote,

> [I]n one sense, ["nature"] means all powers existing in either the outer or inner world and everything which takes place by means of those powers. In another sense, it means, not everything which happens, but only what takes place without the agency, or without the voluntary and intentional agency, of man. This distinction is far from exhausting the ambiguities of the word; but it is the key to most of those on which important consequences depend.[6]

Mill's first meaning of the word, as everything that takes place whether outside or inside the aegis of human agency, arguably had been more pertinent to classical political economy up to his time (DesRoches 2018a, Schabas 2005). François Quesnay (1694–1774) and the French physiocrats, for example, insisted that good political economy required discerning and complying with the laws of nature. T. Robert Malthus (1766–1834) based his political economy on two postulates about the essence of human

[5] For historical discussion of the interplay between nature and the economy, see DesRoches (2015, 2018a), Jonsson (2013), Kula (1998), Schabas (2005), Warde (2011), Wolloch (2017), and Worster (1994). For still broader discussions of the meaning of "nature" and "wilderness" in Western thought, see Coates (1998), Cronon (1995), Daston (1998), Kaufman (1972), Nash (1982), and Smout (2000).

[6] Mill (1874 pp. 8–9).

nature: that (i) food is necessary to sustain human life and (ii) the passion between the sexes is necessary and enduring. These postulates gain their significance when confronting two equally important natural laws of the external world: that the fertility of the earth can increase at most arithmetically, whereas populations, if unchecked, increase geometrically. Thus, Malthus's theory is, in its essentials, about the interplay of human nature and the natural world. Perhaps most importantly, if less famously for economists, Carl Linnaeus (1707–1778) described, in his *Œconomy of Nature* (1791), the interdependence of the earth, the vegetable kingdom, the animal kingdom, and humanity, all bound together by common interest in the functioning of the food web. In the United States, the early conservationist George Perkins Marsh (1801–1882) expressed similar views in his *Man and Nature* (1864), warning that "we can never know how wide a circle of disturbance we produce in the harmonies of nature when we throw the smallest pebble in the ocean of organic life."[7]

Mill himself preferred the second meaning for "nature," as the world external to humans, or the environment in which we find ourselves. As Margaret Schabas (2005) has argued, this move freed humans from natural law, making us the masters of our own destiny. At the same time, it set aside "nature" as something untouched by humans, in contrast to the artificial ways in which we have transformed and, indeed, conquered nature. This meaning of the term arguably had been in ascendance since at least the time of Francis Bacon, whose project was to exert human mastery over nature, to control it. But its importance grew after Mill. According to Schabas, it has reached its pinnacle in neoclassical economics. Dynamically, neoclassical economics essentially assumes that wealth can grow indefinitely, without bound. Statically, it is focused on constrained optimization, but the constraints are so highly abstracted that they lose their connection to real physical objects, objects existing at a point in space and guided by physical laws. As discussed in Chapters 2 and 6, the history of environmental economics is about humanity becoming reacquainted with its dependence on nature while also coming to terms with the effects of its actions on it.

These questions about humanity's place in nature coevolved with questions about the role of nature in economic productivity. What makes nature productive? Is it something inherent in the earth, which humans

[7] On Linnaeus and his importance for political economy, see DesRoches (2018a), Jonsson (2013), Schabas (2005), and Worster (1994). "We can never know…" (quoted in Worster 1994 p. 269). Though receiving attention in the history of ecology, Marsh is an understudied figure in the history of political economy.

receive passively, or something coaxed out of nature by human agency? Donald Worster (1994) organized his classic study of the history of ecological ideas along a continuum, anchored at one end by the Arcadian paradigm of Gilbert White (1720–1793), in which humanity must live a simple agrarian life and accommodate itself to nature, and at the other end by the imperial paradigm of Linnaeus, in which humanity must organize nature to its own ends. Excepting White's emphasis on simplicity, in the canon of political economy, Quesnay and his fellow physiocrats exemplify the former view. They contended that agriculture alone can yield the so-called net product, or a return above costs, making it the sole source of wealth for the economy. It is a free gift from Nature. Its primacy is both temporal, for it sustained humanity before agriculture, and causal, acting as a kind of prime mover putting economic circulation in motion. So humanity can best take advantage of nature's powers by complying with natural laws.[8]

Similarly, Adam Smith referred to the importance of the "spontaneous productions of the earth." For, "No equal capital puts into motion a greater quantity of productive labour than that of the farmer. Not only his labouring servants, but his labouring cattle, are productive labourers. In agriculture, too, Nature labours along with man; and though her labour costs no expense, its produce has its value, as well as that of the most expensive workmen." Yet Smith also argued that "The most important operations of agriculture seem intended, not so much to increase … as to direct the fertility of Nature towards the production of the plants most profitable to man." In other words, humanity needs to direct natural fertility, managing nature to create wealth.[9]

Of course, humanity's direction of nature only accelerated through the invention of the steam engine, the factory system, and other modern arts. Beginning in the nineteenth century, the scientific management of natural resources like forests and waterways emerged as a means of bringing social control to nature through rational planning, with the "conservation" of resources offered as a way to minimize both human and natural waste alike. By the twentieth century, such management increasingly

[8] Banzhaf (2000) discusses the role of Nature in physiocracy in more detail. While humanity is an agent in the production of wealth, the circular flow of exchange requires a first cause, which is rooted in Nature. This motion, not land *per se*, is the ultimate "free gift" from nature. Such gifts, free of human agency, are one way of distinguishing different forms of capital or assets, separating natural capital from man-made capital (e.g., Barbier 2011). DesRoches (2015, 2018a, b) offers further discussion.

[9] Quotations from *Wealth of Nations*, II.iii.3 and II.v.12.

incorporated formal economics, for example in benefit–cost analysis of dams and water projects.

These questions about the "productivity" of nature beg the additional question of what is the good to be "produced," or rather *whose* good. Linnaeus, for all his belief that humans were members of nature's œconomy, believed that "all things are made for the sake of man," though ultimately only as an intermediate good that enabled mankind to glorify God. Marsh too believed that it is a mark of civilization when man subjects the world to his control and subjects it "to his uses." As discussed in Chapter 2, this view was echoed by Gifford Pinchot (1865–1946), the great forester and pioneer of US conservation policy. Pinchot paired his intense utilitarianism with an equally intense materialism, reaching the conclusion that "there are just two things on this material earth – people and natural resources."[10]

This emphasis on human *use* may be contrasted to human *delight* (Smout 2000), not unlike Worster's distinction between the "imperial" and "Arcadian" attitudes to the world. Smout discusses how in Scotland, for example, at the same time improvers were bemoaning the barren wastelands of the Highlands and the Hebrides, Walter Scott was writing panegyrics to such places, "where the proud Queen of Wilderness hath placed … her lonely throne." In the United States, transcendentalists like Emerson and Thoreau emphasized the spiritual value of experiencing wilderness. By the close of the nineteenth century, such views found their way into American political debates about land use. As discussed in Chapter 2, John Muir (1838–1914) in particular elevated natural landscapes, ecosystems, and other species to "sparks of the Divine Soul." Challenging Pinchot's anthropocentricism, he argued that they are good in themselves and should be preserved regardless of any practical use they may or may not have for humanity.[11]

The tension between the imperial and the Arcadian, between use and delight, was a defining feature shaping conservation and preservation in the Progressive Era, leaving a lasting intellectual legacy. But as Hays (1982, 1987) discusses, when "environmentalism" emerged in the postwar era, it was as a new synthesis emerging from these opposing forces. This synthesis allowed a new economics of aesthetic consumption to bridge the gap

[10] On Linnaeus, see DesRoches (2018a) and Worster (1994). Marsh quoted in Worster (1994 p. 173). "People and natural resources" (Pinchot 1947 p. 325).

[11] On romantic views of wilderness, see, in addition to Smout (2000), Cronon (1995). For the American tradition especially, the classic reference is Roderick Nash's *Wilderness and the American Mind* (1982). On the specific case of Scotland and especially the work of the improvers, see Jonsson (2013). "Divine Soul" (Muir [1875] 1980).

between the economics of developing resources for narrowly construed instrumental uses, as advocated by Pinchot, and the anti-economics of Muir. While more radical environmental movements like deep ecology continue to decry human consumption, the postwar environmental movement succeeded by appealing to contemporary consumer movements.

1.2 The Increasing Role of the Consumer: Intangible Quality

Hays's thesis that the postwar environmental movement was, essentially, a consumer's movement, puts it in the middle of other developments that shaped economic thought in the twentieth century. It has been said that the nineteenth century was the century of production, while the twentieth century was the century of consumption. While that may be an oversimplification, certainly mass consumption and marketing were gaining ground like never before.[12] These societal changes were reflected in the writings of economists. Some responded by making the consumer central to their theories. As early as the nineteenth century, marginalist economists like W. Stanley Jevons, as well as Austrian economists like Carl Menger, emphasized the demand side of the supply-and-demand coin, relative to earlier thinkers like Smith, David Ricardo and Mill. Reversing the labor- or cost-of-production theories of value that had come before, they argued that an object's value depends on an individual's subjective evaluation of its utility.[13] Later pushing the idea further, economists like Irving Fisher argued that income is best understood as the abstract services of capital – the shelter provided by a home, the music from a piano, or the nourishment from food. From there, it was no great leap to think about the final services provided by natural capital.

The increasing social prominence of the consumer also was tied up in political questions. Some commentators deprecated various aspects of consumerism, pointing to flaws in the institutional arrangements that encouraged it, with economists such as Thorsten Veblen, J. A. Hobson, John Kenneth Galbraith, and Tibor Scitovsky representing only a few prominent examples. Others, more optimistic, saw it as a way to reverse the social

[12] On the history of consumerism in Western societies, including connections to economic theory and politics, see Cohen (2003), Sandel (1996 Ch. 7), Sassatelli (2007), Thelen (1972), and Trentmann (2016). Brooks (2000) offers a humorous, but perhaps for that all the more insightful, commentary on how Veblen's conspicuous consumption and leisure has become intertwined with environmentalism.

[13] Winch (2006) reviews the role of the consumer in English and French classical and neoclassical economics.

problems associated with industrialization and the plight of workers. Still others saw in an emphasis on consumption a way to overcome the divisions of race and religion, uniting people in their common interest of consuming. Interest in tracking how the consumer was doing led to the creation of cost-of-living indices in the early twentieth century.

Of course, the Great Depression created new challenges for individual consumers – and for the capitalist system generally. According to John Maynard Keynes and others who developed his ideas, economic instability was rooted in an anxious desire to hoard money against bad times, "multiplied" through a chain of forestalled consumption. Keynesian economists and American institutionalists alike developed theories of under-consumptionism, with public works and other types of government spending often promoted as a cure to get the economy going again.[14] As discussed by Cohen (2003), at the end of WW II, fearing a return to Depression, leaders of business, commerce, labor unions, and government collaborated to send the message that it was one's patriotic duty to spend money. An optimistic America, embracing marriage, home ownership, and children, was ready to comply. As but one apposite illustration, *Bride's* magazine assured its readers that, in buying "the dozens of things you never bought or even thought of before … you are helping to build greater security for the industries of this country …. [W]hat you buy and how you buy it is very vital in your new life—and to our whole American way of living."[15]

As an alternative to the Keynesians' political response to the Great Depression, in the 1930s other economists such as W. H. Hutt began to speak of "consumer sovereignty." This language of sovereignty was consistent with the neoclassical view of the consumer making free choices from a set of options, but it also emphasized the role of the market as a social institution that shapes society, an alternative both to the authoritarian regimes

[14] The literature on what constitutes true or bastardized Keynesianism is vast. For my purposes, it is not important what Keynes really meant, only that the social importance of aggregate spending was prominently discussed at the time. Rutherford and DesRoches (2008) and Backhouse (2017) review these ideas in the American context, looking at reactions from American institutionalists and from Samuelson, respectively.

Surveying the increasing role of the consumer in macroeconomics since Keynes, Boulding (1945) made a particularly interesting move. Emphasizing physical measures of the capital stock, rather than financial measures, he argued that when capital stocks grow too large, either consumption flows must increase, or capital must be destroyed (as in war). His focus there on the materiality of resources and the stock-flow relationship of material foreshadows his more famous analysis of the earth as "spaceship," with limited natural resource stocks and limited capacity to store wastes (Boulding 1966).

[15] Quoted in Cohen (2003 pp. 119–20).

threatening at the time and to majoritarianism. Thus, from their view, an individual consumer's choices in the market are analogous to their "votes" in collective bodies, both being ways society "decides" what to produce. Later, economists such as Charles Tiebout (1956) extended this logic even to public goods, with consumers able to "vote with their feet" for a bundle of taxes and amenities when they choose a neighborhood in which to live. As discussed in Chapter 8, whether to incorporate the environment into policy analysis using the logic of the market or the logic of civic republicanism has been an ongoing debate.[16]

This increasing focus on the consumer found its way into many consumer protection laws in the US as well as the creation of private organizations such as the Consumer's Union. Over time, it also caused political leaders and analysts to rethink the rationale for many government regulations. For example, US antitrust laws originally were designed to limit the overall economic and political power of concentrated interests, with workers, competing firms, and the self-government of local communities having as much at stake as consumers. By the 1970s, they were understood solely to protect consumers. Similarly, in the case of natural monopolies like railroads and utilities, where economists believed competition would be inefficient, economic experts would help regulate prices to protect consumers. Interestingly, rational oversight of utilities was sometimes conceptually linked to rational oversight of natural resources, as indicated, for example, by the title of the *Journal of Land and Public Utility Economics*, founded at the University of Wisconsin by Richard Ely. Environmental protection has continued to be wrapped up in the rhetoric of consumer protection.[17]

Even as it was growing in social importance, the very meaning of "consumption" was changing. For example, from the 1930s to 1960s, University of Chicago economists like Margaret Reid, Theodore Schultz, and Gary Becker were blurring the distinction between consumption and production. They introduced theories of household production, in which households are like little firms that buy goods, not so much as ends, but as material

[16] On Hutt and consumer sovereignty, see Desmarais-Tremblay (2020) and Persky (1993). For discussions of Tiebout's work, including his extension of the concept of sovereignty and his reaction to Samuelson's claim that consumers cannot, or at least do not, reveal their demand for public goods, see Weisbrod (1959) for a contemporaneous view and Fischel (2006) and Singleton (2015) for historical discussion.

[17] On the evolving role of consumer protection in the history of US anti-trust provisions, see Sandel (1996 Ch. 7) and Giocoli (2011). On railroad and public utilities regulations, see Rutherford (2000) and Giocoli (2017). Berman (2022) emphasized the rise of the economic way of thinking in government generally.

inputs, which they combine with human capital and time to produce the final services they actually enjoy. More generally, by the 1960s economists were beginning to embrace Lionel Robbins's (1935) definition of economics as the study of how people choose to use limited resources with alternative ends. This definition replaced an older one according to which economics was the study of material welfare. Robbins's definition replaced a definition based on a set of topics with one based on a way of thinking.

Together, these moves simultaneously expanded the consumer's domain to include virtually any activity – any choice of how to use time and skill, even if immaterial and unpaid – while also straying from the original meaning of the word consumption as physically using something up. For environmental economists, the so-called "consumer" thus could now be viewed as combining natural landscapes, time, and other inputs like transportation services, to "produce" a recreation experience (Chapter 1). Similarly, other economists like Zvi Griliches and Kelvin Lancaster were reimaging economic goods as bundles of underlying characteristics, characteristics which in Lancaster's view could be recombined to create new final services. This development provided a way to think about the multiple dimensions characterizing natural environments.[18]

The evolving meaning of "consumption" also had implications for quantitative measurement. For instance, during WW II, labor unions complained that the (then-named) Cost of Living Index understated inflation because it failed to control for the deteriorating quality or unavailability of goods. They pointed to inferior gasoline and tires, which increased the cost of necessary transportation. Such deteriorating quality meant the true cost of maintaining the standard of living was increasing, even if prices appeared to be steady (because of wartime price controls).

[18] Classic references include Becker (1965, 1976), Adelman and Griliches (1961), Griliches (1961), Fisher, Griliches, and Kaysen (1962) and Lancaster (1966). Banzhaf (2001, 2006) provides additional discussion of Griliches's work. Backhouse and Medema (2009a, b) discuss the history of Robbins's definition. The history of the economics of outdoor recreation is covered in Chapters 3 and 4 of this book, but Cicchetti and Smith (1970) and Cicchetti, Fisher, and Smith (1976) are notable for emphasizing the connection to Becker's model of household production.

As discussed by Bianchi and De Marchi (1997) and Bianchi (1998), if united to the theory of the entrepreneur, the household production model invites us to treat the "consumer" as an individual who delights in adventure and novelty, by recombining inputs into new commodities. This insight may provide a potential framework for linking economic models of choice to the themes of delight and exploration in conservation policy and landscape architecture. For example, when designing the landscape around Niagara Falls, Frederick Law Olmsted wanted to assure a visit was "a series of expeditions," with enjoyment coming from each individually but also from the variety (Sax 1980 pp. 23–4).

An outside scientific committee from the National Bureau of Economic Research (NBER), led by Wesley Clair Mitchell, Simon Kuznets, and Reid, reviewed this criticism. Although sympathetic, the committee concluded it knew "no satisfactory way of measuring changes in 'real prices'—that is, the prices of a given quantity of utility, usefulness, or service, such as occurs when poorer qualities are priced." But it recommended a new, less misleading name indicating its focus on prices *per se*. The renamed Consumer Price Index (CPI) came up for another NBER review in 1961, this time chaired by George Stigler. And this time, it recommended interpreting the CPI as a "true cost of living index," or the money needed to hold utility or quality of wellbeing constant. As part of that move, it recommended adjusting the CPI for quality change.[19]

This history of quality-adjusted prices mirrors the history of pricing the natural environment. In the late 1940s, at the same time one government report by external economists rejected the possibility of objectively measuring the quality of priced goods, another rejected the possibility of measuring the quality of a recreation experience and the price it would have in a hypothetical market (Chapter 3). By the 1960s, attitudes to both problems had changed. In general, economists were increasingly eager to measure qualitative features of objects using abstract measurements tied to the microeconomic theory of the consumer, including environmental quality. They used "shadow prices" to adjust market prices for quality differences or market distortions, but also to fill in missing prices for health and the environment.[20]

1.3 A. C. Pigou and the Public Finance Tradition

One way economists understand the problem of pollution is that people can use the natural environment at no cost, when in fact there is a very real one. Consequently, economists often focus on policy solutions that involve "getting the prices right." The standard history of the getting-the-prices-right approach begins with the work of A. C. Pigou (1877–1959), the Cambridge economist famous for his theory of the potential divergence

19 "We know no satisfactory way..." (Mitchell, Kuznets, and Reid 1944 p. 262). On the history of price indices in the US, see Banzhaf (2001, 2004) and Stapleford (2009, 2011a, b), with Banzhaf (2001) and Stapleford (2011a) particularly covering the issue of quality change. Stapleford (2011a) emphasizes the connection between price indices and the consumer movement.

20 Banzhaf (2005) and K. Smith and Banzhaf (2004) discuss the formal connection between quality-adjusted prices and pricing environmental quality.

between private benefits and costs (reflected in markets) and social benefits and costs. Following Francis Bator (1957, 1958), economists today would refer to these effects – especially as they relate to environmental problems – as "externalities." Externalities are famously hard to define, but, roughly speaking, they represent an unpriced effect on third parties uninvolved in an economic transaction or decision.[21]

In *The Economics of Welfare*, Pigou identified three groupings of situations where he thought there is a divergence between private and social benefits and costs. His second grouping is the one closest to what we now think of as externalities. This grouping represents a situation where

> One person A, in the course of rendering some service, for which payment is made, to a second person B, incidentally also renders services or disservices to other persons ..., of such a sort that payment cannot be exacted from the benefited parties or compensation enforced on behalf of the injured parties.

Pigou gives several examples of such services that certainly could be read as a kind of proto-environmental economics. "Uncompensated services are rendered," he says,

> when resources are invested in private parks in cities; for these, even though the public is not admitted to them, improve the air of the neighbourhood. The same thing is true—though here allowance should be made for detriment elsewhere—of resources invested in roads and tramways that increase the value of the adjoining land .... It is true, in like manner, of resources devoted to afforestation, since the beneficial effect on climate often extends beyond the borders of the estate owned by the person responsible for the forest.... It is true of resources devoted to the prevention of smoke from factory chimneys: for this smoke in large towns inflicts a heavy uncharged loss on the community, in injury to buildings and vegetables, expenses for washing clothes and cleaning rooms, expenses for the provision of extra artificial light, and in many other ways.[22]

Thus, Pigou's discussion seems like a natural source for economic thinking about environmental problems.

Pigou's importance to environmental economics cannot be denied, but a story about environmental economics developed through direct applications of Pigou's theory of externalities runs into three difficulties. First, Pigou's analysis was much wider ranging than today's theory of

[21] For background on Pigou, see Medema (2009 Ch. 3), Aslanbeigui and Oakes (2015), and Kumekawa (2017). Classic attempts to wrestle with the definition of externalities include Viner (1932), Meade (1952), Scitovsky (1954), Bator (1958), Buchanan and Stubblebine (1962), and Arrow (1969). For historical overviews of the concept, see Papandreou (1994), Lagueux (2010), Berta (2017), and Medema (2020a).

[22] Pigou (1932 pp. 183–84).

externalities, so it was not obviously focused on environmental harms. It was nestled between two other groupings of situations where, according to him, private and social cost diverge. The first grouping includes situations where productive investments might potentially be made by people who do not own the instrument of production being maintained or enhanced. A notable example is tenant farmers, who do not have the full incentive to enhance the fertility of the land they are renting. To the contrary, they have an incentive to let it depreciate rapidly in the years before their lease expires.[23]

Pigou's third grouping comprises situations, discussed earlier by Alfred Marshall, where there are increasing or decreasing returns at the industry level or even between industries, so one firm's activities effects the productivity of another's. These situations are known as "external economies" or "diseconomies." This portion of Pigou's theory was the most controversial, and Pigou steadily revised his analysis, retreating from some of the stronger versions of the argument that he had espoused earlier in his career, which involved external effects on land and resource rents. Notably from the standpoint of the history of American resource economics, much of this was a transatlantic debate, with Pigou's ideas mediated through such American economists as Allyn Young, Frank Knight, Jacob Viner, Howard Ellis, and William Fellner, as well as the British economist James Meade. Even so, in the fourth edition of *The Economics of Welfare* (1932), Pigou gave the example of the cotton industry, which when it operates on a larger scale takes on a structure of increasing specialization among firms, with some firms weaving and some spinning, some spinning fine counts and others coarse. In such cases, he argued, investment enters the industry to the point where the marginal firm is indifferent to entering, but nevertheless its entrance increases economic rents for other firms, thus creating a divergence between the private value of investment and the social net product.[24]

Pigou's work spawned a large literature sorting out the nuances of these three situations and how they inter-relate.[25] For now, it is enough to note that, because he was writing a large volume about welfare, Pigou's discussion is inherently synthetic, so not all the material found in it is uniquely his.

[23] Pigou (1932 pp. 174–83).

[24] On the controversy surrounding Pigou's analysis and his responses, see McDonald (2013), Aslanbeigui and Oakes (2015), and Medema (2020a). Salient entries in the transatlantic debate include Young (1913, 1928), Knight (1924), Viner (1932), Ellis and Fellner (1943), and Meade (1952). For Pigou's discussion in the 4th ed., see Pigou (1932 pp. 213–28).

[25] For discussion, see Lagueux (2010), McDonald (2013), Berta (2017), and Medema (2020a).

Additionally, while in retrospect it is easy to pick out the bits that resemble a proto-environmental economics, when taken as a whole, at the time Pigou's discussion did not obviously apply to environmental problems.

A second difficulty with a linear history from Pigou to modern environmental economics is that, while it is the second of Pigou's groups that today is most closely associated with the idea of "externalities," that group actually was the one most ignored in the literature until at least the late 1950s, with passing references to smoking chimneys or traffic congestion viewed as "curiosities" or, in William Baumol's words, "freakish exceptions." Even around 1970, with environmental economics on a swift assent, Kneese commented:

> Environmental pollution has existed for many years in one form or another. It is an old phenomenon, and yet in its contemporary forms it seems to have crept up on governments and even on pertinent professional disciplines .... A few economists, such as Pigou, wrote intelligently and usefully on the matter a long time ago, but generally even that subset of economists especially interested in externalities seems to have regarded them as rather freakish anomalies in an otherwise smoothly functioning exchange system. Even the examples commonly used in the literature have a whimsical air about them. We have heard much of bees and apple orchards and a current favorite example is sparks from a steam locomotive—this being some eighty years after the introduction of the spark arrester and twenty years after the abandonment of the steam locomotive.[26]

Thus, there was a large gap between the time Pigou wrote about what we would now call externalities and references to it in the literature, at least by those that took it seriously. This gap raises the possibility that other currents were at work during the period.

The third, and most surprising, difficulty with the Pigouvian origin of environmental economics is that, even as economists like Bator, James Buchanan, Meade, and Scitovsky did begin to talk more about "externalities" with environmental examples, actual specialists in environmental economics hardly referenced Pigou at all until about 1970. When environmental economists in the 1960s did invoke Pigou, it usually was in reference to welfare economics very broadly or to Pigou's discussion of our defective "telescopic faculty" (i.e., proclivity to ignore the future) and the resulting excessively rapid depletion of natural resources.[27] Even more

[26] Quotations from Baumol (1952 p. 23) and Kneese (1971a p. 2). On the treatment of externalities as freakish exceptions, see Lagueux (2010), Lane (2014), Sandmo (2015), Berta (2020), and especially Medema (2020a).

[27] For example, Krutilla (1967a). See Collard (1996) and Kula (1998 Ch. 6) for historical discussion of Pigou's views on resource depletion.

to the point, they rarely mentioned him when discussing pricing access to environmental resources, not only for "green" uses like recreation, but even for "brown" uses like depositing wastes. Though today economists might commonly refer to such prices as "Pigouvian taxes," at the time they called them "effluent charges," without connecting them to Pigou (e.g., Kneese 1964). As discussed in Chapter 6, the Pigouvian terminology didn't enter widespread circulation until the 1970s.

Of course, one possible reason economists might not have attributed their ideas to Pigou is that his ideas had become so embodied in economics, so taken for granted, that they did not warrant citation.[28] If it was merely the negative evidence of what environmental economists did *not* say, that explanation might be satisfactory. However, as discussed in Chapters 2 and 6, the arguments used by first-generation environmental economists suggest stronger links to the agricultural economics literature and institutionalist analysis of common property.

1.4 Agricultural and Natural Resource Economics

Thus, a central theme of this book is that the humble, applied work of agricultural economists played a particularly important role in the formation of environmental economics, both because of the content of their work and their outlook. With respect to outlook, as members of an applied field with a tradition of advising farmers, agricultural economists had a comfort both with normative economics and with diving into messy empirical measurement, even when economic theory could not provide guidance. With respect to content, they worked on many problems related to conservation and development of resources: city, farm, and forest as competing land uses; management of forestry as a crop; the depletion and renewal of soil fertility; development and conservation of water resources; and so forth. Additionally, they had been leaders in estimating and forecasting the demand for commodities. These experiences paved the way for agricultural economics to journey into difficult intellectual terrain such as the value of, or demand for, environmental resources.

A reasonable place to begin a history of American agricultural economics is with Richard Ely (1854–1943). Ely's *Outlines of Economics* (1893, 1908),

[28] Medema (2020a) discusses some evidence in support of the idea of an "oral tradition" as mentioned by Coase (1960). Kneese too noted that "Economists have long held that technological spillovers can be counteracted by levying taxes on the unit 'responsible' for the diseconomy and by paying a subsidy on the 'damaged' party" (1964 p. 56), indicating such a tradition does lie in the background.

was the leading textbook in American economics before WW I, and continued to sell about 14,500 copies a year between the wars, clobbering Marshall's *Principles* in the United States 18-to-1. Methodologically eclectic, Ely gave space in his work to utilitarianism, but in contrast to what he considered the excessively reductionist approach of the *laissez faire* schools of economics, he never considered it the only or indeed the most important motivation. To the contrary, Ely co-founded the American Economic Association in 1885 as an organization for social change, for the "historical and statistical study of actual conditions of economic life" which would work with the state, "whose positive assistance is one of the indispensable conditions of human progress." A leader in the progressive Social Gospel movement as well as economics, Ely advocated thinking in terms of social rather than individualistic categories, for empirical work uncovering social and historical patterns, and for labor reforms to protect workers from the centralized power of capitalists. Thus, Ely's approach laid the groundwork for the institutionalist school of economics, more self-consciously developed by his student John R. Commons and others in the next generation.[29]

Ely had had at least a passing interest in land use and natural resources from early in his career. In his studies under Karl Knies at the University of Heidelberg, he had been introduced to conservation and professional forestry management, then thriving in Germany but as yet non-existent in America. To help close this gap, in 1891 he organized a publication of the American Economic Association around these issues, bringing together Bernhard Fernow, the German-born and trained chief of the US Division of Forestry, and a young Pinchot.[30]

As his career unfolded, Ely increasingly specialized in what he called "land economics." In 1925, he founded the *Journal of Land and Public Utility Economics*. He also co-authored, with colleagues at the University of Wisconsin, two texts on the topic, *Elements of Land Economics* (Ely and Morehouse 1924) and *Land Economics* (Ely and Wehrwein 1940). At Wisconsin, he partnered with Frederick Jackson Turner, the historian famous for his "Frontier Thesis," in training many future leaders of the

[29] See Bateman (1998), Bateman and Kapstein (1999), Kaufman (2017), and Leonard (2016) for background on Ely and his role in the history of economic thought. Quotation from Bateman and Kapstein (1999 p. 253). Textbook statistics come from Rader (1966) and Backhouse, Bateman, and Medema (2010 p. 64). On American Institutional economics generally, see Rutherford (2000, 2001) and Kaufman (2017).

[30] For Ely's recollections of these early episodes, see Ely (1918a, 1938). For the AEA publications, see Fernow (1891) and Pinchot (1891), as well as Bowers (1891).

field. These students included John D. Black, Lewis C. Gray, Benjamin Hibbard, George Wehrwein, Allyn Young, and Henry Taylor, whose dissertation was on land tenure.

More even than Ely, Henry C. Taylor (1873–1969) became the doyen of the new field of agricultural economics, combining his mentor's enthusiasm for applied work in service to humanity with a knack for finding funding and institutional platforms to support the mission.[31] He was the first professor of agricultural economics in a Land Grant institution, the author of a seminal textbook in agricultural economics (Taylor 1905, 1919), and an architect of new academic institutions to support the field. After receiving his PhD in 1902, in 1909 Taylor formed a new department in the School of Agriculture, where it was positioned to tap new government funding. Outside his home institution of Wisconsin, he skillfully managed the relationships between agricultural economists and their rivals in "farm management," whose roots were in agronomy and allied fields, and which had developed at Cornell University under the leadership of Liberty Hyde Bailey and George Warren. Under Taylor's leadership, their respective societies merged to form the American Farm Economics Association (known today as the Agricultural and Applied Economics Association). This merger thus brought economics into closer contact with agronomic field work and applied farm management, creating a new synthesis. Given this background, the economists were almost compelled to further synthesize institutionalist and neoclassical approaches.[32] For, even while fully appreciating the institutional factors that guided the behavior of farmers and the markets in which they operated, they could quite naturally apply the marginalist reasoning of optimization when, say, advising farmers on how much fertilizer to apply to their fields.

In 1919, Taylor left academia to go to Washington, becoming chief of the US Department of Agriculture's (USDA's) new Office of Farm Management and Farm Economics. Again showing his ability to politically maneuver, Taylor soon expanded the office through another reorganization, forming the Bureau of Agricultural Economics (BAE). By 1929, the BAE had a budget of $6.1 million, and the USDA was spending an additional $7.2 million for its extension work and giving grants of $3.8 million to state experiment stations. At this point in time, the BAE had more social

[31] For general histories of agricultural economics including Taylor's role, see Banzhaf (2006), Fox (1987), Glover (1952), and McDean (1983); see Taylor (1922) and Taylor and Taylor (1952) for his own account. Castle et al. (1981) draw a historical connection between agricultural and natural resource economics.

[32] For more on this point, see Banzhaf (2006) and Rutherford (2011).

scientists than the rest of the federal government combined. Through their work at the BAE and academia, agricultural economists became leaders in estimating empirical demand relationships and forecasting prices, using technically advanced statistical methods.[33]

Meanwhile, agricultural economists were beginning to colonize other parts of the Federal bureaucracy. By 1937, they had taken up positions as the heads of the research or statistical divisions of the Treasury Department, the Department of Commerce, and Federal Reserve Board. Particularly important for this story, they were rapidly growing in number at the Department of Interior. As they spread through the bureaucracy, agricultural economists encountered different policy problems, including fights over water resource plans. Water in the American West has always been for fighting, and at the close of World War II the stakes were bigger than ever. By 1955, federal expenditures had risen to $[illegible] million, with some $8 billion of projects backlogged.[34]

As the monetary stakes grew, the bureaucracies managing them developed more elaborate budgetary procedures. Since the Flood Control Act of 1936, the Army Corps of Engineers was required to compute the benefits and costs of its water projects. But over time other federal agencies began to do similar work. As discussed in Chapter 3, differences in procedures and bureaucratic turf wars threatened to undermine the scientific integrity of these benefit–cost analyses of water projects. Thus, to facilitate coordination, in 1946 the Federal Inter-Agency River Basin Committee appointed a subcommittee to codify best practices for benefit–cost analysis. Not surprisingly, given their success in government, the subcommittee was dominated by agricultural economists from the USDA and Interior.[35] Its report, the so-called Green Book (FIARBC 1950, 1958), became the blueprint for benefit–cost analysis of water projects for many years.

33 Budget statistics from USDA (1929). By comparison, from 1923 to 1934 the Laura Spelman Rockefeller Memorial, followed by the Rockefeller Foundation, spent about $3 million annually in support of social science (Craver 1986). In 1939, the Cowles Commission had a budget of $28,000 and in 1945, at its peak, the Radiation Laboratory at MIT had a budget of $13 million (Mirowski 2002 Ch. 4). Statistics on the number of economists and other details of the BAE during the period, together with an interesting comparison to the NBER, can be found in Hawley (1990). The BAE's luminaries included Louis Bean, Mordecai Ezekiel, W. J. Spillman, Howard Tolley, Frederick Waugh, and others. On the statistical work of BAE economists and other background, see Banzhaf (2006), Biddle (2021), Fox (1987), Morgan (1990), and Rutherford (2011).

34 Statistics on agricultural economists as of 1937 from Ezekiel (1937). Statistics on funding for water projects from Eckstein (1958 p. 3).

35 On this history, see Porter (1995 Ch. 7).

Around this time the economists involved faced intense bureaucratic pressures to increase benefit–cost ratios, which forced them into valuing outdoor recreation. This experience with valuing recreation – which seemed so intangible and aesthetic, so outside their usual material domain – represented economists' first foray into pricing the environment. But, perhaps ironically, these early experiences were still in the context of evaluating policies to *develop* resources, with recreation as an added-on benefit, *not* in the context of preserving wilderness or natural environments.

1.5 Postwar Neoclassicism

Although agricultural and other institutional economists dominated resource planning in the first half of the twentieth century, by the late 1940s new schools of neoclassical economics were coming on the scene.[36] These schools emphasized economics as constrained optimization, consistent with Robbins's definition. One was the Chicago school, led by economists like Milton Friedman and Stigler, which brought to bear a rough-and-ready pragmatic approach to economic analysis, an emphasis on simplicity and willingness to ignore "second order" concerns such as the indirect effects of prices on quantity demanded mediated by changes in income. As discussed above, Chicago school economists pioneered the expansion of economics into many areas previously considered outside its scope. They also were one wave of economists flowing into welfare economics.[37]

At Chicago, economists like Ronald Coase and Harold Demsetz forged a neoclassical version of the study of institutions, including those that govern relationships between polluters and consumers. The famous "Coase theorem" states that when property rights are well defined and transactions costs are low, parties will negotiate to reach an economically efficient outcome. Thus, if a factory has the right to emit smoke from its chimney, a downwind neighbor could offer monetary payments or other forms of compensation to induce it to cease emitting, but this will happen only if the neighbor's value of clean air exceeds the factory's value of emitting. Contrariwise, if the downwind neighbor has the right to be free from the nuisance, the factory could negotiate with the neighbor to allow it to emit, but this will only happen if its value is higher. This "New Institutionalist" approach bore some resemblance to the older American institutionalism,

[36] For an overview of post-war neoclassical consumer theory, see Mirowski and Hands (1998) and Mirowski (2002).

[37] On the Chicago school's place in the history of welfare economics, see Banzhaf (2010a).

though with a more neoclassical bent. Still, when it first appeared it was received by many environmental economists in the context of the literature they knew.[38]

In the postwar period, another new school emerged which emphasized economics as constrained optimization, and which incorporated new methods of operations research (OR), linear programming, and game theory. Centered largely around the Cowles Commission, a research institute then based at the University of Chicago, this school viewed the economy as being at a single, general equilibrium coordinated simultaneously by all prices, an equilibrium interpreted in terms of these new mathematical tools, so that the whole economy could be viewed as a planning program. Using these tools, economists shed new light on environmental problems. Kenneth Arrow (1969), for example, drawing on his earlier work with Gérard Debreu, defined externalities by the gap between a situation where some markets are missing and an idealized complete and efficient economy. In this idealized world, gasoline for example and the pollution it causes would trade in separate markets, but in the real world only gasoline has a market. In some ways echoing the ideas of Coase, the implication seemed to be that creating markets would allow economic efficiency, but in this case the creation would have to be planned and deliberate, not emergent.

Earlier, Paul Samuelson (1954) had developed a formal model where participants make tradeoffs between "collective consumption" of a shared public good and "private consumption." Out of Samuelson's work as well as that of Richard Musgrave, a postwar theory of the two-fold nature of public goods emerged. First, public goods are non-excludable. That is, as with commonly owned resources, it can be difficult to exclude people from enjoying them. Additionally, public goods are "nonrival." Whereas one person's extraction of water from a shared aquifer, for example, is "rival" in the sense that it leaves less water for others to use, one person's enjoyment of pure public goods like healthy ecosystems need not reduce another's enjoyment. Samuelson argued that, because of non-excludability, individuals would free ride, or shirk, in the provision of public goods, so government had to play a role. But he also argued that, to provide the right level of a public good, the government would need to know *everybody's* demands or willingness to pay and, because of nonrivalry, sum them together to get

[38] Coase's original argument was published in Coase (1960). Coase's career is physically tied to the University of Chicago and for my purposes the two can be linked, but just how well Coase fits into any single neat "Chicago school" is a matter of debate. For more on Coase and the Coase theorem, see Bertrand (2015) and Medema (2014a, b, 2020b, c).

the total value. As it turned out, this was the same kind of information applied economists working on water projects were already beginning to try to find. Unfortunately, Samuelson concluded pessimistically that this task would be a challenge because, by free riding, individuals had little incentive to reveal their values in the market.[39]

1.6 The New Think Tanks: RAND and RFF

Postwar neoclassicism grew in tandem with new think tanks like the RAND Corporation. Following earlier applications of OR during WW II, at RAND this school developed its most practical contributions to planning. Officially opening in 1946 as "Project RAND," it began as a small think tank within the Douglas Aircraft Company with funding from the US Air Force. Its primary purpose was to forge an interdisciplinary, integrated study of the engineering of weapons systems and of military strategy (the acronym is for "Research ANd Development"), an integration it called "systems analysis." Because of the inherent conflict of interest in an aircraft company appraising military hardware and strategy, RAND soon became independent in 1948 with a $1m capital grant from the Ford Foundation. But it continued to rely primarily on annual support from the Defense Department and was most famous for its contributions to theories of nuclear deterrence.[40]

RAND's place in the history of postwar social sciences is well covered in the secondary literature. In the history of environmental economics, the DC-based think tank Resources for the Future (RFF) plays a larger role. Yet their histories are tied together in many ways.

First, both institutions were born out of Cold War anxieties. Like RAND's, RFF's origins can be found in wartime work, in particular at the National Resources Planning Board (NRPB) and its New Deal predecessors, who were studying the nation's strategic resources. In 1947, war-time

[39] See Cherrier and Fleury (2017) and Desmarais-Tremblay (2017a) for further discussion. Earlier Italian and Swedish traditions had suggested the possibility of market-like revelation of the demand for public goods (see Medema 2009 Ch. 4 for a summary) and more recently economists like James Buchanan and Charles Tiebout were reviving such ideas. Samuelson was impatient with both approaches (Marciano 2013; Johnson 2015; Singleton 2015).

[40] Ford's grant was initially structured as a loan but later changed. Hounshell (1997), Jardini (1996), Kaplan (1983), and B. Smith (1966) provide general background on RAND. Amadae (2003), Berman (2022 Ch. 3), Leonard (1991, 2010), Mirowski (2002), and Sent (2007) provide additional background and discuss RAND's role in shaping modern economics. J. Smith (1991) discusses the history of US think tanks more generally and their place in social sciences research.

production and natural resources boards were reorganized as the National Security Resources Board (NSRB), with the mission to make plans to mobilize natural resources in the event of war or other emergencies. In 1950, the NSRB concluded that "there is nothing more important to the future security of the United States than obtaining, now and in the future, an adequate supply of those raw materials necessary to build up our defenses and maintain our economy …." Based on the NSRB's recommendations, President Truman created the President's Materials Policy Commission, commonly known as the Paley Commission after its president William Paley, to study the problem of natural resource scarcity. The commission's staff included many future RFF staff members and other social scientists of note, including Harold Barnett, Arnold Harberger, Orris Herfindahl, Arthur Maass, and Sam Schurr, among others.[41]

Titled *Resources for Freedom*, the Paley Commission's report opened,

> The question, "Has the United States of America the material means to sustain its civilization?" would never have occurred to the men who brought this Nation into greatness as the twentieth century dawned. But with the twentieth century now half gone by, the question presses and the honest answers are not glib.
>
> The United States, once criticized as the creator of a crassly materialistic order of things, is today throwing its might into the task of keeping alive the spirit of Man and helping beat back from the frontiers of the free world everywhere the threats of force and of a new Dark Age which rise from the Communist nations. In defeating this barbarian violence moral values will count most, but they must be supported by an ample materials base.[42]

In short, the United States and its allies had to develop and conserve their natural resources in order to outlast the communist threat.

Despite Cold War fears, the Paley Commission sounded an optimistic note. Under a market system, it reasoned, resource scarcity would lead to higher resource prices. Higher prices, in turn, would incentivize conservation and recycling on the demand side and incentivize discovery of new resources or development of renewables on the supply side. But the commission argued there was a role for government too. It needed to maintain

[41] On the history of natural resources agencies in government during WW II and the early Cold War, including the Paley Commission, see Goodwin (1981), Landsberg (1987), and Lane (2014). Quotation from Goodwin (1981 p. 52). The understanding that natural resources are an important part of preparedness for war is probably as old as warfare, so it is not hard to find examples earlier than WW II. Still, it is notable that in the preface to *Foundations of National Prosperity*, Richard Ely highlighted the importance of natural resources for the "titanic war struggle" of WW I (1918b p. v).

[42] President's Materials Policy Commission (1952, I., 1).

the general economic environment, regulate natural resource monopolies, regulate resource use during critical emergencies, manage government-owned resources, and maintain foreign relations and international security.[43] Finally, the Paley Commission urged the ongoing documentation and study of natural resource scarcity, perhaps through a new independent organization.

Meanwhile, following the death of Henry Ford in 1947, the Ford Foundation had received a transformative gift from his estate. Accordingly, the foundation created a committee to set its strategic priorities for the funds, chaired by Rowan Gaither. Gaither had served as an administrator of MIT's Radiation Laboratory during the war, had helped found RAND, and had come to Ford in 1948 to request support for RAND's independence.[44] In 1949, the so-called Gaither report outlined the foundation's future priorities. Its central focus would be to "advance human welfare," as understood in a Cold War context. The report called for meeting the communist threat with a mix of hard and soft power, with support for organizations from RAND to the Fund for Adult Education, all part of a cohesive vision. It also highlighted the importance of natural resources, as a strategic necessity but also as an engine of economic growth. Thus, picking up where the Paley Commission had left off, in 1952 the Ford Foundation provided a small seed grant of $50,000 to establish RFF and for it to host a "mid-century conference" on natural resources, a prestigious event attended by President Eisenhower. Beginning in 1953, RFF became a full-fledged think tank, with Paley serving as chairman of the board and Ford providing an average of $865,000 per year for the next ten years. At that point, Ford increased its support further, until it cut its ties with a final large matching grant in 1979.[45]

With their origins thus intertwined, it was perhaps inevitable that RAND and RFF would cover similar intellectual ground. RFF's first work was

[43] President's Materials Policy Commission (1952, I., 8–12, 18).

[44] MacDonald (1956).

[45] On the Gaither report's discussion of natural resources, see Ford Foundation (1949 pp. 34–7). On Ford's plans for a program in conservation, see McDaniel to Eliot 5-27-52 RAC 21.3.4.45; McDaniel to Eliot 8-24-53 with accompanying report "A Program for Resources Conservation and Development to Strengthen the Economy," RAC Ford Fdn, Assoc. Dir. RM Hutchins, II.11; and "A long term program for Resources for the Future, Inc." RAC microfilm, Reel 0387, grant 05300041. For a transcript of the mid-century conference, including discussion questions and summary statements, see RFF (1954). Annual funding statistics come from annual reports, available through the foundation's website at www.fordfoundation.org/about/library/annual-reports/YEAR-annual-report/, where "YEAR" should be replaced by any year, 1952 to 1964. See RFF (1977) for other documentation of its first 25 years.

focused on traditional questions of natural resource scarcity in line with the Paley Commission, as well as benefit–cost analyses of public investments in water projects. By the 1950s, this benefit–cost work began to address questions about the value of unpriced services like outdoor recreation, a theme which was extended during the 1960s (Chapters 4–6). For its part, RAND's systems analysis required assessing the military worth of a weapons system within the context of a particular strategy. Accordingly, RAND too required benefit–cost analysis, as exemplified by Charles Hitch and Roland McKean's book *Economics of Defense in the Nuclear Age* (1960). But, as with resource economists working with outdoor recreation, RAND's analysts faced a number of empirical difficulties that challenged the application of their tools.

Thus, at the same time that resource economists were thinking about the value of non-market goods like recreation, RAND economists were struggling with quantifying the value of the lives of military personnel when weighing military systems (Chapter 7).[46] Meanwhile, with its Air Force patrons greatly displeased about its inability to address this problem, RAND also began to see the wisdom in diversifying away from its work on military matters. Again, it turned to the Ford Foundation for help. In 1952, the same year it first endowed RFF, Ford awarded RAND a second million-dollar grant, this time for a new initiative called "RAND-Sponsored Research," for the study of non-military topics in the public interest. Closing the circle, some of RAND's earliest non-defense projects were applications of benefit–cost analysis to water resource problems.[47]

The postwar think tanks like RAND and RFF were intended to be places that broke down disciplinary boundaries, places where economists could interact with other social scientists, engineers, decision makers, and others. Importantly for the history of environmental economics, they also provided places where economists of different schools could mix, including agricultural and resource economists with institutionalist training, Chicago school economists, and economists trained in OR and other methods associated with RAND and Cowles. For example, RFF hired agricultural economists with substantial experience in government planning agencies, people like Marion Clawson, Joseph Fisher, and Irving Fox. At the same time, it hired economists working on OR problems at RAND, people like Barnett,

[46] This episode is discussed in Jardini (1996 pp. 52–63).

[47] On RAND-sponsored research, see Ford Foundation (1953) and Jardini (1996). For examples of work on water resources, see McKean (1958), De Haven and Hirshleifer (1957), and Hirshleifer, De Haven, and Milliman (1960).

Schurr, and eventually even its president Charles Hitch. As we shall see in this story, such interactions were crucial in shaping the history of environmental economics.

RFF also serves as a microcosm of the history of environmental economics. By 1970, it was helping to develop new tools for measuring the demand for environmental amenities not traded in markets, or the price people *would* pay for them if a market existed. This research agenda was distinctly different from its initial one of studying the conservation of strategic materials. This book tells the story of that shift over the course of the twentieth century, beginning in the next chapter with the state of the American conservation movement circa 1900.

2

Conservation and Preservation

Nature, to be commanded, must be obeyed.

Francis Bacon, *Novum Organum* (1620)

2.1 Conservation and the Gospel of Efficiency

The wise stewardship of natural resources is a virtue universally acknowledged. But in western countries, a distinct science of conservation began in forestry, perhaps because forests so obviously have a long time horizon, while too their decline was so visible (Pinchot 1891; Warde 2011). By the late nineteenth century, there was already a 100-year tradition of professional forestry in Europe, especially in Germany, often traced back through the work of Georg Ludwig Hartig and Johann Heinrich Cotta and the founding of professional schools of forestry there as well as in France.[1]

But in the United States, scientific management of forests and other resources was still a new idea, imported from Europe by immigrants like Bernhard Fernow and by Americans studying abroad like Gifford Pinchot and Richard Ely. Fernow (1851–1923) was a German forester who immigrated to the United States after marrying an American. After early struggles in his new country, he became chief of the USDA's Division of Forestry in 1886. Although not the zealot that his successor Pinchot would be, Fernow steadily championed ideas of sustainability and professional management.

[1] And from there back further to the seminal forestry manual of Hanns Carl von Carlowitz, *Sylvicultura oeconomica* (1713). On the intellectual history of forestry and resource management in Europe, see Bennett (2015), Schmithüsen (2013), and Warde (2011). Crabbé (1983) and Smith (1982) touch on the connection between German forestry and the economics of conservation in the United States at the turn of the century. For contemporaneous histories and appraisals of forestry in Europe from America's first professional foresters, see Pinchot (1891) and Fernow ([1907] 1913).

He authored two influential texts, *Economics of Forestry* (1902) and *A Brief History of Forestry* ([1907], 1913), and an 1891 American Economic Association publication organized by Ely, among other essays. He founded the *Forest Quarterly* (now the *Journal of Forestry*) and served as the first dean of the College of Forestry at Cornell and then at the University of Toronto's Faculty of Forestry. In these ways, Fernow, in his modest fashion, prepared the way for the work of Pinchot to come.[2]

Gifford Pinchot (1865–1946) graduated from Yale University in 1889, still unsure of his future. The son and grandson of wealthy real estate magnates and lumbermen, he longed for an active life in the outdoors. He also felt the calling of Christian ministry. Influenced, as were Ely and the founders of the American Economic Association, by the Social Gospel movement, he combined the two callings, atoning for his family's sin of denuding the land. As Pinchot explained, "among the first duties of every man is to help in bringing the Kingdom of God on earth," which would require "the application of Christianity to the commonwealth," with "loyalty to our country, to the brotherhood of man, and to the future." And the future depended on better management of our resources, for "nothing less than the whole agricultural and commercial welfare of the country" was in the balance. With the zeal of these convictions, he pursued what Hays (1959) has called the Progressive "Gospel of Efficiency."[3]

Pinchot sought training in Europe, formally at the French *École nationale des eaux et forêts* but also informally under the tutelage of Dietrich Brandis, the German-born forester and Inspector General of Forests in British India. After this training, Pinchot's career ascended rapidly: by 1898, he was appointed chief of the young US Division of Forestry (later to become the US Forest Service under his watch), a position he held until 1910. In 1900 he founded the Society of American Foresters. In the same year, he co-founded, with his father, the Yale School of Forestry. A skilled politician, he worked closely with President Theodore Roosevelt to achieve his objectives and, eventually, would become governor of Pennsylvania.

Pinchot advocated "wise use" of natural resources, which he interpreted in utilitarian terms, extending Jeremy Bentham's maxim to emphasize the importance of maintaining resources for future generations. Following W. J. McGee, he defined conservation as "the greatest good to the greatest

[2] For additional background on Fernow, see Twight (1990) and Rodgers (1951).

[3] On Pinchot and his role in the conservation movement, see Hays (1959), Balogh (2002), and Miller (1992, 2001). On his association with the Social Gospel movement, see Naylor (2005). For his autobiographical account, see Pinchot (1947). Quotations from Pinchot (1910 pp. 95–6, 94).

number for the longest time." Note here the subtle shift from Bentham's "greatest happiness" to "greatest good." Though inherently anthropocentric, utilitarianism potentially can celebrate a great range of ends. But Pinchot combined his utilitarianism with a narrow materialism. He argued that "there are just two things on this material earth – people and natural resources."[4]

In identifying threats to the wise use of resources, Pinchot emphasized Progressive Era concerns about waste and inefficiency as well as monopoly control, which concentrated natural wealth so that it would not flow to the greatest number. He wanted to replace the chaos of laissez-faire competition and its "law of the jungle" with rational guidance from experts and the State, a "new order" "based on co-operation instead of monopoly, on sharing instead of grasping," and on "mutual helpfulness."[5]

Importantly, Pinchot did not confine his understanding of waste to excessive harvest and extraction. Although it seems ironic when looking back from today's configurations, he emphasized *developing* resources as much as conserving them. From Pinchot's perspective, development and conservation were two prongs in the progressive attack on waste. Or, rather, development was actually part of conservation. As he explained in *The Fight for Conservation* (1910):

> The first principle of conservation is development, the use of the natural resources now existing on this continent for the benefit of the people who live here now. There may be just as much waste in neglecting the development and use of certain natural resources as there is in their destruction....
>
> Conservation stands emphatically for the development and use of water-power now, without delay. It stands for the immediate construction of navigable waterways under a broad and comprehensive plan as assistants to the railroads. More coal and more iron are required to move a ton of freight by rail than by water, three to one. In every case and in every direction the conservation movement has development for its first principle, and at the very beginning of its work. The development of our natural resources and the fullest use of them for the present generation is the first duty of this generation....
>
> In the second place conservation stands for the prevention of waste. There has come gradually in this country an understanding that waste is not a good thing and

4 Pinchot (1947 p. 325). For Pinchot's formulation of the utilitarian maxim, see Pinchot (1910 p. 48, 1947 pp. 325–7); on his materialism (1947 p. 325). Mill himself had united a kind of materialism to his utilitarianism. He argued that utilities are "fixed" in material object and later extracted. Thus, for example, the violinmaker and violin teacher both are productive, because the fruits of their labor are embodied in the violin and the musician, but the violinist is not productive, because the music is ephemeral. By Pinchot's time, neoclassical economists were obliterating this distinction. See Schabas (2005 pp. 127–8).

5 Pinchot (1947 pp. 506–9).

that the attack on waste is an industrial necessity. I recall very well indeed how, in the early days of forest fires, they were considered simply and solely as acts of God, against which any opposition was hopeless and any attempt to control them not merely hopeless but childish. It was assumed that they came in the natural order of things, as inevitably as the seasons or the rising and setting of the sun. Today we understand that forest fires are wholly within the control of men. So we are coming in like manner to understand that the prevention of waste in all other directions is a simple matter of good business. The first duty of the human race is to control the earth it lives upon.[6]

Thus, Pigou, for example, displayed a common misunderstanding when he stated that "the whole movement for 'conservation' in the United States is based on [the conviction that] the State should protect the interests of the future *in some degree* against the effects of our irrational discounting and of our preference for ourselves over our descendants."[7] In saying that, he was only half right. The half he missed is that, according to the conservation movement, the state should develop resources immediately, so they are not "wasted" by remaining unused. The state also had to protect them from natural processes like forest fires, which lay waste to their productive potential.

This quest to develop more resources arguably was deeply embedded in the American psyche, with the propensity to move west and open new frontiers a central part of its national identity. In his "Frontier Thesis" ([1893] 1920), Frederick Jackson Turner had famously argued that America's civic development was intertwined with a cycle of resource development and depletion. As Americans moved west, Turner argued, taming the frontier first made them strong and self-reliant. Then, when they exhausted the soils, some pioneers remained behind to farm the land more intensively, while others moved on, continuing the cycle. Meanwhile, as settlements grew in the wake of this westward movement, Americans became more civilized as well as independent. In this way, a virtuous balance of self-reliance and civilization was inculcated into the American spirit – thanks to the process of developing, exhausting, and again developing natural resources. Thus, Turner argued America relied on wilderness, but not in its preserved state; rather, it relied on wilderness as a supply of virgin lands available for development.

Whatever the merits of Turner's thesis, it was quite influential. Consequently, when the frontier closed at the end of the nineteenth century, it provoked national angst. When he said "the whole agricultural and

6 Pinchot (1910 pp. 43–5). For additional discussion of development as conservation, see Hays (1959).

7 Pigou ([1932] 1962 p. 29, emphasis in original).

commercial welfare of the country" was at stake, Pinchot was not merely dabbling in hyperbole, the way today somebody today might complain about the price of gasoline. He was issuing a call to arms against an existential threat.

To help meet this threat, Pinchot organized a famous 1908 Conference of Governors on natural resource conservation. The conference was attended by twenty-two governors among other leaders, with addresses from Andrew Carnegie, future president William Howard Taft, and President Theodore Roosevelt. Reflecting the concerns of the times, Roosevelt remarked in his opening address that:

> Every step of the progress of mankind is marked by the discovery and use of natural resources previously unused. Without such progressive knowledge and utilization of natural resources population could not grow, nor industries multiply, nor the hidden wealth of the earth be developed for the benefit of mankind.[8]

In other words, natural resources are not just a material input with fleeting benefits vanishing as they are consumed, but an engine of lasting advancement.

While these luminaries drew national attention to conservation, behind the scenes the conference was supported by an immense research project drawing on experts throughout the federal bureaucracy, published in two massive volumes (some 1,500 pages) of technical reports about the state of the nation's resources. This research was organized around the themes of waste and development. For example, a report on water resources highlighted the fact that only one-sixth of the 215 trillion cubic feet of precipitation that falls on the United States is captured for human use in some way, while about half evaporates and one-third flows to the sea. Not all this water is wasted, the report explained, for even water flowing to the sea is useful in transit for hydropower and navigation. Nevertheless, it estimated that some 85–95percent was indeed totally wasted. To prevent this waste, dams and reservoirs should be built, to control the flow and capture it when needed, preventing floods.[9]

2.2 Conservation Economics in the Academy

Motivated by this policy relevance, academic economists too exhibited increasing interest in conservation issues. Many shared the conservation movement's Progressive vision for economic reforms and government

[8] Roosevelt (1908).

[9] Joint Committee on Conservation (1909), Van Hise (1909), McGee (1909).

control to bring about greater efficiency. Especially for agricultural economists, who were just beginning to form as a distinct field under the leadership of Ely, Henry Taylor, and George Warren, conservation was a natural place to extend their sphere of influence.

The academic literature on the economics of conservation from this period conveys three themes that are an important inheritance of postwar environmental economics. First, as with Pinchot, it started with the premise that resources existed to be developed for the benefit of humanity. It could hardly be otherwise. Political economy arguably is inherently anthropocentric. Moreover, in this time before Lionel Robbins's definition of economics as the study of choice under scarcity, it was materialistic as well, indeed *defined* as the study of material welfare. In the UK, economists like Marshall at Cambridge defined the field as the "study of men as they live and move and think in the ordinary business of life." Moreover, he said, "the steadiest motive to ordinary business work is the desire … for the material reward of work." At the London School of Economics, Edwin Cannan likewise defined economics by the study of wealth and material welfare. In the United States, Ely, in his widely used *Outlines of Economics*, defined its subject around man's "efforts to get a living." Ely interpreted "a living" more broadly than some, going well beyond bread and butter to encompass literature, art, religion, and government. Nevertheless, all these activities, he said, depend "on material things." Even if it wasn't always utilitarian, given its emphasis on the material, at this time economics *qua* economics entailed the efficient *use* of resources.[10]

This posture clearly was reflected in the literature on the economics of conservation. For example, Taylor's (1907) summary of the socially ideal use of resources was to create "the largest gross return from the sum-total of the resources of the country." Similarly, Ely, in *The Foundations of National Prosperity* (1918), wrote that

> *Conservation, narrowly and strictly considered, means preservation in unimpaired efficiency of the resources of the earth, or in a condition so nearly unimpaired as the nature of the case, or wise exhaustion, admits. And broadly considered, it means more than the word itself implies, for it naturally includes an examination of methods whereby the natural inheritance of the human race may be improved.*[11]

[10] Quotations and related statements in Marshall ([1920] 1946 p. 14), Cannan (1922 pp. 1–3), and Ely (1893 p. 3).

[11] Quotations from Taylor (1907 p. 214) and Ely (1918a p. 3, emphasis in original).

Ely's narrow and broad definitions correspond, roughly, to today's notions of "strong" and "weak" sustainability, respectively meaning the sustaining of natural capital *per se* or human welfare, though Ely spoke of "inheritance" here, not welfare.[12] Nevertheless, in preferring the broader definition, he emphasized anthropocentric ends. According to this way of thinking, if, say, the soil has been partially depleted of its fertility, but at the same time new methods of agriculture or forestry have been devised to coax from it a higher yield, then we can say we have conserved resources. Similar logic guides Ely's understanding of a word like "to waste," the antonym of to conserve. In a gentle critique of movement conservationists like Pinchot who he thought focused excessively on physical waste *per se*, Ely countered that allowing a resource to go unused actually is efficient if its economic value is less than the cost of procuring it.[13] Thus, in Ely's hands, the everyday meaning of a phrase like "conservation of resources" is transformed to mean "economically efficient use of resources."

Later, this theme would be on full display in postwar work, such as the 1952 Paley Commission. Like Pinchot, the Paley Commission rejected a definition of "conservation" that would make it synonymous with "hoarding," emphasizing that wise use and expanding supplies are integral to the concept. Like Ely, it also emphasized the role of costs, rejecting, for example, the attitude of devoting a dollar's worth of work to save a few cents worth of waste paper. To the Paley Commission, as to Ely, conservation was synonymous with "efficient management."[14]

A second theme from the turn-of-the-century literature on conservation is the fluidity among the concepts of farmland, other natural resources, and man-made capital. In the first edition of *Outlines*, Ely suggested classifying the factors of production into three categories: *Nature*, labor, and capital. Replacing "land" here with "nature" in the classical land-labor-capital formulation was meant to convey the fact that all natural forces play a role in production. Many of those forces are "free goods," with no scarcity value. "Land," then, can be thought of as those aspects of nature that are priced and exchanged, or the subset that falls under political economy. Viewed this way, land is still a very broad category, encompassing "standing space" (pure Cartesian extension), soil fertility, and subsurface

[12] For more recent discussion and a defense of each respective position, see Ayres, Van den Berrgh, and Gowdy (2001) and Solow (1993). While there are clear parallels between these literatures, they are not perfectly congruent. In particular, today's literature is more explicitly utilitarian.

[13] Ely (1918a p. 27).

[14] President's Materials Policy Commission (1952, I., 21).

minerals and fossil fuels.[15] Over the course of revising various editions of his books, Ely steadily expanded these themes. In the second edition of *Outlines* (1908), Ely et al. disputed Ricardo's notion of the "original and indestructible properties of the soil" as wrong on two counts, first because soil fertility is not indestructible and second because other properties of land not directly related to soil, such as the local climate, are. By 1940, Ely and Wehrwein organized *Land Economics* first around chapters related to land as nature and standing space respectively, then, after a discussion of property rights, around various uses of land.

In Ely's writing and others' in the period, the analogies between land and other resources ran both ways. Just as we can understand many natural resource problems by analogy to agricultural economics, so too can we understand some questions in agricultural economics by reasoning analogically to depletable natural resources. Completing the triangle, both were comparable to capital. In particular, the soil is a resource, with an efficient path of depletion and/or renewal, like depreciating capital. This theme is well represented in the work of Lewis Gray, a student of Ely and Taylor at Wisconsin, who made important contributions to the economics of exhaustible resources. In particular, Gray analyzed the optimal depletion of resources as a function of the time path of the resource's price, the rate of interest, and the cost of extracting it, factors that would be further developed in Harold Hotelling's better known contributions. Using common principles, Gray's treatment of natural resources moves back and forth between applications to farmland and to coal, comparing and contrasting the two cases. For example, whereas coal is necessarily depleted through use, farmland is renewable through cover crops and manuring, but nevertheless, farmers may deplete it depending on their habits, the property rights and other institutions in which they operate, and prevailing prices and interest rates.[16]

Picking up on these themes, Ely and Wehrwein wrote that

> "Indestructible" agricultural land is a myth, and the reason why it has been depleted and destroyed is that it must have paid the farmer to do so. It is useless to argue that it *should pay* to maintain or build up soil fertility unless the operator has a

[15] Ely (1893 pp. 99–100) and Ely and Morehouse (1924 Ch. 2). As Castle (1965) concluded, viewed this way, "there is no difference between land and natural resource economics" (pp. 542–3, n. 1).

[16] See Gray (1913, 1914). Earlier, Fernow had made a similar point about the relationship between mines and forestry (1902 pp. 167, 250). For biographic background on Gray and overviews of his work, see Kirkendall (1963) and Crabbé (1983). Missemer, Gaspard, and Ferreira da Cunha (2022) consider Hotelling's (1931) work in historical context, including Gray's earlier analysis.

long-time interest in the soil. Soil has an exhaustion value similar to a forest or a mine. The American farmer has often found it more profitable to exhaust the virgin fertility of one farm and move to a new farm than to try to maintain or restore the fertility on his old one. The farmer who claimed he was a good farmer because he had worn out four farms already was not far from the truth if judged by narrow "economic" standards.[17]

As a rule, Ely, Wehrwein, and Gray viewed those "narrow 'economic' standards" as altogether too narrow, though they admitted the logical possibility that exhaustion could be socially efficient in some situations. They blamed particular property rights structures that created poor incentives for farmers. Going further, they also argued that in some cases soil exhaustion is not even in the narrow self-interest of the farmer, but is a consequence of custom and habit, which can prolong wasteful practices long after they are in a farmer's self-interest. In these cases, the solutions were expert intervention and/or education.

Similar issues, of course, arise in forestry. Ely and Wehrwein approach this topic by first considering "the forest as a mine," before turning to questions of conservation and reforestation. As developed over the course of the twentieth century, the parallels between forestry and capital became even stronger than those between farmland and capital. For example, as noted by Bowes and Krutilla (1985), optimal rotations for a forest that yields environmental "services" while it grows and timber value when harvested look, mathematically, exactly like the optimal life cycle for a machine that yields a flow of output and has scrappage value.[18]

According to Ely, the upshot of all this is that "there is no absolute line of division between land and capital." "From the case where capital is embodied in the land and entirely assimilated to it in character, we pass by insensible gradations to fences, barns, houses, etc., which more and more assume the character of capital as distinguished from land." Consequently, it follows that the distinction between land rent and interest on capital also is ambiguous. Interestingly, Ely argued that no rent should be attributed to "free nature." While it is productive in some everyday sense, it is only useful when another productive input is applied to it, and technically we should attribute productivity there. Thus, "the wind is not productive, but windmills are." "We harness natural forces to the work of production, but we impute productivity only to the harness." The key test is whether there are property rights of some sort, some rights of control. Common

[17] Ely and Wehrwein (1940 p. 216; see also pp. 390–91).

[18] "Forest as a mine" (Ely and Wehrwein 1940 Ch. 9). See also Gaffney (1957) and Hirshleifer (1970).

property – by which he meant property with open access – can never be thought of as productive.[19]

Such discussions of natural capital are by no means unique to Ely for the time. Fernow (1902) referred to forests as "wood capital," and similarly to "soil capital" and "water capital." They were not even unique to land economics. Hotelling appears to have developed his theory of natural resource rents first through thinking about capital goods, and then applying the model to resources (Missemer et al. 2022). Similar logic was also at work in more general theories of capital and productivity, as in the work of Frank Knight and, earlier, John Bates Clark and Alvin Johnson. Indeed, it easily could be traced through the classical economists back to Adam Smith and Turgot.[20] Though not unique in the history of economic thought, nevertheless the heavy use of these analogies to capital, at this particular time and place, suggests the possibility of a continuous line of reasoning from the conservation economics at the opening of the twentieth century to the metaphor of "ecosystem services" provided by "natural capital" at its close.[21]

[19] "No absolute division" (Ely 1908 p. 350); "wind is not productive" (Ely 1908 pp. 454–6). To say the least, this discussion muddies the waters about the origins of natural capital at the turn of the century, especially if we accept DesRoches's (2018b) definition of natural capital as being (relatively) detached from human agency. On Ely's account, such capital cannot be productive. Perhaps an alternative way to define "relatively detached" would be by the extent to which it is used in conjunction with human-made inputs, or, in economics jargon, the degree of complementarity in production.

[20] For discussions of the later capital theory of Knight, Clark and others, see Henry (1995), Plassman and Tideman (2004), and Emmett (2008). Missemer (2018) discusses Johnson's contributions.

In Book II of the *Wealth of Nations*, Smith gives as one type of fixed capital, "The improvements of land, of what has profitably laid out in clearing, draining, enclosing, and manuring, and reducing it into the condition most proper for tillage and culture. An improved farm may very justly be regarded in the same light as those useful machines which facilitate and abridge labour …" (WN II.i). Too, as discussed by Jonsson (2013 Ch. 5), Smith paints a picture of the rational exhaustion of land (at least as one stage of development) so long as it is abundant relative to the value of produce (WN I.xi.3). Warde (2011) offers additional details on Enlightenment views about soil fertility, nutrient flows and circulation, and the possibility of exhaustion.

[21] On the contemporary concept of ecosystem services and natural capital, and the way they work as a metaphor, see Costanza et al. (1997), Daily (1997), Boyd and Banzhaf (2007), Barbier (2011), and Fenichel and Abbott (2014). For histories of natural capital concepts, including discussion of its role in neoclassical economics and ecological economics respectively, see Christensen (1989), Pearce (2002), Røpke (2004), Gaffney (2008), DesRoches (2015, 2018a, b), Missemer (2018), and Barbier (2021). Missemer's (2018) discussion is especially helpful for his consideration of early 20th C. capital theory, but most other narratives treat natural capital and/or ecologically based economic approaches as late 20th C. inventions, perhaps harking back to the classical era of Smith and Ricardo. The potential importance of Ely and the school of agricultural economics he helped shape is yet to be explored.

The analogies between land and other resources also provided a logical pathway for economists to begin thinking about air and water *quality*. The first step in this logic is the idea, associated with David Ricardo, that more fertile agricultural land earns a rent. The second step is Ely's insistence that the concept of "land" encompasses more than just soil. Ely had already included water availability and quantity within the concept, so including water quality and then air quality as well was not too great a leap. Thus, like differential soil quality, differential water and air quality too could earn a rent. Finally, as Ely argued against Ricardo, even soil fertility is not indestructible, so it is reasonable to consider policy analyses of changes in the quality of any of these attributes. Thus, while air, and sometimes water, were still thought of as "free goods" at the turn of the twentieth century, by embedding resource economics within a broader "land economics," Ely and others paved the way for thinking about the scarcity value of environmental resources. As discussed in Chapter 6, analogical reasoning between land, water quantity, and water and air quality, and the property rights governing them, guided the thinking of economists developing ways to price pollution in the 1960s.

A third theme in the turn-of-the-century conservation literature is the importance of property rights. Again, this is a ubiquitous theme in economics and politics: one could trace the idea through an economic canon of western Greats back through Aquinas to Aristotle.[22] Too, at a popular level, one frequently encounters such aphorisms as "everybody's property is nobody's property."[23] But in the hands of American institutionalists such as Taylor, Katharine Coman, and R. P. Teele, this commonsense notion was analyzed systematically. They brought to bear detailed historical case studies of property rights in natural resources, especially the evolving property rights over water and rangeland in the Western frontier. In the case of water rights, the combination of the arid climate and open-access property rights led to intense pressures. Analyzing this issue, Ely and Wehrwein

[22] "For that which is common to the greatest number has the least care bestowed upon it. Everyone thinks chiefly of his own, hardly at all of the common interest" (*Politics* II.iii).

[23] This quotation enters the academic literature on the economics of common property with Gordon (1954) as if a commonplace observation and is repeated by Scott (1955), Dales (1968a), Crocker (1968), Ciriacy-Wantrup and Bishop (1975) and numerous others since. I do not know the history or origins of this phrase, but it appears now to exist more in the academic literature than in common usage; many sources actually credit Gordon with it. However, it was used in political discussions at least as early as Coffin (1863 p. 168), in the context of land management in the Indian Territories. It also appeared in a debate over public ownership of natural resources in *Debates in the Massachusetts Constitutional Convention 1917–1918* (p. 568).

observed that, like land, water resources too can be distinguished between the space it occupies and the resource itself. But because groundwater flows throughout a basin, a single user can deplete the shared resource, especially in the arid West. Thus, California developed the doctrine of "correlative right," which limits users to a reasonable share.[24]

Open access was similarly problematic on rangelands. W. J. Spillman, director of the Office of Farm Management before it was reorganized under Taylor's leadership, argued that it made it "impossible for the ranchman to conserve in any way a supply of range feed for his animals, even for the near future; for any conservation he may practice is as likely to benefit his competitor as himself." Creating private property by parceling out lands among ranchmen would be required to incentivize conservation.[25]

In thinking about these kinds of property rights arrangements, economists again leaned on analogical reasoning between soil and other resources, and the property rights governing each. With respect to soil, Ely and Wehrwein pointed to tenant farming, which they said misaligns a tenant farmer's incentives for soil conservation. They described a farming cycle in which tenants who were "climbers" up the rungs of agricultural ownership depleted land along the way, in an effort to raise cash to buy their own farm, then, having made it, retired and turned their farm over to tenants. They also pointed to the homestead laws, which made it easy to treat agricultural land as a disposable commodity, cheapened by oversupply and readily replaced by the next government-supplied land.[26]

Starting with his masters and PhD theses, Henry Taylor made the study of tenure systems his particular specialty, with extensive travel abroad, especially in England, both to unearth archival sources and to observe current practices in the field. Taylor agreed with the conventional view that tenant farming led to more rapid depletion of soils than freeholding. However, two strategies could ameliorate these effects. One was longer-term contracting, such as the twenty-one-year lease championed long ago

[24] See, specifically, Teele (1904, 1926), Taylor (1907), Coman [1911] (2011). Taylor and Taylor (1952 Ch. 27) suggest that Teele's work was influenced by an unpublished 1904 manuscript of Ely's, titled "Economics of Irrigation," commissioned by Teele's USDA office. They reproduce extensive excerpts from this manuscript. On correlative right, see also Ciriacy-Wantrup (1956). Franco and Missemer (2023 Ch. 10) also note the importance of institutional analysis in the history of environmental economics, highlighting the importance of Wehrwein.

[25] Quote from Spillman (1918 p. 71). But see also Anderson and Hill (2004) for a historical discussion of how the evolution of property rights among cattlemen helped to overcome such problems.

[26] Ely and Wehrwein (1940 pp. 216–7).

by Arthur Young. Another, and in Taylor's view more effective, strategy was more complete contracting, introducing clauses to pay tenants for assets left behind when the lease expires (Taylor 1919).[27]

These lessons about tenant farming could be used to understand the wasteful use of natural resources. Highlighting the ubiquity of such analogies, President Theodore Roosevelt at the 1908 Governors' Conference stated, "Every one knows that a really good farmer leaves his farm more valuable at the end of his life than it was when he first took hold of it. So with the waterways. So with the forests." But stewardship of the land is grounded in the incentives of property rights. "We should exercise foresight now," he said,

> as the ordinarily prudent man exercises foresight in conserving and wisely using the property which contains the assurance of well-being for himself and his children. We want to see a man own his farm rather than rent it, because we want to see it an object to him to transfer it in better order to his children. We want to see him exercise forethought for the next generation. We need to exercise it in some fashion ourselves as a nation for the next generation.

In this way, care of resources can be understood by analogy to questions of land tenure. Indeed, Roosevelt explicitly linked homesteading, with its privatization of public lands for farming, to forest policy on public lands. But for Roosevelt and Pinchot, as for Ely and Taylor, the analogy did not imply forests and waterways should be privately owned. To the contrary, in their view, as a farmer needs to take private ownership of his land, the nation needed to take public ownership of its public resources.

The logical connection between land tenure for farmers and open access to environmental resources would be developed throughout the twentieth century. Perhaps most famously, at the peak of the environmental

[27] For example, Taylor quotes approvingly from a Yorkshire survey, which recorded the following system:

> The landlord covenants to allow the tenant, on quitting his farm, what two indifferent persons shall deem reasonable, for what is generally called full tillage and half tillage, being for the rent and assessment of his fallow ground, the plowing and the management of the same; the lime, manure, or other tillage laid thereon; the seed sown thereupon; the sowing and harrowing thereof; also for the sowing, harrowing, manuring, and managing any turnip fallow which he may leave unsown; also for any clover seed sown on the premises; and harrowing and rolling in of such seed; and for every other matter and thing done and performed in a husbandry-like manner on such fallow lands, in the two last years of the term; also for the last year's manure left upon the premises; and for any manure and tillage laid upon the grass land. (1919 p. 335)

See also Ely and Wehrwein (1940 Ch. 7). Given these contractual possibilities, Gray and others at the BEA's Division of Land Economics held out a more optimistic view of the potential efficiency of tenant farming than Ely (e.g., Gray et al. 1924).

movement, Garrett Hardin's "Tragedy of the Commons" invited readers to "picture a pasture open to all. It is to be expected that each herdsman will try to keep as many cattle as possible on the commons." The result is ruin for each herdsman, as overgrazing destroys the grass. In the same way, Hardin said, the earth and its ecosystem are a common resource supporting all humanity, a commons being depleted.[28]

Over a decade earlier, Scott Gordon (1954) and Anthony Scott (1955) also had drawn attention to common property problems. Both recognized the wisdom in the popular aphorism that "everybody's property is nobody's property," but demonstrated formally how, under open access, competition would deplete the value of resources. Though their focus was on overfishing, they too made the connection to common tenure in land. Gordon, especially, complemented his formal model with a discursive discussion of hunting and trapping as well as agriculture, and the endogenous formation of alternative forms of property rights when resources become scarcer.

Taken together, these earlier themes in conservation economics have three important implications for how the postwar generations who inherited them would fashion a new environmental economics, as explored in the remainder of this book. First, they created a ready roadmap for agricultural economists to expand their work, not only from questions of farm policy to other natural resource questions, but later to dams and other capital projects involved in water resource development. Agricultural economists had long been applying benefit–cost analysis in a rough-and-ready way in the management of individual farms and in agricultural policy. In making those calculations for water projects, they also could draw on a history of relating economic development to resource exploitation as well as the inter-temporal dynamics of services provided by capital, whether natural or man-made, and their rates of depreciation.

Second, though in retrospect the concept of Pigouvian externalities certainly is one possible lens through which to view environmental problems, American economists working in the 1950s and 1960s had other lenses at hand. With a rich homegrown literature on resource problems, the mystery of the absence of Pigouvian ideas during this period, discussed in Chapter 1, now comes into better focus. To better understand the relationship between these viewpoints, it is useful to employ Pigou's own three-part categorization of situations where private and social interests diverge. The first, recall, comprises situations where productive investments in a resource might be made by people who do not own it, as with tenant

[28] Hardin (1968), with quotation from p. 1244.

farmers. The second is the one refined by later writers into what essentially is the modern theory of externalities, where actions affect third parties not party to a contract. The third category comprises situations where increasing returns to scale extend beyond a firm's boundaries, with one firm's economic activity improving the efficiency of others, perhaps through learning by doing or by facilitating finer degrees of specialization.

It was actually the first and third categories that were most relevant to first-generation environmental economists working at mid-century. Like the conservation economists before them, they were engaged with problems of *developing* resources for use, when the services provided by environmental amenities first came to their attention. The whole idea that developing and conserving natural resources is a matter of public interest, irreducible to the sum of private values, almost inevitably involves logic resembling economies of scale (Pigou's third category). But American economists had other sources for thinking through these issues besides Pigou. Take as an example Turner's Frontier Thesis, for here is a story of external economies projected onto a John Ford-sized screen: the development of resources spilling over to all civilizing and democratizing forces. Such a theme played out in many smaller ways as well. For example, west of the 100th meridian, farming requires irrigation, but even the irrigation ditches dug by early settlers required cooperative construction and management, as a ditch scaled to serve only a single farm would lose all its water to evaporation. Thus, economies of scale at the industry level were present (Teele 1904, 1926; Coman 1911). As recently argued by Leonard and Libecap (2019), the evolution of water rights in the American West from riparian rights to prior appropriation was one organic response to this problem. As discussed in Chapter 3, later the development of ever larger regions, further from water sources, seemingly justified federal support for massive water projects.

When resource economists turned next to studying pollution, they understood the problem in the context of pricing access to common-property resources. This context relates the problem to Pigou's first category, but, again, American economists had other sources for thinking about such issues. Indeed, Pigou himself relied on Taylor's history of English property rights in his own discussions of land tenure.[29] (The importance of these connections to the earlier American literature, and the absence of Pigou, will be revisited in Chapter 6.)

A third and final implication of this earlier history is that economists' long focus on developing resources to increase material welfare, while later

[29] Pigou ([1932] 1962 p. 178).

providing the *occasion* for thinking about the amenities of undeveloped landscapes, also constrained their ability to do so. What did environmental amenities from preserved landscapes have to do with development? Or with material wealth? It seems a clash was inevitable with forces preferring the preservation of wilderness to its development.

2.3 The Great Schism: Conservation versus Preservation

Pinchot and other conservationists fit well into a category that Worster (1994) has referred to as the "imperial" attitude towards nature (Figure 2.1). Represented earlier by such figures as Francis Bacon and Carl Linnaeus, that attitude emphasizes mankind's dominance over nature and acts of management and control of resources for material gain. Worster contrasts this imperial attitude with the "Arcadian" attitude, represented by such figures as Gilbert White and, in America, Henry David Thoreau and Ralph Waldo Emerson, who emphasized either the sublimity of nature and mankind's posture of awe before it, or its beauty and our delight. At the

Figure 2.1 Gifford Pinchot

Figure 2.2 John Muir

turn of the American century, it was John Muir who most famously demonstrated this posture (Figure 2.2).

Relative to Pinchot's privileged upbringing, John Muir (1838–1914) had a very different background.[30] Born in Scotland, he moved to the Wisconsin frontier when he was eleven. He worked on the family farm with his father, then in a machine shop, where he was an expert on managing efficient workflows. He always loved the wilderness but led a fairly conventional life until an accident in 1867 left him blind for one month. After recovering, he decided life was too short to do anything but live for his passion, and so he went to the wilderness. He hiked 1,000 miles from Indiana to the Gulf of Mexico, then famously hiked the Sierra-Nevada Mountains. There, he was inspired to think and write and, soon, to work on the signature project of his life: to preserve as wilderness the area that would become Yosemite National Park. That work yielded fruit in 1890 with the passage of the Yosemite Act, the first act of conservation explicitly tied to preserving land

[30] For biographies of Muir, see Wolfe ([1945] 2003) and Worster (2008).

in its wild state.[31] Understanding the need to watch over this new treasure, Muir founded the Sierra Club in 1892 as an advocacy group and nascent political force.

In contrast to Pinchot's mix of the Social Gospel and utilitarianism, Muir was a transcendentalist, reworking his orthodox Christian upbringing into a spiritual faith in Nature as the path to God (Nelson 2010). He hiked with a well-thumbed copy of Emerson's essays, and his hero would eventually seek him out in Yosemite. To Muir, leaves, rocks, and bodies of water are "sparks of the Divine Soul." Landscapes are "blessed," "waters will wash away sins as well as dirt," and Nature shows material care. Consequently, wilderness is the best avenue to divinity, for it best reflects God's creation, untarnished by human hands: "The clearest way into the Universe is through a forest wilderness."[32]

Consistent with this spiritual view of Nature, Muir opposed anthropocentric world views like Pinchot's. "No dogma taught by the present civilization," he wrote, "seems to form so insuperable an obstacle in the way of a right understanding of the relations which culture sustains to wildness as that which declares that the world was made especially for the uses of man." To the contrary, nature's value was intrinsic, in the sense that it was non-instrumental but also in the sense that it had objective value independent of human valuation. For example, to a question about what rattlesnakes are good for, "[a]s if nothing that does not obviously make for the benefit of man had any right to exist; as if our ways were God's ways," he answered that "they are good for themselves, and we need not begrudge them their share of life."[33]

[31] In contrast, Yellowstone, established in 1872, had been preserved as a "pleasuring ground" for its "curiosities." Earlier, the Yosemite Grant of 1864 had deeded ten square miles to the State of California for a state park at Yosemite, but that small area soon became the center of a thriving tourist business (Nash 1982 Ch. 7). In contrast, the Yosemite Act of 1890 added nearly 1,200 square miles.

[32] "Landscapes are blessed" etc. (Muir [1875] 1980 *passim*). "Clearest way into the universe" (quoted in Nash 1982 pp. 125–6). The encounter with Emerson proved disappointing. Muir invited him to join him "in a month's worship with Nature in the high temples of the great Sierra Crown beyond our holy Yosemite," but Emerson and his companions preferred the comfort of a nearby inn. Emerson later reciprocated, writing from Massachusetts to invite him to "bring to an early close your absolute contacts with any yet unvisited glaciers or volcanoes" and join him as a permanent guest, for solitude "is a sublime mistress, but an intolerable wife." Muir declined (Nash 1982 p. 126; Worster 2008 pp. 210–15).

[33] The term "intrinsic value" itself has many subtleties with distinct meanings that often are conflated (O'Neill 1992; Callicott 1999). These two senses of the term (non-instrumental and independent of a human evaluator) may well have been conflated by Muir. "No dogma..." (Muir [1875] 1980 pp. 235–6); rattlesnakes (Muir [1901] 1980 p. 200).

Initially holding one another in mutual respect, Pinchot and Muir began as allies against the status quo and laissez faire, which Muir referred to as the "gobble-gobble school of economics." But their alliance began to unravel as the necessity of making specific land use decisions exposed their differences. For example, in 1891, the United States had established its first forest reserves, creating some 13 million acres of federal forestland, but how those lands would be used was by no means clear. In 1896, Pinchot and Muir both were appointed to a committee of the National Academy of Sciences commissioned by the Secretary of the Interior, to survey the newly created reserves and to make recommendations about their disposition. Muir envisioned them to be preserved as wild places, like Yosemite; Pinchot favored managed development for wise use. The committee could not agree on a recommendation, and individual members soon turned to working against one another in a game of political chess. In the end, the wise use side won, as Congress declared the purpose of the reserves to be "to furnish a continuous supply of timber" plus ongoing mining and grazing. When they met later that year, a comment by Pinchot supporting the grazing of sheep on federal lands so enraged Muir, who had long viewed sheep as "hoofed locusts" that denuded natural landscapes, that Muir declared "I don't want anything more to do with you." The fault line dividing the leading spokesmen for the romantic and the bureaucratic impulses in American environmentalism had widened to a cleft.[34]

Aptly, the final, epic battle between Muir and Pinchot was fought over a dam. In 1906, shortly after its devastating fire, the City of San Francisco petitioned the federal government to allow the damming of the Hetch Hetchy valley, some 150 miles away in Yosemite, for municipal water supplies. Roosevelt tried to finesse a political compromise that placated Muir, but, in the end, the political forces in San Francisco carried the day, and the Hetch Hetchy was dammed, but not before a seven-year fight that further opened the divide between the development and preservation camps. In retrospect, this fight proved to be only the first of a series of battles, fought over the next seventy-five years, where development and preservation forces clashed at dam sites, from Hetch Hetchy to Tellico, via Hells Canyon and Dinosaur Monument.[35]

[34] "Gobble gobble school" (quoted in Wolfe [1945] 2003 p. 102). On the NAS commission and "hoofed locusts," see Nash (1982 pp. 130–38).

[35] The fight over Hetch Hetchy is one that has been told many times by historians. For excellent accounts, see Hays (1959), Nash (1982), and Worster (2008). It is noteworthy that the fight also was caught up in the so-called "Ballinger controversy" over access to Alaskan mineral rights, which eventually cost Pinchot his job, as he was fired by President Taft for

Muir and his allies launched a furious campaign to preserve their beloved Yosemite. They emphasized its spiritual significance. "Dam Hetch Hetchy!" exclaimed Muir, in the final words of his book, *The Yosemite*. "As well dam for water tanks the people's cathedrals and churches, for no holier temple has ever been consecrated by the heart of man."[36] Interestingly, for its foreshadowing of future debates, Muir and the "nature lovers" also appealed to Yosemite's value as a place for recreation. As Nash (1982) argues, this was a tactical error, for the proponents of the dam could just as well turn this argument to their advantage, with the resulting reservoir providing many more recreational opportunities for boating and fishing.

For his part, Pinchot appealed to science and posed the problem in terms of the utilitarian calculus rather than spiritual values. In his testimony to Congress, he framed the question as centering on "whether the advantage of leaving this valley in a state of nature is greater than … using it for the benefit of the city of San Francisco." While he admitted the idea of preserving the valley was appealing when viewed in isolation, the city's need was "overwhelming."[37]

The clash between Pinchot and Muir extended to the very definition of the word "conservation" and related vocabulary. Pinchot claimed to have personally coined the term, though historians have considered that claim rather dubious.[38] Using Pinchot's vocabulary, "conservation" inherently meant the wise use of resources. Muir and his allies would be said to advocate "preservation" in contrast to "conservation." For their part, Muir and his allies were unwilling to concede the term "conservation" to Pinchot. In their rival vocabulary, the wise-use or utilitarian school and the preservationist school were two sides of the "conservation" coin.

It is tempting to reduce the differences between Pinchot and Muir to a simple difference in values: Pinchot valued timber, Muir preferred wilderness. But as Meyer (1997) argues, there are difficulties with that interpretation. Pinchot in fact first went into forestry as an act of propitiation, motivated by the sense of damage his family's lumbering business had done to the woods. He frequently referred to the sublimity and beauty of nature. Describing his reaction upon first seeing the Grand Canyon, he wrote,

fomenting division over the affair. Subsequent fights over dam projects are described elsewhere in this book, but notable discussions are provided by Berkman and Viscusi (1973), Brooks (2006), Harvey (1994), and Plater (2013).

36 Muir ([1912] 1989 p. 218).

37 Nash (1982 pp. 170–1).

38 On his own claims, see Pinchot (1947 p. 326). Hays (1959 pp. 5–6) appraises their credibility.

"awe-struck and silent, I strove to grasp the vastness and the beauty." By the same token, Muir was hardly the prototype of the misanthropic deep ecologist as some would paint him. At the risk of logical inconsistency for the sake of diplomacy, he frequently conceded the necessity of forestry and development.[39]

On Meyer's reading, the differences between Pinchot and Muir were as much about politics as values. Muir sought a space for wilderness sheltered from the pressures of political economy and self-interest. He built Tocquevillian mediating organizations like the Sierra Club. Given his spiritual view of wilderness, a reasonable comparison for the place of preservation in Muir's politics would be to the space traditionally given to religion in American politics, and for preservationist organizations to institutions like churches. But just as some versions of modern liberalism would remove religion from politics and exile it to a realm of private feeling, Pinchot dismissed love of wilderness as private feelings that had no place in his technocracy. Accordingly, in the debate over the Hetch Hetchy, he conceded private feelings for the beauty of the wild valley, but gave no role to them in public decision-making. "The fundamental principle of the whole conservation policy," he testified to Congress, "is that of use, to take every part of the land and its resources and put it to that use in which it will serve the most people." As love of wilderness – of *non*-use – was by definition omitted from his version of the utilitarian calculus, Pinchot's science of conservation management led inevitably to the recommendation to develop.[40]

In summary, each side recognized the values espoused by the other but could make no room for it in its politics. According to Muir's poetic and spiritual approach, one must serve either Nature or mammon; no one can have two masters. According to Pinchot's scientific approach, spiritual and aesthetic values had no place in the utilitarian calculus.

Thus, on that winter day when the God Committee met to decide the fate of the snail darter, the distrust of the environmentalists was no mere prejudice against economists, it was an expression of feelings and impressions formed from a hundred years of intellectual debate and political maneuvering between the "wise use" of natural resources for human ends and the preservation of wilderness for its own sake. Though their distrust

[39] "Awe-struck and silent..." quoted in Meyer (1997 p. 272). See also Miller (1992) and Nash (1982 pp. 136 ff).

[40] Quoted in Nash (1982 pp. 170–1). Later in life, Pinchot seems to have reevaluated this position. As governor, he preserved the last large stand of virgin hardwoods (Miller 1992).

was understandable, it was by then a little behind the times. As explored in the following chapters, economists wrestled with the unsatisfying impasse left behind by Pinchot and Muir – particularly the exclusion of nonmaterial but no less real values from the utilitarian calculus – for much of the twentieth century. In many ways, dissatisfaction and frustration with it led to the emergence of environmental economists from natural resource economics, as a newer and distinct subfield.

3

Do Economists Know about Lupines? Economics versus the Environment

[T]hat part of social welfare that can be brought directly or indirectly into relation with the measuring-rod of money … may be called economic welfare. It is not, indeed, possible to separate it in any rigid way from other parts, for the part which can be brought into relation with a money measure will be different according as we mean by can, “can easily” or “can with mild restraining” or “can with violent straining.” The outline of our territory is, therefore, necessarily vague.

–A. C. Pigou, *Economics of Welfare* (1932)

The rupture between Pinchot and Muir highlights how unpropitious the circumstances were for the eventual emergence of a field called “environmental economics,” for in the early decades of the twentieth century economics could not help but be on the side of Pinchot in this debate. It defined itself as the study of material wealth and welfare; it employed the logic of utilitarian calculus, property rights, and/or market institutions; and it studied how to *develop* resources. In short, it omitted Muir’s love of wilderness altogether. In this context, “environmental” and “economics” were disjoint concepts that were difficult to reconcile. At that time, “economics of the environment” would have seemed unimaginable. “Economics *against* the environment” would have seemed more apt.

In this chapter, I consider two early reactions to this impasse. Writing the history of thought about US conservation policy forward from the Pinchot-Muir debates, one naturally comes to the work of Aldo Leopold. Best known for his trenchant and heartfelt essays collected in *A Sand County Almanac* (1949), Leopold was an expert in conservation policy with an interdisciplinary training in ecology and economics. After long contemplation about the relationship between them, he concluded that, although it had a role to play in conservation, economics could not quantify the value of wilderness and ecosystems. It could not help determine the right objectives of policy. Those ends had to be defined outside economics. But economics could help with the prudential management toward given ends.

On the other hand, writing the history of environmental economics backward from the present, we come to a quintessential problem in the field: the "pricing" of environmental services that do not trade in markets. Tracing such work back, we find that economists first cut their teeth on these problems when attempting to quantify the value of outdoor recreation as part of benefit–cost analyses of dams and other water projects. But in doing that, something odd happens, for we find we are now in the middle of a story of economists who, far from pricing the value of *preserving* natural environments, were ironically engaged in efforts to bolster the rationale for *developing* western water resources. Those efforts were driven by bureaucrats who were attempting to justify such projects, and who looked to economists to add outdoor recreation to the list of benefits they would provide, to tip the scales in favor of development. And it was the economists who tried to tell them it could not be done.

Although taking place over the same period, Leopold's story and that of the benefit–cost practitioners are very different ones. Yet those differences only highlight the universality of the frustration with the Pinchot-Muir impasse and the problem, at mid-century, of finding anything meaningful for economics to say about environmental policy.

3.1 Do Economists Know about Lupines? Aldo Leopold's Ecological Economics

Aldo Leopold (1887–1948) knew he wanted to be a forester from an early age. He went to a college preparatory school specifically for the purpose of going to Yale so that he could enroll in the School of Forestry, which had recently been founded by the Pinchot family. He arrived at Yale in 1904, first taking courses in the Sheffield Scientific School as preparation for the forestry school, where he did his graduate work. At Yale, Leopold obtained an interdisciplinary education in resource management, which included a healthy dose of economics, with a particular emphasis on Bentham's utilitarianism. He then began his professional career at the US Forest Service in 1909, during a period of time when it was headed by Pinchot himself. Later, in 1933, he took a position at the University of Wisconsin's Dept. of Agricultural Economics, as a professor of Game Management.[1]

[1] Goodwin (2008) provides autobiographical details related to Leopold's economic training. Additional biographical overviews of his life and career include Nash (1982 Ch. 11), Callicott (1994), Meine (2010), and Newton (2006).

Leopold began his career firmly in Pinchot's conservation camp. But during his time at the Forest Service into the 1920s, he increasingly came to feel that forests and other resources needed to be managed for multiple purposes, and moreover that hunting and non-consumptive recreational uses should be given more weight than they were relative to the extractive activities like lumbering. In this respect, Leopold was perfectly in step with trends in natural resource management. The Forest Service had recently commissioned a report from Frank Waugh, a landscape architect (and father of leading agricultural and resource economist Frederick Waugh), which recommended recreation be given weight in management decisions.

While increasingly valuing these kinds of uses or purposes, Leopold still looked at the problem as a manager or economist would. He used marginal reasoning to think about the trade-offs between consumptive and non-consumptive uses. For example, he claimed that "while the reduction of the wilderness has been a good thing, its extermination would be a very bad one." Explaining by analogy, he continued,

> What I am trying to make clear is that if in a city we had six vacant lots available to the youngsters of a certain neighborhood for playing ball, it might be "development" to build houses on the first, and the second, and the third, and the fourth, and even on the fifth, but when we build houses on the last one, we forget what houses are for. The sixth house would not be development at all, but rather… stupidity.[2]

At this point, for Leopold, it was all a question of balancing costs and benefits.

Eventually, however, Leopold became disillusioned with this way of thinking. A decisive moment seems to have come when he and his colleagues killed a wolf, which until that point he had viewed only as a nuisance to deer and other game. As he witnessed at close range the "fierce green fire dying in her eyes," he knew then instinctively that something had been missing from his calculations.[3] After this event, he left the forest service and eventually found his way to the University of Wisconsin. Shortly afterward, he co-founded the Wilderness Society with Benton MacKaye, Bob Marshall, and others.

At one level, Leopold simply moved more to Muir's preservation side of the spectrum from his start on Pinchot's conservation side. He began as a forester, came to appreciate wilderness for its non-consumptive uses, and increasingly came to value wilderness for its own sake. But Leopold did

[2] Quoted in Nash (1982 pp. 187–8).

[3] Leopold ([1949] 1987 p. 130).

not just shift positions in an existing intellectual landscape, he molded new ones. To Leopold, the conservation approach did not give enough credit to the intrinsic value of wildlife. By the same token, the preservation approach of "locking up" wildlife did not give enough credit to human beings. A third way was needed.

Leopold looked to the growing field of ecology as that third way. Man could live with wildlife as part of a complex web of interactions. This would require a new "conservation ethic" or "land ethic" – a "*universal symbiosis with land*, economic and aesthetic, public and private." This land ethic was much more than a realignment between the market and the government. Indeed, after his experience in the forest service, Leopold was wary of public ownership and other government management. In a pair of essays published in 1933 and 1934 in the *Journal of Forestry*, he contended that the public ownership of lands can play a limited role, but simply expanding their scope is not a promising avenue to conservation. In fact, it may only be an exercise in self-delusion. First, according to Leopold, public lands could not possibly cover sufficient territory without impeding other critical land uses like farming. Second, they would be managed with the typical clumsiness of large bureaucracies, with various agencies, each having tunnel vision, working at cross-purposes. Finally, the more radical versions of state ownership embraced by socialism, communism, and fascism were only worse because of their emphasis on materialism, capital, and "salvation by machinery."[4]

At the same time, Leopold argued that markets alone would not work either, because the profit motive privileged benefits that accrue to individuals rather than to the overall community. Thus, "the economic cards are stacked against some of the most important reforms." For example, as discussed by Richard Ely and George Wehrwein, in many cases conservation of topsoil is not sufficiently profitable to the farmer when using a narrow economic calculation. But, Leopold contended, that is because the calculus does not include downstream damages to other landowners, nor the costs of public expenditures designed to mitigate the problem, such as dredging or constructing erosion check-dams. In Leopold's estimation, an ounce of prevention was worth a pound of cure. Thus, "the thing to be prevented is destructive private land-use of any and all kinds. The thing to be encouraged is the use of private land in such a way as to combine the public and the private interest to the greatest possible degree." Leopold consulted

[4] Leopold ([1933] 1991, 1934). "A universal symbiosis..." (Leopold [1933] 1991 p. 639, emphasis in original). Leopold originally referred to his project as the "conservation ethic," later preferring "land ethic." Meine (2010) discusses the subtle distinctions.

and collaborated with Wehrwein, now his colleague at Wisconsin, to try to encourage such combinations. For example, he proposed using tax subsidies to encourage soil conservation.[5]

Leopold believed, then, that private incentives were a critical piece of the preservation puzzle. But, ultimately, the new land ethic would have to appeal to "something deeper, some sub-economic stratum of the human intelligence." In 1947, Leopold proposed a new interdisciplinary research and teaching project at the University of Wisconsin to explore these issues. He envisioned a new school of thought which he dubbed "ecological economics." The project was based on the premise that "industrialization is now bringing on a worldwide conflict between economics and conservation (ecology)" and that people from both sides of that conflict needed to be brought together to overcome the impasse.[6] Unfortunately, Leopold died the next year at the age of sixty-one from a heart attack while battling a wildfire, thus leaving the project unfinished.

That Leopold, trained in conservation management and holding a position in a department of agricultural economics, would frame the problem in terms of a "conflict" between economics and ecology is telling, and helps to set in relief the future developments covered in this book. To Leopold, economics – like Pinchot's calculus – inevitably discounted the intrinsic value of wildlife. As he wrote in *A Sand County Almanac*:

> Sometimes in June, when I see unearned dividends of dew hung on every lupine, I have doubts about the real poverty of the sands. On solvent farmlands lupines do not even grow, much less collect a daily rainbow of jewels. If they did, the weed control officer, who seldom sees a dewy dawn, would doubtless insist they be cut. Do economists know about lupines?[7]

As Muir defended the rattlesnake, Leopold defended the mere existence of creatures lacking narrowly construed utilitarian value. He understood that there were economic arguments for preserving nature, but he found them inadequate:

[5] Leopold ([1933] 1991, 1934). "The thing to be prevented…" (Leopold 1934 p. 542; see also Meine 2010 pp. 387–8). Collaboration with Wehrwein is documented in Meine (2010) and Lin (2014). For further discussion of Leopold's concept of the land ethic, see Callicott (1994), Meine (2010), and Lin (2014).

[6] "Something deeper…" (Leopold [1933] 1991 p. 189). On Leopold's proposal for ecological economics, see Newton (2006) and Lin (2014). "Industrialization is now bringing…" (quoted in Lin 2014 p. 110). Leopold's project does not appear to have direct connection to the school of "ecological economics" that arose in the 1980s, though commonalities can be found, such as their emphasis on living within biological constraints.

[7] Leopold ([1949] 1987 p. 102). See Callicott (1994) and Goodwin (2008) for additional discussion.

The emergence of ecology has put the economic biologist in a peculiar dilemma: with one hand he points out the accumulated findings of his search for utility in this or that species; with the other he lifts the veil from a biota so complex, so conditioned by the interwoven cooperation and competitions that no man can say where utility begins or ends.[8]

Leopold had no doubts about the real choice in this dilemma. The search for arguments based in utility or what today we might call "ecosystem services," while sometimes valid, were too often futile – too ridiculous, even – to be the intellectual basis for conservation. Expanding on this point, Leopold wrote:

One basic weakness in a conservation system based wholly on economic motives is that most members of the land community have no economic value. Wildflowers and songbirds are examples. Of the 22,000 higher plants and animals native to Wisconsin, it is doubtful whether more than 5 percent can be sold, fed, eaten or otherwise put to economic use. Yet these creatures are members of the biotic community, and if (as I believe) its stability depends on its integrity, they are entitled to continuance.

When one of these non-economic categories is threatened, and if we happen to love it, we invent subterfuges to give it economic importance. At the beginning of the century songbirds were supposed to be disappearing. Ornithologists jumped to the rescue with some distinctly shaky evidence to the effect that insects would eat us up if birds failed to control them. The evidence had to be economic in order to be valid.[9]

For Leopold, something beyond mainstream economics clearly was necessary to justify the preservation of natural ecosystems. To be sure, economics had a role to play in illuminating the incentives created by particular property rights and other institutions. It could, for example, design tax incentives for conservation. But economic prices could never inform us about the underlying values of ecological preservation.

3.2 Is Some Number Better than No Number? Valuing Outdoor Recreation

Whereas Leopold, when growing skeptical of the economic concept of "value" that dominated his agency, reconciled the conflict by leaving the Forest Service and moving to academia, others, facing similar conflicts, chose to remain in government. They attempted to harmonize, as best they could within the confines of bureaucratic reasoning, the cognitive

8 Leopold (1939 p. 727).
9 Leopold ([1949] 1987 p. 210).

dissonance between quantifying material values and appreciating the qualities of time spent in nature. Just the analysts that Leopold had had in mind when he designed his curriculum in ecological economics, their story makes up the second part of this chapter.

Developing America's Resources

The development of natural resources was part of the American identity from colonial times. The United States commenced official analysis of water and other civil engineering projects in 1802, when it established the US Army Corps of Engineers (USACE). USACE was modeled after the French *Corps des Ponts et Chaussées*, for, as with forest management, Europe was far ahead of the young United States in the analytical management of such projects. But whereas in the French tradition project management integrated economics and engineering, in the United States it was performed entirely by civil engineers until well into the twentieth century.[10]

Formal benefit–cost analysis in the United States is often dated to the Flood Control Act of 1936, which declared that to investigate potential improvements of watersheds and waterways is "in the interest of the general welfare." The law required that analysts determine whether "the benefits to whomsoever they may accrue" exceed the costs of a project.[11] While this was an important move, as noted by Porter (1995) it did not create benefit–cost analysis *ex nihilo*, for it is hardly plausible that Congress would create a requirement for a wholly unknown practice.

10 Ekelund and Hébert (1978, 1999), Etner (1987), and Porter (1991, 1995 Ch. 6) discuss the French engineering tradition, its place in bureaucratic management, and its relationship to economic practice. Moore and Moore (1989) and Porter (1995 Ch. 7) discuss the history of the Corps of Engineers and flood control policies, while Graves (1995) gives an overview of the role of economists at the Corps in the twentieth Century.

There are suggestive parallels between the nineteenth Century French engineering tradition and the history told in this chapter and the next. Both were a synthesis of engineering and economics for planning public works. On the other hand, Porter (1991, 1995) has emphasized important differences. In particular, because it did not arise in the context of open democratic policy debates, the earlier French tradition did not require standardization to bolster its credibility, whereas the drive to standardization plays a key role in the modern history described here. Porter suggests that, as a consequence, modern French public economics draws more on Anglo-American economics than its own engineering tradition.

11 On the early history of benefit–cost analysis in the US and the prominence of water projects, see Porter (1995 Ch. 7) as well as Castle et al. (1981), Hanemann (1992, 2006), Hufschmidt (2000), and Whittington and Smith (2020).

In fact, engineers at the Corps had conducted such studies on an *ad hoc* level for some time, as the wish list of potential projects always outstripped the ability to complete them, and so the Corps had to devise a bureaucratic form of prioritization.

But USACE was not the only game in town. Although the Flood Control Act largely assigned benefit–cost analyses to the Corps, it assigned the study of aspects related to run off and soil erosion to the Department of Agriculture (USDA). It also carved out an exception for irrigation projects in the arid west, which were managed by the Bureau of Reclamation (BOR). Housed in the Department of the Interior, the BOR was a Progressive Era agency, whose economic experts had close affiliations with the Bureau of Agricultural Economics (BAE). Reclamation economists had long been conducting a kind of benefit–cost analysis, one that followed a different logic guided by the Reclamation Act of 1902. The Reclamation Act established a revolving fund from the sale of western lands, with farmers and other water users repaying construction costs through annual user fees over a set period of time. In theory, these repayments were to replenish the fund, allowing new projects to go forward on a continuing basis. This financial model had naturally led to a kind of benefit–cost analysis within the BOR based on reimbursements, or at least a profit-and-loss forecast, with feasibility studies estimating the present value of projected revenue relative to capital costs.[12]

This political context had important implications for the history of pricing the environment. First, it obviously created the potential for bureaucratic turf wars. These two laws alone attempted to demarcate vague jurisdictional boundaries between USACE, BOR, and USDA. Later, the Federal Power Commission and the Bureau of the Budget would get involved. So did two more preservation-minded agencies within Interior, the Fish and Wildlife Service (FWS) and National Park Service (NPS). Under the Fish and Wildlife Coordination Act of 1946, USACE and BOR had to consult with the FWS on how best to design dams to protect fish populations. Indeed, this change in policy was highlighted by Leopold as an example of how his program in ecological economics could have practical use.[13]

[12] On the reclamation act and the repayment system, see Teele (1927), Regan and Greenshields (1951), Wahl (1995) and Pisani (2003). Regan and Greenshields compare the logic of benefit–cost tests under the Reclamation and Flood Control acts.

[13] Wrote Leopold, "The clearest need for trained men is in the federal bureaus, especially in the Fish and Wildlife Service which administers the new law … requiring the Corps of Army Engineers and Reclamation Service to consult it…" (quoted in Lin 2014 Fig. 2).

Second, it reveals an important reason why benefit–cost practices and research priorities differed across agencies. Under the Flood Control Act of 1936, economic calculations centered on benefits "to whomsoever they may accrue." Later, economists would interpret this language as including unpriced public goods. They also would naturally interpret it as involving the aggregation of benefits across individuals, as in the potential Pareto criterion of the "new welfare economics" proposed about the same time by John Hicks and Nicholas Kaldor.[14] This criterion hinged on winners under a policy receiving benefits large enough that, hypothetically, they could compensate losers for their costs, with everybody better off (under the hypothetical compensation). In contrast, under the Reclamation Act, economic calculation centered on actual repayments and whether they would be sufficient to replenish the fund. As these reclamation repayments only needed to cover irrigation related costs, economists had to devise a way to net out costs related to other purposes, including public goods like recreation facilities. In other words, one context focused on benefits, both priced and unpriced, and whether the hypothetical payments people would be willing to make for them would cover costs; the other focused on whether actual payments would cover costs, after netting out costs associated with the unpriced benefits. Thus, the sets of concerns and patterns of thought, even among economists with similar training, were not always in harmony.

This political context also sheds light on the bureaucratic openings that economists could exploit to start participating in benefit–cost analyses, which to that point had been the domain of engineering. Economists, especially agricultural economists, were well positioned to take advantage of these opportunities. As previously mentioned, they first got a toehold in the USDA at places like the BAE and Forest Service. By mid-century, they were spreading out across the bureaucracy. For example, in 1947, war-time production and natural resources boards were reorganized as the National Security Resources Board (NSRB), with the mission of making plans to mobilize natural resources in the event of war or other emergencies. The NSRB provided a temporary home base for resource economists, before they scattered throughout the government. In the same year, the Whitehouse Council of Economic Advisors brought in Joseph Fisher, a future RFF president, to lend natural resources expertise, and the Secretary of the Interior created a new program staff reporting

[14] Hicks (1939) and Kaldor (1939). Krutilla (1981) also notes the similarity between language of the Flood Control Act and the logic of the potential Pareto test.

directly to him on natural resources issues. Its staff including Harold Barnett, who also later found his way to RFF.[15]

The splitting of benefit–cost work among the USACE, BOR, USDA, and other agencies accelerated the spread of economic expertise throughout the federal government. USACE was the last to fall, long preferring the expertise of civil engineers over economists. It had no economists in its central directorate until the late 1950s, and but a few (and by all accounts poorly trained) in its field offices. In principle, USACE might have turned to any number of economic fields, including business management, industrial organization, and capital theory. But when it made its move, it emulated its rivals and turned to agricultural economics. Specifically, it poached Nathaniel A. Back from the USDA's planning office. Back was an agricultural economist who had represented the USDA on the Federal Inter-Agency Committee on Water Resources when it developed the guidelines in the 1950 Green Book, the mid-century Bible of benefit–cost analysis. Now, he represented USACE for the revised (1958) edition. Under Back's leadership, USACE increased the economists in its field offices from 51 to 77 between 1963 and 1965 and created an economics branch within the directorate.[16]

Agricultural economists were ideally situated to be the go-to source for help with these benefit–cost analyses. First, they were already there, in large numbers, on the government scene. Second, with their fundamental *raison d'être* being service to the farmer, they had always had a constituency and a normative mandate, so they were used to working with stakeholders. Third, as they swelled the ranks of the federal bureaucracy, they developed a culture of statist planning that was comfortable with the institutions involved, including interest group politics and the interactions with Congress, other bureaucrats, and scientific experts.[17] Whereas neoclassical economists and institutional economists like Wesley Clair Mitchell often (if not always) viewed themselves as objective scientists working at arm's length from the policy process, agricultural economists tended to view themselves as

15 On the role of natural resource economists in government during this period, see Goodwin (1981). On the increasing role of economists generally, see Barber (1985), Hawley (1990), and Stapleford (2009).

16 For details on the role of economics at the Corps of Engineers, see Graves (1995).

17 Hawley (1990) particularly emphasizes this theme, contrasting the statism of agricultural economists with the antistatist corporatism of the National Bureau of Economic Research. See also Banzhaf (2006). Hawley suggests that, in this respect, agricultural economists were unique in the federal government, but Stapleford (2009) argues that a similar culture could be found among the social scientists in the Bureau of Labor Statistics.

existing within a decision-making process, self-aware of their constituencies and the way their research was used.[18] Fourth, they had a long tradition of researching water resources. For example, the discussion of water resources in Ely and Wehrwein's textbook (1940) reads like a ready-made outline for benefit–cost analysts, divided into sections covering such topics as flood control, navigation, irrigation, and riparian rights, which included power and outdoor recreation. Fifth and finally, agricultural economists had helped pioneer the empirical forecasting of prices, an essential skill for valuing the future services of water projects.

By the time America was entering its postwar economic expansion, more was at stake economically than ever before. The value of property vulnerable to floods, the demand for electric power, and the traffic on rivers all were increasing. Correspondingly, annual federal expenditures on water projects had risen to $800 million by 1955, giving them the largest share of all the civil public works activities carried on at the federal level. Moreover, some $8 billion of projects were backlogged.[19]

Of course, political pressure followed this money. Water has always been a source of controversy in the Western United States, and by extension so too have water projects that would divert it from one region, or from one group of users, to another. Competition over water resources extended to the many bureaucratic jurisdiction overseeing them.

In such a setting, an objective authority would be needed to adjudicate the conflicting claims. Benefit–cost analysis could play that role (Porter 1995). But to do so with integrity, benefit–cost analysis needed reformation. One problem was that across this wide array of agencies, there was an equally wide array of inconsistent benefit–cost practices. These inconsistencies were unsettling, as they undermined the authority that benefit–cost analysis had to have if it would serve to settle disputes. As Porter (1995), Desrosières (1998), and Stapleford (2009) have emphasized, disputes about the measurement of social facts undermine the utility of those facts in settling social debates. But the participants themselves were well aware of this tension. As J. M. Clark, Eugene Grant (a prominent professor of industrial engineering), and Maurice Kelso (a prominent agricultural economist) would put it in a consultant's report to the BOR: "Democracy has to rely on technicians in matters inscrutable to the non-specialist, but preferably where the specialist is following a well-authenticated technique. In this

[18] As discussed in Chapter 8, as new planning paradigms from neoclassical economics began to dominate benefit–cost analysis in the 1960s, many agricultural economists would bemoan the loss of an appreciation for those institutions.

[19] Figures from Eckstein (1958 pp. 1–3).

case, the disagreements among the specialists are evidence that they do not possess an authenticated technique ...."[20]

To lend benefit–cost analysis more authoritativeness, in 1946 the agencies formed the Federal Inter-Agency River Basin Committee (FIARBC), with a Subcommittee on Benefits and Costs, to coordinate their benefit–cost practices. The subcommittee was staffed by a number of agricultural economists, including Nathanial Back (USDA), Reginald Price (BOR), Mark Regan (BAE), E. C. Weitzell (BAE), George H. Walter (BAE), and with participation of others including Roy Prewitt (NPS).[21] Its 1950 report, the Green Book, is widely considered a landmark in the development of benefit–cost analysis and served as a handbook for practitioners in the ensuing years, as well as a starting point for further discussions. The committee continued to meet through the 1950s and released a revised edition in 1958.[22]

The Green Book reshaped benefit–cost analysis in terms of neoclassical value theory, with prices representing marginal values, both as costs and benefits. In doing so, it adopted the spirit of many agricultural and other economists of the era, who were willing to adopt a methodological eclecticism, embracing marginal value theory for normative problems where appropriate, while ever questioning whether it was appropriate in a particular institutional context.[23] In that spirit, it also acknowledged many situations where marginal values were not relevant. For example, on the cost side, it recognized fixed costs and indivisibilities in the set of realistic investments. It also recognized the existence of joint products, with a dam, for example, providing multiple services simultaneously, and the attending cost-sharing problem of attributing costs to a benefit category. On the benefit side, however, the Green Book assumed that most benefits derived from the marketable

[20] Clark, Grant, and Kelso (1952 p. 11).

[21] Prewitt's name does not appear in the published reports but his participation is evident from the archival records (NA 79.99.70).

[22] FIARBC (1950, 1958). For more on the Green Book and its place in the history of benefit–cost analysis, see Hanemann (1992) and Porter (1995). Not everybody was a fan. Richard Hammond, an analyst at the Stanford Food Research Institute, viewed it as an unhelpful failure (Hammond 1960, 1966). But his criticisms are embedded in an overall critique of benefit–cost analysis as inherently an "artifice," if not of neoclassical economics generally, and were easily waved away by others as being those of a crank.

[23] Porter (1995 p. 188) posed as an unresolved question how and why the Green Book economists began to apply the "high theory" of welfare economics to benefit–cost analysis, when they did not seem to be trained in it. I suggest a simple answer: they didn't. They were applying the marginal value theory of the Cambridge tradition as adapted by American agricultural and resource economists. However, as discussed in the second half of this book, the "new welfare economics" was introduced before long by other economists.

services directly provided by the projects, such as electricity and increased agricultural output. Furthermore, it assumed the project made relatively small contributions to these services, so prices would not be much affected. With these moves, the Green Book could use prices (or forecasted prices) as a constant parameter representing the marginal benefits of the project.

The Green Book further addressed two particularly thorny problems that preoccupied both government and academic economists at the time. One was the question of "secondary benefits," or indirect effects elsewhere, including efficiencies stemming from an increase in the scale of economic activity and downstream multiplier effects on economic activity through a chain of expenditures. On the whole, economists were skeptical of such effects and feared they were open to abuse by those who wanted to fiddle with the numbers, and the Green Book authors were no exception. They suggested such effects were small and tended to reflect costs elsewhere, so from a national perspective they tended to cancel out. However, they recognized that the question was tied up with the "accounting stance" of the analysis, or the question of whose benefits and costs "count." If one objective of the project was to spur regional development, then even shifts in economic activity from one region to another might appear as net benefits to the region of interest (a topic we return to in Chapter 8).[24]

The second thorny question was how to measure so-called "intangible" benefits, or the provision of goods and services that are not traded in markets. Examples include national security, the saving of life from floods, sites of historic importance or scenic beauty, and outdoor recreation. The Green Book authors concluded that, although these goods highlight the limitations of the market price system in reflecting value, there is no other suitable framework for evaluating the effects of public projects in common terms. Money is the common unit in which they can be reconciled. According to the Green Book authors, some things of value, such as preserving wilderness areas or rare or vanishing species of wildlife, probably could never be quantified and would have to be dealt with qualitatively. But for other things, there was a fighting chance. Accordingly, "prevention of loss of life, improvement of health and provision of facilities for recreation should be evaluated in monetary terms as fully as possible."[25] Of those, outdoor recreation received by far the lion's share of the attention and consequently became a prominent context in which economists developed their thinking about pricing the environment.

[24] See for example, FIARBC (1958 Ch. 2).
[25] FIARBC (1950 pp. 7, 26–8, 50–52).

Pricing Recreation Benefits

The FIARBC economists organized their thinking around categories of project purposes, including flood control, irrigation and drainage of agricultural land, navigation, hydroelectric power, and municipal water supplies. Intangible benefits such as recreation were naturally at the bottom of the list and were not included in the early progress reports of the FIARBC. Nevertheless, recreation arguably received disproportionate attention relative to its weight in the benefit–cost numbers, both within the FIARBC and in the contemporary work generally. By 1964, one bibliography listed 160 books and articles on recreation, indicating its policy importance during the period.[26]

The attention given to recreation benefits can be attributed to five factors. First, and most simply, as an intangible good not sold in the market, valuing recreation was one of the most difficult nuts to crack. Second, recreation was becoming increasingly important for the management of federal lands, as participation skyrocketed following the war. In an RFF report, Marion Clawson estimated that from the end of the war to 1955–6, attendance had increased at various land and water resources by the following annual rates:

National parks	8%
National forests	10%
National wildlife refuges	12%
TVA reservoirs	15%
Corps of engineers reservoirs	28%
State parks	10%
City & county parks	4%

Figure 3.1 shows the increase over a longer time horizon. It reveals that while part of the postwar increase reflected a recovery from a wartime dip, much of it was part of a secular trend. Attendance at National Forests, for example, was up approximately fifty-fold from 1920 levels by 1955. The consequence of this increasing popularity of recreation was overcrowding, a strain on land managers, and a demand for more facilities.[27]

[26] Progress report to the FIARBC from the Subcommittee on Benefits and Costs, April 1947, NA 79.99.70. Recreation is included in the second progress report, Nov. 1948, NA 79.99.70. For a bibliography of recreation studies, see Wolfe (1964).

[27] Figures from Clawson (1958 p. 7). See also Clawson (1959a), US Senate (1957 pp. 11–12), ORRRC (1961).

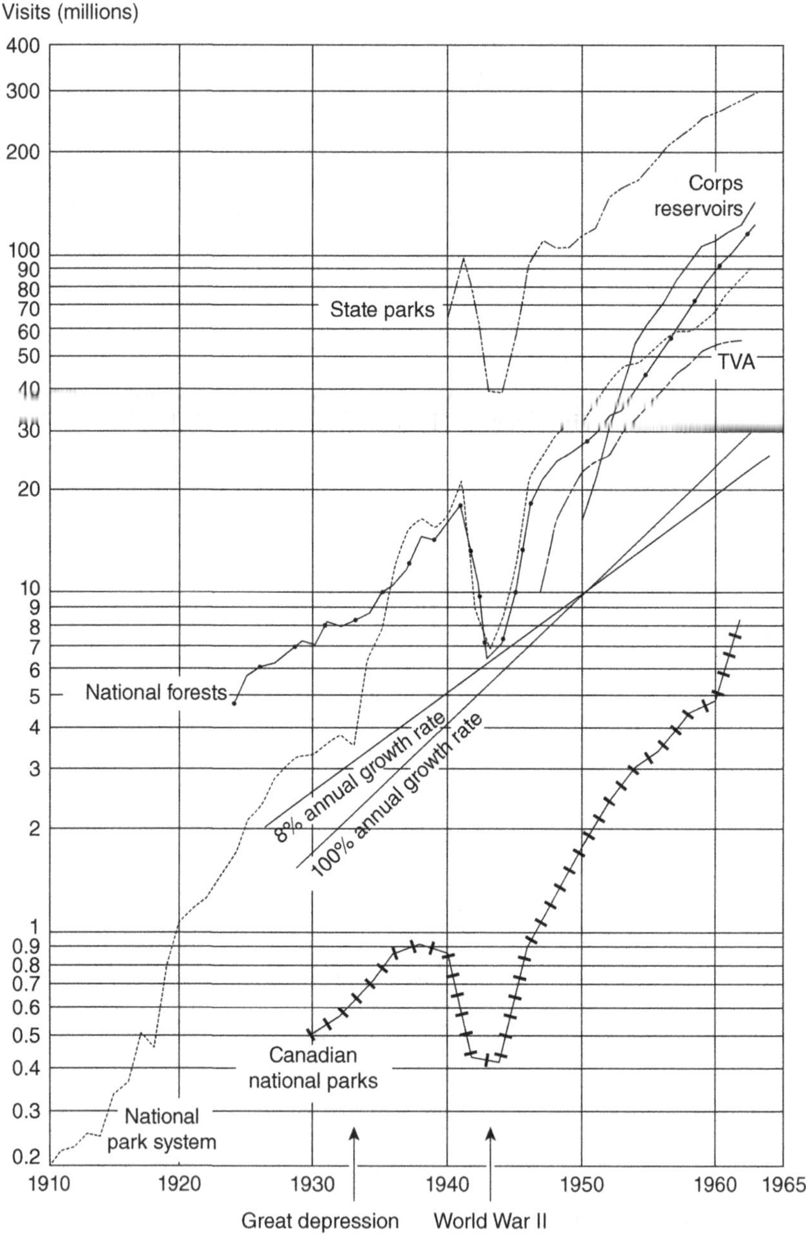

Figure 3.1 Attendance at recreation facilities, 1910–1964 (Clawson and Knetsch 1966)
The figure shows the rapid increase in outdoor recreation in the post-war era.

This "crisis in outdoor recreation" provoked a wide range of federal responses over the following years. In 1956 the Park Service drew up its "Mission 66 plan" to improve facilities to meet anticipated 1966 demand, and the Forest Service followed similarly. In 1958, Congress created the Outdoor Recreation Resources Review Commission (ORRRC), chaired by Laurance Rockefeller. And in the 1964 Land and Water Conservation Act, it created a new source of funds for state and federal conservation acquisitions. Summarized one report from the period, "money is going to be invested in outdoor recreation – large amounts, by all indications."[28]

Third, frankly, including recreation as a benefit would pump up the benefit–cost ratios. Internal memoranda from the period frequently pressured analysts to tweak their methods to improve these ratios, by adding secondary benefits and/or recreation benefits.[29] In this context, finding a satisfactory method to incorporate recreation would uphold the integrity of benefit–cost analysis while at the same time appeasing the more cynical manipulators of the system.

Particularly intriguing, a fourth and related factor was the role of recreation in cost sharing formulae. Since the Reclamation Act of 1902, reclamation projects could only go forward if they could be reimbursed by farmers and other beneficiaries. But costs that were explicitly incurred for other objectives, such as recreation, would not need to be recovered. Moreover, for multipurpose projects, if a portion of joint costs could be allocated to recreation, it would correspondingly reduce the net costs to be recovered from farmers. And since joint costs are by definition inseparable, the only way to allocate them seemed to be through benefit shares.[30] So increasing recreation benefits would reduce the net costs to be recovered. Through this serpentine syllogism, outdoor recreation benefits actually became an

[28] Quote from Clawson and Knetch (1966 p. *vi*). See ORRRC (1961) for a report on its activities. For more on this policy history, see Siehl (2008).

[29] For example, R. D. Searles, acting Sec. Interior, to Commissioner, Bureau of Reclamation, 12-12-51, RCP 88B; Michael Strauss, Commissioner, Bureau of Reclamation, to Sec. Interior, 9-17-52, AMP 68; Michael Strauss to Sec Interior J. A. Krug, 11-1-48, NA 79.99.2299. For a later example, see the discussion of some of the pressures on the Water Resources Council in Chapter 8 and in Berkman and Viscusi (1973 Ch. 8).

[30] Mark Regan, a BAE economist who played a leading role on the Green Book, spent much of his career on the issue of cost sharing (MMR *passim*). He suggested just this approach of allocating costs based on proportional benefits (Regan 1958; Regan and Weitzell 1947). The problem of recovering joint costs continued to be a vexing problem in water resources planning for many years, and other approaches have been proposed. Freeman and Norris (1988) considered pricing outputs above marginal costs, while Loehman and Whinston (1974) follow the axiomatic approach of Shapley. The problem continued to be an area of active research for many years (e.g., Moulin 2002).

indirect subsidy to farmers – always popular in Washington. Congressmen, bureaucrats, and lobbyists understood this logic perfectly well.[31]

Finally, the economics of outdoor recreation was caught up in inter-agency gamesmanship, especially between the NPS and BOR. Here, it played a dual role, provoking the rivalry while also serving as a pawn in the wider competition. The underlying source of the friction was the fact that the NPS and FWS were tasked with estimating recreation values for the BOR. Though all three are within the Department of the Interior, the agencies' incentives were often misaligned.

In particular, the BOR had numerous projects, and it wanted to count the recreation opportunities at reservoirs as benefits, to help justify them. By 1946, USACE, unsure how to satisfactorily incorporate such an intangible service as recreation into its own benefit–cost analyses, was also turning to the NPS for help. Unfortunately, NPS analysts felt they had enough on their plate, thank you, without having to do more work for another agency. If they only had to turn the crank on a well-established model, they might have been merely annoyed by the task. But NPS analysts had no suitable approach to monetizing recreation either, so being forced to come up with a number was the last thing they wanted to do. Yet office memos and other grey literature from the period reveal constant activity and queries from the analysts in the regional offices seeking guidance.

In 1946, growing impatient, Reclamation turned up the heat, with Michael Strauss, the BOR commissioner, sending NPS director Newton Drury an "urgent request" to begin monetizing recreation benefits. Drury appears to have been accommodating at first, suggesting that a particularly promising approach developed by its southwestern regional office be written up, put into practice agency-wide, and shared with the other agencies. But problems remained. Through efforts to communicate their practices to the FIARBC, it soon became clear that the NPS's regional analysts were out of step with one another and with the guidance from their own staff economist, Roy Prewitt. Even more embarrassingly, the gatekeepers at the FIARBC rejected their methods. Drury tried to clean up the mess in-house, wryly suggesting "it would be well to consider the desirability of revising the entire procedure to arrive at a method that would be more acceptable

[31] Congressional hearings on a bill to require including recreation benefits bear this out. See, for example, the line of questioning from Sen. Francis Case of South Dakota (US Senate 1957 pp. 18–9, 35–9, 104–5). The game could get quite devious. For example, in an effort to improve his industry's competitive position, the railway representative suggested that shipping should also pay user fees (p. 103 ff.). (Historically, shipping was exempt from tolls [Ashton, Shabman, and Cooper-Ruska 1976].) See also Porter (1995 p. 163 ff) on the political competition between railroads and water traffic.

from the economist's point of view." Meanwhile, he was (unsuccessfully) trying to push some of the work over to the FWS.[32]

This general tension was only the background to the real elephant – or, rather, dinosaur – in the room: namely, the proposed Echo Park dam in Dinosaur National Monument, in the Colorado River Basin near the Colorado/Utah border. Planning for the dam had begun quietly enough, but eventually would provoke one of the most important postwar battles over wilderness preservation. When first proposed by Reclamation before the war, the dam seemed like a commonsense application of Pinchot-era conservationism, making use of public lands to obtain much-needed water resources in the West. When definite proposals began to be drawn up in 1941, just before the US entered the war, Drury and other NPS staff were supportive and cooperative. It seemed consistent with the idea, unquestioned at the time, that, with the exception of Grand Canyon, the value of scarce water outweighed the region's wilderness.

That same year, the Park Service's regional office in Santa Fe, New Mexico, began a comprehensive study of recreational opportunities in the Colorado River Basin, partially funded by Reclamation under a cooperative agreement. The study would "literally...weigh the monetary benefits" of recreation and "establish a yardstick for evaluating the economic benefits of recreational use." This study appears to have been the first effort to quantify recreation benefits, and it would form the basis of Drury's efforts to cooperate with BOR's benefit–cost work over the next three years. Down in the details, the study focused on expenditures for travel, site fees, and recreational supplies, taking these as a gauge of people's willingness to pay. Up at a high level, Frederick Law Olmsted, Jr. agreed to head the survey. Completed in 1944, Olmsted's report concluded that any lost wilderness could be minimized and was of negligible scenic value anyway, so development would enhance recreational opportunities by making better use of water.[33]

32 Drury to regional directors 6-28-46, Drury to regional directors 4-25-47, Drury to regional directors 4-6-48, and *passim*, NA 79.99.9; Arkansas-White-Red River Basin Interagency Committee, 4-12-51, NA 79.11.2227; Report on Economic Survey of Lake Texoma Recreation Area and Vicinity..., May 1949, NA 79.10.755. "It would be well to consider...," Drury 4-6-48 *op cit*. On USACE's initial struggles, see also Porter (1995 p. 161).

33 "Literally weigh" (quoted in Neel 1994 p. 57). On the Echo Park dam controversy and its history, see Harvey (1994), Nash (1982 pp. 209–19), and Neel (1994), with the latter providing an especially detailed discussion of the recreation survey. Details of the early efforts to monetize recreation can be found in "A Study of a Method for Evaluating Recreation where Recreation is a Collateral Use," 2-15-41, RCP 91. The report may have been conducted in collaboration with the NRPB, in which the NPS participated. His plans to use this report are documented in a memo from Drury to regional directors 6-28-46, NA 79.99.9.

But by the late 1940s, preservationists were coalescing around resistance to the dam. Moreover, popular attitudes and aesthetic tastes were changing. A widely read piece by the essayist Bernard DeVoto, praising Dinosaur's "magnificent scenery" and "great vistas," helped turn national public opinion against the proposed project. Though it remained popular locally, by 1955 the project was dead, killed off by a national movement. The significance of this event is debated by environmental historians. Some see it as an isolated event, an uprising against one particularly ill-chosen site for one dam. Others see it as a watershed moment, a first big "win" for preservationists in a rematch of the Hetch Hetchy controversy.

In any case, importantly for our story, the Echo Park controversy was caught up in the inter-agency clashes inside the Department of the Interior. The whole project was a BOR idea advancing BOR's mission, but on NPS land and sapping the strength of NPS staff. Reclamation was pushing its sister agency around, in big ways, such as the "discussions" about how to site and plan the project, and petty ways, as when its surveyors would show up and begin working without so much as a courtesy call. The Park Service began to resent it. Although the details of exactly when and why are murky in the historical record, there is abundant evidence that Drury began to turn against the Echo Park dam in the late 1940s. Perhaps he was just defending his turf against an increasingly intolerable incursion. Perhaps, sensing new strength behind the preservationist movement in the postwar era, he felt more secure defending a cause he always believed in. Perhaps he just changed his mind about the value of Echo Park's wilderness.

Whatever the reason, Drury began to lobby the Secretary of the Interior against the project and to denounce it publicly. This reversal against a project he had originally supported won him few friends in the department, alienating Michael Strauss and the BOR, and even some in his own agency from the western regional office who still supported it. More ominously for him, he also alienated two successive Secretaries of Interior, Julius Krug and Oscar Chapman, who both backed Reclamation in the dispute. In the end, Chapman forced Drury to resign in 1951.[34]

Intriguingly, during these machinations, Drury exploited the uncertainties surrounding how to measure recreation benefits. In autumn 1948, the NPS made a pair of related moves, one specific to the Echo Park dam, the other more general. First, the regional office issued a report questioning,

[34] The exact reasons for Drury's essential firing are murky, perhaps being because of his infuriating intransigence, perhaps his maddening vacillations (Harvey 1994; Neel 1994).

qualitatively, whether the losses to wilderness in Dinosaur National Monument and the recreations opportunities based on it wouldn't exceed the recreation benefits of a reservoir. Simultaneously, the central office concluded that, in general, the values of park and recreation facilities cannot be measured quantitatively, so they would "no longer attempt to furnish such estimates." Instead, it suggested only a "judgement value" could be made. Furthermore, rather than make these judgments on a case-by-case basis, for expediency the NPS would simply use the blanket rule that benefits were equal to those costs specifically incurred for recreation facilities. (After all, why else would they do it if the benefits weren't at least that amount?) Moreover, no portion of the joint costs would be allocated to recreation.[35] These moves were shrewd, because though it appeared Interior was inevitably moving forward with approval of the Echo Park dam, the project could still be killed by the Bureau of the Budget or the US Congress, and those were precisely the points in the decision-making process where weak benefit–cost numbers would be most damaging.

BOR leaders were apoplectic. Strauss quickly sent a blistering memo to the Secretary of the Interior appealing this decision. As he pointed out, the expediency would dilute benefit–cost ratios, as a ratio of one was being averaged in. Moreover, by minimizing the cost share allocated to recreation, it made farmers and ranchers (i.e., Reclamation's stakeholders) bear more of the burden through their reimbursements. Furthermore, even if any joint costs subsequently were allocated to recreation, because benefits were limited to direct (not joint) costs, the benefit–cost ratio for the recreation portion would be less than one, thus creating a catch-22.[36]

Secretary Krug clearly was also displeased, and Drury eventually had to back off his decision. Thus chastened, the NPS reversed itself: for the next several years, it assumed that benefits were equal to 2x costs! Additionally, joint costs could be allocated to recreation after all, but they would be capped at 5 percent of total costs.[37] This formula had no economic rationale, and it undermined the scientific credibility of benefit–cost analysis. One cynical – but entirely plausible – explanation of Drury's move is that he made it so as to appear to be cooperating with the BOR and the Secretary

[35] On the regional report, see (Harvey 1997 p. 68; Neel 1994). On the decision not to quantify recreation benefits: Conrad Wirth to regional directors, 10-11-48, NA 79.99.70; Straus to Klug, 10-26-48, NA 79.99.9.

[36] Straus to Klug, 10-26-48, NA 79.99.9.

[37] Drury to regional directors, 11-1-49 NA 79.11.2227; NPS "Method of Evaluating Recreational Benefits for Water-Control Projects," 2-16-50, NA 79.11.2227; Trice and Wood (1958 pp. 200–1).

of the Interior, while adopting a plan that he must have known economists and other experts would shoot down, thus doing his dirty work for him. Indeed, economists throughout the bureaucracy rebelled against the decision – in Drury's own agency, the BEA and FIARBC, and even in the BOR, killing the proposal and sending it back to the drawing board.

Seeking Objectivity

Meanwhile, for the economists just trying to keep their heads down and do their jobs, the ultimate problem of quantifying recreation values remained: prices are not observed. NPS economists had been wrestling with this problem since the 1941 recreation survey of the Colorado River Basin. Their attitudes to the problem ranged from a despairing refusal to quantify recreation benefits to the optimistic search for the most justifiable method. Thus, although the expansion of government planning was drawing them into more measurement of more intangible services, they didn't always go along willingly.[38]

In 1947, Arthur Demaray, an NPS associate director, contacted ten leading economists to elicit their opinions about the potential "to evaluate the benefits of the national parks to the national economy, to the states, and to local communities." He also contacted economists in other agencies. Overwhelmingly, the economists discouraged attempts to quantify such intangible services. Edgar M. Hoover, an economist at the University of Michigan who had spent substantial time at the NRPB, was particularly explicit. He concluded, "I don't think the overall utility or justification of the park system can be measured at all in statistical terms, and it would be dangerous to try to argue the issue in dollars and cents." Elaborating the point, he explained his reasoning as follows.

> The park system may justify its existence in two ways:
>
> 1. By increasing the productive efficiency of those who find recreation in the parks, and thus indirectly increasing national income in the form of other products.
>
> 2. By providing more or better recreation per dollar spent than alternative forms would. This involves no change in national money income or expenditure, but means we get more fun out of the money we earn and spend.
>
> It seems evident to me that neither of the above types of ultimate gain is measurable.

[38] Fleury (2010) discusses two factors behind the growing economic imperialism of the 1960s, the changing conception of economics based on Robbins's definition and the expansion of the government's role in society (in his case, with respect to social welfare programs). In Fleury's narrative, economists exploited the opportunity, but as this history shows their volition isn't necessarily a precondition for the process he describes.

However, Hoover conceded that it might be feasible to evaluate the "more restricted question" of local economic impacts.[39]

Reviewing this correspondence and consulting with other federal agencies, Park economist Roy Prewitt thoroughly studied whether it would be feasible to measure recreation benefits. He concluded that it would not be:

> Recreation is, first of all, an intangible—a service. It is not a standardized or homogeneous service; it varies with every individual and it cannot be considered separate and apart from the individual. It is of the mind and body, it cannot be stored or transported, it is a psychic value and it cannot be measured in objective terms. Finally, the recreational values supplied by the National Park Service are not sold for a price under marketplace rules.[40]

Here, Prewitt identifies two obstacles. First, recreation benefits themselves are intangible and personal. They cannot be measured scientifically by an outside observer. Second, conceding that, in fact, the ultimate benefits of many economic goods are psychic and personal – a radio, for example – he noted that, unlike such goods, parks are not priced. While economists can observe the price of radios and infer that people are willing to pay that price, they cannot do so for recreation trips. It seems that while neither obstacle would be decisive alone, in combination they were. On the one hand, regardless of the nature of the service, a market price would reveal its value. On the other, even when unpriced, a very tangible service such as a cost savings could be measured indirectly. Recreation benefits satisfied neither criterion.

Prewitt concluded that "it might be better to forget the words 'economic value of recreation' and focus attention on the expenditures induced by recreation.... It is in this area that an objective approach can be made...." He thus proposed Hoover's less ambitious suggestion to focus on expenditures. However, he extended it to include not just local effects, but the forecasted effects on net national income, based on the net incomes received per dollar of expenditures in various measurable categories (travel, food, lodging, etc.).[41] In fact, this proposal in its essence was to continue down the path NPS analysts had begun with their Colorado River Basin study, albeit with more care about the interpretation of the numbers.

Of the economists initially consulted by the Park Service, one lone dissenter held out hope for measurement of recreation benefits: Harold Hotelling. He was all but ignored by Prewitt, with the exception of a brief

[39] Quotes from Demaray and Hoover in NPS (1949).
[40] NPS (1949 p. 12).
[41] NPS (1949 pp. 19–21).

remark, almost as one remarks upon a curiosity, that "he would use the consumer surplus approach, based on travel costs, from which he would derive a demand curve for park services."[42] Consumer surplus was an old idea in economics, representing the net value to consumers for a good or service, the difference between the most they would be willing to pay and the actual price they do pay. As discussed in the next chapter, the concept had long been criticized by neoclassical economists as theoretically confused, and by institutional economists as unrealistic. It was only just at this time being rehabilitated by the "new welfare economics," but NPS economists were unaware of that fact.

Despite having been inactive in economics for many years, Hotelling was stimulated by the problem, and in his letter hearkened back to his "long term interest" in evaluating public benefits. Hotelling suggested that concentric zones of approximately equal travel times to the park be drawn around it. Then, the trips to the park from each distance would be tallied and interpreted as a point on a demand curve with prices determined by travel distance.

> If we assume that the benefits are the same no matter what the distance, we have, for those living near the park, a consumers' surplus consisting of the differences in transportation costs. The comparison of the cost of coming from a zone with the number of people who do come from it, together with a count of the population of the zone, enables us to plot one point for each zone on a demand curve for the service of the park. By a judicious process of fitting it should be possible to get a good enough approximation of this demand curve to provide, through integration, a measure of the consumers' surplus resulting from the availability of the park. It is this consumers surplus (calculated by the above process with deduction for the cost of operating the park) which measures the benefits to the public in the particular year.

Hotelling went on to suggest that one could also estimate a set of demand functions accounting for the relations between different parks, continuing to use consumer surplus.[43]

As discussed in the next chapter, eventually Hotelling's suggestion would become the basis for pricing recreation opportunities. Nevertheless, it was quite vague. Many of the steps in the logic of the now standard model are missing in Hotelling's letter.[44] Is the operational quantity gross trips from each zone, or trips per capita? Is the integration over travel

42 NPS (1949 p. 12).

43 NPS (1949 Ch. 2).

44 For an introduction to the modern literature, see for example, Phaneuf and Requate (2017 Ch. 17).

costs or park fees, and what would be the respective limits of integration? Whether for its lack of clarity, the awkward insistence on consumer surplus, or some other reason, for the time being, the Park Service shelved Hotelling's suggestion.

So at this juncture, the Park Service was hemmed in. Its own economists were unable to find a way to estimate benefits. Its outside experts were discouraging (or, in Hotelling's case, at best vague and unpersuasive). Its masters in the Interior Department and rivals at BOR refused to allow them to give up. And the FIARB economists, safeguarding the integrity of benefit–cost analysis, disallowed their cynical ploy to arbitrarily set benefits at 2x costs.[45] Seeing no other alternative, the Park Service soon began gathering data on expenditures. It also gathered data on entrance costs at other parks and private recreation facilities that might be considered substitutes, which might provide a proxy for prices that would or could be charged. After all, in Prewitt's words, "it is in this area that an objective approach can be made." And objectivity was necessary to establish a well-authenticated technique. Objectivity gave merit to measures of expenditure, regardless of whether or not they could be interpreted as "benefits" or "values."

Using this approach, the NPS estimated a price of $1.41 for a visit, which they interpreted as a lower bound to value. In 1957, the NPS officially began using this "unit-day" approach. No sooner did they do so, however, than its claims to objectivity were undermined. Doris Carlton (later Doris Knapp), the NPS economist supervising the project, told Congress that "no matter what method you use..., you are bound to come up with arbitrary figures." Accordingly, she supported a bill that would introduce recreation into benefit–cost analysis by valuing trips at $1 per visitor-day on the basis that it would be a conservative lower bound and highlight the arbitrary nature of the calculation.[46]

Although the bill did not pass, soon this method was formalized into benefit–cost practices. In 1962, the Water Resources Council (WRC), the successor to the FIARBC, submitted "Policies, Standards, and Procedures in the Formulation, Evaluation, and Review of Plans for Use and Development of Water and Related Land Resources," or what is better known as Senate Document 97. Following publication of that document, President Kennedy ordered the agencies to "develop specific standards for the measurement of recreation and fish and wildlife benefits."

45 FIARB (1950 p. 51).
46 US Senate (1957 pp. 119–22).

In 1964, the WRC issued its estimates. Its report recognized that

> recreational services of public water and related land resource developments are currently provided to the users free of charge or for a nominal fee, usually covering only a part of the cost. Thus, although it is known that there is a large and growing demand for these services, there is, in the formal sense, no well-established market for them and few data are available on market prices that reflect the value of the service provided by public projects. Under the circumstances, it becomes necessary to derive simulated market prices.

The WRC settled on a range of $0.50–$1.50 per day of recreation, except for very specialized (and expensive) activities where the range might be from $2.00 to $6.00.[47]

As the economist Jack Knetsch wrote at the time, "The time has passed when we can profitably debate whether outdoor recreation should properly be acknowledged as a rightful use of natural resources." But with the WRC choosing arbitrary, round numbers, how to quantify the value of that use would continue to remain a matter of contention.[48]

47 WRC (1962, 1964). "Develop specific standards" (WRC 1964). "Recreational services" (WRC 1964 p. 5), figures (p. 4).

48 Knetsch (1964). This unit-day approach would continue to be used for decades. However it gradually moved from an estimate of daily expenditures on recreation to an estimate of consumer surplus per day. See, for example, Walsh, Johnson, and McKean (1992).

4

Consumer Surplus with Apology

In every department of human affairs, Practice long precedes Science: systematic enquiry into the modes of action of the powers of nature, is the tardy product of a long course of efforts to use those products for practical ends.

–John Stuart Mill, *Principles of Political Economy* (1848)

The economists trying to price the value of outdoor recreation were attempting to follow faithfully, if expansively, the Flood Control Act's bidding to measure the benefits of water projects "to whomsoever they may accrue." But what were "benefits?" Evidently, they were somehow related to well-being or welfare. But that only begged questions about the meaning of "welfare," let alone how to measure it. Many economists felt keenly the sting of Lord Kelvin's dictum that, "when you cannot express it in numbers, your knowledge is of a meager and unsatisfactory kind."

In fact, collectively, economists were ambivalent about the measurement of welfare. Pulled one way, they wanted to attain the methodological purity of modern science. Unfortunately, welfare measurement conjured up vague but embarrassing connotations of the nineteenth century's vision of cardinally measurable utility, long discredited. Pulled the other way, they wanted to be relevant to the policy questions of the day. The struggle between these opposing forces led British economists to develop the modern theory of applied welfare economics in the 1930s. In his *Essay on the Nature and Significance of Economic Science*, Lionel Robbins offered a new interpretation of economics defined by opportunity costs. In doing so, he expanded the scope of economic inquiry to problems that seemed unrelated to material welfare, and so outside the traditional scope of economics. But at the same time, impelled by the pull of methodological purity, he tried to limit its scope to truly scientific questions, and so placed strictures on economists' ability to make normative pronouncements. In the late 1930s, this move sparked a flurry of correspondence in the *Economic Journal* among Robbins, Roy Harrod, Kaldor, and Hicks.[1] Partly in response to Robbins, Kaldor and Hicks developed their potential Pareto test, in which economists could judge an investment or policy as improving the general welfare if the winners could potentially compensate the losers. To them and many others, this test provided a scientifically objective way to make pronouncements about normative questions, thus synthesizing the two opposing forces.

While many economists have continued to maintain what Philip Mirowski has called a "hermeneutic of suspicion concerning welfare," at some point in the 1950s the balance began to swing in the profession from intolerance to permissiveness.[2] As they entered the field of benefit-cost analysis and similar practical work, economists wrestled with the problem of how to define welfare (or changes in welfare) in a way that was quantifiably measurable. Applied economists, even those sympathetic to institutionalist approaches, generally recognized the normative imperatives of neoclassical optimization. In this framework, they could interpret prices as marginal values, that is, values for small changes in the supply of a good or service. But what about values for large, non-marginal changes? Economists today would choose one or another variant of consumer surplus, but this was not an obvious choice in the middle third of the twentieth century, as Marshall's variant was thoroughly discredited and Hicks's variants were perceived as mere theoretical curiosities seemingly of little practical value. Nevertheless, as they increasingly embraced welfare economics in the late 1950s, American economists returned to the previously scorned concept of consumer surplus as a welfare measure. Moreover, for the first time, they actually began to estimate it.[3]

This chapter tells the story of how, motivated by the specific problem of outdoor recreation, environmental and natural resource economists wrestled with broader questions about welfare measurement during the middle third of the twentieth century. It is not a story of pure intellectual progress. Rather it is a very human story of intellectual development through trial and error; of confusion, misunderstanding, and debate; and

1 See Harrod (1938), Robbins (1938), Kaldor (1939), and Hicks (1939).

2 Mirowski (2002 p. 199).

3 Ekelund and Hébert (1985), Hanemann (undated), and Morey (1984) have previously pointed out that consumer surplus was not the obvious go-to measure. The relationship between environmental economics and welfare economics has been emphasized by Hanemann (1992, 2006, undated), Krutilla (1981), Smith (1988).

of tension between academic ideals and bureaucratic imperatives. It is a story of how, as economic science has been acted out, "theory" and "practice" are not disjunctive, but copulative. Progress was conceived in the trenches.

4.1 Consumer Surplus: The Conceptual Legacy

Consumer surplus is an old concept, dating to the work of Jules Dupuit and Alfred Marshall in the nineteenth century. It is the difference between what consumers are willing to pay for a good or service and what they actually have to pay, or the surplus value remaining to them. Figure 4.1 depicts the idea. The demand curve represents the price (on the vertical axis) that would induce a consumer to choose any given quantity of a good (on the horizontal axis). The price also is the consumer's marginal willingness to pay (WTP) for a little bit more of the good, starting from any given quantity. The demand curve is downward sloping, indicating that consumers will purchase greater quantities at lower prices. At the actual price shown,

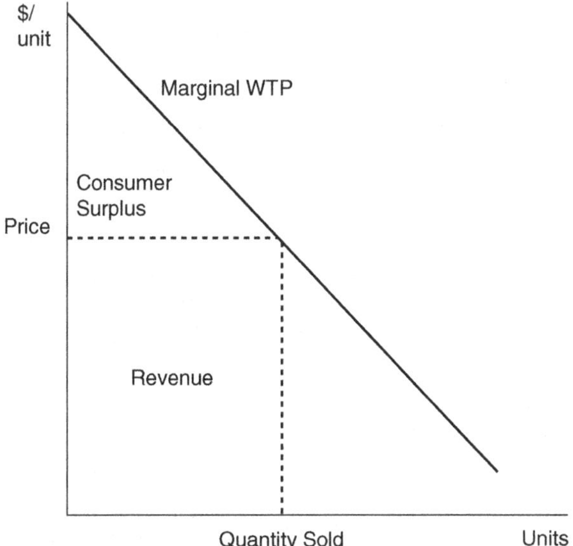

Figure 4.1 Consumer surplus
The figure depicts a downward sloping demand curve, with more units purchased at lower prices. The demand curve indicates the quantity sold at a given price. Revenue is the product of the two (a rectangle). Consumer surplus is the area between the demand curve and the price (the amount by which his WTP exceeds the price that must be paid) up to the quantity sold.

there is a given quantity sold. Geometrically, the price times quantity sold, or revenue, is a rectangle. In contrast, consumer surplus is a triangle represented by the area under the demand curve (i.e., the integral of the demand curve) less the revenue.

Although still new, already by the turn of the century this concept of consumer surplus was under attack on two fronts. First, it seemed incoherent to many. Because a consumer's welfare is different at different prices (i.e., at different points along the demand curve), the change in surplus from a change in prices does not measure the welfare effect of that price change. In particular, it cannot be interpreted as the amount of money needed to keep the consumer at constant welfare. Consequently, taking the area under the demand curve does not "integrate back" to any coherent entity representing welfare, with the potential for nonsensical results, such as the total change in consumer surplus from multiple price changes depending on the order in which the analyst calculates them. Second, in practice consumer surplus required making subjective judgments about the value of money to different people – otherwise, how could one add one person's surplus to another's? Such judgments did not seem to belong to the realm of science. Weary of defending it against such attacks, by the end of his career even Marshall viewed consumer surplus as an intellectual failure.[4]

Thus thoroughly discredited, consumer surplus was dead and almost forgotten as a welfare measure in the first third of the twentieth century. However, it lived on in a weird zombie-like existence in the analysis of pricing structures and market power, as a way of defining the potential maximum revenue that firms could charge. As consumer surplus is the difference between the amount consumers are willing to pay and do pay, tautologically, the highest price a firm could charge would leave the consumer with no surplus. Marshall himself had discussed monopolies' pricing in terms of the consumer surplus they could extract, and later Cambridge economists from A. C. Pigou to Joan Robinson thought of it almost exclusively in those terms. In this way, "consumer surplus," despite its name, was ironically becoming a *revenue* concept in the theory of the firm. Mid-century texts either explained it in those terms (e.g., Boulding 1955), ignored it altogether (e.g., Stigler 1947), or treated it with contempt (e.g., Little 1950; Samuelson 1947). Others, while not disavowing the theory per se, felt it was so far from operational as to be virtually

[4] See Currie, Murphy, and Schmitz (1971) and Ekelund and Hébert (1985) for overviews of the history of the concept of consumer surplus.

useless, at least for groups if not individuals as well (Baumol 1952). Thus, in the judgment of a young William Baumol, Pigou's "measuring rod of money … bends and stretches, and ultimately falls to pieces in our hands."[5]

There were two prominent exceptions to this rule. In the UK, J. R. Hicks attempted to "rehabilitate" consumer surplus in ordinal terms while also accounting for income effects in various ways. He proposed defining consumer surplus using a variant of the demand curve that accounted for adjustments to income needed to keep welfare constant as prices changed. Hicks's proposals overcame a number of theoretical objections, because, unlike Marshall's version, they were a measure of a compensatory payment that maintained consumers at a constant level of welfare. They thus also satisfied the so-called integrability conditions, thereby making consumer surplus independent of the order in which analysts calculated multiple effects. However, Hicks's proposals were all but ignored by applied workers for decades, probably for three reasons. First, it seemed that Hicksian demands are a mere intellectual construct, unrelated to observable behavior and hence unmeasurable. Attacking it on these grounds, Frank Knight for example concluded in his essay on "Realism and Relevance in the Theory of Demand" that, given the incoherence of Marshall's version and the unrealism of Hicks's, consumer surplus is of "extremely little practical significance." Second, as Hanemann (undated) has pointed out, the proliferating variants of Hicksian surplus must have made the exercise to seem all the more absurd. Reflecting this cavalcade of historical interpretations, Morey (1984) has delightfully dubbed the concept "confuser surplus." Third, the problem of aggregating surpluses of different people remained.[6]

The second exception is Harold Hotelling. Like Hicks, Hotelling had a tremendous influence on the development of modern economics. As a professor at Columbia, his indirect influence was substantial, training Kenneth Arrow, Robert Dorfman, Milton Friedman, and other next-generation architects of neoclassical welfare economics. At the same time, through his earlier work at Stanford's Food Research Institute and in his collaboration with Henry Schultz, Hotelling had studied the problems of agricultural economists and was always interested in empirical work. Hotelling rigorously defended the use of consumer surplus. In his paper

5 Baumol (1952 [1965] p. 164).

6 For Hicks's proposals, see Hicks (1941, 1943). "Extremely little" (Knight 1944 p. 311). On the problem of aggregation, see Baumol (1952) [1965] and Little (1950).

on "Edgeworth's Taxation Paradox" (1932), he grounded the social cost of taxation in lost consumer (and producer) surplus. In other work on railway and utility regulation (1938), he followed Jules Dupuit in arguing that it is always optimal to price commodities at marginal costs, which in many cases may be quite low, even if consumers receive a great benefit. Thus, revenues would not be an adequate measure of benefits because of the surplus left to consumers. Hotelling advocated public provision of projects in such cases where marginal cost pricing could not cover average costs, and benefit–cost analysis to help plan them. He girded his case against the "open attacks" on consumer surplus (which were due to "an excessive emphasis on [its] shortcomings") with a model of ordinary demand that met the integrability conditions.[7]

Hicks and Hotelling proposed their variants of consumer surplus in the 1930s. But for the time being, applied economists took a much different track. Consider, for example, the authors of the Green Book. In their conceptual framework, they set up as an archetypical situation an "irrigation project which makes available a supply of water for agriculture. The farmer uses the water in conjunction with land, labor, and materials to produce wheat. The wheat, in turn, is transported to and processed through an elevator and a mill to produce flour which is utilized by a baker to make bread for sale to a consumer."[8] They then defined benefits as the dollar value of the increased output in wheat, net of the costs of supplying that wheat. They generally assumed that the project would not affect output prices but noted that if output prices do adjust to the supply increase, secondary benefits (rents to fixed input factors and Keynesian multiplier effects) might accrue downstream for the mill and the baker. They make no mention of similar downstream benefits for the final-end user who eats the bread. Thus, their central concept of benefits was net income, not consumer surplus. Geometrically, it was the difference between two rectangles, not a triangle.

The popularity of net income as the criterion during this period can be attributed to several factors. First, neoclassical economics focused

[7] Hotelling (1932, 1938). "Open attacks" (Hotelling 1938 p. 246). On Hotelling's significance in the history of twentieth century economics generally as well as his defense of consumer surplus specifically, see Hands and Mirowski (1998), Mirowski and Hands (1998), and Mirowski (2002). Hotelling's model imposing the integrability conditions on Marshallian demands would continue to be used in the literature for many years, including applications to water resources and outdoor recreation (see, e.g., Maass et al. 1962; Burt and Brewer 1971; Cicchetti, Fisher, and Smith 1976).

[8] FIARBC (1950 pp. 7–8).

attention on marginal values, which of course could be identified with price. Price seeming more objective than preference, this move comfortingly put value theory on a more scientific footing (Winch 1972). Second, all the policy priorities during the first half-century were most naturally income concepts rather than concepts related to the "satisfaction" of the consumer. Natural resources policies aimed to "develop" Western resources, while agricultural policy was focused on its farming constituents. More broadly, depression-era policies were of course focused on economic recovery, which gave way to the postwar focus on "growthmanship" (Collins 1990). Finally, and not coincidentally, the national income accounts such as GNP were being developed over the same time period. Significantly, these accounts aggregate otherwise incommensurable goods like apples and oranges into an index by weighting them by their relative prices.

Understanding this context is crucial for interpreting economists at the time, for often they used terms that seem deceptively familiar to us today, but which then had very different meanings. For example, "willingness to pay" for a total quantity of a good often meant marginal value or marginal value times quantity (a hypothetical revenue rectangle), rather than the total value under the demand curve.

Although most economists involved with planning recognized a distinction between marginal value and total value, they believed there was no measurable way to capture the distinction.[9] Consequently, they had no choice but to use the tools at hand. As Mark Regan and E. C. Weitzell, two BAE economists put it:

> [N]o adequate guides are available for the quantitative expression of most social values. Until additional tools are developed, it will be necessary to use those that are available, even though it is recognized that some of these tools are not completely adaptable. As J. M. Clark so aptly states "... simple fiscal calculations must continue to be used, with the proviso that they need adjustment, but that radical adjustments should not be made unless sufficient cause is shown in the particular situation involved. Ordinary economic prudence should continue to take as its point of departure the calculation of whether the works concerned are worth the amount of money spent, in the usual fiscal terms."[10]

In this spirit, income (or expenditure) provided a coherent, empirically tractable, and socially relevant concept for "benefits."

[9] See for example, Clark (1936), Gray and Regan (1940), and Price (1948).

[10] Regan and Weitzell (1947 p. 1289). The Clark reference is to *Economics of Planning Public Works*, National Planning Board, 1935, p. 57.

4.2 "Applying" Hotelling's Suggestion

Regardless of whether benefits were conceived of as income or as surplus, measuring the benefits of outdoor recreation opportunities created the additional problem that the benefit was "intangible." No market prices, let alone demands or WTP, are apparently observed for recreation. As discussed in Chapter 3, when struggling with this problem, economists made several creative suggestions. Edgar Hoover and others opened the door to the possibility that one might measure the impact of recreation for restoring the productivity of workers, an idea consonant with an economics still focused on the supply of material wealth rather than the enjoyment of intangible services. However, Hoover himself rejected the idea as impracticable. Another idea was Hotelling's suggestion to look at travel costs as a kind of price, from which one could estimate a demand curve for recreation and, ultimately, consumer surplus. Obviously pleased with his own suggestion, Hotelling wrote about it to Hicks, expressing hope that the NPS would take it up and use it to pioneer "actual calculations" of consumer surplus.[11]

At the time, the Park Service ignored Hotelling's idea, but eventually it was the one that economists began to pick up and run with. The first to do so were Samuel Wood and Andrew Trice. Wood was a land economist who had earned his MA from Berkeley in 1933 and worked at the consulting firm Pacific Planning and Research, which had the contract for the study. Trice had received his PhD in economics from Berkeley in 1955 and was just starting out as an assistant professor at Sacramento State University. They analyzed a potential reservoir project that California was considering in the Feather River basin, north of Sacramento.

Trice and Wood published their study, entitled "Measurement of Recreation Benefits," in *Land Economics* in 1958. They obtained data originally collected by the California Department of Water Resources and the Fish and Wildlife Service (FWS), based on interviews with recreationists in the region, data which included the location of each recreationist's home. With these data, they traced out a distance-decay function, giving the number of trips taken by people from a given distance. Using an estimated cost of 6.5 cents per mile traveled, they then changed the scale of this function from miles to dollars, calling it the demand curve for trips to the site.

Using this demand curve, Trice and Wood measured the value of the park. But their concept of value was somewhat curious. They invoked a

[11] Hotelling to Hicks, June 24, 1947, Box 3, Hotelling Papers, Columbia University. I thank Philip Mirowski for sharing a copy of the letter with me.

measure that they described as "involving" a consumer surplus concept. Discussing consumer surplus in relation to the perfectly discriminating monopolist, they comment that "the problem is to find a method for determining what a monopolist would charge if he were a mind reader as well as a monopolist."[12] Such wry comments suggest some ambivalence about consumer surplus as a measure of welfare, as well as the continued interpretation of consumer surplus as revenue.

In any case, Trice and Wood actually defined their benefit measure as the difference between the price that would choke off 90 percent of the quantity demanded (about $3) and the median price actually paid (about $1), for a net value of approximately $2.00 per trip. Although they refer to this measure as a "consumer surplus," clearly, it is the difference between one particular price off the demand curve and one price actually paid, not the area under the demand curve. Their confusion seems to have stemmed from Hotelling's suggestion that the benefits are the same no matter what the distance. Today, economists interpret this as meaning that at each point geographically the distribution of demand functions is the same. Trice and Wood interpreted it as meaning that every individual has the same (constant) WTP. They then took the neighborhood of the choke price (the price at which demand falls to zero) to be that homogenous value, in this case going only to 90 percent.

Trice and Wood called this ninetieth percentile price the "bulk-line value." This concept appears to be analogous to Frank Taussig's concept of the "bulk-line price," or the price that would bring forth the bulk (say, 90 percent) of the supply of a commodity. The concept was used in the economics of rationing. Yet this bulk line value seems a very curious way to identify surplus. If demand were binary, *everybody* in the market closer than the bulk line distance would make trips. In that case, their benefit measure would be consistent with consumer surplus, but demand would not slope downward. If demand were not binary, it might slope downward, but it would not make sense to measure only the value of the first trip (i.e., to use something in the neighborhood of the choke price).[13]

In fact, Trice and Wood's article was not well received. In the following issue of *Land Economics*, Lawrence Hines, a well-known public economist at Dartmouth, criticized Trice and Wood for looking at the price of

12 Trice and Wood (1958 p. 198).

13 On Taussig's bulk line price, see Taussig (1919). Taussig may be an underappreciated figure in the history of economic thought. His work on noncompetitive pricing (including agricultural commodities but also monopoly pricing and price discrimination with economies of scale) lurks in the background at several points in the history of

travel, which is an ancillary expenditure only indirectly related to a recreation site such as a park. The only true measure would be a market price of the park itself. Drawing an analogy to the theater, he suggested that the cost of transportation to the theater and other ancillary expenses "may be relevant to evaluation but these data are no substitute for knowledge of the price of the theater tickets." In addition, Hines pointed out that the assumption of identical preferences was "total unrealistic." Finally, he argued that the whole idea of consumer's surplus, though "beguiling," has serious problems, including the assumption of constant marginal utility of income.[14]

Marion Clawson

Nevertheless, economists continued to pursue the idea of valuing outdoor recreation, whether because it was beguiling in itself or, as discussed in Chapter 3, because they were dragged into it by bureaucratic imperatives. Of particular significance, Marion Clawson (1905–1998) re-interpreted Trice and Wood's recreation demand curve, addressing many of Hines's criticisms. Yet Clawson himself at first had no more interest in consumer surplus as a concept of value than did his predecessors.

Clawson was an agricultural economist and lifetime scholar of public lands, who published some thirty-six books in his career. He grew up on small mines and ranches, raised by parents who had not attended high school. He earned his bachelor's degree from the University of Nevada, taking mostly practical agricultural courses, with a little calculus and economics. He then worked at the BAE for eighteen years, winning the patronage of Mordecai Ezekiel. In the meantime, using one year of leave and spare time over six years, he earned his PhD in economics from Harvard, studying under the agricultural economist John D. Black. In 1947, Clawson went to Washington to take the job of Director of the Bureau of Land Management (BLM). After Eisenhower's election, he took a position at RFF, just then being formed, where he published most of his work and spent the rest of his professional career. Although fundamentally a marginalist, Clawson reflected the prewar pluralism of American economics, with interests covering wide ground, from the psychology of preference formation to the historical evolution of social

environmental and natural resource economics. Additionally, as recently emphasized by Giocoli (2018), it also was an important part of similar attempts, around the same time, to construct the value of regulated assets not traded in markets.

14 Hines (1958 pp. 366–7).

institutions. First coming to government work in the New Deal years, Clawson was also a strong believer in planning.[15]

As noted Chapter 3, one of Clawson's chief concerns was the rapid growth in recreation demand and consequent over-crowding (Figure 3.1). He was adamant that more recreational sites were needed, and that careful planning was required to do it rightly. But, initially, he saw no particular role for benefit–cost analysis in making those plans. To the contrary, in the early 1950s, while advocating a kind of qualitative analysis, Clawson had argued that it was "practically impossible to measure the monetary value of recreation." One can infer that people are willing to pay at least the expenditures they make in executing a trip, but that does not speak to their actual value. Elaborating, he wrote,

> Many of the benefits of resource development and land management programs produce benefits which are not monetary in character.... It is impossible to compare the comparative advantage of game with that of domestic livestock, because they do not produce the same kind of benefit. Likewise, the advantages of superlative scenery cannot be directly compared with the advantages of a given amount of hydro-electric power, because the advantages are in different coin. Comparisons can be made, of course, and must be made; but the items compared are different, and no nice balance between them is possible.

In other words, recreation and its various opportunity costs cannot be compared in dollars.[16]

By the late 1950s, Clawson modified this position, believing recreation resources could be priced. Yet benefit–cost tests were never his chief interest. He took it for granted that more lands were needed. Rather, his priorities were to plan the locations and attributes of recreation facilities to meet demand. Obtaining the data to set entry fees intelligently was also a strong concern, both to raise much-needed funds and to manage congestion.[17]

Clawson's first attempt to estimate recreation demand, although widely cited at the time and to this day, circulated only as an RFF discussion

[15] These and other details are from his autobiography (Clawson 1987). In *Uncle Sam's Acres*, written while he was Director of the BLM to explain the history of public lands, Clawson illustrates his faith in planning, breezily commented that all future water development should be done by the Federal Government (Clawson 1951 pp. 326–32). Much later, he would write a (qualified) panegyric to the National Resources Planning Board, suggesting its resurrection (Clawson 1981). In Balisciano's (1998) taxonomy, Clawson was a technical-industrial planner.

[16] "Practically impossible" (Clawson 1951 p. 172); "Many of the benefits..." (p. 336).

[17] On siting recreation lands and designing their attributes, see Clawson (1959b) and Clawson and Knetsch (1963); on revenue collection, see the same as well as Clawson (1959a). The emphasis on revenue collection was largely absent from the travel cost literature for many years, but is beginning to reassert itself (Banzhaf 2022).

paper. Entitled "Methods of Measuring the Demand for and Value of Outdoor Recreation," it was a paper delivered to the Taylor-Hibbard club, a student organization at the University of Wisconsin, in 1959. In this work, after quickly dispensing with expenditures or value added as a measure of benefits, Clawson turned to the method of Trice and Wood as his point of departure.[18]

Clawson made two important adaptations to Trice and Wood's approach. First, he assumed that groups of people, at each location, have the same *distribution* of demand relationships. In contrast, Trice and Wood had implicitly made the stronger assumption that each *individual* has the same demand relationship, seemingly with constant WTP. Second, Clawson distinguished two different demand concepts, the demand for "the total recreation experience" and the demand for "the recreation opportunity per se." The total recreation experience, which he thought Trice and Wood had valued, includes transportation, lodging, and so forth, so its price includes the price of travel. Moving upward along the demand curve from a given point represents the effect on trips of an increase in costs, for people coming from that particular distance. However, Clawson wanted the demand for the recreation opportunity per se. To derive this demand curve, he simulated the effect of charging entrance fees to the site. Depending on the local elasticities of demand for the total experience, the relative drop-off in trips would be different from different points of origin.

At this point in the logic, Clawson had constructed a demand curve for the recreation site per se, pioneering a procedure that is still in use by practitioners to this day.[19] But, to Clawson, having knowledge of this demand

18 Clawson (1959b). It is not clear to what extent Clawson was familiar with Hotelling's original suggestion. It is mentioned in Trice and Wood's paper, and Clawson cites, in a general way, the Prewitt report in which it appeared, but he never directly mentions it. Jack Knetsch (2003), Clawson's junior colleague at RFF, recalls that he had the impression Clawson had never seen it.

19 For summaries of the modern literature, see for example, Parsons (2017) and Phaneuf and Requate (2017 Ch. 17). Clawson's point can be understood with reference to Parsons's Eq. 6.2 (p. 191). If for simplicity we ignore the ceteris paribus factors he includes, Parsons writes each individual n's trip demand as a function of travel costs $f(p_n)$. He then states each individual's consumer surplus is $\int_{p_n^0}^{p_n^*} f(p_n)\,dp_n$, where p_n^0 is individual n's actual travel cost to a site and p_n^* is the choke price that drives the quantity demanded to zero. When summing over people n, Clawson's point was that we cannot use a common p, but must start each individual at his or her own respective $p_n^0 : \sum_n \int_{p_n^0}^{p_n^*} f(p_n)\,dp_n$. Equivalently, Clawson's procedure (using Parsons's notation) was to write each demand as a function $f\left(p_n^0 + t, \ldots\right)$, where t is a hypothetical fee, and integrate over a common t for everybody: $\int_0^\infty \left[\sum_n f\left(p_n^0 + t\right)\right] dt$

curve raised a new set of questions. For the past ten to twenty years, NPS and other economists had been struggling with the fact that they did not know the prevailing market price of a trip to a site. If they had known that price, they would know one point on the demand curve, and could interpret it as a marginal value, as they did other goods. Now, Clawson had knowledge of the entire demand curve, but not a particular price (or point) on it. The first fact seemed an embarrassment of riches, the second an impoverishment.

The question, then, was what to do with the demand curve for recreation once one estimated it. Today's practitioners would take the actual price for each household, which varies based on its distance to the site, and then take the area between the demand curve and that price as the household's consumer surplus. But, like Trice and Wood before him, Clawson did not think that was the obviously right thing to do.

Clawson's concept of benefits was inextricably linked to actual prices. On the one hand, "the value of recreation would provide a ceiling to any fees that might be charged for its use." On the other, the revenues that can be collected represent people's value. To find this value, he computed the revenue-maximizing nondiscriminatory price based on the demand curve – that is, the largest possible revenue rectangle. While conceding that one would never actually want to charge the revenue-maximizing price, he argued that the difference between it and the revenue at a lower price can be considered a socially desirable transfer.[20] Thus, although he shifted the research emphasis from expenditures "associated" with recreation, or the overall trip experience, as Doris Knapp and other NPS economists were doing, to (hypothetical or potential) expenditures on the site per se, Clawson at this point was still focused on expenditures, where, in Prewitt's terms "an objective approach can be made," rather than trying to measure the aesthetic satisfaction of the recreationist.

Considering consumer surplus as an alternative candidate, Clawson observed, as was then commonplace, that it is equivalent to the revenue charged by a discriminatory monopolist. And, like Trice and Wood, he suggested that such a monopolist would have to really exist for consumer surplus to have any real meaning. Wrote Clawson,

> Under a scheme of discriminatory pricing, a monopolist might somehow manage to separate his potential customers or market into groups or segments, and to exploit each to the limit of its willingness to pay.... To the extent that anything like this is possible, the monopolist would reap for himself the consumer surplus.

[20] Clawson (1959b pp. 2, 29, 35).

In practice, pricing of this sort would probably but not always be illegal; perhaps more important, it would be extremely difficult if not impossible to separate the total market so neatly in segments from each other of which a different price could be extracted.

And, continuing after some detailed examples:

In general, consumer's surplus is equal to monopolist's possible gain; to the extent the latter is realized, it reduces consumer surplus. In practice, it is hard to see how consumer's surplus can be captured, by either public or private provider of recreation.

In fact, the usefulness of estimating consumer's surplus is questionable in any situation. Under almost any circumstances some users of outdoor recreation will gain more from it than they would have been willing to pay if necessary. This may be taken for granted; but how can you capture it, would public policy permit you to try, and what is to be gained from estimating its amount?[21]

In other words, the logic was that (i) consumer surplus is the revenue captured by a perfectly discriminating monopolist; (ii) there is no perfectly discriminating monopolist; therefore (iii) consumer surplus is an irrelevant concept. Instead, a single price consistent with the institutions and the level of output is needed. Put another way, by this interpretation consumer surplus is another revenue, rather than a true surplus measure. When viewed in these terms, the single-price monopoly revenue just seemed more realistic than consumer surplus.

To economists working in this field today, Clawson's moves at this point will seem surprising. It is tempting to say he just made a mistake, failing to apply the correct theory (consumer surplus) to the problem at hand. But as discussed above, that theory hardly existed at the time in a form that justified its use. Marshall's version of consumer surplus was discredited. Hicks's version was new and quixotic. There were no ready examples of anybody having applied the theory before. Moreover, Clawson was hardly alone in his interpretation. It is a logic repeated by numerous other contemporary resource economists. Indeed, the set of economists who made the same point comprise an honor roll of applied economists in the 1950s and 1960s: Rendel Allredge (Prewitt's successor at NPS), Dan Bromley, Emery Castle, James Crutchfield, Otto Eckstein, Howard Ellis, Irving Fox, William Lord, Neil Newton, Allan Schmidt, and Richard Tybout.[22]

21 Clawson (1959b pp. 30–1).

22 Allredge, "Review of Clawson/Knetsch," 4-30-65, NA 79.11.1597; memo to Dir. [NPS], 5-26-53, NA 79.11.2227. Bromley, Schmidt, and Lord (1971). Brown, Singh, and Castle (1962). Crutchfield (1962). Eckstein (1958). Ellis in US NPS 1949. Fox, Memo, 12-18-50,

In fact, the intellectual context at the time justified these economists' focus on finding a relevant price, in two ways. First, the interwar period during which Clawson and other experienced scholars had developed intellectually was a time of pluralism in American economics, with the institutionalist and neoclassical schools both thriving and intermingling. If there was one lesson to be learned from the institutional school, it was of course the importance of thinking in terms of historically relevant real-world institutions, rather than abstract constructs.[23] If there was one lesson to be learned from the neoclassical school, it was the importance of thinking at the margin. Moreover, its greatest achievement was to thus reconcile value theory and price theory, with marginal values being synonymous with price. Thus, both institutionalist and marginalist thinking encouraged understanding an increment of value as an increment of revenue. Second, while the Flood Control Act of 1936 famously required the measurement of benefits and costs "to whomsoever they may accrue," earlier benefit–cost work under the Reclamation Act, where agricultural economists had more involvement, required forecasting a future stream of *actual* returns to the government, through reimbursement from water users, and testing whether those revenues exceeded costs after discounting. In other words, this line of work required meeting a revenue-cost rather than a benefit–cost test. For all of these reasons, it was quite natural for economists in the period to think of value in terms of the revenue that realistically could be obtained by a real-world firm.

4.3 Measuring Surplus

But even as Clawson was struggling with these issues, the intellectual context was changing. A new postwar generation of economists was beginning to take leadership of the field, a generation that had much less reticence about measuring welfare. Moreover, somewhat inexplicably, economists of all schools were, simultaneously, beginning to accept consumer surplus as the proper way to do it.

For example, the new operations-research school of economists, centered around the Cowles Commission, held a paradigm infused with

NA 79.11.2227. Lord, Testimony presented to the Water Resources Council Hearings, 9-5-69, NA 315.24.3. Newton, Memo to Asst Dir., Cooperative Activities, 4-16-65, NA 79.11.1597. Tybout, Testimony presented to the Water Resources Council Hearings, 9-5-69, NA 315.24.3.

23 On interwar pluralism, see Morgan and Rutherford (1998). On the Institutional school, see Rutherford (2000, 2001).

welfare interpretations. Its director, Tjalling Koopmans, himself was highly motivated by what he described as "problems of planning, as well as theoretical problems in welfare economics." One of Cowles's early concerns was to shore up the measurability of "utility" for use in games and general equilibrium problems. Equilibrium solutions to these problems then yielded value functions that had clear welfare interpretations. Beckmann and Marschak (1955), for example, showed that when prices were taken as given, the solution to a transportation problem (how to allocate goods from fixed points of supply to fixed points of demand to minimize transportation costs) was equivalent to the solution for a social planner who wanted to maximize national income. With Cowles economists also working on the linkage from demand to utility through the integrability conditions, it was not long before they framed planning problems as maximizing consumer surplus instead. Examples included Dorfman and Marglin in Maass et al. (1962), Takayama and Judge (1964), and – despite his contempt for consumer surplus as a concept – even Samuelson (1952). Arrow too, famous for his result that, axiomatically, social choice rules are logically inconsistent, often advocated benefit–cost analysis for environmental and natural resource planning, using consumer surplus.[24]

More surprisingly, related developments were occurring at the University of Chicago. Representing the school's early roots, Knight, we have seen, was extremely skeptical of both Marshallian consumer surplus (incoherent) and Hicksian consumer surplus (fictional and unmeasurable). Representing the school as fully formed, Friedman (1953) had famously articulated an instrumentalist approach to utility, in which utility maximization would be used only for formulating hypotheses and forming testable predictions. This approach would certainly seem to rule out all welfare measurement. After all, if utility is only a posited "as-if" mechanism for deriving testable predictions, and if demand has ontological precedence over it, it is hard to see how normative prescriptions could be based upon it. Friedman himself seemed to say as much in his articles on expected utility with Leonard Savage from around that time. Nevertheless, by the 1960s, Friedman was measuring the effects of

[24] Koopmans, "problems … of welfare economics" (quoted in Mirowski 2002 p. 263). On measuring utility for game theory, see von Neumann and Morgenstern (1944) and Marschak (1950). On integrability, see Roy (1949) and Wold (1949). Samuelson (1952) constructed an object that he conceded any economist would naturally interpret as consumer surplus, but, to avoid the "strange connotations" of that term, renamed it "a net social payoff function." On Arrow's advocacy of benefit-cost analysis, see, for example, Arrow et al. (1993, 1996).

inflation in terms of how much consumer surplus it eroded, which he felt gave "a rough measure of the magnitude" of its welfare effects. Last but not least, Arnold Harberger, bridging the gap between the Chicago school and Cowles, introduced more structural or utility-theoretic interpretations of ordinary consumer surplus into Chicago's simple price-theory-with-real-world-applications approach to economics, showing how it could be viewed as a reasonable approximation to Hicksian welfare changes.[25]

This new acceptance and interest found its way into numerous applications between, roughly, 1955 and 1965. Harberger measured the lost consumer surplus from monopoly power, barriers to international trade, and taxation, with particular attention over the years to the special tax treatments of the energy and mining sectors. Marc Nerlove studied the effect of agricultural price supports and other commodities programs on consumer and producer surplus. Herbert Mohring studied the costs and benefits of transportation policy, modelling it as a programming problem designed to maximize economic surplus. And so on. Additionally, outside of benefit–cost analysis, related developments were transpiring in the theory of cost-of-living indices. During the same decades, wrestling with the practical problem of quality change in goods, economists began to adopt a welfare-based approach to such indices, replacing an earlier view that they simply measured the cost of a fixed basket of goods, a story with many parallels to this one.[26]

Water resources arguably became the leading arena for applying the new welfare economics, thanks to work by next-generation scholars trained in postwar operations research. Other than Hotelling's, the

[25] Friedman's work with Savage on expected utility (Friedman and Savage 1948, 1952); "a rough measure" (Friedman 1969 p. 14); see also Bailey (1956) for a similar approach. On Harberger's interpretation of consumer surplus as an approximation to a welfare change, which bears close similarities to Hotelling's, see Harberger (1964a, 1971). His synthesis of Chicago and Cowles can be appreciated from his resumé. He received his PhD from the University of Chicago in 1950, at the same time Cowles was there, and was a professor at Chicago from 1953 to 1983. He named Friedman, Jacob Marschak, and Theodore Schultz as his most influential classroom teachers, and had a PhD committee consisting of Arrow, Lloyd Metzler, and Franco Modigliani (Levy 1999) – a health mix of Chicago and Cowles figures! For more on the Chicago school's welfare economics, see Banzhaf (2010a).

[26] For Harberger's estimates of the welfare loss from monopoly power, international trade, and taxation, see respectively Harberger (1954, 1959a, b, [1964b] 1974). On energy and mining, see Harberger ([1955] 1974, [1961] 1974). On agricultural and transportation policy, see respectively Nerlove (1958) and Mohring and Harwitz (1962). On the history of cost-of-living indices, see Banzhaf (2001, 2004) and Stapleford (2009, 2011a, b).

earliest suggestions to use consumer surplus in this context appeared in five books over a five year period, all linked to RFF, the Harvard Water Program, or RAND. The first three appeared in one year (Eckstein 1958; Krutilla and Eckstein 1958; McKean 1958). At this point, the suggestions were still tentative. All three books argued that, for most assessments, marginal values would be sufficient, as projects would be small relative to the market. However, as an aside, they conceded that sometimes large projects might affect output prices. In this case, the quantity of output could be valued at an average of the prices before and after the project. Note there is a certain ambiguity here. Using the average price does give consumer surplus for a linear demand curve, but it could also be viewed as simply splitting the difference between two revenue rectangles (or two index numbers). Moreover, as if embarrassed by its history, none of the authors used the term "consumer surplus," and Roland McKean in particular implied he was building on new ideas from Hotelling and Abba Lerner.[27] Going a bit farther, Hirshleifer, De Haven, and Milliman (1960) advocated consumer surplus by name for large changes in the production of a good or service. Most explicitly, Dorfman and Stephen Marglin modeled a water project as the plan of a benevolent social planner who was allocating resources to maximize ordinary consumer surplus (Maass et al. 1962; see also Marglin 1967 and Dasgupta, Marglin, and Sen 1972). But as of yet none of these economists had actually followed through to produce such estimates.[28]

Moreover, there was still the question of what to do in the case of recreation and other non-market goods. Eckstein, Dorfman, and Marglin were highly skeptical that economists could ever simulate markets for such goods, preferring to leave the judgments to the political process, a point we will return to in Ch. 9.[29] Notably, Eckstein was unimpressed with the work by Doris Knapp and others on recreation expenditures, discussed in Chapter 3. Making the same point as Clawson, Eckstein argued that one had to distinguish between expenditures associated with

27 On taking the average price, see Eckstein (1958 p. 37) and Krutilla and Eckstein (1958 p. 74). Like Clawson, Eckstein too emphasized the single price that would hypothetically prevail if recreational sites were private (1958 p. 41).

28 A student of Hirshleifer's at the University of Chicago during this period did estimate the demand for water associated with one project and computed the area under it, again with no discussion (Dawson 1957).

29 Dorfman appears to have been more open to the question in the early 1960s, supervising a thesis (Merewitz 1966) and organizing a conference (Dorfman 1965) on the subject, but by the close of the decade he had clearly had made up his mind against such efforts.

recreation and WTP for public lands. However, unlike Clawson, he felt it could not be done. Said Eckstein,

> A proper measure of benefits would be to indicate how much managers of the lake could collect in user charges; [but] since there are no charges for the use of the reservoir, … appropriate prices cannot be found…. Such purposes of water projects as recreation must be judged on other criteria, for the use of benefit–cost analysis for them not only is invalid, but casts doubt and suspicion on procedures which can effectively serve a high purpose where they are appropriate.[30]

Thus, in Eckstein's view, it is better not to force the impossible. Echoing the words from the Clark committee, he suggested that forcing invalid numbers into a benefit–cost framework, just because there is an empty slot for them, only undermines the impression that benefit–cost analysis is a well-authenticated technique. Better simply to treat recreation effects qualitatively and allow decision makers to take account of such information through judgment rather than through arithmetic.

Eckstein believed the problem was greater than the specifics of outdoor recreation. He concluded that, in general, it is impossible to learn about individuals' values for public goods such as environmental amenities. As pointed out by Whittington and Smith (2020), in this he was particularly influenced by Paul Samuelson's analysis of the problem. Samuelson and, separately, Richard Musgrave had recently argued that, because individuals can free ride in the provision of public goods, they will not reveal their true preferences for such goods, even if markets existed for them. At any given price, their demand would fall short of their true preferred level of public goods. Reversing the logic, it would seem that at any quantity actually supplied the price would be lower than people's actual value for it.[31]

Despite Eckstein and Dorfman's skepticism, their students would unite the new value theories with the new travel cost model and be among the first to estimate consumer surplus measures. The most important of these is Jack Knetsch (1933–1922).[32] Knetsch had begun his education in

30 Eckstein (1958 p. 41).

31 Samuelson (1954) and Musgrave (1957). For Eckstein's reliance on Samuelson, see Eckstein (1958 p. 74). Cherrier and Fleury (2017) review economic debates on these matters and Desmarais-Tremblay (2017a) further discusses Samuelson and Musgrave's views.

32 Another is Robert Davis. As discussed in Ch. 9, Davis took a very different approach to the problem, pioneering the use of surveys to measure recreation values (Davis 1963a,b, Knetsch and Davis 1966). A third student is Leonard Merewitz. Merewitz actually took up the travel-cost approach in a 1964 undergraduate honors thesis written under Dorfman (Merewitz 1966). He went on to earn his PhD from Berkeley and continued to work in the area (see, e.g., Merewitz 1968).

agriculture, and then moved on to agricultural economics, earning his MA from Michigan State University in 1956. He then began working at the Tennessee Valley Authority, where, in his experience, they (like others) were looking for new classes of benefits to augment the totals.[33] Next, he earned his PhD in economics from Harvard in 1963, working with Eckstein and Dorfman.

In 1962, Knetsch went to RFF, bringing with him a perspective from the newer schools of welfare economics. Knetsch suggested using consumer surplus as the operational welfare criterion, in explicit contrast to Clawson's choice of maximum (single-price) revenue. Although understanding the potential revenues is important, he said, revenues are "a separate matter" from benefits.[34]

Open to new ideas, Clawson partnered with Knetsch to produce the magnum opus, *Economics of Outdoor Recreation* (1966), widely viewed as the pinnacle of this line of literature. Not only was it the Bible of recreation economics, it brought together the best of the various twentieth century schools of economics, combining the careful attention to social and historical context of the institutional school, the meticulous attention to data and statistics of agricultural economics, and the consumer theory of neoclassical economics. In its empirical estimates of the value of a recreation site, it was among the first studies in all of economics to estimate consumer surplus.

4.4 Applied Economics: Application, or Construction?

Given the priority of the policy questions, it is not surprising that the economics of recreation developed largely outside academia. In government, benefit–cost analysis provided a way to mediate disputes among interests, but this in turn created an incentive on the part of interest groups to alter the terms of the analysis to tilt it in their favor. Farmers interested in lower user fees for water and anybody else interested in higher benefit–cost ratios for projects had an incentive to include recreation as a benefit. Ultimately, these groups forced economists to include recreation in benefit–cost analysis. Economists, in government and think tanks as well as academia, then had to develop the practice of working with recreation data and navigating among economic theory, empirical

[33] Knetsch (2003).

[34] See Knetch (1963, 1964). "A separate matter" (Knetch 1963 p. 392). Davis (1963) and Wennergren (1964) made similar arguments.

methods, and bureaucratic imperatives. In this sense, environmental economics has been shaped by the state as much as it has helped appraise it (Furner and Supple 1990).

Agricultural economists like Trice, Wood, and Clawson found creative ways to monetize intangible benefits, but they were confused or ambivalent when it came to specifying precisely just what "benefits" were. In this case, far from being an "application" of a prior theory, measurement came *before* the theory. Policy questions required objective answers urgently – interpretation could come later. This story is by no means unique to natural resource economics. For example, similar problems plagued the pricing of non-traded assets subject to price controls or to government takings (Giocoli 2018).

For the economists, meaningful interpretations of what they were doing – meaningful in the context of economic theory, the context of measurement practices, and the policy context – did not come easily. Concepts such as consumer surplus, its historical pedigree notwithstanding, simply did not appear to be ready for use, off the shelf as it were. Moreover, they were not smoothly passed forward, as disembodied ideas, from Dupuit to Marshall to Hicks and Hotelling. They had to be interpreted within communities of economists speaking the same language, and confusion resulted when they were not in fact speaking the same language. Thus, in the benefit–cost community, these ideas had to be learned on the ground and reinterpreted – almost reinvented – before they could take on meaning in applied work. As when a child works on homework, the theoretical concepts sank in only through the applied problems. Once economists did turn to consumer surplus, they did so – *pace* Willig (1976) – *with* apology, in both senses of the word.

Moreover, natural resource economists did not merely apply or learn established theory. As they wrestled with practical problems, they set important precedents for the profession at large. Their work on the value of outdoor recreation, in particular, was among the very first attempts at actually measuring consumer surplus. In this way, they very much shaped the larger profession.[35]

[35] Smith (1988) also emphasizes the role of applied environmental and resource economics in shaping welfare economics.

5

John Krutilla and the Environmental Turn in Natural Resource Economics

> [S]olitude in the presence of natural beauty and grandeur, is the cradle of thoughts and aspirations which are not only good for the individual, but which society could ill do without. Nor is there much satisfaction in contemplating the world with nothing left to the spontaneous activity of nature; with every rood of land brought into cultivation, … every flowery waste or natural pasture ploughed up, all quadrupeds or birds which are not domesticated for man's use exterminated as his rivals for food, every hedgerow or superfluous tree rooted out, and scarcely a place left where a wild shrub or flower could grow without being eradicated as a weed in the name of improved agriculture. If the earth must lose that great portion of its pleasantness which it owes to things that the unlimited increase of wealth and population would extirpate from it, for the mere purpose of enabling it to support a larger, but not a better or a happier population, I sincerely hope … that they will be content to be stationary ….
>
> –John Stuart Mill, *Principles of Political Economy* (1848)

> The stone age did not end because the world ran out of stones, and the oil age will not end because we run out of oil.
>
> –Don Huberts, Royal Dutch Shell, in *The Economist* (1999)

The turn-of-the-century impasse between the intellectual heirs of Pinchot and Muir continued to mid-century, to the growing frustration of economists trying to chart an intermediate course, one which would incorporate aesthetic and ecological values into policy decisions, without abandoning decision rules framed in terms of materialistic benefits and costs. In the immediate postwar period, their efforts appearing to have failed, many gave up the attempt, concluding that it couldn't be done. As discussed in Chapter 3, Aldo Leopold for example eventually broke with the conservation economics of his youth and tried to create a new synthesis of ecology, economics, and other disciplines. Around the same time, economists in government concluded that the value of recreation per se could never be measured monetarily, so they turned to measuring expenditures on items associated with recreation instead, like transportation and gear. The former backed away from economics in order to incorporate aesthetic and ecological norms; the latter backed away from incorporating them in order to hold to an objective and economic science. Both recognized the impasse.

By the 1960s, economists were reconsidering the problem. As we saw in Chapter 4, work at RFF by Marion Clawson and Jack Knetsch represented one particular path to incorporating aesthetic appreciation of nature into economics. This chapter considers another path, one cleared by their RFF colleague, John Krutilla. Whereas Clawson wrestled with the specific challenge faced by NPS economists like Prewitt and Knapp, Krutilla responded to the broader philosophical challenges posed by people like Leopold. If Leopold's distinctive move was to wed the romanticism of Emerson and Muir to the science of ecology, it was Krutilla who – improbably – wed it to economics.

5.1 John Krutilla

John Krutilla (1922–2003) was a wilderness advocate, an avid outdoorsman who eagerly took field trips to the wilderness areas he studied, hiking and camping, and who at other times escaped to his cabin in the Shenandoahs (Figure 5.1). He read Muir and Leopold and was a friend of such figures as Margaret and Olaus Murie, leading US naturalists. Eventually, he would serve as trustee of the Environmental Defense Fund (1971–74) and as an officer of Leopold's Wilderness Society (1973–76). Like Leopold, he would forge a new synergy of economics and environmental preservation. Indeed, Krutilla was instrumental in founding the Association of Environmental and Resource Economics in the late 1970s and served as its third president. But in contrast to Leopold's interdisciplinary ecological economics, Krutilla's environmental economics put economics at the center.[1]

Krutilla grew up on a Washington farm and earned a BA in economics from Reed College. He earned a PhD from Harvard in 1952, working under Walter Isard (regional economics) and Alexander Gerschenkron (comparative economic systems and development), with a dissertation titled *The Structure of Costs and Regional Advantage in Primary Aluminum Production.* He began his career working with a natural

[1] Personal communication with Kerry Krutilla, Oct. 20, 2015. (Kerry Krutilla is John Krutilla's son.) Details on Krutilla's role in profession organizations are in AERE (1995).

Figure 5.1 John Krutilla

resources development team at the Tennessee Valley Authority (TVA), but went to RFF in 1955, where he remained until his retirement.

With his background in regional and development economics, Krutilla's early body of work represented a fairly conventional, albeit successful, application of economic theory to benefit–cost analysis, construed in narrowly materialistic terms. It included numerous pieces in applied journals and one in the *Journal of Political Economy* (Krutilla 1962). In one piece that would have important echoes later, Krutilla (1955) argued that regional development programs are better evaluated using benefit–cost analysis than by attempting to empirically estimate changes in regional output or income. He also suggested it would be useful to understand a program's effect on the supply functions of factors (like power and water) which are inputs into the production of goods for which demand is likely to increase as income increases. He called these "strategic factors."

Most notably among his early body of work, Krutilla co-authored the book *Multiple Purpose River Development: Studies in Applied Economic Analysis* with Otto Eckstein, a young economist at Harvard, in 1958. The book was a cutting-edge application of benefit–cost analysis to water projects.

To detailed institutional considerations about water, it united a more sophisticated understanding of microeconomic theory than previous practitioners had brought to the topic, including discussions of capital markets, the cost of public funds, external economies, indivisibilities, and so forth. It then applied this analytical framework to four case studies, including Hells Canyon on the Snake River in the Columbia River tributary system.[2]

Hells Canyon was notable as a battleground between two rival philosophies of development: a progressive version of government investment spearheaded by the US Army Corps of Engineers and the Bureau of Reclamation, championed by New Deal Democrats, and a pro-business version led by Idaho Power and championed by Republicans. The Engineers proposed one massive dam, while Idaho Power proposed a series of three smaller dams. Eventually, Idaho power's plan prevailed, and the last of the three dams was completed in 1967.[3]

In *Multiple Purpose River Development*, Krutilla and Eckstein evaluated the relative merits of the two rival projects. Considering such standard purposes of water development as hydroelectric power, flood control, and navigation, they found the Corps' plan to be more efficient, but found that a compromise between the two, a hypothetical two-dam project, would be more efficient than either. Though this work represented the frontier of benefit–cost analysis at the time, the times were rapidly changing. As Krutilla himself would later concede with a note of regret, the book limited its consideration of economic factors to physical production. In particular, it treated the "preservation" of wilderness for its "aesthetic appeal" as an extra-economic consideration, a value "in addition to economic efficiency" rather than one factor in the economic efficiency calculation. Thus, while nodding to the concerns of "preservation," at this point Krutilla, like Pinchot, left such factors outside the economic calculus. In *Multiple Purpose River Development*, the focus was on just that – development.[4]

5.2 RFF: From Scarcity and Growth to Environmental Quality in a Growing Economy

In this, Krutilla was thoroughly in step with RFF and how the Ford Foundation had envisioned it. As we saw in Chapter 1, Ford had established RFF in 1952 to study how best to conserve resources, in order to strengthen

[2] Krutilla and Eckstein (1958 Ch. V).

[3] On political battles over Hells Canyon development, see Brooks (2006).

[4] Krutilla's later regret (Fisher, Krutilla, and Cicchetti 1972). Aesthetic appeal as outside economic considerations (Krutilla and Eckstein 1958 p. 265).

democracy in its struggles against world communism. In Ford's view, this meant RFF would be an intellectual heir to Pinchot. Using words straight from the conservationist's lexicon, it described RFFs mission as the study of the "wise use of natural resources."[5]

RFF's early work fulfilled Ford's expectations. It began by hosting a "mid-century conference" on the future of natural resources, attended by some 1600 people discussing the "mounting pressure on our natural resources," from minerals and energy, to water, to recreational lands. At the close of its first decade, RFF released a magnum opus on *Trends in Natural Resource Commodities*, by Neal Potter and Francis Christy (1962), which compiled some 500 pages of data tables and charts on natural resource commodities from 1870 to 1957.

As Potter and Christy discussed in their report, on the whole, these data gave a surprisingly optimistic message. Their lead chart is reproduced here as Figure 5.2. The figure shows that, overall, agricultural and natural resource prices had not increased (after controlling for inflation). Although timber prices did increase, minerals prices actually decreased and agricultural prices were roughly flat, leaving the aggregate index flat as well. This pattern suggested that supplies were not being constrained. Additionally, as seen in Figure 5.3, employment in natural resource sectors had decreased relative to output (again with the exception of forestry), or, equivalently, the output per worker had increased.[6]

In the influential volume *Scarcity and Growth* (1963), Harold Barnett and Chandler Morse subjected Potter and Christy's data to additional analysis.[7] Barnett was a resource economist who had worked at the Department of the Interior (DOI), where he conducted a large input-output study of America's resources, and at RAND before coming to RFF; Morse was an economist at Cornell University. Their research confirmed Potter and Christy's sense of optimism. Setting their historical analysis in the broad sweep of the history of economic thought, they considered Malthusian and Ricardian hypotheses of resource scarcity driving growth to a halt. In Ricardo's theory, for example, the pressures

5 Ford Foundation (1954 p. 48). Also, "Resources Conservation and Development," recommendations of H. M. Albright, E.J. Condon, W. S. Davis, and F. Osborn, 1952?, and memo from Charles W. Eliot to Joseph M. McDaniel, Jr., May 27, 1952, both in RAC, Office of President Files, Gaither, Box 4, Folder 45.

6 Potter and Christy (1962 pp. 3, 15).

7 The work continued to be a touchstone in RFF's history, with volumes like *Scarcity and Growth Reconsidered* (Smith 1979) and *Scarcity and Growth Revisited* (Simpson, Toman, and Ayres 2005).

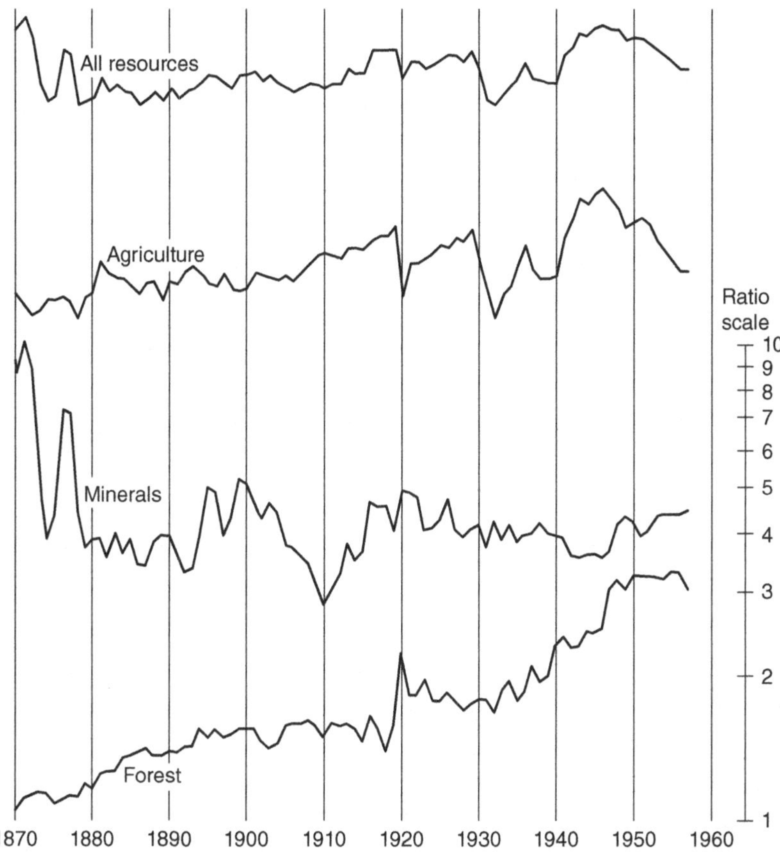

Figure 5.2 Natural resource prices, 1870–1957 (Potter and Christy 1962)

from population and economic growth would force agriculture onto less fertile land, or alternatively force more intensive farming of existing lands, with similar forces operating in the extraction of minerals, fuels, and other resources. Thus, through diminishing returns, labor productivity would fall and the marginal cost of production would increase. However, as seen in Figures 5.2 and 5.3, in actual fact prices were falling and productivity increasing.

Barnett and Morse consequently rejected these classical theories. While they agreed particular resources might be depleted, they concluded that natural resource scarcity, writ large, is not an impediment to growth. In large measure, this was because people innovatively found new substitutes for a particular resource as it became depleted. They wrote,

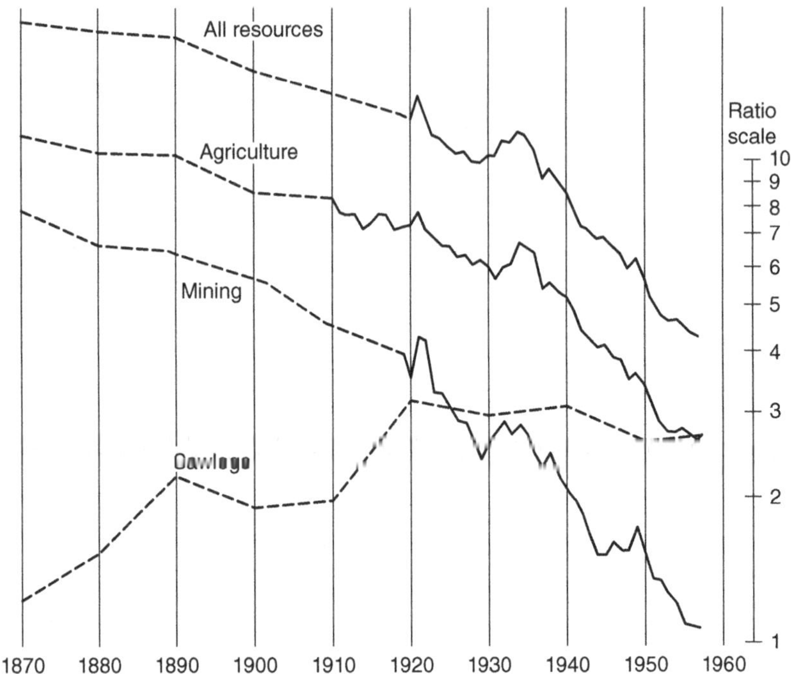

Figure 5.3 Employment-to-output ratios in natural resource sectors, 1870–1957 (Potter and Christy 1962)

[T]he resource problem is one of continual accommodation and adjustment to an ever-changing economic resource quality spectrum. The physical properties of the natural resource base impose a series of initial constraints on the growth and progress of mankind, but the resource spectrum undergoes kaleidoscopic change through time. Continual enlargement of the scope of substitutability—the result of man's technological ingenuity and organizational wisdom—offers those who are nimble a multitude of opportunities for escape....

Continuing on they said,

That man will face a series of particular scarcities as the result of growth is a foregone conclusion; that these will impose general scarcity—increasing cost—is not a legitimate corollary. The twentieth century's discovery of the uniformity of energy and matter has increased the possibilities of substitution to an unimaginable degree, and placed at man's disposal an indefinitely large number of alternatives from which to choose.... The finite limits of the globe, so real in their unqueried simplicity, lose definition under examination.[8]

[8] Barnett and Morse (1963 pp. 244–5). Barnett had long been interested in the theme of resource substitution, going back to his earlier work at DOI (Goodwin 1981 pp. 37–9).

This optimistic tone was echoed in a number of other RFF reports and books over the next five years or so, most notably in a series of studies by Hans Landsberg and colleagues, including *Resources in America's Future* (Landsberg, Fischman, and Fisher 1963), *Natural Resources for US Growth* (Landsberg 1964), and *Energy in the United States* by Landsberg and Sam Schurr (1968). Landsberg also argued that new substitutes would come online. For example, shale oil and gas would eventually replace conventional supplies. Still, these substitutes would not appear magically. They required continued technical innovation, free trade, and political and economic stability.[9]

Nevertheless, the message emerging from this line of work was that natural resource scarcity was not a limit to growth. The logical corollary was that Pinchot's branch of conservation was no longer a priority for public policy. More specifically, the logic was that future resource scarcity would increase future prices, creating an incentive to (i) decrease the quantity demanded in the future, finding new ways to do with less, (ii) save today's supplies for the future through inter-temporal arbitrage, and (iii) find new substitutes. Over the next two decades, this logic became the basis for rebuttals from optimistic economists like Julian Simon when contesting neo-Malthusian warnings from the Club of Rome and others: even as particular physical resources are depleted, in the final analysis, humanity itself is the "ultimate resource."[10]

This was a startling conclusion for RFF scholars to reach. Essentially, they were rejecting the very rationale for RFF's founding just ten years previously. However, their conclusions were not all butterflies and rainbows. They sounded warnings about a very different kind of resource scarcity and, accordingly, a new research agenda. Having rejected Malthusian and Ricardian scarcity, Barnett and Morse suggested that a more plausible concern was Mill's, encapsulated in this chapter's epigraph, that unchecked growth would begin to undermine environmental quality. They suggested

[9] Landsberg and Schurr both began their careers at the NBER working on a project on manufacturing productivity. Like Potter and Christy's report, Landsberg et al.'s 1963 report was a staggering 1,000 pages of facts and figures in the old NBER style. For a retrospective appreciation of the work of Landsberg and Schurr along with biographical details, see Darmstadter (2003).

[10] On Barnett's influence on Simon, see Sabin (2013). Simon's views are represented by his book, *The Ultimate Resource* (Simon 1981). He was responding to such works as *The Population Bomb* (Ehrlich and Ehrlich 1968) and the Club of Rome's *Limits to Growth* (Meadows et al. 1972). My summary of Barnett and Morse's historical summary is not meant to imply that their optimism or Simon's were entirely new on the scene. On earlier strands of population optimism in classical political economy, see Kern (2003).

that such issues related to quality of life – to the distribution of income and to "the intangible satisfactions derived from the appearance of the environment" – may prove to elude the same solutions as material inputs, with fewer possibilities for substitution.[11]

Thus, in the 1960s, RFF began to turn from studying the conservation of natural resources to the preservation of environmental quality. For example, in 1962 it hired Allen Kneese to lead a new quality-of-the-environment division. A 1966 forum organized by Kneese represents one characteristic example of this new line of work. It was titled *Environmental Quality in a Growing Economy*, clearly a twist on the titles of earlier works like *Scarcity and Growth* or *Natural Resources for US Growth*. In one prominent contribution to the volume, Kenneth Boulding offered his essay, "The Economics of the Coming Spaceship Earth." Boulding argued that the old mode of economic thinking emphasized the one way throughput of resources through the economy, crudely measured by GNP. Although that thinking was sensible in a time when the world could be viewed as an open system, it was now outdated. A new mode of thinking now needed to emphasize the feedbacks of pollution and waste onto the quality of the environment, in a closed system.[12]

RFF's leaders were well aware of the import of the moves they were making, as was Ford. In the introduction to those 1966 proceedings, the editor wrote that, all over the world, the "pressing problems of natural resources … are coming to be those of quality rather than quantity." Elaborating,

> This change of emphasis has come quickly. As recently as 1951, when President Truman established the President's Materials Policy Commission, fears of natural resource scarcity were uppermost in the minds of most people. The commission's main assignment was to inquire into whether there would be enough food and raw materials at reasonable prices over the next twenty-five years to support continued economic growth and meet the requirements of national security.
>
> Today, in the middle 1960's, many of the worries over supply have subsided.… Instead, the most troublesome questions are likely to concern the cleanliness of water and air; the effects of heavy use of pesticides upon soil and water; availability of suitable surroundings for outdoor recreation; the beauty of the countryside; and the effects of urban living upon the human body and spirit. These make a mixed bag of problems, but all of them can come under the tent of a single phrase: "quality of the environment."[13]

[11] Barnett and Morse (1963 p. 252).

[12] The forum papers were edited and published by Jarrett (1966a). "The Economics of the Coming Spaceship Earth" (Boulding 1966).

[13] Jarrett (1966b pp. *vii–viii*).

At this historical juncture, not long after Rachel Carson had published *Silent Spring*, the need to address the troublesome questions about the quality of the environment should have been obvious to anybody. However, economists were still struggling to gain purchase on what remained an elusive problem. In their conclusion, Barnett and Morse had suggested that, in the long run, what was needed was a more objective approach to our "value problem," a way to incorporate the trade-offs between distribution, intangible benefits, and material wealth into the economic calculus.[14] Many economists were now beginning to agree. But with the promising innovations in the economics of outdoor recreation excepted, they were still no closer to reconciling this "value problem" than were Pinchot and Muir, Leopold, or the NPS parks economists heretofore.

5.3 Conservation Reconsidered

Arguably, nobody did more to impose economic forms on these inchoate issues than John Krutilla. Sometime in the mid-1960s, Krutilla appears to have made a deliberate pivot to address what he now viewed as the deficiencies of his early work in benefit–cost analysis, with its omission of environmental quality as an "extra economic" consideration. He now endeavored to combine his outdoor avocation with his economics profession, an intellectual move that would characterize the rest of his career. For example, with his wife, Shirley Krutilla, he began to take a series of courses offered by the USDA Graduate School and the Audubon Society, courses on ecology, meteorology, geology, soil science, and so forth.[15]

The intellectual fruits of this pivot first appeared in 1967, when Krutilla published "Conservation Reconsidered" in the *American Economic Review*.[16] There, he borrowed the language of "conservation" and "preservation," which still carried the historical echoes of the dispute between Pinchot and Muir and their respective intellectual heirs. Specifically, he argued that economists, by ignoring the concerns of the preservationists like Muir, implicitly had biased benefit–cost calculations in favor of wise-use conservationists.

[14] Barnett and Morse (1963 p. 252–66).

[15] Personal communication with Kerry Krutilla, Oct. 4, 2015. Further evidence in J. Krutilla, Testimony before the Federal Power Commission in the matter of Pacific Northwest Power Company and Washington Public Power Supply System, project no. 2243/2273, 1970[?], EDF 1.V.1, Litigation Files G-I, Box 2. On the historical importance of the USDA graduate school, see Rutherford (2011).

[16] Krutilla (1967a). See also the more discursive version published in *Daedalus* (Krutilla 1967b).

In making this case, Krutilla's most fundamental point was that there was a trade-off between developing a resource and preserving it. In other words, developing a resource came at the *opportunity cost* of preservation, potentially meaning the loss of a unique or special landscape.[17] And these costs were very real – just as real as the reciprocal cost of foregoing development when preserving landscapes. Said Krutilla, "When the existence of a grand scenic wonder or a unique and fragile ecosystem is involved, its *preservation* and continued availability are a significant part of the real income of many individuals." By these "individuals," he clarified that he meant "the spiritual descendants of John Muir, the present members of the Sierra Club, the Wilderness Society … and others to whom the loss of a species or the disfigurement of a scenic area causes acute distress and a sense of genuine relative impoverishment." These spiritual descendants of Muir valued the "mere existence of biological and/or geomorphological variety and its widespread distribution."[18] Such values would come to be known as "existence values" or "non-use values" in the environmental economics literature – values for the simple existence of a thing rather than for what it could do instrumentally.

Through this seemingly simple move, Krutilla brought the intrinsic values emphasized by Muir, Leopold, and others into the utilitarian calculus of economics. *Contra* Pinchot, preservation didn't inevitably decrease economic efficiency or national income. It could *increase* "real income" if people put a high enough value on preserved landscapes.

To this overarching point, Krutilla added two specific reasons why analysts should consider weighing the benefit–cost scales more in favor of preservation. The first centered on uncertainty about the future. Krutilla noted that whereas a decision to preserve always left open the possibility of developing later, in contrast a decision to develop had *irreversible* adverse consequences for preservation, since the landscape would be irretrievably lost, a point that would be further developed by Anthony Fisher and Kenneth Arrow.[19] Furthermore, Krutilla suggested that even

[17] Smith (2004) comments that the historical use of the term "undeveloped" for natural environments seemed to give the impression that there were no opportunity costs of development, whereas labeling them as "preserved" conveyed a very different impression.

[18] Krutilla (1967a pp. 779, 781, emphasis added). Muir, and his followers in the Sierra Club, and Leopold, and his followers in the Wilderness Society, appeared often in Krutilla's writings from this point on. Additional instances include Krutilla and Cicchetti (1972), Fisher and Krutilla (1974), Fisher, Krutilla, and Cicchetti (1974) and many others.

[19] For example, Fisher, Krutilla, and Cicchetti (1972) and Arrow and Fisher (1974).

if preservationists had no value for the resource at present, the possibility that they might in the future would generate an "option value" in the presence of such irreversibility.[20] All this implied not only that benefit-cost analyses of development projects were biased in favor of development whenever they ignored these opportunity costs, but suggested that many market transactions involved the problem of free-riding on the preservation side of the ledger.

Second, as an empirical matter, Krutilla believed that preservation values were increasing, because of both demand and supply factors. Demand for preserved landscapes was increasing as people gained more disposable income, and it would continue to increase as they took part in outdoor recreation, gaining tastes for more such activity. Meanwhile, the supply of such landscapes was dwindling because, as public goods, they could not compete on a level playing field in the land market. Moreover, there were no private substitutes to take their place. In contrast, private markets were quite adept at providing substitutes for those scarce resources which served as material or energy inputs in private production. Consequently, the value of developing natural resources was decreasing over time, relative to preservation.

This logic reversed the traditional emphasis in natural resource economics on conservation. Referring to Barnett and Morse and picking up where *Scarcity and Growth* left off, Krutilla wrote,

> the traditional concerns of *conservation* economics—the husbanding of natural resource stocks for the use of future generations—may now be outmoded by advances in technology. On the other hand, the central issue seems to be the problem of providing for the present and future the amenities associated with unspoiled natural environments.[21]

Here, Krutilla seems to have been hearkening back to his earlier notion of "strategic factors," in which he had suggested that public investments in development should target resources that were inputs into the production of outputs with growing demand. Only now those inputs were reinterpreted more broadly to include preserved environmental landscapes.

20 Here, Krutilla was drawing on earlier arguments by Burton Weisbrod (1964).

21 Krutilla (1967a p. 778, emphasis added). Krutilla opened his essay with references to Potter and Christy and especially Barnett and Morse, and these citation patterns appear to be more than mere nods to RFF's canon. Krutilla's young protégés at RFF, Charles Cicchetti, Anthony Fisher, and Kerry Smith, all recall that Krutilla was deeply affected by *Scarcity and Growth*. See Smith (2015) for additional discussion of its influence on Krutilla's thinking.

As Smith (2011) has noted, in "Conservation Reconsidered" we see Krutilla coming to grips with the same problems that had so vexed Leopold. Leopold had argued that "one basic weakness in a conservation system based wholly on economic motives is that most members of the land community *have no economic value*.... When one of these *non-economic* categories is threatened, and if we happen to love it, we invent subterfuges to give it economic importance."[22] These concerns had led Leopold to forge compromises between economics, ecology, and other disciplines into a new land ethic. In contrast, Krutilla argued that if indeed we do happen to love one of these categories in the land community, then that qualifies as economic value. In his taxonomy of subjective values, the "mere existence" of a beloved object is one category. For Krutilla, development brings benefits but comes at the opportunity cost of foregoing preservation values (and vice versa); thus, the choice between development and preservation is itself an economic question.

5.4 Hells Canyon Revisited

Krutilla soon had a chance to put his new ideas into practice. In 1957, just about the time *Multiple Purpose River Development* appeared in print, Pacific Northwest Power, a consortium of four private utilities, proposed yet another project in Hells Canyon, downstream from the earlier three, at what was known as the High Mountain Sheep site. The Washington Public Power Supply System soon proposed a rival project nearby; then in 1962, the DOI proposed an alternative federal project at the High Mountain Sheep site. Thus, three parties maneuvered to develop the same area. In 1962, the Federal Power Commission (FPC) ruled in favor of the Pacific Northwest Power. In response, DOI, headed by Secretary Stewart Udall, sued the FPC, in part on grounds that its plan would better protect anadromous fish, as required by law. While an appeal to the FPC and a trial upheld the initial decision, the case eventually went to the Supreme Court of the United States. In 1967, in *Udall v. FPC*, the court decision remanded the case to the FPC in a 6–2 decision, ordering it not only to reconsider *which* development proposal was in the public interest in light of further evidence about fish protection, but also whether *any* development was in the public interest in light of such concerns.

The majority opinion, authored by progressive jurist William Douglas, stated,

[22] Leopold ([1949] 1987 p. 210, emphasis added).

> The issues of whether deferral of construction would be more in the public interest than immediate construction and whether preservation of the reaches of the river affected would be more desirable and in the public interest than the proposed development are largely unexplored in this record. We cannot assume that the [Federal Water Power] Act commands the immediate construction of as many projects as possible.... The grant of authority to the Commission to alienate federal water resources does not, of course, turn simply on whether the project will be beneficial to the licensee. Nor is the test solely whether the region will be able to use the additional power. The test is whether the project will be in the public interest. And that determination can be made only after an exploration of all issues relevant to the "public interest," including future power demand and supply, alternate sources of power, the public interest in preserving reaches of wild rivers and wilderness areas, the preservation of anadromous fish for commercial and recreational purposes, and the protection of wildlife.[23]

Thus, for the first time in the bureaucratic turf wars over river development, preservationists now had a seat at the table. In a very real sense, the modern era of environmental politics in America was born.[24]

When the case was remanded to the FPC, Krutilla entered as an expert "Friend of the Commission" in 1969.[25] In contrast to his earlier work on Hells Canyon in *Multiple Purpose River Development*, Krutilla now applied the arguments of "Conservation Reconsidered" to the problem. In particular, he emphasized the importance of option value, reflecting the asymmetry in the fact that preservation maintains the option to develop in the future, whereas developing the canyon would irreversibly harm the ecosystem. Along with his younger colleagues Charles Cicchetti and Anthony Fisher, Krutilla would continue to develop the idea of option value, and its application to the Hells Canyon case in particular, in a series of publications in the early- to mid-1970s.

The basic argument from this line of work is illustrated in Figure 5.4 (from Fisher, Krutilla, and Cicchetti 1972). The curve $D^*(t)$ is a hypothetical

23 *Udall v. Federal Power Commission* 387 U.S. 428 1967, p. 449.

24 Hays (1982) considers the Hells Canyon episode the most dramatic example of the transition from the old politics of conservation to the postwar politics of environmentalism. For more on the history of the Hells Canyon episode, see Brooks (2006) and Ewert (2001). For a contemporary perspective, see Lyons (1955). Additionally, Goodwin (1983) discusses the proposed idea for a Columbia Valley Authority to develop the region, modelled after TVA.

25 On his testimony to the FPC, see Krutilla, John, Testimony before the Federal Power Commission in the matter of Pacific Northwest Power Company and Washington Public Power Supply System, project no. 2243/2273, 1970[?], EDF collection, RG 1, SG V, Ser. 1, Litigation Files G-I, Box 2. See also Cicchetti, Charles, testifying before the same commission. On later collaborations with Cicchetti and Fisher, see Fisher, Krutilla, and Cicchetti (1972), Krutilla and Cicchetti (1972), and Krutilla and Fisher (1975).

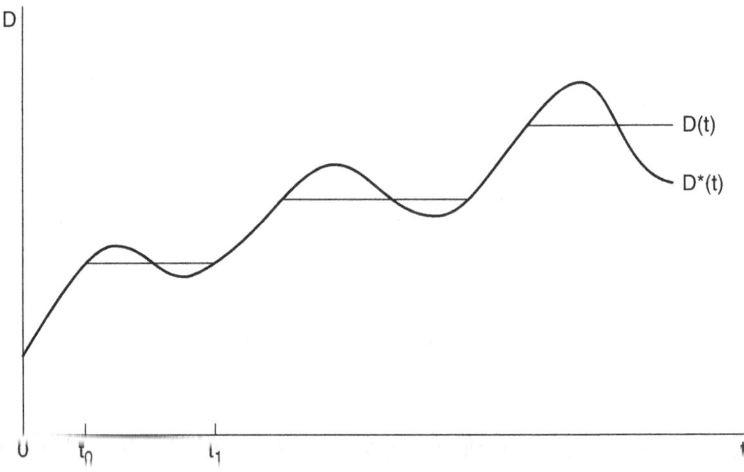

Figure 5.4 Irreversible development
Source: Fisher, Krutilla, and Cicchetti (1972 p. 609)

path depicting what the optimal development over time would be *if*, theoretically, it were possible to reverse development. The path shows periods of increasing development followed by periods of decreasing development. But as development is irreversible, the downward-sloping portions of this myopic path are impossible. Ruling those out, the optimal path becomes $D(t)$. To maximize the present value of net benefits, the constraint imposed by irreversibility leads to a smoothed path which, relative to the myopic one, undershoots development for a time where the myopic path would be at its peaks but then overshoots it where the myopic path would be at its troughs. As an empirical matter, Fisher et al. then asserted that the gross benefits of preservation are growing over time, while the gross benefits of development are shrinking, as technological change reduces the costs of substitutes, as Krutilla had argued in "Conservation Reconsidered." That is, we are currently at a point like t_0 in the graph. Consequently, $D^*(t)$ is declining monotonically or soon will be. Since that is impossible, the optimal $D(t)$ entails a so-called bang-bang (or on-off) solution, with development up to the present and no further development in the foreseeable future, until perhaps a time like t_1 comes along.

Fisher et al. employed a fairly complicated simulation model to apply this analysis to Hells Canyon. The model involved parameters representing a rate of technological change in private substitutes for the natural resource, growth rates (and deceleration in growth) in intercept and slope terms of a demand function for preservation, population growth rates, plus the by-then-conventional benefit–cost parameters related to development benefits and costs and interest rates. They found that given the simulated rates of change, a base-period annual preservation value of $52,000–$147,000 would be enough to tip the balance toward preservation and away from further development of Hells Canyon. Since this critical value was a fraction of the best estimates of recreation values, they concluded that the economics supported preservation.[26] In a repudiation of Pinchot's conservationism, rational utilitarian management of natural resources no longer presupposed development; it also could come out on the side of preservation.

5.5 A Shifting Landscape of Economic and Environmental Thought

These changes in Krutilla's thinking and others' occurred within the context of three larger intellectual developments in both economics and the environmental movement in the 1950s and 1960s. First, in economics, Lionel Robbins's (1935) definition of the field in terms of opportunity costs was rapidly displacing rival "classificatory" definitions. Those classificatory definitions had demarked the territory of economics as limited to the business or material realms of life. For example, Marshall, recall, had defined economics as "a study of men as they live and move and think in the ordinary business of life." Elaborating, he said, "it concerns itself chiefly with those motives which affect ... man's conduct in the business part of his life .... [And] the steadiest motive to ordinary business work is the desire ... for the material reward of work." Other definitions at the turn of the century were similar.[27]

When viewed in those terms, what economists sometimes referred to as intangible or spiritual considerations such as the love of wilderness were decidedly non-economic. But when viewed through the lens of Robbins's definition, wilderness looks like a scarce resource, so the choice to develop it or preserve it entails opportunity costs, making it an economic choice. The distinction is illustrated in Figure 5.5. From the economics-as-material-welfare point of view, depicted in the top panel,

[26] For the most detailed account of the model, see Krutilla and Fisher (1975 Chs. 5 and 6). The basics are also present in Krutilla's testimony, where Krutilla reached similar conclusions (*op cit.*).

[27] Marshall ([1920] 1946 p. 14).

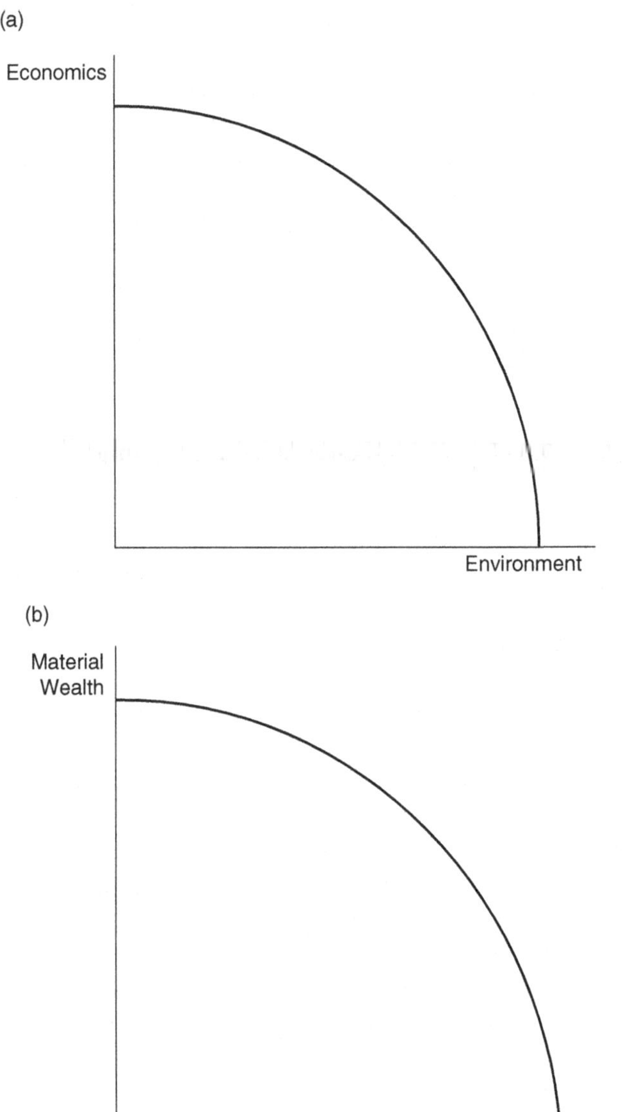

Figure 5.5 (a) Economics vs. the environment contrasted with (b) Economics of the environment

there is a trade-off between economics (material welfare) and wilderness. Economics is one factor to consider, preserving wilderness is another. The figure shows the possible combinations of the two, which include any point on or below the curve. The downward slope of the curve represents the fact that more preservation comes at the cost of less material welfare (or vice versa). In the economics-as-opportunity-cost view (on the bottom), economics itself is about such trade-offs, so it transcends the axis and is elevated to govern the trade-off between material welfare and wilderness. As Robbins had put it, "there is still an economic problem of deciding between the 'economic' and the 'non-economic'."[28] This logic paved the way for allowing a new "economics *of* the environment" to replace the stalemate of an "economics *versus* the environment."

As Backhouse and Medema (2009a, b) have shown, economists on both sides of the Atlantic were coming to embrace this new definition of economics in the late 1950s and 1960s. Thus, it is no coincidence that Krutilla's intellectual journey from *Multiple Purpose River Development* to "Conservation Reconsidered" occurred at the same time that Gary Becker was pushing labor economics to consider crime, the allocation of time, and so forth. Both developments were an expansion of economics to new ranges of topics: suddenly, opportunity costs were everywhere.[29]

As Backhouse and Medema further discuss, Robbins's definition was simultaneously liberating and restricting. It liberated economists to consider new topics, but it restricted them to using the tools of constrained optimization. In evaluating economics, Leopold had seen a discipline that could not yet conceive itself addressing the environment in the way Krutilla would later do. But at the same time, to forge a new ecological economics, Leopold had been able to draw on a profession willing to embrace a wider set of human motives and a greater appreciation for institutions and history.

Interestingly, Robbins's essay may have contributed to the history of environmental economics in a second way as well. As previously noted, the strictures Robbins tried to place on normative economics provoked responses from Kaldor, Hicks, and others, who developed the potential Pareto test in response, as a scientific form of welfare economics. Those tests became the basis for most applied benefit–cost analysis. Near the end of his career, Krutilla (1981) would place his own work in this context, as an effort to address Robbins's critique of applied welfare economics.[30]

[28] Robbins (1935 p. 11).

[29] Others, besides Krutilla, were making similar points at the time about trade-offs among so-called intangibles. See, for example, Schelling (1968) (discussed in Chapter 7) and Schmid (1967).

[30] Krutilla (1981).

A second change in the intellectual context was that US economists were, around the same time, increasingly embracing the idea of empirically measuring economic values for environmental services and for other goods not traded in markets. Such work began with government economists incorporating outdoor recreation into benefit–cost analyses of dam projects, a context obviously important to Krutilla's work, but by the time of "Conservation Reconsidered" Krutilla's RFF colleagues were rapidly developing these ideas in new directions. These earlier moves would have made the idea of measuring the economic values of foregone natural environments at least conceivable to Krutilla and his audience. At the same time, Krutilla's idea of nonuse values created a new category of values to be estimated, one which in turn elevated the importance of new measurement tools such as survey-based contingent valuation. Indeed, soon after "Conservation Reconsidered," Krutilla began to lead a new Natural Environments Program at RFF to investigate methods for measuring the value of environmental amenities. Staffed by future leaders in the field like Cicchetti, Fisher, Kerry Smith, and others, the program further explored the idea of option value, the implications of congestion for the quality of a recreation experience and hence willingness-to-pay, and the generalization of recreation benefits to multiple sites.[31]

Finally, these changes in economics coincided with important historical developments in environmentalism. Indeed, properly speaking, one can hardly even speak of "environmentalism" before this period. Until World War II, the schism in American conservationism, represented by the rift between Pinchot and Muir, pitted natural resource managers pursuing efficiency against lovers of nature who approached it on spiritual, rather than rational, terms. While those tensions remain with us today, the two categories of conservation and preservation rearranged and reconfigured themselves in important respects. On one side, elements from the "preservationist" camp dropped Muir's spiritual focus and embraced the new science of ecology to bolster the case for preservation. For example, when Leopold transitioned from being a disciple of Pinchot to a lover of wilderness, he hardly dropped science in favor of spiritual transcendence. Rather, he fused a love of wilderness to new arguments for its importance drawn from ecology, while simultaneously urging people to abandon the zero-sum fight between development and

[31] On option value: Fisher, Krutilla, and Cicchetti (1972), Krutilla and Cicchetti (1972), and Krutilla and Fisher (1975). On recreation and environmental quality: Cicchetti and Smith (1973). On multiple sites: Cicchetti, Fisher, and Smith (1976).

preservation in favor of a new harmony between man and nature. On the other side, the "conservationist" camp, which previously defined scientific management of resources only in terms of material uses, soon adapted to the new political realities driven by popular tastes. As but one small but revealing example, during this period many state agencies simply swapped out their shingles reading "game managers" for ones reading "wildlife managers."[32]

As Hays (1982, 1987) notes, the new "environmentalism" that emerged during this period was thus a fusion of ecology and the political economy of aesthetic consumption, rather than production. Furthermore, while the appearance of Rachel Carson's *Silent Spring* in 1962, the fire on the Cuyahoga River in 1969, or the first Earth Day in 1970 may have been adopted as important symbols of American environmentalism, the real strength of the movement was found in the political groundswell focused on public health, recreation opportunities, and a reaction to "overdevelopment." These were the concerns of an increasingly urban culture. As William Cronon has put it, "country people generally know far too much about working the land to regard *un*worked land as their ideal. In contrast, elite urban tourists and wealthy sportsmen projected their leisure-time frontier fantasies onto the American landscape and so created wilderness in their own image."[33]

At the crossroads of these three movements stood John Krutilla. Taking a little bit from each of them, he helped re-organize earlier debates framed in terms of economics-versus-the-environment into a new field studying the economics of the environment. Shortly after "Conservation Reconsidered," Krutilla and Cicchetti made the point quite explicitly and succinctly, arguing that the "nub of the analytical problem" for many conservation questions was a trade-off between two alternative purposes.

> One purpose, associated with extractive activities, would convert the natural environment into intermediate products to satisfy the requirements of industrial raw materials used in production of final consumption goods. The other purpose involves the retention of the natural environment for the provision of a flow of services which enter directly into the utility function of final consumers.[34]

Thus, economics could handle "intangible" values for nature by reinterpreting nature as something that provided services directly to consumers,

[32] On Leopold's fusion, see Callicot (1994) and Goodwin (2008). Hays (1982) makes the observation about wildlife managers and game wardens.

[33] Cronon (1995 p. 79).

[34] Krutilla and Cicchetti (1972 p. 2)

as well as to producers of material goods. This approach represented an almost 180 degree turn from economists' consensus position around 1950, when, starting from a focus on material development in the spirit of Pinchot, they ironically were dragged into considering recreation values by political pressures to nudge benefit–cost ratios in *favor* of development – *against* their better judgment that economics should be limited to material considerations and avoid such intangibles. But now that they were computing recreation benefits and related values, it was no great leap to credit them to the preservation side of the ledger.

In this way, Krutilla brought the intrinsic values emphasized by Muir, Leopold, and others into the utilitarian calculus of economics. As Krutilla himself showed, environmental values thus could be incorporated into benefit–cost analyses of government programs, a research project that is now routine for governments and intergovernmental agencies around the world. Such values also have been incorporated into litigation over environmental damages and even national- or global-level indices of landscapes. Many biologists and ecologists have applauded the quantification of such ecosystem services as a way to give the environment a seat at the economic table, precisely Krutilla's objective.[35]

But in the very act of incorporating the intrinsic values of nature into utilitarian economics, Krutilla also narrowed the sense in which they could be considered intrinsic. They remained so in the sense that they could be viewed as ends in themselves, without any instrumental value or any particular "use." But to be compatible with utilitarianism their value still had to be rooted in the subjective judgment of people, a position Callicott (1989, 1999) describes as "truncated intrinsic value." Or, to put it in other terms, values need not be anthropocentric – not centered on human uses – but they must still be anthropogenic, with their source in human judgments.[36] Accordingly, other ecologists and philosophers remain highly skeptical of the commodification of nature that Krutilla's research program advanced.[37] So have some economists. Not long after Krutilla wrote "Conservation Reconsidered," the development economist E.F. Schumacher, advocating for a *Small is Beautiful* approach to economics, argued that benefit–cost analysis

[35] For an example of Krutilla's work on bringing preservation into benefit–cost analysis, see Fisher and Krutilla (1975). For an example from litigation, see Bishop et al. (2017). For examples of indices, see Bateman et al. (2013) and Costanza et al. (2014). On support from natural scientists, see for example, Daily (1997).

[36] See Rolston (2002) and Schröter et al. (2014) for further discussion of such issues.

[37] For example, McCauley (2006), Robertson (2006).

is a procedure by which the higher is reduced to the level of the lower and the priceless is given a price. It can therefore never serve to clarify the situation and lead to an enlightened decision. All it can do is lead to self-deception or the deception of others; for to undertake to measure the immeasurable is absurd and constitutes but an elaborate method of moving from preconceived notions to foregone conclusions … The logical absurdity, however, is not the greatest fault of the undertaking: what is worse, and destructive of civilization, is the pretence that everything has a price or, in other words, that money is the highest of all values.[38]

Thus, although Krutilla brought the concerns of Muir and Leopold into economics in his own way, not all "the spiritual descendants" of Muir or Leopold, whose values Krutilla strove to represent, have embraced that way.

[38] Schumacher (1973 pp. 43–44).

6

Pricing Pollution

You get what you pay for.

–Gabriel Biel, *Expositio Canonis Missae* (1576)

Even as economists such as Krutilla were thinking about how to calculate the economic values of nature in the absence of markets, others were thinking about how to introduce pollution prices into the actual economic calculations made by households and firms. Numerous economists jumped into this space, from Robert Solow and Joseph Stiglitz to Kenneth Boulding and Nicholas Georgescu-Roegen on questions of sustainability, from Kenneth Arrow to James Buchanan on externalities, and William Baumol, Wallace Oates, and Martin Weitzman on pollution pricing, among many others. But of all economists working on pollution pricing in the era, Allen V. Kneese (1930–2001) was the widely acknowledged leader. In *The Economics of Regional Water Quality Management* (1964), Kneese, an economist at RFF, introduced detailed proposals for "effluent charges" on emissions of pollutants into waterways. Extensively cited, the book was considered the first systematic treatment of the topic and certainly the most definitive. Shortly thereafter, Thomas Crocker (1966) and John Dales (1968a, b) introduced proposals for trading pollution rights, later known as the tradable permit or cap-and-trade approach. This body of work extended economic thought about pricing the environment from benefit–cost analyses of government projects and regulations to actual pollution markets.

6.1 Allen Kneese and Effluent Charges

Allen Kneese earned his Ph.D. in economics from Indiana University, with a dissertation on market power and exclusive dealing in the farm machinery, automobile, and petroleum industries (Figure 6.1). After graduating,

Figure 6.1 Allen Kneese

he worked at the University of New Mexico and at the Federal Reserve Bank of Kansas City, where he first turned to researching water resources problems in the American West. In 1961, at what was still an early stage in his career, Kneese moved to RFF. He established himself as a leader in the field, artfully using grants and conferences to shape the community's research agenda. He also built up many of its institutions. For example, he was a founding editor of the journal *Water Resources Research*. Later, as environmental economics was becoming a distinct sub-discipline in the 1970s, Kneese was front and center, serving as the first president of the Association of Environmental and Resource Economists and founding editor (along with his collaborator, Ralph d'Arge) of its flagship publication, the *Journal of Environmental Economics and Management* (JEEM).[1]

Kneese's first forays into the economics of water resources addressed the traditional problem of developing them as inputs into

1 Dissertation (Kneese 1956). See Kneese (1988) for a brief autobiographical statement, including a summary of early intellectual influences. See Nishibayashi (2019) for a historical discussion of Kneese and his work.

material production, particularly in the context of water shortages in the American West (Kneese 1960). Like other works at the time on this subject, Kneese adopted a welfarist perspective on the problem. As a logical point of departure, he began with what he characterized as Pigouvian welfare economics. But here he was clearly referring to the interpretation of market prices as marginal social values generally, as in Pigou's national dividend (essentially an interpretation of GDP as a proxy for welfare). He did not refer to the divergence of private and social values specifically. Furthermore, Kneese's next move was to dismiss this older Pigouvian approach as too simplistic in its treatment of interpersonal comparisons of utility, it now being superseded by the "new welfare economics" of Hicks and others. In this respect, Kneese took a similar path as Krutilla, his long-time RFF colleague, who depicted his own career retrospectively as having played out against the backdrop of innovations in welfare economics.[2]

Kneese also identified Pigouvian external effects as a key concept in normative project evaluation, but only as refined by Howard Ellis and William Fellner and others. Interestingly, at this stage, he barely mentioned pollution and externalities. Instead, he emphasized external economies (more so than diseconomies) from increasing the scale of resource development. For example, surface-water irrigation recharges aquifers used by neighboring farms for irrigation; upstream storage improves the efficiency of downstream hydro-electric power; and so forth. Most generally, an expanding market in a rural area may contribute to an increase in regional economic efficiency by facilitating the division of labor.[3]

Soon after turning his attention to these issues, Kneese moved to RFF. As discussed in Chapter 5, RFF was evolving at this time, from a think tank focused on the scarcity of natural resources needed for development and economic growth, to one focused on the scarcity of environmental amenities. Hired by John Krutilla and Irving Fox, Kneese joined RFF as part of this evolution, leading a new research program on water quality. After his move to RFF, Kneese turned immediately to the study of water pollution, publishing initial thoughts on the subject (Kneese 1962; Kneese and Nobe 1962). Kneese wanted to apply a welfarist, benefit–cost perspective on the pollution problem, but he also wanted to replace the traditional approach of evaluating a policy already formulated by engineers with one that embeds the economics into the *design* of multipurpose development of entire river

[2] See Krutilla (1981).

[3] Kneese (1960 pp. 311–12).

systems. Here too, Kneese was following recent trends in the field, including work by Krutilla and especially by the Harvard Water Program led by Arthur Maass, which Kneese later singled out as the "apogee" of work on the design of multiple use water systems.[4]

Kneese identified several characteristics of water resources that raised unique policy problems, including, among others:

1. Water resources are highly mobile and highly variable in quantity and quality in time and space, so water quality must be treated probabilistically;
2. They do not respect political boundaries;
3. They have multiple purposes, provided by the same resource simultaneously and/or sequentially;
4. A particular use provides benefits and imposes costs on different groups separated geographically; and
5. They are (at least nominally) publicly owned.[5]

According to Kneese, distortions from the marginal-benefit-equals-marginal-cost rule arise because, given these realities, private producers cannot enter the market and produce socially desirable services while still covering their costs. Economies of scale, indivisibilities in jointly supplied outputs, and external economies and diseconomies all impede the potential to collect sufficient revenue. Examples of such external effects include the recharging of aquifers, resulting in land drainage problems; decreases in dissolved oxygen, resulting in fish kills; hydroelectric power altering stream flow, which in turn hinders navigation; and irrigation which results in sedimentation of water, thereby increasing treatment costs for municipalities. Thus, whereas Kneese's RFF colleague Marion Clawson wrestled with how to think about measuring benefits of investments in public lands, in a paradigm where norms were determined by the revenues that could be raised in a realistic market institution, here Kneese thought about the problem in reverse: how realistic revenues fail to capture the normative benefits, as determined outside the market by an economic model of optimization. Nevertheless, Kneese's difficulty lay not so much in identifying the appropriate "shadow prices" as developing the institutions to generate or respond to them.[6]

4 Krutilla and Eckstein (1958) and Maass et al. (1962) exemplify work in this area by Krutilla and the Harvard Water Program. "Apogee" (Kneese 1988).

5 Kneese and Nobe (1962 pp. 46–7).

6 Others were thinking along similar lines. For example, Castle (1965) makes this point explicitly.

In Kneese's view, all this creates a role for planning, but logically consistent plans would require two forms of aggregation. First, geographically, the planning area must be sufficiently wide to encompass these and other relevant effects, so that upstream and downstream trade-offs were captured in the planner's field of vision. Second, to trade off the competing ends of water resources (e.g., for deposition of wastes upstream or recreation downstream), the planner would have to aggregate across services. Obviously, Kneese argued, one cannot maximize a mix of different services measured in incommensurate physical units. So "the question of weighting alternate physical outputs in some meaningful commensurable manner inevitably arises and the weights logically must represent some measure of relative social worth." If pollution damages and abatement costs both are denominated in dollars, then marginal costs can be equated across abatement alternatives and to marginal damages of foregoing abatement. This commensurability, Kneese said, could be achieved through "a system of charges and bounties."[7]

This system of effluent charges, mentioned only in passing in 1962, evolved by 1964 into the centerpiece of Kneese's best-known work, *The Economics of Regional Water Quality Management*, which was further revised and expanded in collaboration with Blair Bower, an engineer, in 1968 as *Managing Water Quality: Economics, Technologies, Institutions*. These works were perceived at the time to be the definitive statements of pollution pricing.[8] As indicated by the subtitle of the 1968 book, Kneese combined (i) the economic logic of external diseconomies and property rights; (ii) physical constraints requiring the balancing of physical material across production, residual wastes, and transport of those wastes across space; and (iii) the constraints of operating within realistic institutions. He wrote,

> [The] economic institutions on which we customarily rely to balance costs and returns—the interaction of market forces in a private enterprise system—do not perform this function satisfactorily for waste disposal. Aesthetic nuisance in a stream destroys public values that are not marketable. In deciding how to dispose

[7] "The question of weighting..." (Kneese and Nobe 1962 p. 449); "A system of charges" (p. 459).

[8] But there were predecessors. In a piece obscurely published in *Sewage and Industrial Wastes*, Edward Renshaw (1958), just graduating from the University of Chicago, also recommended a system of pollution penalties. The piece was forgotten and neglected, but in hindsight appears to be an impressive forerunner. Additionally, Fort et al. (1959) presented a proposal for a "smog tax," published as a RAND report, but it too did not circulate widely and appears to have been forgotten until its rediscovery ten years later. For those interested in trivia, the report was the first "publication" for both William Niskanen and William Sharpe.

> of its wastes, an upstream firm or city is not forced to take into account the costs imposed upon downstream water users.... Under some circumstances there are economies of scale in waste disposal that cannot be realized by an individual firm or city acting independently.
>
> Because of these features of waste disposal, market forces are supplemented in a variety of ways. Appeals are made to civic responsibility.... Damaged parties may resort to adversary proceedings in courts of law. Financial inducements to encourage waste treatment by municipalities are offered by the federal government, and storage to augment low flows is provided at federal expense.... But in the application of these practices there has not been a systematic balancing of costs and returns to achieve optimum benefits....[9]

In short, when market institutions fail to equate marginal costs and benefits of an activity, other institutions must take their place. But so far, he said, the array of regulatory responses, while perhaps moving the outcome in the right direction, were not efficient.

Kneese's preferred solution was a system of spatially differentiated effluent charges, ideally set at the marginal damages of emissions.[10] Although he was optimistic about progress being made in the nonmarket valuation of pollution damages, especially in the areas of outdoor recreation as advanced by Clawson, Knetsch, and others, and environmental health (e.g., Weisbrod 1961), he conceded that it was not yet practical to estimate the marginal damages from pollution.

Accordingly, Kneese proposed the alternative of ambient quality standards, in which a regulatory authority mandates a minimum level of water quality to be maintained downstream. Discussing the duality between prices and quantities, he argued that this standard too could best be met by charging fees equal to the marginal costs of meeting it. Although not equating the marginal costs of pollution control to marginal damages, this more pragmatic approach would still have the virtue of equating the marginal costs of reducing downstream injuries across various margins of adjustments (reductions in the output of dirty goods, changes in the production process, end-of-pipe controls, water storage, and dilution, etc.). Kneese proposed a trial-and-error approach that involved groping for the unknown "supply" schedule of pollution abatement. That is, the

9 Kneese (1962 p. 4).

10 Kneese also considered subsidies (or bounties) for pollution abatement as an option, but felt it raised additional implementation issues. For example, if under optimal resource allocations a firm reduced its pollution by exiting the market, the owners of that nonexistent firm would still have to receive their subsidy. The extent of the symmetry between pollution taxes and subsidies became an active research question around this time. See Baumol and Oates (1975) for a literature review from the period and summary.

regulator would impose initial prices on upstream effluent, observe the reduction in pollution at various downstream points, and then adjust the prices to meet the target.

From his discussion, it might appear that Kneese's vision was a grand plan requiring the superior knowledge of a social planner, including marginal abatement costs across various activities, all spatially differentiated. In fact, Kneese disavowed any such interpretation. To the contrary, he stressed the fact that with effluent charges, the market – not a planner – would find the way to reduce pollution (or just pay the charge if pollution reductions were too expensive). In a static world of given abatement costs, the charges provided the incentive for firms to select those abatement technologies that were most cost-effective. More importantly, in the long run, they provided dynamic incentives to find new ways to reduce pollution at lower cost.

Academic demonstrations using Kneese's approach soon followed. For example, Edwin Johnson (1967) employed a linear program to find the least-cost solution of achieving water quality standards in the Delaware estuary, given abatement cost functions and a source-receptor matrix relating effluent released at one point in the estuary (the source) to water quality effects at various down-stream points (receptors). This least-cost solution involved heterogenous charges on effluent sources proportionate to their respective down-stream effects. Relative to this hypothetical least-cost solution, Johnson found that the conventual uniform effluent standard cost 62 percent more to achieve a moderate ambient quality standard. In contrast, even a simple, spatially homogenous effluent charge would only cost 12 percent more and furthermore distribute the costs more equitably, while a zone-specific charge would only cost 7 percent more. Thus, even if it was not literally possible to equate marginal costs of abatement across all sources of effluent, pragmatically designed effluent charges were still much more efficient than traditional regulations on emissions.[11]

Robert K. Davis (1968) similarly employed a linear program to find least-cost solutions for pollution reductions in the Potomac River basin. Critiquing an Army Corps of Engineers plan that had relied on constructing sixteen reservoirs to store water to dilute pollution during times of low flow, Davis found a wide range of costs across abatement alternatives, many of them much cheaper than constructing reservoirs. This analysis supported Kneese's basic argument that, to achieve environmental improvements, policy makers should not try to pick preferred

[11] Johnson (1967 p. 297, Table 1).

technologies. Even if one doubted his actual estimates, Davis's deeper point was to demonstrate how wide ranging costs could be across technologies, and thus the potential gains markets could realize when given the proper incentives.

6.2 Effluent Charges as Pigouvian Taxes

Viewing the history of economics in retrospect, it is natural to interpret Kneese's effluent fees as an application of Pigouvian remedies to market failures, albeit one enriched with technical and institutional details.[12] But, as discussed in Chapter 1, one problem with this conventional narrative is that it's impossible to trace an unbroken line from Pigou to the environmental work of the 1960s (Medema 2020a). In the intervening decades, Pigou's ideas on external (dis)economies had evolved into today's concept of externalities, but without much reference to real-world applications. As Medema tells the story, the line was lost but then reconnected: when environmental applications began to loom larger, the revised Pigouvian theory was simply "grafted into" the emerging field of environmental economics. However, this explanation soon confronts another difficulty: when Pigou's ideas supposedly reappeared and were incorporated into the environmental literature, Pigou himself was not actually much mentioned.

Kneese's work underscores these issues. After his discussion of normative problems in the evaluation of water development projects (Kneese 1960), which discussed Pigouvian welfare economics as a stage in utilitarian thinking generally, Kneese did not cite or mention Pigou at all until the end of the decade. But Kneese was not alone in this. According to JSTOR, the term "Pigouvian tax" (and related variants) appeared first in Buchanan and Stubblebine (1962), not long after Coase (1960) referred to Pigou's "standard example" of factory smoke as an external effect and to the "traditional approach" of imposing fees, an approach he set up as a foil to his own analysis.[13] The term was used only twelve times in the decade of the 1960s (see Figure 6.2). By this point, this neglect cannot be attributed to a general disinterest in the topic. Until about 1972, others working on similar topics

[12] This is in fact the standard interpretation. See, for example, Berta (2019, 2020), Pearce (2002), Sandmo (2015), and de Steiguer (2006).

[13] Related variants Include "Pigovian" instead of "Pigouvian," "taxes" as well as "tax," and "Pigou" in conjunction with "corrective tax" or "effluent fee" or "effluent charge." Notably, other early proposals like Renshaw (1958) and Fort et al. (1959) also never mention Pigou.

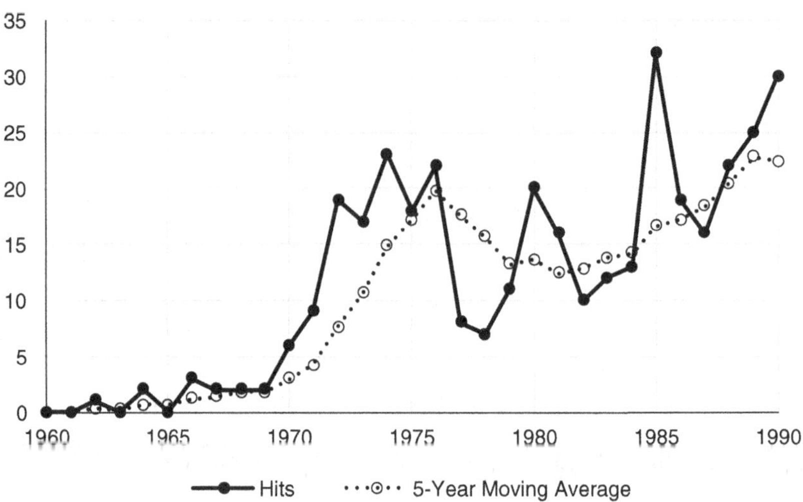

Figure 6.2 Annual JSTOR hits related to "Pigouvian tax"

or commenting on policy proposals to levy fees on pollution, from humble practitioners to Nobel laureates, cited Kneese without mentioning Pigou, apparently treating his work as original. A Google Scholar search yielded only sixty-five hits mentioning Kneese *and* Pigou between 1962 and 1972, 982 hits mentioning Kneese but *not* Pigou, and 2,110 mentioning Pigou but not Kneese.[14] So it appears that, at this time, the environmental literature on effluent charges and the Pigouvian literature on externalities were operating in quite distinct spheres.

So when did the literature make the connection to Pigou? In 1970, the term "Pigouvian tax" appeared in Baumol's review of Buchanan's *Cost and Choice* and soon after in a paper by Baumol and Oates (1971). As discussed by Berta (2020), Baumol and Oates provided a formal proof of Kneese's argument that an effluent fee could induce the least-cost method for meeting an arbitrary environmental objective, even if it was not optimal in the sense of equating marginal costs to marginal damages. In doing so, they described Kneese's work as part of a "Pigouvian tradition." At this point, references to Pigou increased rapidly, as seen in Figure 6.2. Soon, Kneese himself was using the term "Pigouvian" and it was enshrined in textbooks and prominent

14 Examples of prominent papers or authors citing Kneese but not Pigou include Crocker (1968), Dales (1968a, b), Davis (1968), Freeman and Haveman (1972), Johnson (1967), Mills (1966), Montgomery (1972), Ostrom and Ostrom (1965), and Solow (1971). The search was conducted on May 28, 2020 and excluded hits where Kneese was author or editor.

literature reviews. Thus, the idea that pollution prices are almost synonymous with "Pigouvian" may have been a *re*interpretation first made by Coase and Buchanan, and then consolidated by Baumol and Oates. But it was a reinterpretation of an existing body of work already developed separately.[15]

Rather than talk about his approach as Pigouvian, Kneese was, ironically, more apt to talk of it in Coasean terms (Nishibayashi 2019). In *Regional Water Quality Management*, his opening moves in his economic analysis (after a chapter on "technical and engineering facts") were to take the reader through a tour of market efficiency, with external diseconomies presenting a potential exception to the superiority of markets. He then quickly introduced Coasean bargaining (Coase 1960) as one possible way for markets to consider downstream costs of waste disposal, making this one of the first treatments of Coase's negotiating result in the environmental economics literature.[16]

Interestingly, Kneese interpreted the negotiating result in terms of Coase's earlier logic from the "Nature of the Firm" (Coase 1937). Wrote Kneese,

> When such technological links are "internal" to a decision unit, the result may be considerably different than if they are external. To take a simple example, a farmer may find that a small stream on his property will irrigate either an upstream plot A or a downstream plot B, but not both.... In deciding whether to irrigate plot A, the farmer will consider the return lost on plot B, and plot A will be irrigated only if its return is higher. Consequently, the resource will be allocated in the way that maximizes the value of production. If, however, plot B is on another farmer's land and the owner of plot A cannot sell his right to the water, the owner of plot A will not consider the return lost on plot B in determining whether to irrigate plot A. If plot B actually presents the superior productive opportunity, failure to irrigate it because the water is preempted upstream is a technological external diseconomy.
>
> Now suppose that the owner of plot A *can* sell his right to the water and that the farmer owning plot B can afford to, and has an incentive to, pay more for the water than it is worth if applied on plot A. In this case, the efficient result would once again be produced.[17]

15 In Kneese and Mäler (1973), we now hear of "the traditional Pigovian solution of taxing an externality-causing activity" (p. 705). Baumol and Oates (1975) and Fisher and Peterson (1976) are examples of a textbook and prominent literature review, respectively that helped put a stamp on the idea. Medema (2020a) suggests that, ironically, it was perhaps Buchanan's and Coase's attacks in the 1960s on Pigouvian economics that built up the idea that the approach was inherently Pigouvian.

16 Kneese's summary of Coase (Kneese 1964 pp. 40–47). See Medema (2014a, b, 2020b) on the Coase theorem in the environmental economics literature of the 1960s and 1970s, including Kneese's role.

17 Kneese (1964 p. 41).

In this way, Kneese believed the question of external diseconomies is intrinsically intertwined with questions of property rights and market institutions, so it cannot be examined solely through technical relationships. Erstwhile diseconomies can be internalized either through merger (Coase 1937) or through negotiation (Coase 1960), but either way the logic is similar.[18]

Because of high transactions costs, Kneese thought that, in practice, Coase's negotiation result was unlikely to be relevant to water pollution problems. He also thought that the idea of a single firm internalizing all the services provided by water within a relevant drainage basin was as undesirable as it was unrealistic. Operating so many enterprises would have high administrative costs. Additionally, the benefits of internalizing externalities would be at least partially offset by the creation of monopoly power.

Nevertheless, Kneese found this notion of the basin-wide firm to be a useful organizing principle, and it was an idea he would continue to revisit throughout his career.[19] As with the single farm with plots A and B, Kneese suggested the basin-wide firm would be a "natural decision unit" in the sense that it would internalize externalities. It could own upstream plants that benefit from releasing wastes, but also charge levies for downstream recreation use. Then the firm would equate the marginal costs of pollution control at the upstream plants to one another, but also to the marginal damages of effluent on foregone recreation values. In making this point, Kneese drew on Coase's "Nature of the Firm" as well as George Stigler, Otto Davis, and Andrew Whinston, on how firms can internalize externalities within their boundaries.[20]

[18] See Bertrand (2015) for the connections between Coase's two classic articles. Her discussion is highly pertinent to Kneese's treatment.

[19] For example, Kneese and Schultze (1975).

[20] Specifically, Stigler (1946) and Davis and Whinston (1962). "Natural decision unit" (Kneese 1964 p. 48).

As noted previously, Kneese (1964) is an early application of the Coase theorem, or at least of Coase's negotiating result. How this theorem came into the environmental economics literature is a matter of some speculation (Medema 2014a, b, 2021). Given Kneese's graduate training in industrial organization, and his later citation to Stigler and to an edition of Coase's paper reproduced in a 1952 Stigler-Boulding reader, Kneese was probably already familiar with "The Nature of the Firm." Coupled with the fact that Kneese (1962) had earlier discussed the idea of the basin-wide firm without mentioning the negotiating result, a likely explanation is that Kneese was already thinking along these lines by working through the logic of "The Nature of the Firm" – not the "Problem of Social Cost." Medema (2021) suggests that Jerome Milliman, who was visiting RFF around this time, may have pointed Kneese to the "Problem of Social Cost." If so, it is plausible that it fit

Kneese drew three lessons from this artifice of the basin-wide firm. First, administrative agencies ideally would operate at the geographic scale of the water basin. In this way, they would have jurisdiction over all the relevant effects, internalizing them. Second, they should think in terms of economic incentives, such as those provided by effluent charges. Third, like a firm, they should think in terms of maximizing economic value, by minimizing costs and making economic trade-offs between upstream and downstream activities. In this sense, Kneese was extending the logic of Coase's theory of the firm, but whereas Coase limited the institutional choice to either expanding the boundaries of the firm or trading among firms, Kneese enlarged it to include regulatory agencies with their own optimal boundaries *and* the ability to change the terms of trade among regulated firms.

Kneese was no more Coasean than he was Pigouvian. My point is not to place him in the Coasean box instead of the Pigouvian one, but to suggest that, when we see (i) that the quintessential texts on effluent fees from the period do not even mention Pigou, (ii) that they spend more time talking about Coasean models, and yet (iii) that they relate those models to decidedly non-Coasean policy remedies, then we should begin to suspect that more is going on here than a simple Pigouvian-Coasean dichotomy.

Kneese's work offers an alternative solution to the "problem" of the disappearance of Pigou from the literature on external diseconomies. Namely, in the first half of the twentieth century, Pigou's ideas about the divergence between the private value of investments and social net product, although important, never really were as unique as the later literature came to imply. And, by extension, Coase's analysis was not the only alternative to Pigou's. Though the *moniker* "Pigouvian" was adopted around 1970, a name is not hereditary lineage. In fact, there *were* continuous lines of thought running through the period in American economics, but the lines run back to the economics of land use and resource development, not to Pigou. These traditions had developed their own distinctive schools of thought about the economies of scale of resource development and the poor incentives of open access to common resources.

Kneese's analysis of the basin-wide firm reveal three important links to this earlier literature. First, he thought in terms of rich and detailed political, legal, and economic institutions. Ideas like external diseconomies were not just technological relationships, they were embedded in social

comfortably into Kneese's existing thoughts on the subject. The fact that Coase himself made the connection between "Problem of Social Cost" and his own earlier work on the "Nature of the Firm" (1960 pp. 16–17) underscores the ambiguity.

relationships, which required a comparative analysis of which institutions could deliver more value. Kneese combined microeconomic theory with detailed case studies, such as his study of the *Genossenschaften*, the cooperative associations governing water in the Ruhr Valley, which used pollution prices among other tools.[21]

Second, just as he tended to institutional details, Kneese modeled the physical details of the production process, in contrast to most neoclassical models that treat production at a high level of abstraction.[22] These details included attention to spatial relationships, such as the locations of economic activity and waste disposal, the delivery of services, and the effects of upstream wastes on downstream water quality. They also included how energy and materials are passed through the production process. Because of the fundamental laws of the conservation of matter, wastes inevitably are produced jointly with marketed outputs.

Once the balance of materials and energy were introduced as economic constraints on the joint production of material wealth and environmental quality, Kneese's logic later led him to conclude that, even if deposition was decreased in a watershed, wastes still had to go somewhere. Thus, the typical US policy approach of focusing on water quality, air quality, and solid waste separately was misguided because the flow of materials could cross over from one medium to another. Together with Robert Ayres, a physicist, he developed general equilibrium models in which, by tracking flows to and from the environment, physical materials always balance. Incorporating physical constraints on production in this way, became, as with related work at the time by Georgescu-Roegen emphasizing the importance of entropy laws, a key part of the logic of an alternative ecological economics that developed in the 1980s. Kneese himself never became as radical, and for the time being he was content to observe that, because wastes are an inevitable part of all material production, and because they have to go somewhere, pollution problems or "residuals management" are a pervasive part of modern economies, not the "freakish exceptions" that most economists had assumed they were.[23]

Finally, Kneese thought in terms of economies and diseconomies of scale among firms as much as external effects like Pigou's chimney smoke,

21 Kneese (1964 Ch. 7) and Kneese and Bower (1968 Ch. 13).

22 On this point, see RFF (2001 quoting Kerry Smith) and Nishibayashi (2019). Nishibayashi interprets Kneese's work as following a two-step approach that begins with engineering-economic studies followed by institutional studies.

23 Ayres and Kneese (1969), Kneese, Ayres, and d'Arge (1970). Compare Georgescu-Roegen (1971). On the place of this line of work in ecological economics, see Røpke (2004).

and moreover, he sometimes conflated them. Within the internal logic of the model of the basin-wide firm, upstream water development does not so much affect the public good of individual recreational users as it affects the productivity of the recreation *industry*. It affects the supposed downstream firm selling recreation services (tickets to a private beach). At the same time, efficient solutions like water storage and dilution involved economies of scale, so no single upstream firm would be likely to adopt them. Thus, through the fiction of the basin-wide firm, Kneese could address pollution questions using the same benefit–cost framework that resource economists had constructed to address questions about resource *development*, questions of economies of scale and scope that were inherent to large-scale water projects. It was all a question of how to develop water resources to maximize the value of the set of services they provided. It was the kind of question that the first generation of environmental economists, like Kneese, had been trained to address earlier in their careers. The question had always involved trade-offs (e.g., diverting water for agriculture vs maintaining flow for navigation). Only now the trade-off between material production and the harms created by the residuals was more salient.

6.3 Pollution Permits: Thomas Crocker and John Dales

In the Pollution Pricing family tree, the first cousin to effluent charges is the tradable permit approach, now often called cap-and-trade, under which the right to pollute a fixed quantity is allocated to a group, and the members of the group can trade those rights to one another in a market, while maintaining the cap on total pollution. Mathematically, cap-and-trade can be shown to be similar to effluent charges in many respects, but qualitatively the idea of trading pollution like any other commodity seems much more novel. For that reason, real-world applications for the idea were slow to develop, but they tentatively began to appear in the late 1970s and 1980s, first through a US "offset" program for air pollution and then for leaded gasoline. In 1990, with bilateral support, the US Clean Air Act Amendments introduce a full-fledged cap-and-trade program for reducing sulfur dioxide (SO_2), a cause of smog and acid rain. Today, it is the primary approach taken around the world for the most aggressive policies addressing climate change.

Whereas effluent charges or pollution taxes set a price on pollution, allowing the market to determine the quantity demanded at that price, tradable permits set an upper bound on the quantity of pollution, allowing the market to determine the price at that quantity supplied. Shortly after Kneese began writing on effluent fees, two economists introduced the idea of such pollution markets, Thomas Crocker and John Dales. Of the two, Crocker eventually had a longer and more active career in environmental economics, yet Dales's work on pollution prices was more immediately influential, with Crocker's early contributions largely recognized in retrospect as tradable pollution permits entered mainstream policy discussions.[24]

Thomas Crocker (b. 1937) received his Ph.D. in agricultural economics from the University of Missouri in 1967, working predominantly with Mason Gaffney, whom he followed to the University of Wisconsin-Milwaukee, where he completed his dissertation and other early work on pollution pricing before eventually landing at the University of Wyoming, where he spent most of his career.[25]

John Dales (1920–2007) was a natural resource economist who spent most of his career at the University of Toronto. He received his Ph.D. from Harvard in 1953, working with Walter Isard, a leading economist in regional studies. Thus, perhaps not coincidentally, he graduated in the same year, with the same advisor, as John Krutilla. Like other economists of the period who began to work on environmental issues, much of Dales's early work focused on water resources development, with a strong historical-institutionalist flavor. A sampler of his published titles reveals their essence, starting with his dissertation, *The Hydro Electric Industry in Quebec, 1898–1940* (1953), and such other publications as "Fuel, Power, and Industrial Development in Central Canada" (1953), *The Protective Tariff in Canada's Development* (1966), and a comment on "Primary Products and Economic Growth" (1967).

While on a sabbatical leave in the late 1960s, Dales turned to the economics of pollution problems, publishing his thoughts in *Pollution, Property and Prices* (1968b), by far his best-known work. The book, which he described as an "economico-legal" proposal for dealing with pollution, introduced the benefit–cost logic of pollution abatement, but also limited it to a logical organizing principle. Setting benefit–cost analysis up as a strawman, Dales knocked it for having a host of measurement problems that prevent it from being a reliable empirical guide in practice. In language echoed in Harold Demsetz's "nirvana fallacy" (1969), Dales argued that benefit–cost logic had the potential to be deceptively simple, seemingly "solving" difficult social problems when, in fact, "they were solved because we took great pains to adopt assumptions that made

[24] See Berta (2021) for a recent comparison of Crocker's proposal and Dales's.

[25] See Crocker (2011) for autobiographical details.

them solvable." Unlike the blackboard, realistic solutions to real-world problems, he said, required humility and recognition that ignorance is endemic to policy making.[26]

Rather than focus on the intractable question of what is to be done, then, Dales turned to the "economico-legal question" of *how* it was to be done. His answer: devise a system of property rights and other incentives that would let the market solve the benefit–cost problems. Even here, he said, there is no perfect solution, because private agents in the market, free riding, still will not fully reflect social values in their decisions, just as public agencies do not know the true values. Dales's proposed compromise was that a Water Control Board (or respectively Air Board) set up a market by creating a certain number of pollution Rights, each giving the bearer the right to discharge one ton of wastes. If the number of Rights is binding on pollution emitters, they will have scarcity value. This approach would have the advantage, he argued, of (i) having lower administrative and policing costs than traditional regulations; (ii) providing more certainty over the level of environmental quality than pollution charges, which would require a good deal of trial-and-error to find the price that induced the desired quality; while (iii) still achieving that level of environmental quality at the lowest cost possible.[27]

Whereas Dales proposed what today would be called a system of emissions rights, Crocker proposed what today would be called ambient rights. The former lumps a group of polluters together and allows them to trade emissions 1:1, regardless of where those emissions end up. The latter lumps together all polluters who affect a specific region and allows them to trade at a ratio commensurate with their effect on that region. In Crocker's scheme, each source would have to buy permits in separate markets for each region it affects, with relative prices between sources proportionate to their relative effects in each region. Thus, if Source 1 is further upwind from Region A than Source 2, it might need to buy fewer Region-A permits for each ton of its emissions than would Source 2. Similarly, Crocker wanted to allow inter-temporal variation in prices (with permits earmarked to specific seasons of the year or times of day). Thus, he envisioned a much more elaborate system of rights than did Dales.

Nevertheless, Crocker conceded, as did Dales, that there was no perfect system, so the real question was the relative merits of a given

[26] Quotes and summaries from Dales (1968b pp. vi, 34–8, 44–50, 36, 39–40).

[27] Dales (1968b pp. 82, 93). Note Dales's use of big-R "Rights," in contrast to the "tradable permits" that later developed in US policy. Dales had envisioned a stronger property right than the privileges granted by permits.

institutional design. But tradable pollution rights, he felt, have the compelling advantage of leveraging the information-signaling power of the market price system while sidestepping "all the guesswork involved in attempting to estimate individual estimator and receptor preference functions." He also felt they were much more practical than effluent charges or subsidies. "Although the theoretical results of varying taxes and/or subsidies and of observing actual market-determined prices may be similar," he argued,

> Unless the control authority is willing to vary its taxes and subsidies over rather wide ranges for each receptor and emitter site and for each time period being considered, it will be posed with the technically impossible problem of estimating ranges of preference functions for which it has no information."

As Crocker recalls it, his ideas initially were developed in reaction to Kneese's proposals, and he soon would take Kneese on more directly. Crocker took it for granted that achieving an ambient standard was the most important goal of pollution pricing, so he felt pollution charges were too indirect a method, requiring knowledge about the price-abatement relationship or excessive experimentation to learn it. Curiously, he did not seem to feel his own system had similar difficulties, though it required information about the transmission of pollution from each source to each receptor to set the correct trading ratios.[28]

6.4 Pollution Trading as Coasean Bargaining

How shall we situate pollution trading in the context of the contemporary literature on externalities and property rights? The seminal authors offered few clues. Dales did note his intellectual debts to Coase's "Problem of Social Cost" as well as to Charles Reich's "The New Property" (1964) and Scott Gordon's work on "The Economics of a Common-Property Resource" (1954). He also cited Kneese's book as an important point of reference. For his part, Crocker was sparing in his citations in his early work, but later too discussed his proposals in relation to Kneese's and Gordon's model of the commons.[29]

What is clear from the outset is that neither cite Pigou at all. Of course, they contrasted their ideas to Kneese's effluent charges, but Kneese's work,

[28] "All the guesswork" (Crocker 1966 p. 81), "Unless the control authority…" (p. 82). Crocker (2011) documents his recollection of reacting to Kneese. He critiqued Kneese's work in Crocker (1968, 1972).

[29] Dales (1968b pp. 110–11), Crocker (1967, 1968, 1972).

as I've argued, is not obviously Pigouvian either. If anything, its institutional approach bore some affinity to Coase's.

That brings us to the Coasean origins of marketable pollution rights, if any. Many standard summaries of environmental economics do draw the connection.[30] On the other hand, Berta and Bertrand (2014) and Medema (2014a) have taken the opposite view, arguing that while cap-and-trade bears passing resemblance to Coase's (1959) proposal to auction bandwidth, it is closer in spirit to Arrow's (1969) model of complete competitive markets (which included hypothetical markets in all effects on all parties) than to Coase's vision of bilateral bargaining. While Dales acknowledged "owing much" to "The Problem of Social Cost," it appears to be more for its general connection between law and economics.

As I've argued elsewhere, personally I do believe there is enough affinity between Coasean ideas and pollution trading to warrant making the association, if for no other reason than that Coase himself was proud to accept credit for the idea. Although Coase's vision was more about bilateral bargaining than today's liquid permit markets, in fact, in the US, actual pollution trading policies *did* evolve out of experience with bilateral trades, in particular the US Environmental Protection Agency's (EPA's) "bubble" and "offset" programs.[31] More generally, pollution trading can fairly be described as Coasean insofar as it (i) clarifies property rights to environmental resources like the atmosphere and introduces enforcement mechanisms for violations of those rights; (ii) reduces transactions costs by commodifying pollution, with clear units of measurement and centralized market platforms; and (iii) allows trading. Such trading becomes more Coasean in character the more salient are trades between greens and browns, which endogenize the final quantity of pollution released – that is, when the "cap" in "cap-and-trade" is an *upper bound* on pollution, which environmentalists can buy down, in contrast to fixed caps allocated only among polluters.

30 For example, Tietenberg (2010), Stavins (2011).

31 In the US, the 1970 Clean Air Act prohibited new sources of emissions in counties designated as being in "non-attainment" with ambient air quality standards, while also regulating emissions of existing sources more stringently. To lighten the costs of these regulations, in the mid-1970s the US EPA introduced an offset program to allow new sources in non-attainment areas if they could find an existing source to reduce its emissions by 1.2 tons for each ton of new emissions. In 1979, the program was extended to include trades among existing sources. These programs had narrow geographic scopes, involved bilateral trades with no central market, and had to be individually approved by EPA. But it is widely believed that experience with these programs created a level of comfort with pollution trading that paved the way for later cap-and-trade programs such as the 1990 acid rain program. See Tietenberg (2006) for details.

In a Coasean worldview, such green-brown trades are linked to the idea of reciprocal harm associated with the opportunity costs of using the water or the atmosphere for one use versus another (e.g., deposition of wastes vs. maintenance of health, property, and ecosystem services).[32]

Such reciprocal costs were a linchpin in Crocker's presentation of pollution trading. Even if, he said, a marginal decrease in pollution increased net benefits, yet still,

> We are no more justified in making the would-be emitter endure all the costs of "pure" air while the would-be receptor receives all the benefits than we are in burdening the receptor with all the costs of "dirty" air while the emitter collects all the benefits.

In this, Crocker disagreed with Kneese, who held up the polluter-pays principle of effluent charges as one of its virtues. Elaborating, Crocker added that

> One would therefore expect the market to allocate the air's two value dimensions according to the criteria of economic efficiency. Receptors and emitters could be expected to exchange rights to the life- and property-supporting dimensions and the waste-disposal dimension until … the difference between total cost savings to emitters and total damage costs to receptors was maximized.
>
> However, so far society has generally been unable to define property rights to air …."

Such green-brown trades have signaling potential, he said, to reveal the economic value of air resources. Although they also face free rider problems on the green side of the market, at least early on Crocker appeared to be sanguine about the potential to overcome such issues.[33]

Dales too cracked open the door to such trades between the green and brown sides of the market. "Conservation groups," he said, "might well want to buy up some rights merely in order to prevent their being used. In this way at least part of the guerilla warfare between conservationists and polluters could be transferred into a civilized 'war with dollars'." Elsewhere, though, he minimized this possibility, characterizing his proposal as nothing more than an administrative tool. In contrast to "true" or "natural" markets, which involve "two-way communication between sources of supply and demand," he described his artificial market as providing only one-way communication, transmitting the government's decisions about the cap on pollution to the users but without the reverse feedback, so that the

[32] For expansion of the points summarized here, see Banzhaf (2010b, 2020) and Banzhaf, Fitzgerald, and Schnier (2013).

[33] Quotations from Crocker (1966 pp. 62–3, 65 respectively; see also pp. 66, 84).

resulting scarcity value has no effect on the quantity of pollution supplied, nor any relation to marginal damages of pollution. "In the end," he said, "it is you and I who are going to elect the politicians who are going to decide how much pollution we are going to have."[34]

Before long, Crocker came to the same conclusion, arguing the free rider problem would undermine green-brown trades (Crocker 1972). As pointed out by Berta (2020), at this point, then, cap-and-trade proposals resembled the pollution charges suggested by Kneese and Baumol and Oates insofar as they were a program for efficient cost-minimization, rather than for achieving optimal pollution levels. Soon, additional work extending Dales's model would place it more in the style of work by the Cowles Commission, which highlighted the duality between Kneese's prices and Crocker and Dales's tradable quotas. In particular, David Montgomery (1972), picking up on Dales's emphasis on the artificiality of the markets, essentially crossed Dales's model with Arrow's model of complete markets, embedding it in an Arrow-Debreu model of competitive equilibrium.[35] Martin Weitzman (1974a) reimagined it as an application of socialist command-and-control over quantities, interpreted as dual to Lange-Lerner price controls.[36] Such interpretations tend to minimize the potential for green-brown trades, emphasizing allocation among polluters of a fixed aggregate quantity.

At most, then, Coase was but one touchpoint in the intellectual network in which pollution trading operated, as it was for Kneese's proposals for effluent charges. And Pigou was hardly mentioned. If we are hunting for the intellectual history of pollution pricing, perhaps the recurring references to Gordon's (1954) work on common property are a more promising lead to follow.

6.5 Pollution Pricing in the Context of American Economics

As discussed throughout this book, the pioneers of American environmental economics were trained in agricultural and natural resource economics or regional economics, and they had their own tradition of applied

[34] "Conservation groups..." (Dales 1968b pp. 95–6); "two-way communication" (Dales 1968a pp. 803–4); "In the end..." (Dales 1968b p. 104).

[35] See Berta (2017, 2020) and Berta and Bertrand (2014) for discussion of this approach to modeling externalities and its relationship to cap-and-trade.

[36] Even here, the connection to property rights remains: Weitzman, interestingly, at the time was also working on common property and enclosure movements, albeit from a more heterodox perspective (Weitzman 1974b; Cohen and Weitzman 1975).

economics on which to draw. These traditions included engagement with many situations where property rights, institutional arrangements, and economic systems writ large provide poor incentives for managing resources. Because Pigou thought about such situations as well, it is understandable that some would make the connection back to him. But the question of incentives pervades all of economics, not uniquely Pigou's.

Consider the notion of external economies (or diseconomies) from one firm to another within an industry, or from one industry to another, with expansion by one firm changing the supply price of others. These kinds of effects were historically important for environmental economics because of its roots in studying the development of natural resources. Pigou had covered these issues in his third grouping of situations where there is a divergence between private and social values, but by the 1960s they had been refined and developed over the previous half century by such economists as Allyn Young, Frank Knight, Jacob Viner, Howard Ellis, William Fellner, and James Meade. For the most part, this literature addressed issues of external economies in the context of trade and/or development.[37] Young, a student of Richard Ely, initially developed his critique of Pigou's theory by distinguishing real costs from the price effects of changing land rent (Young 1913), an argument taken up by Knight as well. Later, he analyzed economies of scale through the lens of Adam Smith's theory that expanding the extent of the market could facilitate the division of labor (Young 1928). But such forces, he said, depended on the availability of natural resources. Natural limits in their supply and indivisibilities in tapping them create barriers to such scale economies, while the discovery of new natural resources and the growth of scientific knowledge reinforce them. "[O]ut of better knowledge of the materials and forces upon which men can lay their hands there come both new ways of producing familiar commodities and new products."[38]

The spatial scale of spillovers also was an important consideration. As Ellis and Fellner (1943) emphasized,

[37] See, specifically, Young (1913, 1928), Knight (1924), Viner (1932), Ellis and Fellner (1943), and Meade (1952). Currie and Sandilands (1997), Boianovsky and Hoover (2009) and Alacevich (2020) discuss Young's place in neoclassical models of growth and development. McDonald (2013) discusses Knight's debate with Pigou. Medema (2020a) discusses how Meade's distinction between "unpaid factors of production," including his famous discussion of bees and orchards, and "atmosphere" effects were worked out in the context of trade and development.

[38] Young (1928 p. 535).

Certain industries must usually reach some stage of growth before a geographical region starts to develop significantly and also before human and material resources become more specialized. But it is rarely true in these cases that a contraction of the output of any one industry would lead to a loss of the economies in question.[39]

In their thinking, these irreversible external economies prevented competitive markets from allocating resources optimally and justified inducements to develop resources and spur regional growth.

At mid-century, these concerns about resource development began to occupy the interest of the economists who would shape environmental economics in the coming decades. Consider just the titles of three key works in benefit–cost analysis published in 1958 alone:

- *Multiple Purpose River Development*, by John V. Krutilla and Otto Eckstein;
- *Water Resources Development: The Economics of Project Evaluation*, by Otto Eckstein; and
- *Efficiency in Government through Systems Analysis with Emphasis on Water Resource Development*, by Roland McKean.

As mentioned previously, Kneese published "Normative Problems in the Evaluation of Water-Resources Development Projects" (1960) around the same time. Thus, before they were calling attention to the deleterious effects of development on environmental amenities, Kneese, Krutilla, and others were focused more on the *beneficial* spillovers of development, mentioning environmental externalities only in passing. Instead, they identified the crucial issue that created departures from competitive conditions as being large external economies from indivisibilities and jointness in production technologies, as well as interdependence of the production functions of independent producers.[40] Jointness meant that most water projects were multipurpose, so could be thought of as direct inputs into several industries simultaneously, with no one industry (let alone one firm) having the full incentive to invest in them. Interdependencies implied further indirect effects from one firm to another. For example, both Krutilla and Eckstein (1958) and Kneese (1960) mention the possibility that irrigating some farms from surface water would recharge the aquifers used by other farmers. Similarly, upstream storage presents external economies to downstream hydroelectric power. At a larger scale, development of sparsely populated

[39] Ellis and Fellner (1943 p. 507).

[40] Krutilla and Eckstein (1958 pp. 42–77).

areas can enhance productivity by increasing the extent of the market and so extending the division of labor.[41]

Even when their focus turned from natural resource scarcity to scarcity of environmental amenities, this pattern of thought continued to guide economists' thinking. For example, as we've seen, Kneese often thought in terms of the joint effects of firms on pollution levels within a collectively shared water resource, which in turn affects downstream industries like outdoor recreation. Earlier, questions about how to measure the monetary value of such recreation – arguably the first exercises in pricing the environment – arose from thinking about ancillary benefits of building reservoirs in order to justify more development projects. Finally, Davidson, Adams, and Seneca (1966) and Krutilla (1967a) introduced the possibility of external economies from learning-by-doing in outdoor recreation, as investments in environmental amenities induced participation that would then beget more participation, increasing the value of the initial investment. Thus, in these ways, early work in environmental economics often was framed in terms of increasing returns to scale.

Just as important as jointness and interdependencies in the American tradition of resource economics are the twin issues of common property and land tenancy. Pigou too had addressed these issues, placing them in his first group of divergences between private and social values, but at points even he relied on the work of Henry Taylor, another student of Ely's and a central figure in the creation of American agricultural economics.[42] Taylor (1919) had discussed how certain contractual arrangements that can help overcome land tenancy problems.

That common property resources are germane to environmental problems is self-evident. More specifically, as discussed in Chapter 2, resource economists had been wrestling with common property problems throughout the twentieth century and developing theories about them. Indeed, in the 1950s and 1960s those resource economists still grappling with the older issue of water *quantity* in the American West were highlighting the commons problems. They noted the relevance of Gordon's model of taking fish from a shared sea to their problem of the race to pump groundwater over a shared aquifer. They also proposed increasing the fee schedule for water

[41] Krutilla and Eckstein (1958 pp. 56–7), Kneese (1960 pp. 311–12). As discussed in Porter (1995) and further in Chapter 8, quantifying such secondary benefits was hotly contested in applied benefit cost analysis. The FIARBC's green book (1950) downplayed their importance.

[42] Pigou (1932 [1962] p. 178). On Taylor's importance in the history of applied economics, see Banzhaf (2006).

use as an economic remedy (Milliman 1956; Renshaw 1963). Thus, situated in the middle of these policy discussions, American economists in the 1960s would naturally think along similar lines when turning to issues of environmental *quality*.[43]

Still, connections are not the same as identities: quality is not the same as quantity. Among all the tangled analogies, land tenancy, with its connection to the qualitative properties of the soil's fertility, provided a useful bridge between the two. Economists had long studied the implications of the qualitative differences in agricultural land, for example developing Ricardo's theory that especially fertile land could command an economic rent (relative to less fertile land). Unfortunately, land tenancy could potentially dissipate these rents, if tenant farmers did not have the incentive to maintain soil fertility. At the turn of the century, economists felt that air and sometimes water were different, as they were abundant and never commanded a rent. They were free, noneconomic resources. But when quality differences in air and water became more evident, it was possible, by analogy to land, to see how higher quality air and water also could command a social rent, unless it too was dissipated by common ownership and neglect.

Kneese, recall, employed his own analogy between agriculture and the natural environment, segueing from a discussion of the farm with Plots A and B to the basin-wide water firm. Certainly, like Pigou, he considered situations where an exchange between two parties affects a third party. But, reasoning with categories of natural resources that have alternative uses, Kneese considered how such effects are mediated through misaligned incentives to allow a resource to depreciate: "*Failure of municipal and industrial waste dischargers to consider that subsequent water uses may be made more expensive or foreclosed entirely by the discharge is perhaps the basic element of the pollution problem.*"[44] In other words, polluters depreciate a resource that has alternative uses downstream, such as fishing. These downstream users thus face a degraded resource, just as some users of common Western water resources face a depleted resource, or subsequent users of farmland faced a degraded resource after the tenant has depleted the soil.

As his thinking evolved, Kneese became more explicit about situating his work in the context of common property resources. He explained that,

[43] Of contemporary commentators, Castle (1965) may have been the most explicit about these connections. Later, Krutilla also commented on them. As he saw it, "environmental economics was largely the extension of resource economics into previously neglected areas involving rival demands for common property resources" (1981 p. 8).

[44] Kneese (1964 p. 42, emphasis in original).

while it is natural for economists to begin thinking about environmental problems through the lens of "externalities," his own approach could better be described as "*the management of common property resources* approach." Kneese characterized the externalities approach as inherently limited to two-party situations, whereas the common property approach focuses on the degradation of a resource used by many. Concomitantly, whereas externalities have the appearance of being rare exceptions to the economist's ideal competitive market, the logic of materials balancing compels us to recognize that depositing wastes in the environment is a pervasive aspect of production. Accordingly, drawing on Gordon, he argued that, now that the natural environment is itself a scarce resource, "we are confronted with a vast asymmetry in the ability of our property institutions to form the basis for efficient resources allocation."[45]

Explaining his proposals for effluent charges to the US Congress in 1969, Kneese framed it in similar terms. "I think we must devise ways of reflecting the costs of using resources that are the common property of everyone, like our watercourses," he said.

> Because our property institutions cannot adequately be applied to resources like watercourses, and for that matter the air and space, they are in fact unpriced and treated as free goods, even though they are in fact resources of great and increasing value in the contemporary world.... [T]his unfortunate situation cannot be remedied unless we move toward the implementation of publicly administered prices for waste discharge to watercourses and for the use of other common property resources.[46]

Like Kneese, Crocker, and Dales also reasoned from these misaligned incentives of common property, with Gordon being one of the few references provided by either. Dales emphasized that, because they are fluids that fail to respect boundaries, air, and water seemingly will inevitably be held in common. Crocker made a similar point, adding that whereas with land, people can modify its characteristics to mitigate consequences of misaligned incentives (e.g., by regarding a slope to prevent a tenant from eroding the soil), with air we are subject to its whims.[47]

45 "Management of common property..." (Kneese 1971b p. 153, emphasis in original); depositing wastes as pervasive (Kneese 1971b; Ayres and Kneese 1969); "we are confronted..." (Kneese 1971b p. 155). See also Kneese (1968) for a clear account of his approach to finding "desirable institutional arrangements" given production externalities and economies of scale in pollution control.

46 Kneese (1969 p. 347).

47 References to Gordon include Crocker (1967, 1968) and Dales (1968a, b). Crocker's point that we have less control over air is at (1966 p. 63).

Crocker additionally stressed the distinction between "air" and "air space," the former referring to the gasses that move about in space and time, and the latter to the space through which they move. This distinction is interesting because it echoes the one Ely had made between "land" and "standing space." By the latter Ely meant pure Cartesian extension to be occupied by people and economic activity, whereas in the former he included all the quality-differentiated resources of the land. Extending this logic, Ely said that, like land, water too can be distinguished between the space it occupies and the resource itself. Because underground water flows throughout a basin, a single user can deplete the reservoir, denying others use, particularly problematic in the arid west. Thus, California for example developed the doctrine of "correlative right," which limits users to a reasonable share.[48]

Earlier in his graduate career, Crocker had been assisting his advisor on just this issue, and he recalls it being an important inspiration for his work on rights to the air. Highlighting this connection, Crocker wrote that the current treatment of property rights to air obviously resembles "the problems caused by the old absolute-ownership doctrine of groundwater." This old doctrine of absolute ownership, Crocker explained, "defines the groundwater user's rights in terms of reservoir space, but fails to define his rights relative to the rights of other groundwater users in the water that percolates through that space." Even if users had *de jure* rights, they would have no economical means by which to defend them. For air as with groundwater, "the result is that the owner of the space uses the resource within the space until such time as for him and him alone the present value of its marginal value product is zero."[49]

Crocker and Dales both suggested that, although historically it was appropriate to treat air or water as a "free good," the demands on their use were now too high to do so. Crocker summed up the problem with the commons by mashing together quotes from Ellis and Fellner, Gordon, and Francis Bator, stating that the "'divorce of scarcity from effective ownership' brings about a situation in which 'the conservative dictum that everybody's property is nobody's property' appears to be fulfilled."

[48] On Ely's distinction between land and standing space, see Ely (1893 pp. 99–100) and Ely and Morehouse 1924 Ch. 2). On his parallel distinction for water, see Ely and Morehouse (1924 Ch. 9) and Ely and Wehrwein (1940 Ch. 11). On the doctrine of correlative right, see also Coman [1911] (2011) and Ciriacy-Wantrup (1956).

[49] On Crocker's early work with his advisor, see Gaffney (1961 p. 30) and Crocker's recollection in Crocker (2011). "Old absolute ownership doctrine" (Crocker 1967 p. 36); "owner of the space..." (Crocker 1966 pp. 82–3).

Such a statement could have been made by the participants at Pinchot's 1908 governors' conference, where, for example, Roosevelt had stated, "We want to see a man own his farm rather than rent it, because we want to see it an object to him to transfer it in better order to his children." "So with the waterways."[50]

This history has broader implications for our understanding of externalities and public goods. In the 1950s and 1960s, the definition of public goods was crystallizing around the idea that they simultaneously involve non-excludability and either jointness in production or nonrivalry in consumption. At the same time, a definition of an open-access commons was crystallizing around the idea that it too involved non-excludability, but rivalry in consumption (so users can't be excluded, even though their use detracts from others). Throughout that process, Samuelson, Musgrave, and others debated the relative importance of free riding and jointness, and how to overlay the theory of externalities. At the same time, Buchanan, Tiebout, and others offered alternative perspectives with the potential for voluntary mechanisms to overcome these problems.[51] Despite the neatness of conceptual categories like non-excludability and nonrivalry, environmental resources are notoriously difficult to categorize in this scheme. For example, "air quality" would appear to be a public good, as people cannot easily be excluded from enjoying it and their enjoyment does not detract from others. On the other hand, "the atmosphere" appears to be an open access commons good, as firms cannot easily be excluded from using it for depositing wastes, yet their use detracts from others' enjoyment. The history of natural resource and environmental economics suggests the postwar public finance literature was part of a broader discussion about the range of property rights institutions for addressing jointness and open access.

[50] Crocker (1968 pp. 247–8); for the original quotes, see Ellis and Fellner (1943), Gordon (1954), and Bator (1958). Roosevelt (1908).

[51] On both these issues, see for example, Berta (2017), Desmarais-Tremblay (2017a), Fontaine (2014), Johnson (2015), Marciano (2013), and Singleton (2015).

7

Lives, Damned Lives, and Statistics

I took one Draught of Life—
I'll tell you what I paid—
Precisely an existence—
The market price, they said.
-Emily Dickinson, *Complete Poems* (posthumously collected, 1955)

While economic theorists were still debating the interpretation of public goods and externalities, planners were moving forward with the application of the basic economic logic of benefits and costs (including a wide range of opportunity costs) in a variety of settings. For example, in the 1950s and 1960s, analysts at RAND were urging the US military to make plans using "systems analysis," an approach that would embed optimized use of military hardware into the decisions about what hardware to obtain, given a fixed budget and other constraints. RAND then faced the problem of valuing or pricing these constraints, as well as the "benefits" of meeting military objectives. As discussed in this chapter, questions about how to do this brought RAND economists into contact with resource economists wrestling with pricing the environment. This contact was especially spurred by RAND's struggle to value the lives of military personnel. Valuing lifesaving was a question that cut across a number of public settings at that time, including flood control provided by dams, transportation policy, and of course health policy. Later, in the last decades of the twentieth century, it became an important consideration in benefit–cost analyses of pollution control as well. This chapter tells the story of how economists extended pricing to even human life.[1]

[1] Berman (2022) discusses the spread of benefit-cost thinking in government in the post-war era. On lifesaving in evaluating flood control, see FIARBC (1950, 1958), Krutilla and Eckstein (1958 p. 265).

7.1 The Value of a Man

Until about 1970, quantitative estimates of the value of life saving – if ventured at all – were almost invariably based on the so-called human capital approach. The human capital approach calculates the present value of the discounted stream of future labor market earnings that is lost when somebody dies prematurely. According to the theory, this stream of earnings is equivalent to the value of the stock of capital embodied in a person. Some variants tack on the additional cost of funeral expenses (or at least of incurring them earlier). Other variants deduct a person's consumption, to arrive at the *net* contribution to the income of others.[2]

For years, the exemplar of this approach had been *The Money Value of a Man*, first published in 1930 (with a revised edition in 1946) by Louis Dublin and Alfred Lotka, two statisticians at the Metropolitan Life Insurance Company. Dublin and Lotka identified three (potential) applications for their research.[3] First, it was useful for quantifying how much life insurance to purchase. Calculations of lost income were perfectly fitting for this question because insurance is not necessarily intended to compensate for the bereavement of losing a loved one, but merely to replace the lost income of a family's breadwinner so that the survivors may continue to live in their accustomed manner. Second, it similarly could serve as at least one factor to consider in jury awards related to wrongful death. By the middle of the twentieth century, the consensus among economists and other analysts appeared to be that the human capital approach was indeed useful for these kinds of questions.

A third, more controversial, application was to policy evaluation of investments in human health. This kind of application was controversial even among the authors. Dublin was enthusiastic about the potential to use their figures to support his view, encapsulated in the slogan "Health Work Pays," that investments in hygiene made good business sense for the country. Lotka was more dubious, as was the NBER economist W. I. King with whom they consulted. As Lotka saw it, value was a relative

[2] In addition to *Money Value of a Man*, other prominent examples of the human capital approach include Fein (1958), Weisbrod (1961), Klarman (1965), Rice and Cooper (1967), and Ridker (1967).

[3] For discussion of Dublin and Lotka's work, see Bouk (2015 Ch. 6) and Hood (2017). Although Dublin was the senior investigator in the study, Lotka was by the far more famous scientist, with important contributions to energetics and population dynamics, including the Lotka-Volterra predator-prey model. On Lotka's place in the history of economics, see Weintraub (1991 Ch. 3) and Kingsland (1994). Three potential applications (Dublin and Lotka 1930 pp. *v*–*vi*).

concept, so there were different values for a man to his wife and children than to the community, state, and world at large.[4]

By the 1960s, economists wrestling with valuing investments in public health tended to attack the problem by starting from the observation that investments in life-saving, whether private or public, do have associated opportunity costs. Consequently, just as at the same time Krutilla was arguing that the preservation of natural landscapes is an economic choice, so too economists argued that an investment in life-saving is an economic choice.[5] So much economists could agree on. But whether the human capital approach represented those trade-offs appropriately was another matter. Collectively, they posed two interrelated questions. First, what benefits and costs did the human capital approach trade off, and did they fit the relevant social trade-offs? And, second, who was supposed to be making the trade-offs?

Supporters of applying the human capital approach to social policy conceded that it didn't capture all of the relevant factors, but felt it captured the relevant economic ones, insofar as "economic" referred to material welfare. Thus, just as GNP is a useful gauge of the annual value of goods produced by an economy, but is no ultimate measure of The Good, so too the human capital approach is a useful gauge of a person's economic value, but not, in Dublin and Lotka's words, of the "deep significance of valuation, of a kind given to intangible things." Refraining from "dealing with such spiritual values," Dublin and Lotka instead focused on "practical tangible quantities capable of numerical estimate in dollars and cents."[6]

Many economists proceeding along these lines into the 1960s. For example, in one prominent French application, Abraham and Thedié (1960) estimated the cost of fatal road accidents. In the United States, Rashi Fein (1958) quantified the value of labor time lost to mental illness. Burton Weisbrod (1961) quantified the cost of various illnesses and Ronald Ridker (1967) quantified the health costs of air pollution. Dorothy Rice and Barbara Cooper (1967) provided tables of values by age and sex. Herbert Klarman (1965) enshrined the idea in his influential textbook on health economics.

Others proceeded with more caution. For example, the Green Book economists monetizing lives saved from flood control concluded that

4 Bouk (2015 Ch. 6).

5 The point was made by, among others, Weisbrod (1961), Mushkin (1962), Fromm (1965), Schelling (1968), and Spengler (1968).

6 Dublin and Lotka (1930 [1946] p. 3). (The term "spiritual values" appears only in the 2nd ed., but the omission from the 1st ed. appears to have been a misprint.)

human capital measures were at least a starting point from which they could work. However, echoing Lotka's view, they cautioned that, "From a public viewpoint … this economic consideration is incomplete, and the value of human life over and above any economic value placed on it must continue to be regarded as intangible," to be considered qualitatively. The fact that human capital values could capture some but not all value of life seemed to justify including them as a lower bound. At about the same time, engineers writing guidelines for benefit–cost analyses of transportation investments (the 1951 "Red Book") expressed a similar feeling. They felt that, though in principle values for reduced traffic accidents could be plugged into benefit–cost formulas, for the time being no satisfactory values were available. Thus, like Doris Carlton working on the value of a recreation day, they felt that only arbitrary "reference" figures, or placeholders, could be used, to be filled in later if and when a satisfactory method could be devised to quantify values.[7]

Still other economists were highly critical of the human capital approach, arguing that it failed to capture the relevant trade-offs. Prominent critics included Jacques Drèze, Gary Fromm, Charles Hitch, Roland McKean, E. J. Mishan, and Thomas Schelling.[8] Taking a position that gained increasing traction during the 1960s, they argued that the relevant trade-offs had to be evaluated in light of who had the agency, or standing, to make them. That is, trade-offs can only be evaluated in light of who was doing the trading off. Following the twentieth century theme of moving from reasoning in terms of the producer to reasoning in terms of the consumer, they further argued that we shouldn't value people based on how much income they produce, but on their willingness to pay (WTP) to extend their own lives or their loved ones'. That is, the individuals themselves have standing to determine the values of their own lives. Driving home their point, they raised the uncomfortable but obvious questions about the implications of the human capital approach. For example, if we focus on market earnings, doesn't that imply housewives have no value to society? Even if we think in terms of labor productivity more generally (including unpaid work), doesn't that still imply retirees and the severely disabled have no value? If we discount future earnings, doesn't that imply young children have less

[7] Green Book (FIARBC 1950 p. 27); Red Book (American Association of State Highway Officials 1951 pp. 36, 57, 100–103).

[8] Hitch and McKean (1960), Drèze (1962), Fromm (1965), Schelling (1968), and Mishan (1971).

value than teens? And, finally, if we use *net* earnings, after deducting consumption, doesn't that imply the social value of some of these groups would be *negative*?[9]

Earlier, Dublin and Lotka had anticipated such questions and had tried to head them off with their claim to be focused on economic value rather than the "deep significance of valuation." But that response didn't address the fact that their method would still suggest investments in the lives of the very sick or elderly do not pay. So, here, they relied on the fact that "the normal man is naturally possessed of sufficiently powerful instincts of altruism to urge him to right action in these matters, without economic coercion, and, in fact, where necessary, at an economic sacrifice." Obviously, such a reply would hardly be satisfactory to anybody trying to quantify the prices for "right action."[10]

Other economists worked more creatively to respond to these criticisms, bending the human capital approach to adapt to them. Some conceded that, though it might make sense for insurance purposes to focus on people's net income, it makes much less sense for social purposes if the enjoyment of life is part of the social objective. Thus, they suggested using gross rather than net incomes when applying the human capital approach to public policies.[11] Additionally, extending the concept of "income" to include unpaid work, Rice and Cooper, economists and statisticians in the US Social Security Administration, imputed value to the work of housewives by estimating the time spent on homemaking and valuing it at the going wages for domestic work.[12]

Despite these efforts, by the 1980s the human capital approach had largely lost out to approaches based on individuals' WTP. In 1981, President Reagan issued Executive Order 12291, which increased the use of benefit–cost analysis in federal rulemaking. As a result, a wide range of US federal agencies were forced to reconsider how to value life-saving investments and regulations. Beginning with the EPA and Occupational Safety and Health Administration, agencies adopted consumer-based or

[9] Devons (1961 p. 108) and Mishan (1971) are particularly pointed.

[10] Dublin and Lotka (1930 p. 72). They also anticipated questions about how to value homemaking, suggesting rule-of-thumb relationships to men's labor (1930 pp. 39–40; see also discussion in Bouk 2015 Ch. 6).

[11] For example, Fein (1958), Klarman (1965), Rice and Cooper (1967), and Ridker (1967).

[12] Rice and Cooper both had distinguished careers, with Rice later becoming director of the National Center for Health Statistics. The intellectual relationship between shadow values for nonmarket work and for nonmarket environmental improvements, highlighted today by the work of Nancy Folbre and others, may have an interesting history that is yet to be explored. Some of the connections are highlighted in Abraham and Mackie (2005).

WTP measures of value, in some cases switching from human capital values. In particular, they turned to a variant known as the "Value of Statistical Life" (VSL).[13]

The VSL terminology was first introduced by Thomas Schelling (1968). Schelling's crucial contribution was to focus on *statistical* lives – really, mortality risks – in contrast to the lives of specific, identified individuals. His insight was that economists could evade the moral thicket of valuing "life" by focusing instead on people's willingness to trade off money for small risks. Thus, for example, if a reduction in air pollution in a city of one million people reduces the risk of premature death by one in 500,000 for each person, then, *ex ante*, the policy would be expected to save two lives over the affected population. But from the individuals' perspectives, the policy only reduces their risks of death by 0.0002 percentage points. Schelling suggested the policy question (using this example) was the value of a 0.0002 mortality risk for one million people, rather than a life-or-death choice for two people. In his opinion, this move not only sidestepped the difficult ethical questions, but it had the further advantage that, as previously pointed out by others, people do make choices trading off small risks with money and other goals all the time – every time, say, they choose to spend money to inspect their car or the health of large trees surrounding their property. So, as an empirical matter, economists could look to people's behavior to infer their values for these risks.[14]

This distinction between lives and risks is widely considered to be the critical intellectual move supporting the introduction of values for (risks to) life and safety into benefit–cost analysis.[15] Yet despite the importance of this distinction between lives and risks, the VSL maintains an important rhetorical link to the value of life. Specifically, it divides the average individual's WTP for a given reduction in risk by that risk reduction, to normalize the value on a "per-life" basis. Thus, continuing with the

[13] On the importance of EO 12291, see Smith (1984). On the history of this switch to the VSL in the US bureaucracy, see Scodari and Fisher (1988) and Hood (2017). For introductions to and reviews of the modern VSL literature, see Blomquist (2015), Cropper, Hammitt, and Robinson (2011), and Viscusi (2011). The VSL also has been used to help augment the national income and product accounts to accommodate non-market goods (e.g., Muller, Mendelsohn, and Nordhaus 2011) and to appraise the costs of war (Bilmes and Stiglitz 2006).

[14] The point had previously been made by Weisbrod (1961), Drèze (1962), Mushkin (1962), and Fromm (1965).

[15] For example, Ashenfelter (2006), Hammitt and Treich (2007), Viscusi (1993).

previous example, while actually valuing a one-in-500,000 mortality risk and multiplying that value by the one million people experiencing it, the VSL approach then divides the resulting value by the two "statistical lives" expected to be saved, to put it on a per-life basis. This rhetorical link to the value of a life may be the key reason Schelling's proposal gained the most traction in policy debates and why he has received the most credit for the modern approach to valuing life, even though economists like Drèze (1962) and Fromm (1965) had previously made proposals that, mathematically, were effectively the same. Schelling's VSL terminology, though potentially confusing, effectively finessed the distinction between public agencies choosing among policies, which would seem to affect lives lost and saved, and individuals choosing over private actions, which seem to affect risks.

To better understand these issues, it is useful to back up some twenty-five years before Schelling's essay, to consider a particular case where the debate over how to value life was especially intense. The case takes us to the very first years of the RAND Corporation, when the question of valuing lives became crucial to its own institutional life. Although only one case, delving into this debate is useful because it encapsulates well the questions economists had about valuing life and reveals the connections between RAND's military work and the work of natural resource economists at the time. It also became the proximate context for Schelling's own contribution.

7.2 RAND's "Criterion Problem"

From its initial focus on science and engineering, soon after its founding in 1946 RAND incorporated economics and policy studies into its design of military systems. Warren Weaver, a member of RAND's board, established a new research section on the "evaluation of military worth," patterned after his Applied Mathematics Panel (AMP), which was viewed as a success in WW II. The idea, explained Weaver, was to explore "to what extent it is possible to have useful *quantitative indices* for a gadget, a tactic or a strategy, so that one can compare it with available alternatives and guide decisions by analysis…." Building on his previous accomplishments, Weaver brought in his protégés from the AMP, John Williams and Edwin Paxson. In previous work for the Naval Ordnance Test Station, Paxson had worked with John von Neumann to model a submarine-destroyer duel, possibly the first application of formal game theory to military problems. In that particular application, the payoffs were tons of shipping saved or lost. In general, though, similar quantitative measures of the costs and benefits were required to subject a choice to RAND's vision of rigorous Operations Research (OR).[16]

Weaver also brought in a number of economists. Among the first were Allen Wallis and Armen Alchian, who began to work with RAND as early as 1946. By 1948, the economists were constituted as their own division inside the section on evaluation of military worth. The division was headed by Charles Hitch, who in turn brought in Stephen Enke, Jack Hirshleifer, Roland McKean, David Novick, and Albert Wohlstetter.[17] In the long run, Hitch's vision for systems analysis proved to be a success. In the 1960s, Secretary of Defense Robert McNamara was so taken with it that he brought Hitch to the Pentagon to build an inhouse systems analysis group, which led to the so-called Planning-Programming-Budgeting (PPB) System, a major expansion of economic analysis in government. But, of course, that future success was by no means guaranteed when the economics division was first starting out.

Meanwhile, Paxson began a project on strategic bombing, constructing a special Aerial Combat Research Room to simulate aerial maneuvers in a game-theoretic context. By 1947, he and Williams found the computational requirements of their research so demanding that they, along with von Neumann, persuaded RAND to acquire one of the first EDVAC binary computers for their work. Soon, too, George Dantzig was on the scene to apply his simplex algorithm for linear programming. In this way, RAND was reshaping OR and economics in the image of John von Neumann, while using the latest and most powerful technology available. These were heady times for the new think tank.[18]

RAND's first big opportunity to showcase its new analytical capabilities came in 1949, shortly after the Soviet Union detonated its first atomic bomb. The US Air Force (USAF) asked RAND to apply systems analysis to design a first strike on the Soviets. The "Strategic Bombing Systems Analysis," led by Paxson, attempted to find the optimal mix of atomic bombs and bombers. Specifically, it sought to solve a classic OR problem formulated in terms of choosing bombs and bombers to maximizing

[16] On Weaver and the evaluation of military worth, see Hounshell (1997), Leonard (2010), and Mirowski (2001). "Useful quantitative indices" (quoted in Kaplan 1983 p. 72, emphasis added).

[17] Jardini (1996), Leonard (2010), Mirowski (2002). Note the pragmatic and/or empirical approach of the economists associated with Hitch's group. Game theorists such as Arrow, Shapley, and others, by contrast, were housed in the mathematics section of RAND.

[18] Jardini (1996 p. 86), Mirowski (2002 p. 212).

damage, subject to a fixed dollar budget (to procure, operate, and maintain the force) and a fixed budget of fissile material.[19]

Paxson and RAND were initially proud of their optimization model and the computing power that they brought to bear on the problem, which crunched the numbers for over 400,000 configurations of bombs and bombers using hundreds of equations. The massive computations for each configuration involved simulated games at each enemy encounter, each of which had first been modeled in RAND's new aerial combat research room. They also involved numerous variables for fighters, logistics, procurement, land bases, etc. Completed in 1950, the study recommended that the US fill the skies with numerous inexpensive and vulnerable propeller planes, many of them decoys carrying no nuclear weapons, to overwhelm the Soviet air defenses. Though losses would be high, the bombing objectives would be met.[20]

While RAND was initially proud of this work, pride and a haughty spirit do go before a fall. RAND's patrons in the USAF, some of whom were always skeptical of the idea that pencil-necked academics could contribute to military strategy, were apoplectic. RAND had chosen a strategy that would result in high casualties, in part because they had given zero weight to the lives of airplane crews in their objective function, as they seemingly could not be quantified. In itself, this failure to weigh the lives of crews offended the USAF brass, many of whom were former pilots. But moreover that failure led RAND's program to select cheap propeller bombers rather than the newer turbojets the USAF preferred. For all of RAND's scientific equations, modern computing power, and vain boasting, in the eyes of its USAF patrons its first product was a classic case of garbage in, garbage out.[21]

[19] Jardini (1996), Hounshell (1997). Three alternative models minimized the dollar cost per unit of damage, tons of aircraft lost per unit of damage, or lives lost per unit of damage.

[20] Kaplan (1983), Jardini (1996). An early, but ignored, warning sign that RAND might have been on the wrong track was the fact that these models of aerial duels predicted kill ratios of 60 percent, though actual experience in WW II suggested 2 percent was more realistic (Kaplan 1983 p. 88).

[21] Hirshleifer (1950), Jardini (1996). The problem was compounded by what the USAF perceived as other errors as well. RAND's analysis had unnecessarily (indeed, unrealistically) restricted the bombers to North American bases, even though actual plans called for using America's many forward bases as refueling points (Kaplan 1983). Additionally, it had assumed the US had a window to make only a single strike. Both assumptions tilted the analysis in favor of propeller planes. Moreover, because the "game" was over after the first strike, crews did not have value for additional flights.

RAND adapted to this debacle in three ways. First, in the short run, recognizing that its first major study could well prove to be its last, it quickly retreated and adopted a more humble posture. To cut its losses, RAND rushed a follow up study, this one from Paxson's assistant Edward Quade, which incorporated some of the criticism from the Pentagon. In particular, it narrowed the question to the choice of bomber type, adopted the USAF's attack plan, and assumed the possibility of multiple strikes.[22]

At the same time, RAND quickly altered course for its proposed second major project, this one an analysis of air defense systems. Headed by Edward Barlow, the first draft of this project proposal had been a massive 100-page document filled with lots of math, but with dangerously simple assumptions, such as a single strike and a lack of submarines. As RAND began to feel the full force of the USAF's displeasure, the proposal was cut to a slim sixteen pages, devoid of offending expressions or arrogant self confidence in its own scientific method. Indeed, Barlow now explicitly admitted that a weakness with their approach was the potential to ignore non-quantitative factors. "The great dangers inherent in the systems analysis approach," he said, "are that factors which we aren't yet in a position to treat quantitatively tend to be omitted from serious consideration." It is a lesson that was to be emphasized by many early advocates of linear programming methods.[23]

Second, as a matter of long-run strategy, RAND reacted to the debacle of the strategic bombing analysis by diversifying its research portfolio outside of military work. Realizing that all its eggs were in one very risky basket, RAND looked for research sponsors outside the Pentagon. Over time, it increasingly diversified into work in health, education, and other areas of social policy. In 1952, the same year it began RFF, the Ford Foundation provided RAND with a $1m grant to begin a new program, known as RAND-Sponsored Research, in part to take up nonmilitary topics "in the public interest." Not coincidentally, the earliest nonmilitary work seriously occupying RAND staff appears to have been applied work on water resources (De Haven and Hirshleifer 1957;

[22] Jardini (1996 p. 64).

[23] For example, Robert Dorfman, a leading advocate of operations research, was visiting RAND around this time (Jardini 1996 p. 92). Perhaps from the lessons he learned from this episode, throughout his career Dorfman always emphasized the importance of being pragmatic about what can be quantified and about the weight that can be placed on policy recommendations that ignore important, but unquantifiable, elements. Dorfman's dedication to this principle is picked up again in Chapter 8. On Barlow's proposal (Barlow 1950), including the quotation, see Jardini (1996 p. 67).

Hirshleifer, De Haven, and Milliman 1960), followed later by projects in transportation and education.[24]

Evidently, Hirshleifer and other RAND economists recognized the thematic link between their problem of military worth and the problems resource economists were having with valuing water projects, insofar as both involved nonmarket valuation. The Ford Foundation's combined interests in military planning and resource planning must have been another factor behind the scenes. Interestingly, there would be quite a bit of coming and going between RAND and RFF over the years, including Hitch's eventual move to RFF as its president, as well as moves by Harold Barnett and Sam Schurr.

Most importantly for this story, RAND's third response to the debacle was to delve deeper into this question of non-market valuation, that is, to try to put actual weights on airplane crews in its objective functions. Inside RAND this came to be known as the "criterion problem" – essentially the problem of specifying what today are often called "indicators" for imperfectly observed or measured objectives, on both the cost and the benefit side. This was the perfect opening for RAND's economists to exploit. Hirshleifer was particularly fast off the mark, expressing his opinions on the debacle in internal memoranda almost immediately.[25]

From Hirshleifer's perspective, the bombing study failed because of two issues, both of which economists understood well. The first was the distinction between short-run and long-run analysis. Paxson's bombing study imposed unnecessary constraints on the problem, especially the available quantity of fissile material. In the short-run, such constraints may be reasonable, but for long-run strategic planning, they should be subsumed in the budget constraint. That is, given the monetary resources, and enough time, one could acquire more fissile material. The needless constraint on

[24] Jardini (1996) explores these moves in some detail, dating the decisive steps as occurring in the mid to late 1960s. In fact, however, they occurred much earlier, as indicated by the water resources work in the 1950s. The earliest nonmilitary work I can find with any RAND involvement was theoretical research on transportation problems (Beckmann and Marschak 1955; Beckmann, McGuire, and Winsten 1956). However, that work was begun and carried out at the Cowles Commission under Tjalling Koopmans, with RAND serving only as a sponsor. Even recognizing that RAND was always noted as a place where scholars came and went, it is hard to view this work as a RAND product. If we discount that project, RAND's first work in transportation came eight years later, with research on land use and development (e.g., Niedercorn and Kain 1963). Later, by the time Schelling was addressing the problem of statistical lives, RAND was sponsoring a great deal of work on traffic safety (e.g., Lave 1968; Wohl 1968). These dates confirm that RAND's first area of expansion was in water resources. See also Goldstein (1961).

[25] On economists using the criterion problem as an opportunity, see Leonard (1991). For Hirshleifer's early moves, see Hirshleifer (1950).

fissile material, coupled with a large monetary budget, contributed to the use of numerous decoy planes serving little purpose except to be shot down.

The second problem Hirshleifer emphasized was missing prices. The basic idea of linear programming, Hirshleifer reasoned, was to maximize net benefits, which in turn is analogous to maximizing profits. But profits can be maximized in practice because sales and inputs are priced in dollars, so revenues and costs are in common coin. Unfortunately, in military applications like the bombing study, prices are missing from both sides of the ledger. On the benefits side there is the question of quantifying damage to the enemy. But, said Hirshleifer, the main question raised by the bombing study centered on the "cost concept (dollars, crews, or planes) to be used."

Hirshleifer noted that airplane crews can be priced by the cost of training and replacing them, but we may "set a value on human life higher than the mere training cost of a replacement." Thus,

> A man may cost $10,000 in terms of a training cost to replace, but we may prefer to lose $15,000 in materials or machines if we can save the man. This sentence points the way to costing loss of men, if the condition described actually holds true. Obviously, there is a limit to the materials or machines we will sacrifice to save the man, and our losses in men should be valued in terms of this limit, cold-blooded as it may sound. In many respects lives and dollars are incommensurable, but unfortunately the planners must compare them.[26]

Hirshleifer followed up on this issue along with other economists (including Alchian, Enke, and Hitch) a few months later. "In our society," they wrote,

> personnel lives do have intrinsic value over and above the investment they represent. This value is not directly represented by any dollar figure because, while labor services are bought and sold in our society, human beings are not. Even so, there will be some price range beyond which society will not go to save military lives. In principle, therefore, there is some exchange ratio between human lives and dollars appropriate for the historical context envisioned to any particular systems analysis. Needless to say, we would be on very uncertain ground if we attempted to predict what this exchange ratio should be.[27]

Thus, Alchian et al. rejected the human capital approach but left open the door to thinking in terms of economic trade-offs in some other way.

In the short term, the best response to this dilemma that RAND could come up with was to let go of its goal of a general theory of air warfare, and instead focus on smaller subsidiary problems where apples could be

[26] Hirshleifer (1950 p. 5).
[27] Alchian et al. (1951 p. 20).

compared to apples. Incommensurables – like dollars and human lives – would not need to be compared in the "sub-problem." The basic notion was to isolate a smaller portion of the system to be analyzed, taking one set of variables as given, and maximize the objective over the remaining variables, taking the first set as constraints in the problem. The results of such "sub-optimization" would not be fully optimal, as the trade-off between the two sets of variables would not be optimized, but it would be efficient. To put it in other terms, the analyst could simply trace out the efficient frontier between dollars and lives. Ultimate decision makers in the Pentagon or the civilian government could eventually make the call.[28]

This notion of sub-optimization was a major theme in much of Hitch's work and his colleagues' for the next decade, and the lives of bomber crews remained the quintessential example motivating the work.[29] For example, discussing "incommensurables" in *Economics of Defense in the Nuclear Age* (1960), Hitch and McKean considered "the comparison of alternative strategic bombing systems that are to be maintained in a state-of-readiness to deter attack." In this context they further supposed

> that the preferred (that is, minimum-cost) method of achieving the objective is expected to involve the loss of more lives than some alternative method that is more expensive in dollars—even when the costs of recruiting and training the additional personnel required are included...."

Hitch and McKean suggested this is a problem if high casualty rates affect morale. But more fundamentally it is problematic because "we are interested in lives for their own sake," so the human capital lost to the USAF was only part of the picture. Thus, although it was no longer on the front burner, clearly the problem raised by Paxson's strategic bombing study was still simmering at RAND ten years later.[30]

That said, the wisdom of seeking "missing prices" so that incommensurables like dollars and human lives could be put into the same equation was not a settled matter at RAND. For their part, Hitch and McKean thought it ought not to be attempted. Precedents for valuing human life based on the values of human capital, court awards, or the cost of life-saving investments "may be useful in particular problems, but none provides a generally valid and appropriate measure of 'the' value of human life." Instead, they

[28] Alchian et al. (1951), Hitch and McKean (1960 Ch. 10).

[29] The bomber example comes up in Hitch (1953, 1955), Hitch and McKean (1960), and McKean (1963).

[30] "State of readiness" (Hitch and McKean 1960 p. 185); "preferred ... method of achieving the objective" (p. 183); "lives for their own sake" (p. 183).

recommended several variations on the sub-optimization approach, by which policy makers could make choices that saved the most lives with the least sacrifice of other objectives (or vice versa). That is, they identified the trade-offs among incommensurables, or the efficient "frontier" from which policy makers could choose, but they did not try to optimize by choosing from the frontier themselves.[31]

Others were more hopeful that the seeming incommensurables could be made commensurate by examining the revealed preferences of the USAF. Earlier, the Alchian et al. memo had made many of the same points found in Hitch and McKean's book (Hitch had been one of the authors on the memo). But Alchian et al. had argued that, once the efficient frontier is identified,

> Presumably it will be the responsibility of the Air Force or the [Joint Chiefs of Staff] to select one of the points as the most sensible one. Of course, any such selection implies a definite exchange ratio between lives and dollars. If this ratio could be revealed to the designers of bombing systems at an early stage they could explicitly determine the most effective system in terms of job done for a combined cost. While probably impossible in this particular case, we ought to avoid whenever possible the presentation of results only in efficient combination form. This yields the weakest possible ordering of the results given minimum rationality assumptions. All effort should be made to utilize whatever information we have about the relative values of the various inputs.[32]

Note two things in this passage. First, Alchian et al. presumed that it is the responsibility of the USAF to make the trade-offs between lives and machines. Second, all effort should be made to understand those "exchange ratios" and build them into the design phase, rather than merely to present decision-makers with an efficient frontier to choose from. That effort would soon come from Thomas Schelling and his student Jack Carlson.

7.3 Carlson and Schelling

Thomas Schelling (1921–2016) was a Nobel prize–winning economist famous for his work on cold war strategy and conflict (Figure 7.1).[33] Schelling received his BA from Berkeley in 1944 and his Ph.D. from

[31] Hitch and McKean (1960), quotation at p. 184.

[32] Alchian et al. (1951 p. 29).

[33] For background on Schelling and appraisals of his career, see Sent (2007) and Zeckhauser (1989). For interviews, see Breit and Hirsch (2009) and Carvalho (2007). Later, Schelling turned his expertise in international relations to studying global environmental challenges such as climate change (e.g., Schelling 1992).

Figure 7.1 Thomas Schelling

Harvard in 1951. During the last years of the war, he served in the fiscal division at the Bureau of the Budget under Harvard economist Arthur Smithies, an advisor to many second-generation architects of applied welfare economics. Schelling joined RAND as an adjunct fellow in 1956, then spent the summer of 1957 there followed by a whole year during 1958–59 with Hitch as his host, a year which he recalled as the most productive in his career. He also had direct connections to the Pentagon, working with it in the early 1960s to construct war games and advising on the Vietnam conflict. In other words, Schelling joined RAND a few years after the debacle of the strategic bombing analysis, and he visited with Hitch during years when Hitch continued to reflect on the criterion problem and continued to illustrate it with the formative example of valuing the lives of airplane crews.[34]

Jack Carlson (1933–1992) was a former Air Force fighter pilot who completed his dissertation, entitled "The Value of Life Saving," in 1963 under

[34] On the visits to RAND, see Breit and Hirsch (2009); on access to the Pentagon, see Sent (2007).

Schelling and Smithies. After first beginning his academic career at the Air Force Academy, Carlson went on to a career in government – in the Council for Economic Advisors, the Office of Management and Budget, and as an assistant secretary of the interior, then later as head of the National Association of Realtors. Whether the idea to address the question of valuing the saving of lives first came to Carlson and Schelling via RAND or via Carlson's experience in the Air Force is not clear, though to the best of Schelling's recollection the initial idea for the dissertation topic was Carlson's.[35] What is clear is that the issue had been one of considerable policy relevance to the USAF for some time.

All the questions about what trade-offs are incorporated into various approaches for valuing life, and about who gets to make the trade-offs, arose in Carlson's dissertation. Lifesaving, he said, is an economic activity because it uses scarce resources. For example, he noted that the construction of certain dams resulted in a net loss of lives (more than ever were expected to be saved from flood control), but apparently, in proceeding with the projects, the public authorities revealed that they viewed those costs as justified by the benefit of increased hydroelectric power and irrigated land. There are choices to be made, and those choices do not necessarily maximize safety, but a broader objective. In considering how to evaluate those trade-offs in formal benefit–cost analysis, Carlson considered the human capital approach to be "usable as a first approximation" but also as falling short of the full contributions of a person to society. A better approach was to find people making actual choices that revealed their willingness to trade lives for other social goods.[36]

Not surprisingly, given his own career and his advisor's connections to RAND, Carlson considered choices about lifesaving entirely within the context of USAF applications. Taking the approach Hirshleifer had outlined ten years earlier, Carlson considered the USAF's willingness to trade off costs and machines to save men. He considered two specific applications. One was a study of the USAF's recommended emergency procedures when pilots lost control of the artificial "feel" in their flight control systems. The USAF manual provided guidance on when to eject and when to attempt to land the aircraft, procedures which were expected to save the lives of some pilots at the cost of increasing the number of aircraft that would be lost. This approach yielded a lower bound on the value of life of $270k, which Carlson concluded was easily justified by the human capital

[35] Personal correspondence with Thomas Schelling, Nov. 16, 2013.

[36] See Carlson (1963); "first approximation" (p. 86).

cost of training pilots. (Note this is an estimate of the lower bound, as the USAF revealed, in specifying the choices to be made, that lives were worth at least that much.) Similarly, Carlson's other application was a study of the B-58 capsule ejection system. The USAF had initially estimated that it would cost $80m to design an ejection system for the bomber. Assuming a range of typical cost overruns and annual costs for maintenance and depreciation, and assuming one to three lives would be saved by the system annually, Carlson estimated that in making the investment the USAF revealed its "money valuation of pilots' lives" to be at least $1.2m to $9.0m. This was another lower bound, but a tighter one.[37]

Why were these values seemingly so high? One reason Carlson gave (among others) was that "valuation placed on a pilot's life must be more closely tied to the decision-makers involved," which here were the commanders of the USAF, "and must include their criteria and preferences." Carlson pointed out that in the USAF important decision makers like General Lemay were often former pilots, who identified with the individuals affected. Additionally, he noted that some of the value might not have been for the lives per se, but for the implicit message the investments sent to air crews that they were highly valued, a message that might boost morale.[38]

Importantly, in both applications just considered, Carlson took the public perspective: it was a matter of either the government generally, or the USAF specifically, to make trade-offs between lives and equipment.[39] Recall this was the perspective also taken by Hirshleifer and Alchian et al. at RAND a decade earlier. This perspective is particularly natural for military applications. Somebody like General Lemay would certainly factor casualty rates into his decision making, but he would hardly weight those casualties by the preferences of his men. It would be his decision to make based on his own willingness to trade off damage to the enemy for *lives*. Again, I emphasize "lives" here because from the standpoint of the public agency, the outcome is the number of lives saved in the aggregate population, not individual risks. Consequently, it was perfectly fitting for Carlson to call these estimates the value of

[37] The figures are in Carlson (1963 p. 92).

[38] Quotes from Carlson (1963 p. 105).

[39] From a positive perspective, Carlson clearly felt it was the USAF making the trade-offs. From a normative perspective, he seemed to be somewhat ambivalent on this point. He sometimes wrote as though there might be what we would now call an agency problem, with the USAF overvaluing pilots' lives. In this case, USAF decisions should be reviewed by higher levels of government (p. 119).

"lifesaving" or the "value of human life" and even the "costs and benefits…of preserving a particular life or lives."[40]

Interestingly, however, Carlson had earlier in his dissertation briefly considered the case of hazardous duty pay, in which an individual reveals information about his willingness to accept added on-the-job risk for a compensating increment to income. Here, the decision maker was not a public agency, but an individual choosing a job. Carlson gave examples from the private sector as well as volunteer positions in the military. For example, he figured that a pilot willingly increases his annual risk of dying (during peace time) by 0.00232–0.00464 percentage points, for some $2,280 of increased pay.[41] *If* he followed the methodology he had used when considering the public choice applications, he *might* have divided $2,280 by those risks to estimate a per-life value of $491k–$983k. Tellingly, Carlson did not do so in this case: he left it as $2,280 as the willingness to accept for that range of risks. The crucial (albeit implicit) distinction here appears to be one of perspective, whether from the individual's or society's. For the individual as a decision maker, it was a matter of evaluating risk – and only risk, so there was no point in aggregating up to per-life values. In contrast, when the public agency was the decision maker, it was a matter of the realizations of the individuals' risks aggregated over the group (expected lives), hence it made sense to convert the values to dollars per life.

Taking up the subject himself five years after his student, Schelling's crucial move was to finesse this distinction. At the outset of his essay, Schelling wanted to make clear that he was by no means tackling the question of the "worth of human life" itself. That question, he suggested, was rightfully tied up in moral questions and was too "awesome" for the economist to even begin to address. Rather, Schelling made clear that his more modest objective was to value the postponement of deaths; and not the death of a particular, known person, but "statistical death." "What is it worth," he asked, "to reduce the probability of death – the statistical frequency of death?"[42]

After defining the question in these terms, Schelling next asked, "Worth to whom?" Now, Schelling was clearly addressing the problem of evaluating *public* investments (indeed, his essay was part of a conference and

40 Quotes from Carlson (1963 pp. 89, 96, 1, respectively).

41 Economists remain interested in such decisions. Recently Greenberg et al. (2022) have computed the willingness of soldiers to reenlist in the US Army based on the hazards and compensation associated with specific duties.

42 Schelling (1968 p. 127).

book volume dedicated to this topic). Although writing solely about public investments, he took the view that those public investments should be evaluated in terms of the *private* worth they had to the *individuals* who would be affected: "Worth to whom? ... I shall propose that it is to the people who may die."[43]

Elaborating on this point, Schelling addressed the oft-articulated view that life and death are moral – or at least intangible – matters that cannot be priced. Responding to one particular commentator who had argued that it is beyond the competence of economists to assign values to pain, fear, and suffering, Schelling argued:

> The same is true of cola and Novocain.... If they were not for sale it would be beyond our competence, as economists, to put an objective value on them, at least until we took the trouble to ask people. Death is indeed different from most consumer events, and its avoidance different from most commodities.... But people have been dying for as long as they have been living; and where life and death are concerned we are all consumers. We nearly all want our lives extended and are probably willing to pay for it. It is worth while to remind ourselves that the people whose lives may be saved should have something to say about the value of the enterprise and that we analysts, however detached, are not immortal ourselves.[44]

In other words, consumers' sovereignty must reign when evaluating public investments: it is their preferences which count, not the preferences of public officials.[45] Because it was recognized that individuals do make choices over risk, once consumer sovereignty was embraced it became possible to look to such choices as the basis of social values. These exchange ratios can be observed, Schelling suggested, from either the price system itself or through surveys, both methods that were followed up on in the coming years.[46] While public policies would still have the effect of costing or saving lives in the population, from the individual's perspective, these effects were measured as risks, and that was what mattered for valuation.

7.4 Lives or Risks?

Although the VSL methodology and its attendant "statistical lives" terminology are now mainstream, they have never been without controversy. Later, one prominent example of a controversy arose in the United States

43 Schelling (1968 p. 127).

44 Schelling (1968 pp. 128–9). Schelling was responding to Reynolds (1956).

45 Mishan (1971) would soon make the point even more forcefully.

46 Schelling's suggestions to look at market behavior or to use surveys are at (1968 pp. 142–3). Applications of these ideas include Thaler and Rosen (1976) and Jones-Lee (1976).

in 2003 with the debate over the "senior death discount," in which the US EPA set a lower value for the VSLs of elderly citizens than for younger citizens, to account for their fewer remaining life-years. Popular outcry against this senior death "discount," given full voice in the US Congress, forced the EPA to retreat. Dismayed, economists in turn criticized Congress for political interference with rational, economic policy making.[47]

Commenting on their reaction, Fourcade (2009) has argued that too often economists fail to recognize that they are but one voice in wider political debates about both social values and, materially, the allocation of resources. Indeed, as Porter (1995) has argued, the historical rise of benefit–cost analysis stems from its very appeal as a way to mediate such political conflicts. Consequently, it is not surprising that benefit–cost analysts sometimes find themselves caught in the middle of them. In any case, Fourcade argues, the public has a right to enter the political debate, even if it is to reject monetization as demeaning.[48]

Recognizing that economists are operating in a marketplace of ideas in which their paradigm is but one competitor, Cameron (2010) has called for "euthanizing" the term "value of a statistical life" and statistical lives as a unit of account. She argues that this unappealing term is a colossal failure of marketing. It misleads the public, who interpret "value" as intrinsic worth rather than a monetary measure and who understandably interpret "lives" as just that, rather than risks. It is, after all, a lot to ask of the adjective "statistical" to not only modify the noun "life" but to transform it into "risk!" Inevitably, this conflation of the notion of "lives" and "risk" leads to misunderstanding and, in turn, to needless political controversy.[49]

47 See for example, Viscusi (2009a).

48 In response, Viscusi (2009b) argues that to monetize VSLs is not demeaning at all, but rather gives a voice to health and longevity in policy debates. Thus, for example, Viscusi recounts how he began his career critiquing US benefit-cost analyses of dams and related water projects, which were biased in favor of development in part because they ignored difficult-to-monetize ecological effects. Monetizing them, he argues, gives them an equal seat at the table. Viscusi's view has a long tradition among economists (see, e.g., Schultz's [1961] use of the argument, in turn quoting an argument from von Thünen, in the context of monetizing the value of lives). Of course, this response presupposes the economists' paradigm of benefits, costs, and optimization, which Fourcade would argue is itself open to social debate.

49 The point has come up in the context of VSLs before. See, for example, the debate sparked by Broome (1978), much of which is in, or cited in, Jones-Lee (1982). Linnerooth (1982) provides a particularly interesting discussion of the tensions Schelling's VSL approach raises: particular lives will be lost, yet if we value risks instead of lives, and if risks are valued less than their equivalent in whole lives, policy would seem to be biased against health, as if we are "murdering statistical lives." See also Heinzerling (2000).

Cameron suggests replacing the VSL terminology with "willingness to swap" money for "microrisks." Based on focus groups both with the public and with analysts, Simon et al. (2020) similarly recommend speaking of the "value of reduced mortality risk."

As this chapter shows, such controversies are nothing new. Schelling's VSL terminology did not rise out of a vacuum. It too was born out of political controversy, but, ironically, it was pressure from the USAF that forced RAND to even think about the role of lives in its optimization framework in the first place, a problem that eventually attracted Schelling's attention. Moreover, this history suggests a further irony: perhaps it was the very finessing of the distinction between lives and mortality risk, which so exacerbates political tensions today, that originally overcame political problems and facilitated the monetization of mortality risks in benefit–cost analysis.

Consider an applied problem like measuring the benefits of reducing air pollution. It is entirely natural to approach that problem by asking what the effect would be of the policy, and to proceed by answering that it would save *x* lives, perhaps with some confidence interval around *x*. The next logical question would be, what is the value of those lives? Thus, to measure the benefits of policies that would save lives would seem to require a value of life, but that raises difficult measurement issues. On the other hand, values for risk reduction are measurable, but answer a different policy question. Until Schelling's essay, there was no clear connection between those individuals' trade-offs over risks and the apparent policy-relevant question of the value of lives. Not surprisingly, the literature in the 1950s and 1960s was quite vague about whose values were at stake.[50]

Schelling was not the first to think in terms of individual's trade-offs between money and risk, nor to express them on a per life basis. The same idea was previously expressed by Fromm (1965) and, most clearly, by Drèze (1962). Why did Schelling receive most of the credit? Relative to Drèze, perhaps the timing was better. Certainly, it helped that he published in English rather than French. But more substantively, Schelling's "value of statistical life" terminology creatively established an intellectual middle ground. By bridging the gap between the value for *lives*, which was what seemingly was required for social benefit–cost analysis, and the value for *risks*, which was what consumers could reveal either through the market or through surveys, the VSL terminology was an appealing and persuasive way to make the case for introducing those values into benefit

[50] For example, Fromm (1965), Mushkin (1962), Valavanis (1958), Weisbrod (1961).

cost analysis. In other words, conflating "lives" and "risks" may have been exactly what it took at the time for economists to persuade government officials and the public on the idea of pricing those policy impacts.[51]

This synthesis was critical because valuing lives was, as Schelling put it, too "awesome" a problem, but valuing risks had not, up to that point, seemed relevant to many public investments. Schelling was still talking about lives, but a peculiar kind of lives – "statistical lives." This was a new coinage, but it would have had a familiar ring. It likely resonated with the notion of the "statistical life" of a product – how long a light bulb, for example, could be expected to live.[52] Only in this case, consumers were not valuing light bulbs, but themselves.

[51] Hood (2017) argues that economists like Schelling essentially reframed policy questions to give themselves more authority over the models. In contrast, I'm suggesting that economists created new models to more persuasively fit existing questions. If I'm right, the point was not necessarily appreciated by people working within existing frameworks at the time. Initial comments on Schelling's essay were stunningly dismissive as lacking rigorous analysis of risk, as well as for overlooking the existing literature (Bailey 1968; Fromm 1968).

[52] A JSTOR search uncovers dozens of articles using this term in this way in the decades before Schelling, especially in statistics, economics, and engineering journals.

8

Benefit–Cost Analysis: Objective or Multi-objective?

Non-market Valuation and Incommensurability

His conclusions, whatever be their generality and their truth, do not authorize [the Political Economist] in adding a single syllable of advice.

–Nassau Senior, *Political Economy* (1850)

8.1 Introduction

In her classic study of social science, Furner (1975) highlighted the tension the economics profession has long felt between the pulls of policy advocacy and scientific objectivity. This tension has been felt at many times in the history of economics. It was present at the founding of the American Economic Association in 1885, when Ely and others believed they could be both scientists and advocates. It was present at the founding of the National Bureau of Economic Research in 1920, with Wesley Clair Mitchell embedding the principle that economists should stick strictly to the objective facts and leave *all* policy judgments to the political authorities. (To this day, the NBER forbids policy recommendations in its publications.) In response, Robert Lynd, Mitchell's colleague at Columbia, criticized such purist positions in his *Knowledge for What?* (1939), a polemic for purposively conceived social science. A similar exchange followed the American Economic Association's Presidential address from Howard Ellis in 1949, which received comments from Bushrod Allin, Frank Knight, and others.[1]

Economists have been particularly ambivalent about welfare measurement. On one hand, a profession seeking the status of science in the modern age needed to maintain theoretical and methodological purity.

[1] On the founding of the AEA, see Bateman and Kapstein (1999) and Furner (1975). For discussion of the *Knowledge for What?* debate, see M. Smith (1994). Ellis's address and subsequent commentary can be found in Ellis (1950, 1953), Allin (1953), and Knight (1953).

Consequently, large parts of the profession argued that economists should avoid the interpersonal comparisons of welfare inherent in normative economics. On the other hand, economists of all stripes and schools have yearned to contribute to policy-making, which inevitably requires such comparisons. Disagreements about which side of this divide to fall, along with attempts to have it both ways, created some of the most important methodological debates in modern economics. For example, Lionel Robbins took a purist position in his *Essay on the Nature and Significance of Economic Science* (1935), arguing that economists were not competent to weigh the gains and losses to different people inherent in any policy reform. In response to Robbins, Hicks and Kaldor proposed their potential compensation test. A foundational concept in postwar benefit–cost analysis, the potential compensation test asks only whether a policy creates enough value that it could *potentially* be distributed in a way to make everybody better off, with winners hypothetically compensating losers. This seemed to many like a normative question that could be answered scientifically. On the other hand, others pointed out that whether the answer to such a hypothetical question has normative significance is itself a normative question.[2]

Despite such collective ambivalence, economists generally became more accepting of applied welfare economics over the middle decades of the twentieth century. Agricultural and other applied economists, Chicago school economists, Walrasian economists at Cowles – all took up the task of welfare measurement in the late 1950s, in one way or another. Yet they still had to balance their twin goals of upholding scientific integrity while informing public policy.

Maintaining that balance was most difficult when questions arose about how to account for the *distributional* effects of policies, if at all. Of course, if a policy redistributes wealth from one group to another, this effect will obviously be important to the interest groups involved and to the decision makers representing them. But incorporating such effects was challenging. After all, the entire logic of the Flood Control Act's directive to measure benefits and costs "to whomsoever they may accrue," encapsulated by the Hicks-Kaldor potential compensation test, was to combine all benefits and costs into one net measure, obliterating the distributional effects. Accordingly, there is, in a certain sense, a contradiction at the heart

[2] On the initial debate over Robbins's essay and the resulting proposals for potential compensation tests, see Harrod (1938), Robbins (1938), Kaldor (1939), and Hicks (1939). Criticisms of the claim that hypothetical compensations have normative significance are legion, but classic examples include Little (1950) and Sen (1987).

of any effort to incorporate distributional effects into benefit–cost analysis. Benefit–cost analysis only achieved scientific status by shutting down such questions.

Dissatisfaction with this state of affairs lead to a methodological debate in the 1960s, which arose between two competing visions for benefit–cost analysis. One vision was more traditional, emphasizing individuals' willingness to pay for various benefits that could be reconciled, in Pigou's phrase, by "the measuring rod of money." The other was a new alternative, emphasizing the incommensurability of different types of benefits and the importance of political decision-making. Rather than aggregating individual preferences and individual-level optimization into a social choice, as benefit–cost practitioners were doing, and as Arrow and Samuelson were attempting to do in their own ways, this alternative would constrain the role of analysts to what Hitch had called "sub-optimization" (Chapter 7), maximizing each objective given constraints on the other, without making trade-offs across objectives. Then, when it came to making those trade-offs, it emphasized public reasoning and civic republicanism over economic analysis.[3]

Though obscured by many details, the ultimate point of disagreement in the debate was the role of policy analysts: whether they were to simply make the relevant trade-offs known to policy makers, who had the ultimate authority to make the political judgments, or whether they could make normative recommendations and ultimately judge the decisions of policymakers. Although many individuals were involved in the debate, two key organizations formed the core of each camp, RFF and the Harvard Water Program. More than an academic debate, the stakes became very real when the Water Resources Council proposed a version of multi-objective planning to be instituted for water resources.[4]

8.2 The Harvard Water Program

Begun in 1950 as a modest interdisciplinary seminar on the "wise use" of natural resources, the Harvard Water Program expanded with a grant from the Ford Foundation in 1953, around the same time Ford began RFF. Over

[3] Insofar as it allows for group-level rationality and preferences, as distinct from the sum of the group's individuals, the civic republican approach bears some resemblances to the organismic or communal approach of earlier German *Finanzwissenschaft*. See Cherrier and Fleury (2017), Desmarais-Tremblay (2017b), and Sturn (2010) for summaries of *Finanzwissenschaft* and discussions contrasting it to the postwar neoclassical analysis of public goods.

[4] For previous overviews of this history, see Castle et al. (1981) and Hufschmidt (2000).

Figure 8.1 Arthur Maass

the next decade, the program received sustained support from Ford (sometimes indirectly through RFF), the Rockefeller Foundation, the Bureau of Reclamation (BOR), and the US Army Corps of Engineers (USACE). From 1955 to 1965, its director was Arthur Maass (1917–2004), a professor of government and a vocal critic of decision-making at USACE (Figure 8.1). In *Muddy Waters* (1951), Maass had strongly criticized it for its cozy relationship with Congress and lack of accountability to the chief executive. Since that time, however, the Corps had undertaken some reforms, and endeavored to establish a cooperative relationship with Maass, sending visitors to, hiring students from, and supporting the research of the Water Program.[5]

Maass built the Water Program around a large interdisciplinary team of economists, engineers, and himself as a political scientist. The core of this team comprised, in addition to Maass, Maynard Hufschmidt of the School of Public Administration; Gordon Fair and Harold Thomas of engineering;

[5] See Huffschmidt (1967) and Maass et al. (1962 Table 1.1) for additional details on the Harvard Water Program. The initial Ford grant is documented in Ford Foundation (1954). On Arthur Maass, see Maass (1989) for a biographical sketch and interview.

and economists Robert Dorfman, Otto Eckstein, and Stephen Marglin. Many other individuals from Harvard and other organizations participated as well, including Blair Bower, a civil engineer who also worked with Allen Kneese, and the economist Peter Steiner.

Otto Eckstein (1927–1984) was an expert in benefit–cost analysis who had received his Ph.D. from Harvard, working with Arthur Smithies. He had published two previous books on the appraisal of water projects, including one with John Krutilla.[6] Stephen Marglin (b. 1938) was a young economist who first joined the Harvard Water Program as an undergraduate student. After becoming one of the youngest professors to earn tenure, he became noted later for rejecting neoclassical economics and taking a more radical turn. But of the economists, the most important for our story is Robert Dorfman (1916–2002). Dorfman earned a BA in mathematics (1936) and an MA in economics (1937) from Columbia, where he worked with Harold Hotelling. He worked in operations research (OR) for the US Air Force from 1943 to 1950, where he met George Dantzig and was introduced to linear programming, and visited RAND around the time of its debacle over the bombing study. He then earned his Ph.D. in economics at Berkeley, where he was a faculty member before leaving for Harvard in 1955.

One of Dorfman's missions was to spread the gospel of OR. He sought to explain it in simple terms, reveal its spiritual affinity with traditional neoclassical economics, and persuade the economics profession that it had advantages over marginal analysis. He pointed out its close connection to welfare economics (a competitive equilibrium could be viewed as a solution to a linear program) and its ability to handle discrete, discontinuous activities. Most importantly, this ability made it more pragmatic and useful for private and public planning. As he explained,

> The central formal problem of economics is the problem of allocating scarce resources so as to maximize the attainment of some predetermined objective. The standard formulation of the problem—the so-called marginal analysis—has led to conclusions of great importance for the understanding of many questions of social and economic policy. But it is a fact of common knowledge that this mode of analysis has not recommended itself to men of affairs for the practical solution to their economic and business problems. Mathematical programming is based on a restatement of this same formal problem in a form which is designed to be useful in making practical decisions in business and economic affairs.

[6] Eckstein (1958) and Krutilla and Eckstein (1958). Eckstein seems to be a forgotten figure in the history of economic thought, but he was editor of the *Review of Economics and Statistics*, member of the White House Council of Economic Advisers, and a prominent macroeconomist.

This interest in planning – and in particular the hands-on tools needed by "men of affairs" – made him the ideal partner for Maass.[7]

This team met together regularly to educate themselves about problems in water resources planning and to share disciplinary perspectives. Their first five years of work culminated in the release of their book, *Design of Water Resource Systems* (Maass et al. 1962). This work, as unified as can be expected from six authors, is an exemplar of interdisciplinarity, integrating economics, engineering, and hydrology into a single planning problem. Dorfman and Michael Barnett (an MIT physicist) and others introduced programming problems and provided computer code. Thomas and others introduced methods for addressing the stochastic nature of stream flows, simulating possible futures by taking random draws from stream flow distributions, rather than simply replicating history as was conventional practice.

But the most important contribution of *Design of Water Resource Systems* was the place at which it positioned itself in the policy process. In contrast to the other recent books on water policy, its focus was on the actual *design* of water systems, not in the evaluation of a given proposed (or developed) system. Moreover, in designing these systems, it stressed the importance of multiple objectives.

To the members of the Harvard Water Program, the idea of "multiple objectives" meant more than the long-recognized fact that water systems have multiple *purposes* or joint outputs (irrigation, flood control, electric power, navigation, and recreation, for example). As we have seen, traditional benefit–cost analyses, whenever possible, aggregate these outputs together into a single objective, using market prices or shadow prices (the price people would be willing to pay for a little more of them). Nevertheless, some outputs cannot be assigned shadow prices with any confidence, and traditional benefit–cost analysis tends to de-emphasize those outputs.

Maass et al. argued that this focus on the single objective of economic benefits was therefore misplaced. In holding to it, traditional benefit–cost analyses missed Congress's stated intent, which included inter-household equity in the distribution of income, regional development, and other contributions to social welfare, such as the saving of human life from floods. In general, the participants of the Harvard water program especially emphasized the two objectives of efficiency and redistribution. Moreover, Marglin pointed out that, in addition to the size of the pie and its division,

[7] See Dorfman (1997) for additional biographical details. For examples of his advocacy of OR, see Dorfman (1953, 1960) and Dorfman, Samuelson, and Solow (1958). Quotation from Dorfman (1953 p. 797).

people also cared about the *method of slicing* it. Thus, the standard practice of invoking the potential for pure income transfers, as implicit in the Hicks-Kaldor criterion, or of separating out the efficiency and redistribution purposes of government as enshrined in Musgrave's public finance text, not only was not pragmatic, it was not desirable. After all, "Many, perhaps most, people would be willing to give up a bit of efficiency to see the living standards of Indians of the X River Basin improved by their own labor rather than by the dole." Accordingly, it was essential that the redistribution objective be incorporated into projects at the outset.[8]

But although these were the kinds of considerations Congress rightfully had in mind, benefit–cost analysis did not fully take them into account. The resulting disjunction between the true project objectives and the basis for evaluation created two problems. On the one hand, because they would be judged by the sole efficiency criterion, planners did not have the incentive to design projects for these other objectives. On the other hand, when projects were so designed, perhaps because of legal constraints, their benefit–cost ratios would be lower than they would otherwise be if they had been planned without these constraints. The use of a single net-benefit objective thus weakened policy at both the design and the evaluation stages.[9]

Consequently, though still much needed as a tool to conquer complex problems and to objectively promote true public goods over mere rent seeking, benefit–cost analysis did not have the authority it should have. As Dorfman would later put it, "sensible men do not relinquish a project they desire just because an arithmetic requirement is not met, when they are perfectly aware that the arithmetic ignores the considerations that are really motivating them." Together with the fact that legislative language about benefits and costs was vague enough to admit a wide range of interpretations, this weakness allowed engineers to design water systems as large as possible and to confine the economic considerations solely to cost minimization.[10]

In their alternative vision, Maass et al. viewed policy analysts, in USACE for example, as agents of the Executive and Congress. They were to discern the various objectives articulated by these democratic representatives

8 "Many, if not most..." (Maass et al. 1962 p. 67).

9 Writing a little later, Bromley and Beattie (1973) illustrated this point well with the example of reclamation projects that were limited by law to small farmers. The benefit–cost ratio of these projects would have been higher had large farms been allowed to participate (since their greater efficiency translated into higher willingness to pay for water), but this missed the point that one of the objectives of American agricultural policy had been to protect family farmers.

10 "Sensible men..." (Dorfman 1978 p. 279). Designing systems as large as possible (Maass et al. 1962 p. 6).

of the people and design a project to meet them as optimally as possible. This vision involved four basic steps. First, the analysts would identify the various objectives. Second, they would develop design criteria formalizing the objectives with observable (and wherever possible, quantifiable) indicators. Third, they would design the system(s) to be built, integrating the engineering and the economics. Fourth and finally, the analysts would evaluate the designs using a multi-objective version of benefit–cost analysis.

Again, it was at the design stage where the book's chief contribution lay. As Dorfman explained in one of his chapters, the design of a project would begin with a multi-objective "production possibilities frontier," which shows the inherent trade-offs among social goods such as marketed products, equity, and outdoor recreation. The trade-offs would incorporate stochastic hydrological constraints and perhaps even policy constraints, as well as economic opportunity costs. Figure 5.5 depicts a simple production possibilities frontier showing the trade-offs between material welfare and the environment. Any point on or below curve (the "frontier") is physically possible. However, points below the curve are inefficient, because it would be possible to have more of everything. Thus, an efficient design would be somewhere on the production possibilities frontier.

The next concern, then, was optimizing a system for multiple objectives, that is, deciding how to trade-off one objective for another, or where on the frontier to be. In linear programming, only one objective can be maximized, but other objectives can be integrated as constraints. Thus, if there are *N* objectives arbitrarily partitioned into sets *n1* and *n2*, a weighted average of the *n1* could be maximized subject to *n2* constraints. Introducing these ideas in Chapter 2 of *Design*, Marglin considered an example with two objectives, net public benefits and benefits to a specific group, such as a Native American tribe inhabiting a river basin. One could (i) maximize net public benefits subject to a constraint that the net benefits to the Native Americans be above some level; (ii) do the opposite, maximizing benefits to the Native Americans subject to a constraint on net public benefits; or (iii) maximize a weighted average of the two objectives. Marglin's analysis here was similar to Hitch's idea of "sub-optimization," in which, say, lives saved could be set at a minimum level while optimizing other factors. As Marglin pointed out, the duality of the control problem guarantees that these three approaches can be made to be equivalent with suitable choices of constraints and weights.[11]

[11] See also Marglin (1967).

Valid as it is, this logic does not provide much insight into the practical problem of where the weights or constraints are to come from. In other words, how are analysts to decide where on the production possibilities frontier to locate? Moreover, when framed this way, the question seems to return one to the methods of traditional benefit–cost analysis, in which the shadow prices of non-market objectives are perfectly consistent with the programming weights described by Marglin.

The participants in the water program differed on the specifics of how to resolve these issues, but they were generally united in the belief that economists would not be able to observe individuals' relative weights for different objectives by observing their behavior – or that individuals' weights were not the ideal measure even if the practical problems could be overcome. Rather, they emphasized collective, social choices arising from the political process. Accordingly, even if objectives were aggregated together using weights, the social nature of those weights differentiated multi-objective planning from traditional benefit–cost analysis. This emphasis on social choices, as distinct from individuals' choices which Krutilla and others had emphasized, was perhaps the most fundamental point distinguishing the participants in the water program from other benefit–cost practitioners.[12]

For example, in the context of inter-temporal trade-offs and discounting, Marglin (1963a) argued that social rates of time preference had more normative significance than private market rates. To Marglin, these social discount rates were built up from the interlocking of altruistic utility functions, including the utility of future generations. Consequently, future consumption took on the nature of a public good. In one sense, social rates of time preference thus reflected more than the sum of their individualistic parts, but yet they were strictly tied to them. Marglin argued that it is "axiomatic that a democratic government reflects only the preferences of the individuals who are presently members of the body politic." However, he left open some ambiguity on this point, conditioning it on the premise that he was playing "the neoclassical, or rather neo-Benthamite, game." In light of his earlier comment that he had already given "away more to neoclassical welfare economics in the assumption of well-defined utility

[12] In addition to the ideas of the main figures discussed below, see the very clear and concise statement by Steiner (1969a). Book-length treatments of this multi-objective perspective on benefit–cost analysis, subsequent to *Design*, include Marglin (1967), Steiner (1969b), Dasgupta, Marglin, and Sen (1972), and Major (1977). Amartya Sen has continued to show interest in what he calls "public reasoning," which he views as consistent with his capabilities approach to welfare (e.g., Sen 2009).

functions" than he should like, and in light of his later more radical break with economic orthodoxy, Marglin's actual thinking on the importance of individual preferences is open to speculation.[13]

Eckstein and Dorfman were less ambiguous. Eckstein (1961) argued in favor of a multiple objective approach on the ground that it was more realistic and left to policy-makers

> the all-important weighting of the various objectives, giving them the results of the technical analysis in the most usable forms.... [I]n no event should the technician arrogate the weighting of objectives to himself by presenting a one-dimensional answer after burying the weighting process in a welter of technical details.

Going further, he suggested that the economist "interpret the desires" of the policy makers and maximize them. "In this manner, the economist can play the role of technician and bridge the gap between the positive quantitative research which is the main stock-in-trade of the economist, and the normative conclusions which policy requires." For example, in the context of efficiency-equity trade-offs, he suggested that the social values for increased equity could be identified from Congress's choice of marginal tax rates on different income groups.[14]

At first, Dorfman seems to have been at least open to the idea of measuring benefits and costs of intangible environmental improvements. He supervised a thesis and organized a 1963 Brookings conference on the topic, with applications to such areas as outdoor recreation and transportation. Apparently, he was unimpressed with those efforts. Before long, he was echoing the views of Eckstein. Throughout the remainder of his life, Dorfman argued that the relative values of human life, endangered species, and jobs in a particular way of life are

> not questions of fact that might admit expert answers, but questions about social values and public preference, that only the elaborate and clumsy procedures of democratic decision-making can answer. Such answers are not data to be fed into decision-making processes but, rather, outputs of those processes.

In other words, like Eckstein, Dorfman argued that economists simply are not in the position to collapse multiple objectives into a scalar-valued function. Together with engineers, they can only make the trade-offs known to the true decision makers.[15]

[13] Quotations from Marglin (1963a pp. 95, 97).

[14] Quotations form Eckstein (1961 pp. 446, 449).

[15] The undergraduate thesis, by Leonard Merewitz, was published as Merewitz (1966), while the conference proceedings were published as Dorfman (1965). Quotation from Dorfman (1997 p. 373).

This attitude may be surprising for somebody so associated with OR and planning. But Dorfman always articulated the principle that linear programming was best used for narrow problems, quoting a certain Glen Camp to the effect that "...best results will be obtained if the scientist meticulously avoids the evaluation of intangibles." Consistent with these beliefs, he suggested that analysts first design systems only for economic efficiency (i.e., confining themselves to the truly quantifiable) and that political representatives then modify the design to account for other objectives – a lesson he may have learned from his time at RAND.[16]

Finally, as the political scientist on the team, it is not surprising that Maass too emphasized the role of the political process. In a concluding chapter to *Design*, Maass discussed, in detail, the role of the various branches of government at each step of the planning process. Picking up where he left off, Maass returned to these issues in a 1966 article in the *Quarterly Journal of Economics*, on "Benefit–cost Analysis: its Relevance to Public Investment Decisions." Maass began by critiquing two aspects of "the new welfare economics." First, methodologically it tended to de-emphasize distributional issues by focusing on *potential* compensations, or imagining that a distributive branch of government would rectify any adverse distributional effects of a policy via pure transfers. But this, he argued, was a completely unrealistic artifice, one which ignored the constraints on transfers and, as Marglin had argued, society's concern with the method of redistribution. He argued that even Dorfman's proposal to simply begin with a system designed around the efficiency criterion would be a mistake: it unjustifiably privileged that criterion and it would be too easy to skip the necessary step of adjusting the design for other factors. Second, Maass challenged the reliance of the new welfare economics on consumer sovereignty. Here, he argued that people's preferences were context-dependent, and that the relevant context for public investment was the political community, not individual choice. Thus,

> the great challenge for welfare economics is to frame questions in such a way as to elicit from individuals community oriented [preferences]. The market is an institution designed to elicit privately oriented responses from individuals and to relate these responses to each other. For the federal government the electoral, legislative, and administrative processes together constitute the institution designed to elicit community oriented responses.[17]

[16] Glen Camp quotation, Dorfman (1960 p. 614, see also p. 620, plus his 1974, 1978, 1996). First design for efficiency (Dorfman 1963).

[17] Maass (1966 pp. 216–7).

But these processes would have to work in harmony.

To coordinate them, Maass proposed a three-step procedure in which, first, agency analysts represent the trade-offs among various objectives, as embodied in alternative projects; second, the executive proposes a program to Congress; and, finally, Congress accepts, rejects, or modifies this program. In other words, initially, analysts would merely make the production possibilities curve known, while elected representatives would make social choices. Maass further envisioned the process iterating back, with agency analysts improving their design of project alternatives based on Congress's past social choices. Similar approaches were advocated by Marglin (1967 Ch. 2) and Dasgupta, Marglin, and Sen (1972) in their work for the UN, and by Rothenberg (1967) in the context of urban planning.[18]

To assess the potential for this iterating, Maass surveyed Congressional actions with the aim of identifying patterns in their choices. Citing work by his student, David Major, on US housing and highway programs, he tentatively concluded that an examination of the record could give a rough gauge of Congress' willingness to trade off efficiency and distributional objectives. But Maass also emphasized that Congress could have made these trade-offs more systematically (and, hence, inferring the signal could have been made easier) if the agencies had actually made the trade-offs explicit, as Maass suggested be done in his first step.

Even against the backdrop of earlier twentieth century battles between those who advocated a normative science and those who would confine the social scientists to providing information to the true policy-maker, Maass's vision represented an audacious maneuver: a positivist Trojan horse smuggled into the heart of the normative citadel. While traditionally benefit–cost analysis was a tool that would inform policy-makers about the trade-offs they should make, and which could then pass judgment on the quality of their choices, Maass and his colleagues restricted it to informing policy-makers only about the nature of those trade-offs, and to then reflect back their social choices. In short, they would shear even benefit–cost analysis itself of normative trade-offs between objectives.

These ideas were quite new for the times and were not always well received by practitioners of benefit–cost analysis. Moreover, the paradigm of thought in which Maass et al. operated was different enough to cause much confusion. Indeed, a full-fledged debate over multi-objective planning would soon arise, a debate that consumed both the policy world and the academic literature.

18 Cherrier and Fleury (2017) point out the relevance of Rothenberg's work.

8.3 The RFF Economists

Meanwhile, two other economists, just beginning their careers, were writing their dissertations on the question of efficiency-equity trade-offs in the context of water resources policy: Robert Haveman and Myrick Freeman. Though working on separate tracks initially, they would soon unite while spending the 1969–70 academic year at RFF. Together with other RFF economists, they would also engage Maass and some of his colleagues in a major debate over the shape and role of benefit–cost analysis.

Robert Haveman (1936–2022) received his Ph.D. in economics from Vanderbilt in 1963, studying under Rendigs Fels. He first worked in the economics department of Grinnell College, but spent much of his early career in Washington, DC, at RFF (1965–6), as Senior Economist on the US Congress's Joint Economic Committee, Subcommittee on Economy in Government (1968–9), and again at RFF (1969–70), before settling at the University of Wisconsin-Madison in 1970.[19]

Haveman's dissertation was published as a book, *Water Resources Investment and the Public Interest*, in 1965. An evaluation of USACE projects and Congress's pattern of funding them, it was by far the most detailed empirical look at the efficiency-equity trade-offs in water projects. The dissertation can be thought of as addressing the issue from two angles, the first being the *intentions* of Congress and the second being the actual *consequences* of its actions. From the first angle, Haveman looked at the set of USACE projects funded by Congress in relation to the larger set of all those for which the Corps had conducted benefit–cost analyses. The idea here is that even if they were biased, the Corps's estimates were the best information Congress had available when making its budget, so that Congress's use of them provided insight into its objectives. Haveman found that, based on the Corps's estimates, the weighted average benefit–cost ratio of the entire set of potential projects was 1.8, while the projects that Congress funded had an average ratio of 2.2. This comparison suggested that Congress did favor projects with higher net benefits. However, had it chosen to, it could have allocated the same budget in a way so as to reach an average benefit–cost ratio of 3.4, suggesting it was not maximizing efficiency benefits. From this, Haveman concluded that Congress also had other objectives.

Consistent with that interpretation, Haveman found that the pattern of state-level net fiscal flows from water programs (expenditures minus

[19] At Wisconsin, he soon became Director for the Institute for Research on Poverty, and has continued to pursue the theme of equity and welfare throughout his career.

estimated tax costs) had a strong and negative correlation with state-level per capita income (–0.63), suggesting that Congress also had the intention of using the programs to move toward a more equitable distribution of resources. Expenditures were particularly targeted to the southeastern region of the country, the nation's poorest.

Haveman's second perspective on the matter was a more critical look at how effective the Corps's planning and Congressional budgeting processes were in achieving these objectives. To do so, he revised the Corps's benefit–cost estimates using alternative assumptions about the discount rate, a standard point of criticism as the 2.5 percent rate it was using probably underestimated the opportunity cost of capital. Focusing on projects in the southeast from 1946 to 1962, he found that 144 of 147 projects had benefit–cost ratios exceeding one according to the Corps's estimates, but that only 65–100 met this criterion when he used other discounting approaches in the literature. Haveman thus concluded that the current planning process left much to be desired from an efficiency standpoint.[20]

And how effective were those projects in redistributing resources to poorer regions? Haveman essayed two additional exercises to explore the issue. First, he analyzed the hypothetical effect on the southeast if these inefficient projects had not been funded. Here, he found that three of the ten southeastern states *would* have been better off without these projects, but that seven – and the region as a whole – were better off with them. Second, in what he viewed as his most important contribution methodologically, Haveman empirically implemented Eckstein's (1961) suggestion to weight individuals' benefits by the inverse of their marginal tax rates, interpreted as an indicator of marginal social welfare. Using these weights, he found that net benefits from 1946 to 1962 Corps projects were \$1.5b–\$4.7b, and that now 122 of the 147 southeastern projects passed a benefit–cost criterion, even when using a higher discount rate.

Haveman was thus forced to conclude that "given the multidimensional welfare function based upon the estimate of the marginal utility

[20] As pointed out by numerous economists, when taxes impose a wedge between the government's cost of borrowing and the private return to investment, the opportunity cost of foregone future income will be higher than the government's rate of borrowing. Eckstein (1957), Marglin (1963b), and others suggested ways to combine these opportunity costs with subjective preferences into a single model (see also Krutilla and Eckstein 1958). Since water projects like a dam have high up-front capital costs and long-lived returns, benefit–cost ratios are highly sensitivity to such alternative approaches to discounting. Accordingly, the rate of discount is an issue which, then and now, has attracted the attention of some of the top public economists, from Arrow to Weitzman. It was also a rallying point for criticism of the Corps's practices, since the low discount rate would tend to raise benefit–cost ratios.

of income function which was adopted from the policy-makers, construction of ... economically inefficient projects may well be an efficient means of securing desired redistribution." However, he could not shake his gut feeling that there was a lot of inefficiency in the Corps's program. He noted that

> [I]nsofar as either economically efficient projects or pure income transfers exist as possibilities for regional aid, the redistribution of income by means of the construction of such economically inefficient projects is an inefficient means of effecting such redistribution.

Notice that there is a particular ambiguity in Haveman's argument. Clearly, it does follow as a matter of logic that a pure transfer, which by definition has no net aggregate costs, would be more efficient than a project with negative net national benefits. But are pure transfers of this kind actually available? And would this method of slicing the pie, to use Marglin's phrase, be socially desirable? Haveman, while noting Marglin's emphasis on its importance, did not commit himself on the question. Instead, he noted that "under any circumstances...the most desirable condition would exist if an abundance of economically efficient projects are available in the favored region." Clearly, this would be so too, but again, it is not clear that such projects were available. Haveman had only shown that some funded projects were inefficient from a national standpoint, not that there were efficient projects left unfunded.[21]

Haveman's contemporary and future colleague, Myrick Freeman (1936–2022) received his Ph.D. in economics from the University of Washington in 1965, working with James Crutchfield and Walter Oi, and spent the bulk of his career at Bowdoin College, with several visiting appointments at RFF. In his dissertation, he pursued themes similar to Haveman's. Like Haveman, he adjusted official benefit–cost estimates for such factors as the discount rate, real increases in future operating costs, and the opportunity cost of farmers' time. In case studies of six BOR projects, all of which passed Reclamation's original benefit–cost test, he found that only one would survive the adjustments. Freeman also similarly emphasized the importance of distributional issues. Indeed, he argued that "Evaluation of these programs with conventional benefit–cost techniques seems...to miss the point, since there is implicit in the public discussion of these programs the notion of a social welfare function embodying income distribution in some way." (A "social welfare function" is like a utility function for

[21] Quotes from Haveman (1965 pp. 151, 120, and 120n), respectively.

a society, aggregating the utility of individual members, potentially in a way that favors more equity.)[22]

Freeman tackled the problem in a way not unlike Haveman. However, he argued that marginal tax rates were not a logically consistent indicator of a social welfare function. After all, if they were really set so as to equate households' marginal utility of money, taxes would have to be 100 percent on the richest and zero on the poorest until equity was achieved. Obviously, this was not the case. Freeman instead preferred to follow another suggestion from Eckstein (1961), to impose an arbitrary but reasonable functional form on the social welfare function (1967a, b). However, he followed Marglin's model of intergenerational discounting by building up the social welfare function from interdependent altruistic preference functions, so that redistribution took on the character of a public good (Freeman 1969a). In this way, unlike Eckstein, he viewed the social welfare function as grounded in individuals and (in principle) observable by economists.[23]

Freeman adjusted BOR's benefits estimates by using a social welfare function that was additive in the square root of individual incomes. To implement this model empirically, he obtained data on the distribution of local landholdings and aggregate farm income, and he assumed baseline farmer incomes and project benefits were uniform across land (1967b). Freeman found that the transfers were in the "right" direction, in the sense that the marginal social welfare of income was higher for the subsidized farmers than for the taxpayers, on average. However, he also found that the effect was so small as to fail to overturn any of the benefit–cost decision rules. As with the "pure efficiency" (unweighted) approach, only one in six projects passed the test after the appropriate adjustments. Accordingly, the projects' inefficiencies could not be excused on distributional grounds. Moreover, Reclamation's initial benefit–cost ratios did not correlate well with the welfare-weighted ratios, suggesting the biases in its benefit–cost analyses were not surreptitious proxies for distributional objectives.

What then was to be made of BOR's planning process and Congressional budgeting decisions? Freeman considered the possibility that regional distribution was emphasized over individual distribution, but argued that such an objective was inconsistent with both accepted ethical norms and

22 Freeman's analysis can be found in Freeman (1966). Quotation from Freeman (1967a p. 507).

23 Later, Freeman would back off this position to some extent, suggesting that, if not consistent with the principle of equal marginal sacrifice, the graduated income tax was consistent at least with equal absolute sacrifice (in which everybody gives up the same quantity of utility), and may be the most useful signal from the political process (Freeman 1969a).

with Reclamation's practice of shifting costs within regions via various repayment schemes. Indeed,

> Any effort to explain the Bureau's behavior in terms of an economic model such as the one developed here seems bound to be unsuccessful. No doubt such noneconomic factors as the pork-barrel, logrolling, and empire building play an important role in explaining the Reclamation Program as it is developed by the Bureau and Congress. It is suggestive that since 1950 Congressional authorizations in election years have exceeded those in odd-numbered years by a ratio of 7 to 1.[24]

The political outcomes were simply not consistent with the best interests of the nation.

Among all the similarities of interest and in the details of their empirical analyses, two larger themes stand out to unite the work of Haveman and Freeman. First, in their philosophical posture, they believed in reducing multiple objectives to a single social objective function, a function that aggregated the preferences of individuals over social states. Second, they believed that the political process was a poor way to meet these objectives, because of the familiar problems of the "pork-barrel, logrolling, and empire building." As Haveman would later add, the free rider problem was simply too difficult for individuals to overcome in the political process, so that the concentrated interests of industry, government agencies, and other large stakeholders won out over the more diffuse interests of taxpayers and consumers.[25]

While uniting them together, these themes served to separate Haveman and Freeman from Maass. This became more than clear when, over the next few years, they would have two occasions to clash. The first occurred when Haveman commented on Maass's 1966 *QJE* article. An initial draft of the comment, at that point in time co-written with John Krutilla, was highly critical. Maass then drafted an angry reply which effectively declared war, a war which Krutilla escalated in a separate rejoinder (Haveman's being more restrained).[26] The final published exchange was only moderately sanitized (Haveman 1967; Maass 1967), but provoked a further unpublished comment from Freeman (1968).

24 Freeman (1967b p. 331).

25 Freeman (1967b), Haveman (1973).

26 AMP 96. For example, Maass begins his reply: "Krutilla and Haveman do indeed misread me, but I believe this results as much from their traditional and inflexible modes of thought as from my lack of clarity." Krutilla concludes his rejoinder: "There is a certain playing with words outside their conventional meaning that has been at the root of the lack of clarity in the position Maass originally advanced which also plagues his reply." In between are numerous insults and jabs.

Taken in isolation, this exchange was probably no more than the typical academic tempest-in-a-teapot, but it was not the last. The second was broader and had higher stakes, arising when in 1969 the Water Resources Council created a special task force to create new *Procedures for Evaluation of Water and Related Land Resource Projects.*[27]

8.4 The Water Resources Council

The successor to the Federal Inter-Agency River Basin Committee, the Water Resources Council (WRC) was established in 1962 by a Senate resolution requesting from President Kennedy a joint document from the Secretaries of the Army; Agriculture; Interior; and Health, Education, and Welfare agreeing to "Policies, Standards, and Procedures in the Formulation, Evaluation, and Review of Plans for Use and Development of Water and Related Land Resources." Soon after, it was given further clout with formal creation under the Water Resources Planning Act of 1965, with the Secretary of Transportation and the Chairman of the Federal Power Commission added to the list. In that same year, the Bureau of the Budget (BOB), under economist Charles Schultze, expanded the Planning-Programming-Budgeting (PPB) System from the Pentagon to the entire federal bureaucracy, including Johnson's Great Society programs, elevating the prominence of economic analysis.[28]

The WRC's purpose was to assess the state of the nation's water resources relative to needs, recommend water policies, and set planning standards, providing uniformity across agencies. In 1969, the WRC created a special task force to draft new "Principles and Procedures" for evaluating water projects. At that point, the latest standards were enshrined in a memo requested by President Kennedy and approved in 1962, later adopted as a resolution by the US Senate and hence known as Senate Document 97. Eliciting public comments for its revision of the discount rate, the WRC

[27] WRC (1969). The exact titles changed at least twice over the 1969–1971 period. By the end, the document was split into two parts, an executive summary titled *Proposed Principles and Standards for Planning Water and Related Land Resources* and the detailed *Procedures for Planning Water and Related Land Resources* (WRC 1971a, b). I follow the convention of referring to this body of work collectively as "The Principles and Procedures."

See Cobb (1973), Castle, Kelso, and Gardner (1963), and Castle et al. (1981) for an overview of the WRC and the broader water policy and planning context of the times.

[28] On the PPB System, see Berman (2022 Ch. 3) and, for one participant's account, Enthoven (2019). As Berman points out, the PPB system made a major splash but most analyses were superficial. Moreover, as benefit–cost analysis was already long entrenched in the analysis of water projects, PPB's impact was limited.

received hundreds of more general comments pertaining to its evaluation procedures. This, coupled with the recent adoption of numerous new laws stating different objectives for water policies, convinced the WRC that it was time to revisit its principles and procedures for design and evaluation of water systems.

In doing so, the council opened up several issues. The first issue was the appropriate discount rate. At a minimum, it needed to be adjusted to account for rising market rates. More basic was the issue of the appropriate principle. Was it the rate at which consumers traded off future consumption for today's, or the opportunity cost of capital? Was it the social rate of discount, as Marglin advocated? A second issue, less controversial, was the treatment of so-called "secondary benefits," a perennial concern since at least the 1950 Green Book.[29] Confusing the issue, the term was variously used to mean "all unpriced benefits," "all downstream (or induced) economic impacts," or "downstream increases in income." By this time, the consensus among economists was to use this term to refer to downstream increases in income, and to point out that these would be mere transfers unless there were economies of scale or unemployed resources giving rise to a Keynesian multiplier. Increasingly too, most economists felt that, in the usual order of things, these conditions were not met. Instead of "secondary," "non-market" benefits was the preferred term to differentiate unpriced from priced benefits.

But the issue opened up by the Council that gained the most attention during the work of its task force was that of multi-objective planning. As noted previously, since his initial polemic against the Army Corps, Maass had developed a number of individual ties with that organization, one of the most important of which was his former student David Major (b. 1938). Major had been an economics student officially supervised by Eckstein, but he worked primarily with Maass. He was an economist on the engineering faculty at MIT but was on leave with the Army Corps during this period. Other potential allies at the Corps or on the staff of the WRC included Henry Caulfield, a political scientist and executive director of the council, and Robert Gidez, Jim Tozzi, and David Allee in the US Army's Systems Analysis Group, which monitored USACE from the Secretary's office as part of the PPB System.

In its initial draft, the WRC's task force proposed enshrining four objectives into its Principles and Procedures: "national economic development" (their term for what was essentially the economic efficiency objective),

[29] FIARBC (1950). As discussed in Chapters 3 and 4, the so-called Green Book was the bible on benefit–cost analysis for US water projects for many years. See also Porter (1995).

regional economic development, environmental quality, and other human welfare objectives (such as equity and health).[30] Of course, without specific guidance on minimum levels for each of these objectives or relative weights for trading off one against the other, the WRC had no hope of employing anything like the linear programming routines envisaged by Dorfman, Marglin, and the other authors of *Design*. But it captured that spirit by suggesting that planners design a few or several systems to optimize over a reasonable range of these four objectives.[31] In addition, an analysis would be conducted on the effect of each alternative proposal on each objective, with the results displayed in a matrix. Using this menu, the White House and/or Congress could then pick from the alternatives, further revealing its willingness to trade off among objectives. This, of course, was precisely Maass's vision for the planning process.

As the news of the WRC's new move reached them, Maass and his colleagues were beside themselves with excitement. At the first hint, David Major wrote to his mentor to inform him that the revision "represents a thorough-going commitment to multiple-objective programming in water resource investment, almost entirely on the lines proposed in Design." "All this is a very exciting development."[32] Throughout the process, Maass and Major monitored the situation closely, visiting Washington, writing and telephoning members of the WRC, building coalitions, and in short drawing on every possible connection to build momentum behind multi-objective planning.

8.5 The Debate

Those efforts were every bit required, for a great clash developed over the issue. In the political arena, support for multi-objective planning came from pro-development interests that frankly saw a way to expand the range of benefits and hence justify more projects. The National Waterways Conference, for example, represented navigation and industrial interests, and its newsletter, *Criteria News*, documented the developments in minute detail. They had support from Southern and Western Governors and Congressmen and in some of the Cabinets represented on the WRC.[33]

30 See WRC Special Task Force 1969, AMP 77.

31 Gidez, in a letter to Maass dated 6-17-69, explained this evolution in their thinking (AMP 78).

32 Letter 3-30-69, AMP 77.

33 For example, William Guy, Governor of North Dakota, claimed that news of a proposed higher discount rate "swept across this arid Upper Midwest like the crack of doom" (Letter to Don Maughan, US WRC, 2-4-72, National Archives, RG 315, Entry 24, Box 1).

On the other side, William Proxmire, budget hawk extraordinaire and chairman of the Senate Subcommittee on Economy in Government, led the fight in Congress to kill the proposed Principles and Procedures, while BOB and its successor, the Office of Management and Budget (OMB), led it in the Executive Branch. Allied with them were anti-tax or pro-consumer advocates, including Ralph Nader, as well as environmental groups like the Sierra Club. These groups agitated for higher discount rates to block development and objected to padding benefit–cost ratios with secondary benefits and double-counted regional benefits. Economists working with these groups included Robert K. Davis (Audubon Society) and W. Kip Viscusi (Center for Study of Responsive Law) and many others. Those who follow these debates today will be struck by the irony. Now, benefit–cost analysis is typically a hurdle for environmental rules, weighing the costs of the upfront investments (such as a cleaner power plant) against the future environmental gains. In this setting, environmentalists have advocated lower discount rates. But in the 1960s and early 1970s, environmentalists viewed benefit–cost analysis as a potential hurdle for environmentally destructive investments like dams and dredging.[34]

A wide range of academic economists and other social scientists joined the debate as well, sometimes in active coalition with political forces, sometimes simply as commentators. Generally sympathetic were those associated with Maass in the Harvard water program, as well as systems analysts and some agricultural economists of a more institutional persuasion (W. B. Lord and Daniel Bromley, e.g., at Wisconsin and Allan Schmid at Michigan State). This latter group was attracted to the descriptive realism of the political process, which gave rise to the distinct role for policy analysis in Maass's version of multi-objective planning. They would also have appreciated the fact that economic efficiency certainly was not the basis for agricultural policy.[35]

On the other side were mainstream neoclassical economists and agricultural economists, often practitioners of traditional benefit–cost analysis, including a number of economists at or closely connected to RFF. Particularly central to the academic opposition to multi-objective planning were Haveman, Freeman, and Jack Knetsch. As noted previously, Haveman was on leave in Washington from 1968 to 1970, first as the Senior

[34] Ralph Nader's Study Group issued a damning report on BOR practices, including its benefit–cost procedures for justifying projects (Berkman and Viscusi 1973). Pairing political action with this research, these groups flooded the WRC public comment boxes with postcards from members.

[35] See for example, Bromley, Schmid, and Lord (1971) and Bromley and Beattie (1973).

Economist for Proxmire's Subcommittee on Economy in Government, then at RFF, while Freeman was also on leave at RFF at the same time as Haveman. A student of Dorfman and Eckstein, Knetsch earned his Ph.D. in economics from Harvard in 1963. He joined RFF in 1962, then departed for the economics faculty of George Washington University in 1966. With RFF's Marion Clawson, Knetsch had helped pioneer the estimation of nonmarket values for recreation (Chapter 4). As discussed in Chapter 9, Knetsch eventually would become a skeptic of many aspects of welfare measurement, but at this stage he was still very much a traditionalist.

While at the Subcommittee on Economy in Government, Haveman coordinated hearings on the Water Resources Council's proposed standards. These hearings including testimony from five expert witnesses, including Dorfman, who advocated for multi-objective planning on the grounds that objectives were incommensurable, and Knetsch, who favored traditional benefit–cost analysis. They also included written responses to a letter from Proxmire eliciting comments and answers to six questions. These questions probed the nature of the concept of benefits, the meaning of "secondary benefits" and whether they were a legitimate concept, the best way to handle distributional concerns, and the best way to "measure and value" non-market benefits of projects.[36] The report from this committee was released in February 1970 and was generally critical.

Maass, sensing strong opposition, moved swiftly to combat what he called the "BOB-Knetsch-Haveman (Proxmire) axis."[37] Upon receipt of Proxmire's questionnaire, he wrote to Major that it "looks as if Haveman is trying to torpedo all of your good work" and asked for advice on how to play it.[38] Maass chose to respond aggressively, rejecting the questions as biased toward the traditional benefit–cost perspective, which favored "national income benefits" as the sole objective. Interpreting the question about secondary benefits as pertaining to all unpriced benefits rather than the narrower Keynesian meaning, he simply argued that "of course" they are legitimate and should be included; likewise benefits related to equity. Finally, he argued that it was only *valuation* – not *measurement* of the effects – that was a problem for most unpriced benefits. But to Maass, this

[36] Letter to Maass 5-5-69, AMP 78.

[37] Marginal note on letter from Henry Caulfield 7-17-69, AMP 79. Maass was correct to suspect a connection to BOB. Jack Carlson, a Harvard-trained economist and then Assistant Director for Program Evaluation, and who we met in Chapter 7, first suggested the paper and tried to "discretely and anonymously encourage RFF in this effort" (Memo to Sam Hughes, 11-18-68, NA 51.135.1).

[38] Letter 5-8-69, AMP 78.

was not a serious limitation, because the virtue of multi-objective planning was that it would incorporate values from the elected representatives or allow them to choose among alternatives. Wrote Maass to Proxmire, "For pity sakes, what is the political process all about? Shouldn't you and your colleagues be debating the tradeoff weights to be used in the design of projects and programs, more than simply authorizing, and appropriating funds for, projects that have been designed for objective functions about which you have had no discussion and judgment?"[39] Maass circulated his response widely, and it was reprinted in the *Criteria News*.

The debate over multi-objective planning was joined in the academic press as well, with numerous pamphlets and journal articles on the subject. The intensity of the debate can be seen by the large number of articles generated over a short period of time just by the Harvard Water Program participants and RFF economists alone, let alone other figures. As previously noted, Maass and Haveman had already debated in the pages of the *QJE*. Now, Knetsch, Haveman, Krutilla, and two other RFF economists published a pamphlet critiquing the Principles and Procedures.[40] There followed the pattern of article-comment-reply in no less than three more journals, in addition to the *QJE*. These included an article by Major in *Water Resources Research* (1969), suggesting a strategy for benefit–cost analysis that incorporated regional weights for benefits, commented on by Freeman and Haveman (1970); a historical perspective on benefit–cost analysis and multi-objective planning by Maass in *Public Policy* (1970), commented on by Freeman and Haveman (1971); and, finally, at the end of the process, a critique of the final rules from RFF economists Charles Cicchetti et al. in *Science* (1973), commented on by Major (1975).

Collectively, the two groups differed on four key issues. First, and most narrowly, the RFF critics argued the specific objective of regional benefits was invalid. They argued that while redistribution was important, it was more properly framed as a question of *individual* equity – the perspective taken by Haveman and Freeman in their dissertations.[41] Benefits to a region, in contrast, were either offset by costs to another region or were already counted as a net efficiency benefit to the nation. These regional impacts could only have any additional significance outside of the national efficiency benefit if Congress valued one region over another. But of course, Congress would

39 Letter to Proxmire 5-29-69, AMP 78.

40 Knetsch et al. (1969); see also RFF (1970).

41 See Knetsch et al. (1969), Freeman and Haveman (1970), and Cicchetti et al. (1973), plus Kalter et al. (1969) as well. Kalter and Stevens (1971) synthesized the two approaches, looking at benefits by socio-economic class and region.

never explicitly state such preferences. Maass replied, somewhat feebly, that it was good for the nation to aid undeveloped regions.[42]

Second, the two groups differed on how different objectives were to be weighted. Haveman, Freeman, Knetsch, and their colleagues argued that different objectives (food production, protecting property from floods, protecting lives from floods, etc.), should, wherever possible, be collapsed into a single objective function with market prices (or, for non-traded goods, shadow prices) as weights. Thus, separate analysis of multiple objectives was only required when some objectives could not be assigned a shadow price. But, they argued, nonmarket valuation methods inferring the willingness to pay of households for public goods were rapidly improving and could provide such prices in more cases than Maass, Major, or Dorfman acknowledged. Shadow prices for equity could be developed along the lines of Haveman's and Freeman's dissertations. Other outputs, for which shadow prices could not be estimated, could still be listed in "side displays," but they theoretically belonged under the efficiency criterion, and as nonmarket evaluation improved might be so treated.[43]

By contrast, of course, the participants of the Harvard Water Program and the architects of the Principles and Procedures believed that reconciling different objectives should be left to the political decision makers, or that designers should use the weights held by those decision-makers. In reply, Haveman and Freeman argued that, as a practical matter, the trade-offs between efficiency and equity would be difficult to work out from the policy process. In their response to Major's proposal for incorporating regional benefits, Freeman and Haveman wrote that Major "blithely asserts that 'the present legislative process can yield the kind of decision required to give content to the preference curves' of his model. We judge this assertion to be naive, unworkable and undesirable." Even if a stable social preference function existed, they argued, the analyst would need to know the rate of transformation between efficiency and equity to infer preferences from choices. Moreover, Congress is simply not stable enough to yield consistent signals about social preferences. Maass countered that Congress was in fact very stable. Moreover, if it changed, it was only because the mood of the people changed.[44]

[42] Freeman and Haveman (1970) and Cicchetti et al. (1973). Maas's reply: letter to Freeman 6-11-68, AMP 97.

[43] Knetsch et al. (1969), Cicchetti et al. (1973).

[44] Haveman (1967), Freeman (1969b), and Freeman and Haveman (1970). Quotation from Freeman and Haveman (1970 p. 1538). Maass's reply can be found in Maass (1967).

Haveman here seems to have moved away from his guarded optimism about using Congressional choices (as reflected in tax rates) to measure equity weights, an approach

Discussion of the weighting issue was hampered by misunderstanding between the two groups. In the benefit–cost literature, the efficiency criterion was often called a "national income" criterion, and this was the term adopted by Maass and Major. When benefits and costs had been restricted to changes in the quantities of marketed outputs or in the real costs of production, using constant prices, this nomenclature was reasonable. But with the increasing use of both consumer surplus measures and non-market valuation methods in benefit cost analysis, "national income" was becoming a misnomer. Cicchetti, Freeman, Haveman, and others labored to explain this point, and to emphasize that their interpretation of economic benefits and costs – in short, of "efficiency" – was comprehensive, including even non-market effects. Thus, for example, if people valued the environmental improvement of a program more than the costs, the program was efficiency enhancing and met the efficiency criterion.[45]

Dorfman, of course, understood this point well, but simply did not believe that there was any hope of ever pricing such goods and formally bringing them into the efficiency account.[46] Maass and Major, for their part, seemed to others almost willfully to misunderstand. For example, Maass insisted on reading "secondary benefits" as "nonmarket benefits" even though he was aware of economists' alternative usage of the term as induced increases in real income from employing underutilized resources.[47] Accordingly, Maass interpreted critiques of secondary benefits as critiques of any unpriced benefits. Similarly, members of the water program tended to use the term "national income" interchangeably with "efficiency" or "economic development," whereas others tended to draw a sharp distinction between income (a rectangle or price-times-quantity measure) and efficiency benefits, which would include consumer surplus. The Harvard economists were well aware of the issues, but tended to prefer the use of "income" as a casual shorthand.[48] For example, in an apparently unpublished comment on Arnold Harberger's defense of consumer

he had taken in his dissertation. According to his recollection, his experience at the Joint Economic Committee made him more skeptical of Congressional actions (personal correspondence, Aug. 24, 2007). Nevertheless, Haveman also made a distinction between identifying distributional values from Congressional decisions where the distributional effects were front and center (as with tax rates) and identifying them from decisions where such issues were more latent, as with water policies. For the latter point, see Haveman's (1966) comment on Weisbrod (1966).

45 Freeman and Haveman (1970), Cicchetti et al. (1973).

46 See Dorfman (1974, 1978, 1996).

47 For example, Maass (1966 p. 211n).

48 Maass et al. (1962 pp. 27–8), Major (1977 pp. 22–3).

surplus, Major began by asserting that Harberger advocated the national income approach to benefits estimation.[49] In fact, although Harberger did advocate a single objective benefit–cost analysis, nothing could be further from the truth than that he advocated an income criterion. Indeed, he was arguing that consumer surplus measures were superior to a GDP-type income analysis. Although there was still plenty of room for discussion, this confusion over terminology obscured the real disagreements.

At the same time, other observers likewise misunderstood the deference of multi-objective planners to policy makers. Corry Azzi and James Cox (1973), for example, misread Eckstein as advocating that equity-efficiency trade-offs be totally ignored in policy, rather than left by economists to others. These misunderstandings, in turn, widened the gap the participants perceived between the single and multiple objective approaches.

A third point of disagreement was on the practical importance of equity based criteria for planning water projects. Although they emphasized the importance of equity as a social objective, Haveman and Freeman argued that the empirical evidence from their dissertations suggested that water projects were not a good way to meet this objective. In addition, they argued that most benefits would be capitalized into land values, where they would most likely benefit the rich. Consequently, planners could focus on the efficiency criterion alone.[50]

Maass, in response, argued that because of the institutional constraints imposed by benefit–cost analysis, past projects had not been *designed* for redistribution (at least not optimally so). If analysts had been allowed to explicitly consider this additional objective – as Maass et al. advocated – the programs might have looked better on this score. Indeed, Congress would have been in a position to make a more intelligent selection of projects.[51]

One might comment here that it seems odd to use an *empirical* argument against a *methodological* procedure: the fact that, in most cases, water projects on average did not improve the distribution of income or welfare need not preclude the importance of formally quantifying the effect (positive or negative) of each specific project. But this brings us to the fourth and final point made by the critics of multi-objective planning: pragmatically, benefit–cost analysis, even restricted to only those sets of benefits that could be priced, was the most useful tool because it was the most *objective*. As Porter (1995) argued, one of the chief appeals of benefit–cost analysis was

49 Manuscript dated 2-28-1972, AMP 84. The piece is a response to Harberger (1971).
50 Haveman (1967), Freeman and Haveman (1970), and Haveman (1973).
51 Maass (1967).

that it was an objective criterion that could settle disputes. Contemporary participants were well aware of this appeal. The Clark-Grant-Kelso report discussed in Chapter 3 represents one early example of such self-awareness; an essay by Robert Kalter et al. (with an all-star team of applied economists) represented another in the current context.[52]

From this point of view, benefit–cost analysis captured the biggest benefits and costs that deserved first consideration, whereas allowing multiple objectives in an analysis, some of them unpriced, would open up the process to political manipulation and abuse. Moreover, looking to Congress for weights was an interesting exercise descriptively, but it could not provide a normative signal about what the weights *should* be, which would be crucial for improving policy. In fact, it was circular, and could always justify Congressional action.[53] Of course, Maass et al. had already argued the opposite: namely, that designing and evaluating projects on the basis of a single efficiency objective, when Congress wanted to make its choice on the basis of multiple objectives, was more wasteful, and that the job of benefit–cost analysis was to help Congress make better decisions according to its own weights.[54] The importance of this difference in outlook was overlooked by many of the participants in the debate, but was rightfully identified by others, including public finance economists like Steiner and Julius Margolis, as a key difference in the respective paradigms.[55]

In the midst of this debate, a third group, representing something of a "middle way," emerged. Agricultural economists at or from Cornell (Allee and Kalter) and Oregon State (Bromley and Emery Castle), with others, issued their own pamphlet (Kalter et al. 1969). According to Allee, they considered theirs a response to the pamphlet of Knetsch et al.[56] Indeed, in their opening statement, they firmly supported the notion that benefits and costs had to arise out of a framework of objectives, and that decision-making would be improved if the true range of objectives were embraced rather than hidden. They also argued that the criticism of "double counting" only makes sense if one has already adopted a single object. If one is thinking in terms of multiple objectives, there is no problem in noting how an action might contribute

52 The team included Allee, Bromley, Castle, Siegfried Ciriacy-Wantrup, Kelso, Lord, Stephen C. Smith, and Weisbrod.

53 Knetsch et al. (1969), Freeman and Haveman (1970), Cicchetti et al. (1973), Knetsch testimony 9-9-69 NA 315.24.3. On the latter point especially, see Haveman (1966).

54 Hence, this chapter's title, intended to capture what each side viewed as the ultimate strength of its methodological approach. It is not my intention to evaluate which approach is more realistic, more objective, or in any other way better.

55 Steiner (1969a, b), Margolis (1969).

56 Letter to Maass 9-18-69, AMP 78.

to more than one of them. Thus, in principle, a benefit could be counted as meeting both a regional objective and a national objective. However, they were actually dubious of the merits of a separate regional benefit. Among other reasons, they noted that most secondary benefits cancelled out and that many regional benefits were offset elsewhere. Accordingly, siding with the RFF economists on the point, they too felt that a regional objective boiled down to expressing a preference for one region over another.

Writing as individuals, some of the authors of the Kalter et al. pamphlet had expressed or would soon express additional reservations about some aspects of multi-objective planning or the draft Principles and Procedures. Castle and Youmans (1968) argued that, because increasing private consumption would not make people happier, the net benefits measured in the national income or efficiency account were not an end in themselves, but a means to an end. Other objectives, like equity or the environment, were ends and thus were at a higher stratum than income. National income could be used to promote one objective or another, so, in this sense, it was like a unit of account (or numeraire good) for objectives, among which the real trade-offs needed to be made. Following this reasoning, plus the fact that income accounting was more advanced than accounting for the other objectives, in his testimony before the WRC, Castle (1969) suggested that one of the formulated plans, a "plan A," would always be the efficiency-maximizing (single objective) plan.[57]

The WRC took account of many of these suggestions and criticisms when it considered the recommendations of its special task force. It supported the central premise of multi-objective planning, as well as the four specific objectives of national economic development, regional development, environmental quality, and human welfare, but it de-emphasized secondary benefits. Higher political powers were more decisive, however. BOB, and later OMB under Casper Weinberger, had multiple objections to the multiple objectives, and delayed its approval. At one point in 1970, BOB impounded the WRC's funding for its assessment of the adequacy of water supplies. A compromise was seemingly reached in 1971 that would allow

[57] This would seem to privilege the efficiency criterion as a central case, and Maass and Major (1970) responded to Castle and Youmans under the assumption that they opposed the consideration of multiple objectives. Castle and Youmans (1970) had to explain that this was a complete misreading, and that they had only meant that the comparison should be made. For their part, however, Castle and Youmans seemed to have misunderstood the role of the political process in Maass's vision for multi-objective planning. They suggested there was no way to identify a definitive social welfare function yielding weights for the objectives, and that the political process would have to make this choice. But this was precisely what Maass envisioned, as Maass and Major (1970) explained.

planning for two objectives, efficiency and environmental quality, and a third, regional development, if explicitly authorized, but with impacts on all four original objectives quantified.[58] However, OMB continued to obstruct WRC's plans. The debate descended to an impasse over the discount rate, with OMB wanting an immediate jump to 7 percent and eventual increase to 10 percent and the WRC holding out for 6 percent. Again, politically, this debate was largely a case of pro-development interests lobbying for lower rates (so more projects would meet benefit–cost criteria) and budget hawks, environmentalists, and other anti-development interests lobbying for higher rates. In the end, OMB had its way and the rule was published in the Federal Register for public comment at the higher discount rate.[59]

This final comment period in 1972 attracted over 200 witnesses and over 4,500 written responses, included 100 Congressmen, and very heavy mail from environmentalists in support of the high discount rate. Despite some of the compromises, the RFF economists continued to recommend rejection. For the members and alumni of the Harvard Water Program, the glass was half full or half empty depending on one's temperament. Dorfman, Hufschmidt, and Major all endorsed the new Principles and Procedures. Writing later, Dorfman would call it an "order of magnitude increase in political sophistication and realism" and projected that the "stranglehold of the benefit–cost ratio will be relaxed." Maass, however, preferred that the new draft be rejected in favor of the original version with four objectives. Particularly unnerving to him was the fact that plans could be made for environmental quality but not for human welfare effects. Thus, "one could presumably design a project to save the lives of fish and birds and moose... but not the life of man. Gentlemen," he exclaimed, "this is madness." Over a year later, in 1973, the Principles and Procedures were adopted.[60]

8.6 Benefit–Cost Analysis and Political Sovereignty

The story of the debate over multi-objective planning is one that sounds several themes. Against the backdrop of Porter's (1995) thesis of the importance of benefit–cost analysis for adjudicating competing interests, we see

[58] The impounding of funds is documented in *Criteria News* 2-13-70, AMP 81. The compromise in *Criteria News* 12-22-71, AMP 85.

[59] The footballing did not end there, however. Congress reasserted control with the 1974 Water Resource Development Act, which reinstated the formula of Senate Document 97 (with its lower rates).

[60] RFF economists continued to recommend rejection (Cicchetti et al. 1973). "Order of magnitude increase..." (Dorfman 1978 pp. 282–3). "...Gentlemen...this is madness" (Maass, quoted in *Criteria News* 48 4-25-72, AMP 86).

how a formal debate over the competing merits of various procedures – a debate argued in full public view – could be unsettling. We see how personal rivalry can mingle with intellectual differences to fuel the fire. And we see how, even as economists were becoming more involved in benefit–cost analysis, and normative analysis more generally, the trend was neither smooth nor steady. Indeed, social scientists working in the same small field, well-acquainted with one another, and corresponding personally at length could still misunderstand one another.

But there were bigger issues at play: nothing less than the fate of two competing visions of liberalism and the role of the "expert" within them. Cicchetti, Haveman, Freeman, Knetsch, and others emphasized the importance of *consumer sovereignty*, according to which benefits (including the satisfaction of preferences for more equity) accrued to individuals. From this perspective, the task of benefit–cost analysis is to make inferences from individuals' behavior, and on that basis to give advice to policy-makers. It can also be a basis to judge the performance of the political decision-makers, who can be too easily manipulated by special interests into making policies contrary to the commonweal.

In contrast, Dorfman, Eckstein, Maass, Major, Marglin, and others emphasized the importance of collective choice, civic republicanism, and *political sovereignty*, in which elected officials represented the will of the people. Their view was that the good to be obtained was not just the sum of individual goods, and that government investments were not necessarily about public goods as defined by economists. Rather, it was the common good, collectively and socially determined. From this perspective, the task of benefit cost analysis is to observe policy-makers, infer their objectives, and provide them with the best information to facilitate their decision-making.[61]

As noted in the introduction to this chapter, economists up to this point had been ambivalent about welfare economics, torn between competing desires to be dispassionate scientists and yet to make a difference in public policy. Multi-objective planning might have provided one way for economists to reconcile this dilemma. According to its vision, economists and other social scientists would essentially focus on the "positive" tasks of describing the necessary trade-offs among objectives (the production possibilities curve) and of observing elected officials for insights into their willingness to make those trade-offs. They would then design a menu of

[61] For further discussion of the relationship between these two paradigms, see Banzhaf (2011a) and Cherrier and Fleury (2017).

programs for politicians to consider, but they would not have to make normative recommendations.

Yet, by and large, that route was not taken. When it came to a choice between keeping either its newer fashion of objective, positive science and its more comfortable suit of utilitarianism, it was no contest: a more traditional form of benefit–cost analysis won both the intellectual and the political debate.

9

Constructing Markets

The Contingent Valuation Controversy

That is the essence of science: ask an impertinent question, and you are on the way to a pertinent answer.

–Jacob Bronowski, *The Ascent of Man* (1973)

Ask me no questions, and I'll tell you no fibs.

–Oliver Goldsmith, *She Stoops to Conquer* (1773)

9.1 Introduction

In the mid-to-late twentieth century, economists applied increasingly abstract economic constructs to increasingly intangible objects. For example, as discussed in Chapter 4, they moved from measuring value with market prices to using various forms of consumer surplus. At the same time, from an initial point of measuring values of a given *quantity* of material goods, they moved on to value the *quality* of those goods. Environmental economists were carried along by these trends, but also contributed to them. Their quintessential problem of measuring the value of preserving the natural environment is a particular case in point. For how could they observe such values when there were no markets and so no prices to observe?

One seemingly simple answer to that question is to ask people through surveys. Over the years, a broad cross section of economists had suggested doing just that in various contexts. In the context of natural resources, S. V. Ciriacy-Wantrup and Irving Fox made two early suggestions in the immediate postwar period.[1] In the late 1960s, Thomas Schelling and Howard

[1] Ciriacy-Wantrup (1947). Memorandum from Irving K. Fox, Dec. 18, 1950, Box 2227 (River Basin Studies – Economic & Recreational Benefits, 1949–1953), Entry 11, Record Group 79 (National Park Service), National Archives Building, Washington, DC.

Raiffa made similar suggestions for measuring the willingness to pay (WTP) to avoid health risks.[2] Ragnar Frisch (1946) recommended using the "interview method" to recover structural economic equations of all kinds, an idea that appears to date back to his work on measuring marginal utility in the 1920s (Boumans 2009). Arthur Bowley (1920) suggested doing so to make cost-of-living indices.

In his *Manual of Political Economy* (1906), Vilfredo Pareto proposed using surveys to measure people's willingness to trade-off one good against another (or their "indifference curves"), a proposal that L.L. Thurstone (1931) later took up. Pareto suggested that surveys could give direct access to these indifference curves. However, he believed that in the real world people wrestled with the confusing complexity of market institutions and had to discover their preferences through experience. Surveys could test a realm of pure theory, where people were indistinguishable from machines. In contrast, working with market data was messier yet more interesting for an empirical social science.[3]

Despite these earlier suggestions, environmental applications of what later became known as the contingent valuation (CV) method really took flight in the 1960s and early 1970s.[4] The CV method became especially important when, around that time, John Krutilla introduced the notion of "existence values," or the value of preserving a resource simply for its existence, regardless of how people might interact with it behaviorally, thus taking the abstract and intangible to a new level.[5] The CV method was crucial to measuring existence values because, practically by definition, existence values involve no behavioral actions that can be observed in the world outside a survey.

Nevertheless, the CV method faced an uphill battle for acceptance within the wider intellectual community of academic economics. Notwithstanding occasional suggestions to use them, the mainstream of the profession had long been skeptical of surveys. For example, Milton Friedman strongly opposed them, both as used by Richard Lester to interview businessmen about their behavior and as used by Thurstone to estimate utility functions over consumer goods. He argued on methodological grounds that

2 Schelling (1968), Raiffa (1969).

3 On Pareto's ideas about surveys and preference discovery, see Giocoli (2003 pp. 71–5 ff) and Bruni and Sugden (2007). On Thurstone, see Moscati (2007).

4 Johnston et al. (2017) provide a recent overview of the state of the art of the CV method. Carson and Hanemann (2005) and K. Smith (2006) discuss the method in historical context.

5 Krutilla (1967a).

individuals' own understanding of their actions need not match a scientific description of them. Additionally, Paul Samuelson had argued that selfish agents would give deceptive signals about their value for public goods to influence the outcome. Because of the free rider problem, when "buying" public goods (or "contributing") at a set price, their choices understate their values. On the other hand, the same incentives push them to overstate their values when asked how much they'd like to see others contribute. Though opposition to surveys was by no means unanimous, if Friedman and Samuelson agreed to team up against something, it was bound to face tough sledding.[6]

In addition to the general skepticism of surveys, CV faced a more specific barrier to widespread acceptance. Precisely because it measures such abstract entities, a CV survey does not merely elicit opinions or record concrete behaviors. It creates a hypothetical market for goods not normally traded in markets, asks respondents to think about their behavior "contingent" on the market being real (behavior which generates bids), and observes the generated bids. Thus, unlike simpler surveys, it is not merely a recording device documenting relatively objective behavior. Too, unlike statistically estimating a demand curve, the CV method does not involve observing behavior or using data that existed prior to the creative work of the economist. To the contrary, as with experimental economics, a field in which economists observe the behavior of volunteers in a laboratory setting, CV is built around the idea of constructing observations.

Historians of economics are used to the idea of economists constructing their observations (Boumans 2005; Maas and Morgan 2012) but economists are not, or certainly were not in the 1970s and 1980s. Thus, CV put economists in an unfamiliar and uncomfortable position. Borrowing language from Callon (1998) and MacKenzie, Muniesa, and Siu (2007), to the economists involved CV was all too obviously "performative" – meaning it does not just measure something, it does something in the economy. Indeed, although the term has been used somewhat promiscuously, CV perfectly fits J. L. Austin's original linguistic meaning of "performativity:" the respondent to a CV survey literally *speaks* economic values into being.

The natural question then becomes, just what has been spoken into being? Do the objects look like the kinds of values that would be generated

[6] On Friedman's criticism of surveys, see Boulier and Goldfarb (1998), Giocoli (2003), McCloskey (1983), and Moscati (2007). Wallis and Friedman (1942) went further and criticized the entire usefulness of indifference curve analysis. On Samuelson's views, see his (1954). For further discussion of the issues he raised, and the economic analysis of public choices, see Cherrier and Fleury (2017).

by *homo economicus*? Economists began asking such questions early on, sometimes out of skepticism of the method, sometimes out of a sympathetic effort to calibrate the market institutions to make sure they had the right one in place. A CV survey judged to be successful would generate behavior consistent with microeconomic theory of behavior, with consistent preference orderings, sensitivity to prices, and modest sensitivity to income. Various anomalies in the pattern of stated values, however, suggested it was more difficult to use CV surveys to fabricate values from genuine *homo economicus* than environmental economists originally had hoped. Over the course of the 1980s, these anomalies attracted greater scrutiny from the wider profession, and environmental economists soon found themselves enmeshed in broader debates about experimental economics and behavioral economics, a school beginning to challenge some neoclassical assumptions.

To generalize, environmental economists had three options open to them when interpreting these anomalies: (i) CV potentially could generate data consistent with *homo economicus* once best practices were determined, while in the meantime poor CV practices occasionally generated particular anomalies; (ii) CV could be inherently flawed, incapable of generating the correct data; or (iii) CV could be generating the right data while still creating the anomalies, so the fault lay not with the procedure but with the economic model of behavior. Behavioral economists like Daniel Kahneman, who teamed up during the 1980s with Jack Knetsch, an environmental economist working with CV almost from the beginning, argued for the latter position. Once CV appeared to support such criticism, skeptical economists who might otherwise have ignored CV were motivated to attack. These incentives were magnified when, first, a series of regulatory moves and, second, the *Exxon Valdez* oil spill increased the stakes for CV.

This chapter tells the story of these debates. Along the way, it considers the relationship between so-called "applied" fields such as environmental economics and "pure" or "theoretical" economics.

9.2 Robert K. Davis and the "Interview Method"

The first study using what would come to be called the CV method was proposed as an alternative to the travel cost model for valuing outdoor recreation, earlier suggested by Hotelling and implemented by Clawson. For his dissertation in economics at Harvard University, Robert K. Davis estimated the economic value of outdoor recreation in the Maine woods using what he called "the interview method" (Davis 1963a, b). Davis had received a BS and MS in agronomy from Ohio State University and worked at Harvard under Otto Eckstein, with assistance from John Kenneth Galbraith and Edward Banfield (a political scientist). Apparently unaware of earlier suggestions to use surveys, Davis developed his ideas while taking a course from Stanley Stouffer, one of the leading US survey researchers. He was supported by an RFF fellowship and completed his dissertation there. While at RFF, he worked with Knetsch to compare the CV method with the travel cost method applied to the same resource, finding surprisingly similar results.[7]

Davis's work followed an outline of four basic steps that has been used in most CV surveys ever since. First, ask "warm up" questions about the respondents' general attitudes toward the subject matter, to get the respondent in the right frame of mind. Second, provide information about the specific policy context to be valued. Third, at the heart of the survey, construct the market mechanism for "eliciting" values (as some would have it) or "constructing" them (as others would put it). This market has two crucial components, the "payment vehicle," which is the hypothetical channel through which households would make their payment (e.g., taxes, user fees, etc.), and the "elicitation question," which is really the rules of behaving in the market (e.g., stating a value, submitting a "bid," or accepting/rejecting a set cost). Fourth and finally, ask follow-up questions about how respondents perceived the survey and about their income and other demographic characteristics.[8]

From a historical perspective, we can see three themes in Davis's work that would set the context for much of the future debate. First, CV applications were, from the beginning, applied to measuring the benefits of intangible services, like outdoor recreation, which economists until that time had largely said could not be quantified and indeed were not even economic. Previous applications to outdoor recreation using travel costs were still quite new and controversial. Consequently, in his dissertation, Davis felt the need to directly address the idea that recreation belonged to the realm of the aesthetic rather than the economic, arguing there should be no distinction: as Prewitt had noted with his example of the radio, many market goods have intangible or aesthetic dimensions to them.

Second, unlike other early work in the valuation of outdoor recreation up to that time, Davis showed no hesitation about the relevant construct in

[7] The influence of Stouffer is reported in Carson (2011). Davis's early work with Knetsch was published in Knetsch and Davis (1966).

[8] See Mitchell and Carson (1989) for a state-of-the-art overview as of the period covered here.

economic theory that he wished to measure: Hicksian compensating variation, or the most that a consumer would be willing to pay for a resource and be no worse off than he would be without it. In doing so, Davis tied CV to a particular economic theory of individual welfare, one which, in principle, carried with it a set of testable hypotheses. However, the theory entailed very abstract constructs that, to most economists at the time, seemed unobservable. As Hicks had shown, WTP could be viewed as a variant of consumer surplus, in which income is adjusted along the demand curve in such a way as to hold utility constant. However, since such adjustments are never made in the real world, such demand curves seemed to most to be highly artificial. To overcome this problem, Davis created an artificial world in his survey where such entities could be measured. Thus, the survey involved two departures from the standard practices of the time: a highly abstract construct like WTP was being applied to a highly intangible object like outdoor recreation.

Third, like Clawson and Kneese before him, Davis was interested in the market institution that would be created, not just WTP in the abstract. His overarching strategy was to create an "approximation of the market." But that strategy only begged the question of what market. What institution, with what hypothetical allocation rules, should he create? Davis employed what he called a "bidding game." Interviewing people who already visited recreation facilities in the Maine woods, he asked respondents to consider their recreation experience and whether they would still have come if their transportation costs for reaching the destination were $X higher. If they answered "yes," Davis raised the cost by predetermined increments until they said no; if they answered "no" originally, he lowered the cost until they said yes. In this way, he converged on their maximum WTP. From the distribution of responses and the distribution of days-per-trip, he then constructed a demand curve for visitation days. Finally, he computed the consumer surplus under this demand curve.[9]

A number of environmental economists soon picked up the CV method. Particularly influential was a series of studies by Alan Randall, a resource economist working during this period at the University of New Mexico and University of Kentucky. Randall's work represents a continuation and extension of these three themes in ways that would prove significant for the future history of CV.

[9] Davis (1963a). As Davis recognized, he was essentially asking for an all-or-nothing deal, in which respondents could come or not come but not vary the length of their stay in response to their added cost.

First, Randall, Ives, and Eastman (1974) applied CV to an even more abstract commodity than had previously been tackled: namely, the aesthetic benefits associated with cleaner air, including improved views of the landscape.[10] They used photographs to communicate the aesthetic levels that would be obtained under different policies regulating a power plant. These aesthetic benefits were an example of Krutilla's "existence" or "nonuse" values – reasons for valuing the natural environment that have nothing to do with how it might be used (for outdoor recreation say), but simply because people appreciated them for their beauty or uniqueness. In this way, the intangibility that first confronted resource economics was now being taken to a whole new level. Importantly for this story, this move increased the importance of CV in the policy context because, as Randall et al. understood, CV was the *only* possible tool available for measuring such nonuse values. Whereas other methods for measuring environmental values relied on observing actual behavior (e.g., trips in the travel cost model), for nonuse values, there is no such connection to observable behavior such as trips. For example, one might value the existence of, say, a pristine Alaskan wilderness without ever visiting it. In this way, the objects created by CV surveys became even more divorced from observable behavior. They could only exist in the contingent world constructed by the survey.

Additionally, Randall tightened the connection between CV and the microeconomic theory of individual welfare, while simultaneously emphasizing the importance of the institutions created in the hypothetical world of the survey. Randall's work is notable for combining an interest in CV with work on markets, transaction costs, and property rights, with a particular focus on the Coase theorem. This combination of interests was important for two reasons. First, it meant that Randall and his colleagues were particularly sensitive to the design of markets and the way people operated in them. Second, from his earliest work on the Coase theorem, Randall was thinking about how initial property rights allocations could affect market prices and market transactions. If households lack the commodity initially, in the hypothetical world of the CV survey it would be natural to ask them to buy it, so the survey should elicit their WTP. If they do have a property right to the commodity, it would be more natural for them to sell it in a market setting, and so the survey should elicit the lowest willingness to accept (WTA) money in exchange. Microeconomic theories predicted that

[10] Around the same time, Cicchetti and Smith (1973) similarly evaluated WTP for the *quality* of the recreation experience.

these differences should be small. Nevertheless, as we shall see, WTP/WTA comparisons became a major source of controversy for CV.[11]

More generally, Randall's body of work focused attention on how to create what Randall, Ives, and Eastman (1974) called a "contingent market" (apparently thereby first coining the term "contingent valuation"). Randall et al. argued that to do this successfully, the hypothetical situations had to be "realistic and credible" and "concrete rather than symbolic." Second, the contingent market should involve "institutionalized or routinized behavior, where role expectations of respondents are well defined," a criterion they thought was met by the bidding game. Third, the payment vehicle had to be realistic and relevant to the respondents. In alternative versions of the survey, they thus used either sales taxes (realistic, as people are used to paying sales taxes to finance public goods, and relevant, especially to tourists) or alternatively higher electricity bills (also realistic, as the cost of controlling air pollution feasibly could be passed onto customers, and relevant to local residents).[12]

This overriding concern for constructing a realistic contingent market was echoed in the first major effort to review and standardize best CV practices, conducted by Ronald Cummings, David Brookshire, and William Schulze. They wrote:

> [F]or most pure public goods … market institutions do not exist. The CVM [contingent valuation method] is then used as a substitute for the "missing" market; it is used to simulate the market in the sense of eliciting revelations of preferences (a willingness to pay) analogous to those which would have resulted under market conditions. Like the market institution, the CVM must then be viewed as an "institution." *Thus, the general criterion against which to assess the CVM becomes clear: the extent to which the CVM institution, and preference revelations drawn therein, approximates the market institution and values derived therein.*[13]

In other words, the task of CV is to create a (hypothetical) market in which, in Randall et al.'s words, behavior was "institutionalized or routinized" and "where role expectations of respondents are well defined." Those expectations, of course, were to behave like *homo economicus*. CV studies could thus be judged by whether the CV institutions mimic

[11] On his work combining these interests, see Randall (1972). On property rights and market prices, see additionally Randall and Stoll (1980) and Brookshire, Randall, and Stoll (1980). Medema (2014a) discusses Randall's instrumental role in bringing the Coase theorem to environmental economics.

[12] Quotations from Randall, Ives, and Eastman (1974 p. 136).

[13] Cummings, Brookshire, and Schulze (1986 p. 72, emphasis added). Maas (2021) discusses the Cummings et al. review in the context of the public policy moves of the time.

markets and, furthermore, whether people behaved in them the way economic theory suggested they should.

9.3 Testing Contingent Valuation, Testing Economic Man

In his study of experimental economics, Guala (2007) distinguishes between experiments designed for building institutions and those for testing theories. In his view, experimental economics, or at least that branch of it which has been most successful, worked by institution building, and thus "by creating *homines economici*, not by questioning their existence." Guala quotes Charles Plott:

> "The task is to find a system of institutions—the rules for individual expression, information transmittal, and social choice—a 'process' that mirrors the behavioral features of the mechanism. The theory suggests the existence of processes that perform in certain (desirable) ways, and the task is to find them. This is a pure form of institutional engineering."[14]

Although the goal of experimental economics is not necessarily to test the existence of economic man, nevertheless, whether the institutions – or the agents – it builds in the lab have successfully been created is an important empirical question requiring testing.

That there is a parallel here between CV and experimental economics should not be surprising. CV and experimental economics grew up together during the 1970s with common motivations: at heart, both are concerned with understanding behavior that cannot be directly observed in markets, often surrounding questions related to public goods.[15] Some first-generation experimental economists such as Vernon Smith and James Cox began their careers as natural resource economists. Indeed, many economists have stood at the boundary between CV and experimental economics, including Brookshire, Don Coursey, Cummings, Glenn Harrison, Schulze, and, more recently, John List. The intersection was attractive, because laboratory experiments became one way of testing whether the hypothetical market institutions created in a CV survey successfully created *homo economicus*. Too, experimental economists like V. Smith and Charles Plott were drawn into debates over CV, which was something of a rival endeavor.

[14] Not questioning their existence (Guala 2007 p. 143). Charles Plott (1981, quoted by Guala 2007 p. 147).

[15] On the history of experimental economics, see Guala (2005, 2007), Moscati (2007), and Svorenčík (2015).

While both experimental economics and CV seek to create market institutions that reveal demand, differences in their ultimate objectives motivate concomitant differences in the institutions they construct. Experimental economics often begins by inducing preferences with the incentives of material rewards. It then proceeds to test how different institutions perform at processing those incentives and producing desirable (rational and efficient) outcomes, which V. Smith called the "Hayekian hypothesis." Thus, the institution (or machine) does the work. The job of experimental economists is to build the machines and to find the ones that produce desirable outcomes and that can be applied to real-world problems.[16]

In contrast to this Hayekian approach (as V. Smith put it), the CV method takes a regulatory approach. It is predicated on a preexisting regulatory institution, such as benefit–cost analysis or an effluent fee, already performing in the real world. The objective of CV then is to build a kind of temporary machine that can measure (or construct) WTP values that can be plugged into the institution to compute, say, the benefit–cost test or the optimal fee. That is, while the experimental economist produces machines that can themselves be exported to the market economy where they can do their work, the environmental economists using CV produces a machine that does work in the field producing an intermediate output (the WTP value) that can be exported to the planned economy. In this context, getting the appropriate WTP values naturally requires actual (or "home grown") preferences, not induced preferences. Consequently, quantitative measurement plays a much more important role in CV.

Of course, sometimes experimental economists also want to measure a parameter like WTP. But such cases inevitably involve a good that can be delivered to participants in the lab, such as foods made from non-GMO plants.[17] Consequently, the machine built to measure them does not need to be realistic. Rather than replicate a supermarket, the machine can be a highly artificial auction that has been shown to work well with induced values and then turned loose in the lab to measure WTP. In that context, realism in the pursuit of an abstract parameter is no virtue. In contrast, environmental economists using CV typically cannot actually deliver the environmental quality at stake. Instead, they create a fictional counterfactual world in which consumers can purchase (or sell) the environmental

16 On the so-called Hayakian hypothesis, see V. Smith (1982) and, for commentary, Guala (2007) and Muniesa and Callon (2007).

17 Muniesa and Callon (2007) discuss this example. K. Smith (2006) discusses the distinction between evaluating institutions with induced preferences and using an institution to measure home grown preferences.

resource of interest. Since the respondents do not have the incentive of actually obtaining the good, CV researchers must maintain credibility by keeping the scenario as realistic as possible. They must tell a story in which there is a credible mechanism for improving the natural environment and a credible payment vehicle through which respondents might pay for it. In Randall et al.'s case, for example, this meant describing regulation of the power plant, showing photographs, and hypothetically paying through taxes or power bills.

Nevertheless, a common feature of both fields is that the institutions (or machines) must be tested to ensure they are performing as intended. If they are not, they must be recalibrated or redesigned. Whereas experimental economics has succeeded by demonstrating that its institutions do work in the created environment, numerous tests seemed to indicate, at least to some, that CV was not performing as intended, that it was not creating economic man. A decades-long debate ensued over whether these were the result of particular CV practices that could be rectified or whether CV was inherently, irredeemably flawed.

In this debate, one line of work implemented CV studies in the lab and compared the results to those from experimental institutions that were supposed to replicate economic man more faithfully. The initial premise was than any deviations were the fault of CV, or at least the particular CV design tested. But then something surprising happened. In some cases, the experiments found no differences – both CV and the experiments failed to produce economic man. To some practitioners of CV, this result was reassuring, as it seemed to confirm the problem was not to be found in CV. To others, however, the result was much more troubling: it seemed to suggest that *homo economicus* did not exist or could not be created.

At this point, the anomalies in the CV literature began to attract the attention of behavioral economists, a school of thought more willing to challenge orthodox theories.[18] Ironically, it was Jack Knetsch, in the 1960s and early 1970s a leading figure in bringing the new welfare economics to the environmental literature, who, more than any other person, built a bridge from CV to behavioral economics. At some point in the late 1970s, Knetsch became suspicious of nonmarket valuation and its behavioral

18 For a history of behavioral economics, see Heukelom (2012) as well as Edwards' (2010) work on happiness economics. Surprisingly, the connection between behavioral economics and CV has been neglected in that literature, but I would suggest it was quite important, especially in the early 1980s as behavioral economics was gaining traction. A recent search on Google Scholar turned up thirty-five articles written by Dan Kahneman alone containing the term "contingent valuation." The sheer volume is instructive.

foundations. His partnership with Kahneman began in the early 1980s with work on CV, and their later work with Richard Thaler on the endowment effect, published in a series of articles around 1990, remained motivated by problems in the CV literature. At this point, the CV literature had crossed a line. As long as the troublesome results from CV experiments undermined only CV, it could be relegated to a subfield of environmental economics and ignored by the rest of a skeptical profession. Once those results were perceived as undermining the postulates of rational economic behavior, CV attracted more powerful opposition.[19]

At the risk of oversimplification, the various tests of CV and its institutions can be grouped into four key categories. The first went right to the question of strategic behavior posited by Samuelson. Would people reveal their WTP even in the context of a market institution that was not "incentive compatible" (i.e., that gave no incentive for households to reveal their true values)? Early experimental work by Peter Bohm (1972) and V. Smith (1979) seemed to imply that respondents did not free ride as much as Samuelson had predicted, and researchers sympathetic to the CV agenda interpreted this finding as support for CV. However, these results weren't persuasive to skeptics. In particular, failure to free ride in a market setting (even one lacking incentive compatibility) was hardly the same as answering truthfully or accurately to a hypothetical question.[20]

The second category of testing involved sensitivity analyses of the elicitation format. How much difference did it make how the WTP question was asked, and if it made a difference, which format performed better? Davis (1963a) and Randall, Ives, and Eastman (1974) had used a bidding game, in which respondents are first asked to accept or reject a bid, and the bid is adjusted until they (just) accept it. However, research showed that the starting point in this bidding process biased the results, as respondents anchored on the starting value, and similar results were found for other methods. The open-ended approach ("how much would you be willing to pay…?") seemed to be the most unrealistic, to invite strategic responses, and to impose the heaviest cognitive burdens on respondents, who had to find their own WTP rather than react to one.

19 Knetsch's growing skepticism is apparent in Gordon and Knetsch (1979). On the timing of his partnership with Kahneman in the early 1980s, see Kahneman (1986). Published articles on the endowment effect include Kahneman, Knetsch, and Thaler (1990, 1991) and Kahneman and Knetsch (1992).

20 See Dufwenberg and Harrison (2008) on Bohm's place in experimental economics. For examples interpreting the lack of free riding as supportive of CV, see Cicchetti and Smith (1973) and Cummings, Brookshire, and Schulze (1986).

By the 1990s, the consensus opinion of CV researchers converged around the dichotomous-choice format, in which respondents answered yes or no to a single WTP offer, perhaps with a single follow up. The approach had the downside of providing the least information (yes/no to a single value) and thus posing econometric challenging requiring various rival economic interpretations of the error terms. However, it obviously imposed the weakest cognitive burdens, was a familiar market institution (the posted price, or take-it-or-leave-it deal), and was incentive compatible (Mitchell and Carson 1989).

A third pair of tests surrounded so-called part-whole bias. Part-whole bias is the potential for respondents to "embed" a whole set of concerns unrelated to the specific environmental resource at stake. For example, a study of water quality at a particular Lake A might, psychologically, prompt thoughts about Lakes B and C, leading the respondent to value all three lakes instead of just A. In work circulating by 1984, Kahneman and Knetsch had found that WTP to stock fish in either of two lakes was similar to the WTP to stock all the lakes in Ontario.[21]

The fourth category surrounded differences between WTP and WTA, an issue raised earlier by Randall and others in their consideration of property rights and the Coase theorem. With respect to these property rights, WTP fits a setting in which people must buy a commodity to obtain it. In contrast, WTA fits a setting where people already own a commodity but may sell it. As a matter of abstract theory, any with-vs-without comparison can be valued using either WTP or WTA. From a Hicksian perspective, WTP and WTA differ by an income effect (the income associated with the different utility levels obtained with and without the commodity). From a Coasean perspective, they differ by the property right: whether one came to the hypothesized market transaction owning the property or not. Standard theory suggests the income effect of the property right should be small, especially for most of the commodities hypothetically bought or sold in CV markets. For example, the money one would be willing to exchange for a permit to hunt geese should hardly be affected by the wealth associated with that permit. Famously, Robert Willig (1976) showed that the WTP and WTA for *price* changes should be small. Randall and John Stoll (1980) extended his results to exogenous changes in *quantities* of things consumed outside of markets, like environmental quality, a result that seemingly suggested the differences should be small in CV applications as well.

[21] The research appears never to have been published, but results were reported in Kahneman (1986).

And yet, numerous CV studies in the 1970s found very large WTP-WTA disparities, on the order of 4x–16x.[22] CV researchers and others had diverse reactions to these findings. Some believed that respondents rejected as implausible the WTA frame, and so used their responses to express moral outrage rather than to seriously submit an asking price in a market. Others believed that Randall and Stoll misinterpreted their extension of Willig's results from price changes to quantity/quality changes, and that, in fact, there was nothing in economic theory that suggested WTP-WTA differences should be small. Michael Hanemann (1991) developed this point, showing that, when the public good and private goods are highly complementary, WTA for the public good could be much larger than WTP.

Still others believed these results were part of a pattern of evidence consistent with the "endowment effect" proposed by Thaler (1980), namely, the idea that people valued things more once it was theirs or part of the status quo. Kahneman and Amos Tversky's (1979) prospect theory was one way to explain this finding. Kahneman and Tversky argued that real human beings value gains and losses differently and tend to avoid losses, for psychological reasons that have nothing to do with the income effects that are needed to explain the differences according to neoclassical theory. Thus, whereas neoclassical economics focused on the utility people received from a state, Kahneman and Tversky suggested these states needed to be evaluated in the context of some reference point, relative to which other states represent gains or losses. In a series of laboratory experiments, Knetsch and Sinden (1984), Knetsch (1989), and Kahneman, Knetsch, and Thaler (1990) found that WTP bids and WTA asks differed even in the lab, with induced preferences for raffle tickets or homegrown values for small items like candy bars and coffee mugs. These tests seemed to confirm the presence of an endowment effect. Interestingly, these tests clearly were motivated by the CV literature, but they had much broader implications for human behavior.

To assess these and other issues with CV, in 1984 the EPA sponsored a meeting organized by Cummings, Brookshire, and Schulze. Cummings et al. provided a large volume of background material, and a group of expert environmental economists offered their perspectives on the issues, including Randall, Richard Bishop, Myrick Freeman, Thomas Heberlein, and Kerry Smith. Of these, only Randall felt that CV was a method successfully proven to measure WTP, but the others were cautiously optimistic. A further group represented the larger economics profession, comprising

[22] See Hammack and Brown (1974), Bishop and Heberlein (1979), and Rowe, d'Arge, and Brookshire (1980).

Kenneth Arrow, Kahneman, Sherwin Rosen, and V. Smith. Arrow was the most "sympathetic" to the CV method (to use his own word). He viewed potential errors in the estimates of +/− 50 percent, such as had been documented by Cummings et al., as informative and within the same order of magnitude as errors in the natural sciences' ability to estimate the physical effects of pollution.[23]

Kahneman's response was nuanced and diplomatic. He was surprised the CV method performed as well as it did and accepted the method in principle. However, he urged more caution in thinking about the appropriate social setting in which the surveys were used. In particular, he said practitioners should think more about "the purchase structure" and whether a scenario involves, in people's minds, compensation for a loss or purchase of a gain (or avoidance of a loss). This distinction involves not only the property right inherent in the WTP/WTA comparisons, but also the cause of the changes in environmental quality to be evaluated and the reference point they would create for prospect theory. For example, he suggested that people would require compensation for the loss of a scenic view caused by the government, but expect to pay to avoid the loss if it were caused by an insect. Kahneman felt that the data suggested that CV produced nonsensical results when constructing WTA, so it should be restricted to WTP, but he also felt that WTP questions should not be imposed on contexts where people will feel entitled to compensation. In this way, he supported the use of surveys and CV for policy making, but in such a way that one expected neither to meet nor to construct economic man.[24]

Like Kahneman, V. Smith did not expect CV to construct *homo economicus*, but for that reason he was much less enthusiastic about it. He cited an experiment in which individuals had bought and sold lottery tickets, providing bids and offers that could be interpreted as WTP and WTA. He showed that individuals' offered WTP and WTA were, in his words, "all over the map," even when incentivized, but that the market institution cleared at prices close to the inherent value. Drawing on that lesson, he concluded, "As I read the CVM work, it seems to me that what you are mainly working on is proposals for some sort of a substitution for the market, a calculation substitution. I really think we ought to devote a little time to thinking about whether there might be the possibility of creating markets where they don't now exist, and let the market do the calculation."[25] He concluded

[23] Cummings, Brookshire, and Schulze (1986 p. 185).
[24] Cummings, Brookshire, and Schulze (1986 pp. 186–90).
[25] Cummings, Brookshire, and Schultze (1986 pp. 202–3).

with a proposal in which rights to resources could be assigned and people could bid for them. Thus, he favored the design of real markets such as those discussed in Chapter 6, rather than using hypothetical markets to inform government planning.

In short, the perspectives of the wider profession at the 1984 CV conference reflected a reasonable cross section of views: Arrow wanted to muddle through with benefit–cost analysis to inform policy as much as possible; Kahneman viewed CV through the lens of his brand of behavioral psychology rather than economics; and V. Smith wanted to forego the entire CV project of "calculation substitution" for benefit–cost analysis and introduce market mechanisms into the real world.

This debate and discussion might have gone on in the same spirit, mirroring differences in the larger profession, while CV practitioners continued their applied work out of the spotlight. But meanwhile, economic abstractions like existence value entered benefit–cost and liability rules, upping the stakes for the applications.

9.4 The Exxon Valdez

The increased stakes for CV developed through a series of US regulatory moves and court cases over, roughly, the decade of the 1980s. First, in 1979, the US Water Resources Council again revised its "Principles and Standards" for water resources planning, which now allowed for CV as one possible method for estimating recreation values. This precedent took on added importance when, in 1981, President Reagan issued Executive Order 12291, greatly expanding the role of benefit–cost analysis in agencies such as the EPA. As with the earlier episodes for outdoor recreation in the immediate postwar period, this order gave agencies like EPA added incentive to quantify ever more abstract and "intangible" benefits, such as the existence values introduced by Krutilla.[26]

That incentive was further extended to the DOI by regulatory actions surrounding the 1980 Comprehensive Environmental Response Cleanup and Liability Act, better known as "Superfund." Superfund created a liability provision, known as the Natural Resource Damage Assessment (NRDA), whereby DOI, the states, and tribes act as trustees who can sue potentially responsible parties for damages suffered by the public from hazardous releases.

[26] On Reagan's executive order, see K. Smith (1984).

Charged with promulgating the NRDA rules, DOI wrestled with the key question of what constitutes "damages." Importantly, it argued that the economic concept of consumer surplus was the appropriate conceptual framework for defining damages, and it included use values as objects to be measured. But, hedging its bet, DOI took a more ambivalent position on the question of existence values, even though by this point they were tied up with the economic theory of consumer surplus. Calling out the inconsistency, a US Court of Appeals ruled in *State of Ohio v. US Dept. of Interior* (1989) that NRDAs should indeed include existence values. Furthermore, it authorized the use of CV to do so.

These legal moves made CV a very valuable tool to federal agencies. Forced to consider existence values, the agencies turned to CV as the only game in town for measuring such values.[27] However, a countervailing force soon came into play.

Just before the *Ohio* ruling came down, the *Exxon Valdez* ran aground in Alaska, spilling at least 11 million gallons of oil, the largest spill in US waters until the 2010 *Deepwater Horizon* spill. As the spill affected an area little used for recreation or other public activities but widely characterized as pristine, existence values were, in the wake of *Ohio*, bound to play a large role in the case.[28] Indeed, the trustees sponsored a CV study of nonuse damages, which were estimated to be as high as $2.8 billion. Surprisingly, in response Exxon eschewed the usual NRDA strategy of critiquing the trustees' estimates of damages and supplying its own from its own economic experts. Instead, it took a more radical approach: it invested large sums to fund research investigating the inherent flaws in CV as a measurement tool, and thus the impossibility of adequately supporting claims for nonuse values in court.[29]

Exxon's strategy gained a second purpose when, in 1990, Congress passed the Oil Pollution Act, giving the National Oceanic and Atmospheric

[27] Whereas Berman (2017) suggests *de*regulation strengthened economists' position in US antitrust policy, I am suggesting the opposite is true in environmental economics. The difference may be that, in the environmental context, EPA's constituency valued the consumer benefits that come from regulation, whereas in the antitrust context they come from deregulation, but in either case documenting consumer benefits required economic analysis. An alternative view is that regulations beget deregulatory watchdogs (as with Reagan's executive order) and economics emerges in the synthesis.

[28] As discussed by Fourcade (2011), these legal developments differentiated liability for oil spills in the US from France and other countries, but were consistent with the older culture of US benefit–cost practices.

[29] The estimates of the trustees' NRDA damage estimates were published, after much delay, in Carson et al. (2003). See Maas and Svorenčík (2017) for a discussion of this episode.

Administration (NOAA) a similar NRDA role for coastal oil spills. In promulgating its regulations, NOAA convened a blue-ribbon panel to judge the academic research on CV and make recommendations about the role it should play in its regulations. The panel comprised Arrow; Robert Solow; Paul Portney, a leading environmental economist shortly to be appointed President of RFF; Edward Leamer; Roy Radner; and Howard Schuman, a survey researcher. Exxon realized that its sponsored research, if released quickly, could help not only its own case but also influence the new NOAA regulations. When Exxon settled its NRDA case in 1991, this secondary purpose became the primary one.

The research supported by Exxon was presented at a meeting held in 1992. Authors included, among others, Peter Diamond and Jerry Hausman, Daniel McFadden, environmental economists William Desvousges, Reed Johnson, and Kevin Boyle, and psychologists David Schkade and John Payne.[30] Commentators included Arrow, Zvi Griliches, Plott, and Randall. Numerous other economists attended the meetings, including Bishop, Richard Carson, Hanemann, Robert Mitchell, and K. Smith. Yet, discussion time was limited and tightly controlled. Additionally, many of the environmental economists present were offended by the claim made by some new to the issues that they were the first to introduce certain economic innovations, innovations that some of the environmental economists felt they had introduced long ago. In general, the meeting became infamous as an occasion for bad feelings. As Portney later put it in a 1994 symposium in the *Journal of Economic Perspectives*, the entire post-Exxon debate was "spirited (and occasionally mean-spirited)."[31]

Three particularly prominent studies introduced evidence that, in their authors' minds, proved CV to be fatally flawed. First, McFadden and Leonard (1993) found that different market institutions and question formats gave different WTP estimates, suggesting that current practices were not converging on the same construct. They also found that people seemed to anchor on the WTP suggested to them in dichotomous choice questions. Second, Diamond et al. (1993) applied CV to the value of preserving wilderness areas in Montana, using different versions with different combinations of areas threatened. To simplify, they theorized that, except for a small income effect, the WTP to preserve Area A when Areas A and B are

[30] In the interest of disclosure, I worked at Research Triangle Institute with Desvousges, Johnson, and Richard Dunford during these years.

[31] See, for example, the discussion in Hausman (1993 pp. 364–8). "Spirited" (Portney 1994 p. 3).

both threatened plus the WTP to preserve Area B when only B is threatened should equal the WTP to preserve Areas A and B. They found that CV results failed to meet this "adding up test."

Third, Desvousges et al. (1993) found that CV studies were not sensitive to what they called "scope." They used CV to estimate the public's WTP to avoid deaths to migratory waterfowl from landing in uncovered oil ponds. Employing three versions of the survey, they measured WTP to avoid, respectively, the death of 200,000 birds, 20,000 birds, and 2,000 birds. They found that the WTP estimates were not significantly different across the three versions, a result similar to Kahneman and Knetsch's earlier work on Ontario lakes. Following up on this work, Schkade and Payne (1994), the psychologists in the group, used the Desvousges et al. survey to conduct "verbal protocols," in which people think out loud during their responses to surveys. In response to the open-ended question in which they have to state their own maximum WTP, respondents indicated a great deal of confusion and difficulty arriving at a number, groping for various external cues to guide their thought. To Schkade and Payne and other critics of CV, the work implied that people do not have well-defined preferences that can be searched out and measured; rather, those preferences need to be constructed when encountering new decisions and decision contexts. That itself seemed a fatal flaw.

Respondents including Hanemann and Randall argued that CV studies were reliable if done properly; if Exxon studies obtained inconsistent results it was because they were done improperly. For example, in some cases, Exxon researchers used open-ended question formats that were cognitively burdensome and were not incentive compatible, so the results of Schkade and Payne were hardly surprising. Additionally, they argued that many of the results for adding up tests, embedding, and WTP/WTA did not necessarily violate neoclassical preferences.[32]

NOAA's blue-ribbon panel considered all these arguments and more in its deliberations. After weighing the evidence, it concluded that CV studies do convey useful information for benefit–cost analysis. The authors stated, "We think it is fair to describe such information as reliable by the standards that seem to be implicit in similar contexts, like market analysis for new and innovative products and the assessment of other damages normally allowed in court proceedings." Note here the faint praise. As Arrow expressed "sympathy" at the 1984 EPA conference, the panel here

[32] Randall's comments are at Hausman (1993 pp. 445–50), Hanemann's at (pp. 297–9). See also Hanemann (1991, 1994) and K. Smith (1992).

expressed the view that, though it is hardly a clean application of economic theory, CV is good enough for government work. In their view, some number is better than no number, and CV's numbers are good enough. Or, rather, given the ubiquity of benefit cost analysis, the question is not so much whether "some number is better than no number," but whether it is better to use an informed estimate than the number zero, which is the implicit weight given to nature when no value is included. But the panel also offered a number of tests and criteria to ensure CV constructs the values of *homo economicus.*[33]

9.5 Economic Theory and "Applied" Economics

The legacy of the *Exxon Valdez* debate for CV has been mixed. In the halls of mainstream economics departments at research universities, CV afterward became decidedly unfashionable. Nevertheless, authorized by the NOAA panel, the tool continues to be used by academic economists in other parts of the university (like agricultural economics or health policy departments), government economists, and other applied researchers, with, at one count made around 2010, over 7,500 studies and papers from over 130 countries.[34]

This mixed legacy is wrapped up in questions about the relationship between a so-called "applied" field like environmental economics and economics as such. As Backhouse and Biddle (2000) and Backhouse and Cherrier (2017) discuss, the term "applied economics" is as ambiguous as it is ubiquitous. Sometimes it means fitting theoretical abstractions to concrete instances in the real world; sometimes it is a synonym for empirical work; and, I would add, sometimes it is merely a euphemism for mediocrity. The ambiguity arises because "applied economics" has been defined in opposition to a vague set of antonyms, including "pure," "theoretical," or "abstract" economics. Moreover, the realms of behavior over which economics can be applied legitimately are also ambiguous and depend on a shifting understanding of "economics" itself. The varied reactions to the CV debate serve to illustrate the range of potential interpretations for this relationship when applied work does not go as expected. Consider four key positions.

Following the logic of hypothesis testing, one reaction is to accept that CV is a legitimate empirical tool and interpret the anomalies as a rejection

[33] Arrow et al. (1993 quotation at p. 4610). For one articulation of the number-zero-vs.-no-number argument, see Haab et al. (2013).

[34] See Carson (2011) for a bibliography.

of the underlying neoclassical economic theory, at least in some important contexts. As we have already seen, Knetsch began to travel down this road sometime around 1980. Eventually, even McFadden, who won a Nobel Prize in economics for his work uniting theories of utility-maximization to the econometric analysis of choices, seemed to abandon the economic theory of the utility-maximizing consumer. He had already begun his own journey down this road at the Exxon conference. There, he commented that "if people really have this willingness-to-pay, [the values] should shine through" all the variations in the CV studies. McFadden clearly was troubled by the Exxon results. In 1999, he published an article titled "Rationality for Economists?" in which he argued that *homo economicus*, or what he called "Chicago man," "is an endangered species." Notably, he suggested that public goods were a case in point and that "nowhere has this been more evident than in economists' attempts to value nonuse public goods, such as endangered species or wilderness areas." He concluded by arguing that, for economics, "the challenge is to evolve Chicago man in the direction of K-T [Kahneman-Tversky] man."[35]

From this perspective, applied economics and the broader field are in dialogue. As idealized by the scientific method, a (perceived) failure to apply one theory leads to a rejection of the theory, at least for a particular choice context, and to new attempts to apply other theories. In this case, neoclassical economic theory *ought* to apply to "non-use public goods, such as endangered species or wilderness areas," so if it doesn't there is something wrong with the theory.

Reacting to this critique, a second interpretation would protect the integrity of neoclassical economics by severing it from the difficulties raised by CV. Diamond and Hausman concluded their article in the *Journal of Economic Perspectives* symposium, subtitled "Is Some Number Better than No Number?" by arguing that

> contingent valuation is a deeply flawed methodology for measuring nonuse values, one that does not estimate what its proponents claim to be estimating.... It is precisely in the lack of experience both in markets for environmental commodities and in the consequences of such decision that makes contingent valuation questions so hard to answer and the responses so suspect.

They further explain that their skepticism comes, not from flaws in survey methods, but from the "absence of preferences." In other words, the

[35] Exxon conference (Hausman 1993 p. 214). "Rationality for Economists?" (McFadden 1999, quotes from pp. 97, 99). More recent work along these lines includes McFadden (2013).

problem with CV is that it puts people in a situation where they have little experience. Apparently, according to them, economics does not apply to such situations. Thus, CV is doomed to fail. The hypothetical nature of the market, which created the need for CV in the first place, inevitably precludes the possibility of measuring values. Consequently, CV is an illegitimate tool and not competent to challenge neoclassical theory. Hausman, never one to mince words, later suggested that, with its reliance on CV, "environmental economics is to economics what military music is to music" – thus separating the applied from the pure.[36]

A third interpretation, represented by Plott, strikes a balance between the first two. Like McFadden, but unlike Diamond and Hausman, he believed that economic theory ought to apply to nonmarket valuation, so CV anomalies are disturbing. In his comments at the Exxon conference, he confessed that "the problem here is that the fundamental consistency property, the transitivity of preferences that is required of all theories of optimization, is absent." He concluded that CV does not "measure what the underlying philosophy of welfare economics and preference theory requires it to measure." Potentially going further, he raised the possibility that those theories are not "sufficiently well-grounded in scientific evidence" but then pulled back from that conclusion. Evidence pointing that way should be ignored, for now, he said, on the grounds that welfare theory is too far rooted in real-world institutions to uproot until there is a better theory to replace it. But he argued that "economists must begin to deal systematically with this … issue."[37]

Plott soon advanced a theory that neoclassical economic theory can accommodate the idea that agents learn or *discover* their own preferences in new situations, through trial and error. But it is incompatible with the idea that preferences are actually *constructed*, as that would defy the economic logic of optimization. In the ensuing years, Plott has pursued a research agenda based around this theory. In a series of studies, he has argued that WTP/WTA disparities in the environmental literature and elsewhere disappear when experimenters use incentive-compatible mechanisms and give subjects practice and training. Additionally, he has suggested that Knetsch's finding on preference reversals can be explained by incorporating preferences for gifts without resorting to prospect theory or by failure to understand the market institution. Thus, Plott's view is

[36] "A deeply flawed methodology" (Diamond and Hausman 1994 p. 62). "Military music" (Coy 1997).

[37] Quotations from Plott (1993 pp. 468, 471, 468, and 477 respectively).

that CV fails to help people discover their preferences appropriately, but other institutions can.[38]

It is interesting to compare Plott's position as well as Diamond and Hausman's to Pareto's. Pareto agreed that, when they are confronted with unfamiliar market settings, people have to discover their preferences, so initially they may not behave in accordance with neoclassical consumer theory, until they have had sufficient practice. Taking CV as a kind of market setting, as its proponents claimed it to be, these critics emphasized the unfamiliarity of that setting and the difficulty of applying neoclassical theory. Whereas Diamond and Hausman stopped there, Plott sought to find alternatives to CV that do apply the theory. But Pareto himself had viewed surveys as an alternative to markets that were actually more tightly linked to neoclassical theory, bypassing the institutions to go straight to preferences.[39]

A fourth perspective would agree that neoclassical theory ought to apply to unfamiliar settings like nonmarket valuation, but that, in fact, when done correctly, CV successfully applies that theory. Hanemann, for example, was willing to concede that people do not have preexisting preference mappings that a survey can access, so the survey has to construct them. But, in contrast to Diamond and Hausman, he argued that such constructions in surveys are no different than constructions in markets, for people are always constructing their preferences in new market settings. Here, Hanemann quoted Robert Solow, who, when reacting to the Schkade-Paine verbal protocols, commented that they "sound a lot like Bob Solow in the grocery store." Thus, said Hanemann, "[t]he real issue is not whether preferences are a construct but whether they are a *stable* construct." From this perspective, hypothetical CV markets, like other markets, have the potential to construct meaningful values, and thus be a successful application of economic theory.[40]

This range of reactions to the CV debate shows that economists have continued to wrestle with the question of whether, or to what extent,

38 On preference discovery, see Plott (1996) and, for commentary, Bruni and Sugden (2007). On Plott's later empirical work, see Plott and Zeiler (2005, 2007) and Cason and Plott (2014). List's research has also emphasized the importance of market experience (e.g., List 2003).

39 See Giocoli (2003 pp. 72–3) and Bruni and Sugden (2007).

40 Hanemann (1994, with quotation from p. 28). Schkade and Payne were willing to accept this point of view. Later, they suggested a set of guidelines for constructing stable preferences (Payne, Bettman, and Schkade 1999). Hanemann and Payne et al. may have used "construction" the way Plott was using "discovery," without emphasizing the distinction. The way Payne et al. discuss their work in relation to Plott's does suggest this (p. 264).

economic theory applies to intangible goods like environmental quality, a question they have been grappling with since the mid-century debates about pricing outdoor recreation – or, indeed, since the turn-of-the-century disputes between Pinchot and Muir. All economists would agree that there are opportunity costs when it comes to environmental preservation. But what about *measuring* consumers' willingness to make trade-offs? Like the economists surveyed by Roy Prewitt about recreation, economists like Diamond and Hausman conclude that it is impossible to measure such intangible objects as existence values. Like the government economists working in Prewitt's wake, others have forged ahead with creative suggestions to overcome the problem.

Epilogue

The Future History of Pricing the Environment

The future ... seems to me no unified dream but a mince pie, long in the baking, never quite done.

–E. B. White, *One Man's Meat* (1942)

The history of environmental economics and pricing the environment, as told here, sounds eight concordant themes, which seem likely to continue to be of relevance in the future. They can be summarized as follows.

1 The Rise of the Consumer

The first theme is the rise of the consumer in both environmental and economic thinking, twin developments that facilitated their harmonization. From the turn-of-the-century impasse between Pinchot's materialism, promoting the efficient use of physical resources, and Muir's transcendentalism, deprecating human ends, the postwar environmental movement gained traction by appealing to a new, more aesthetic sense of consumption, one that encompassed tastes for clean air and water, for outdoor recreation opportunities, and even for pristine environments – enjoyed all the more by people for the fact that they were leaving them untouched. At the same time, economics was shifting its own emphasis from the supply side of the economy to the demand side. Although it has always been commonplace to note that consumption is the ultimate end of production, turn-of-the-century economics frequently concluded its analysis with the distribution of income to households, without delving into what households did with it. In contrast, postwar economics increasingly emphasized choice and optimization, highlighting the active role of households. Thus, households could now be thought of as "producing" recreation services from a mix of time, transportation, and environmental resources, opening up the possibility of modeling household's demand for environmental quality.

2 The Changing Definition of Economics

Economics was redefining itself in other ways too. At the turn of the twentieth century, it usually was defined as the study of material welfare. Under this definition, it could hardly include "intangible" considerations like natural beauty and wonder. But by the 1960s, the profession had largely accepted Lionel Robbins's definition, based on a way of thinking in terms of opportunity costs. Environmental economists like John Krutilla exploited this change in thinking, observing that there is always a trade-off between preserving wilderness and developing it, so preservation falls under the umbrella of economics. Thus, by his account, even John Muir's values have economic standing.

Now, over fifty years later, the economics profession may be in the middle of another shift, from emphasizing opportunity costs to emphasizing *ceteris paribus* logic – that is, analyzing the effects of an isolated factor (or group of factors) holding everything else constant. The "credibility revolution" in economics has sought to estimate the causal effects of various factors using just such logic. How this revolution will affect environmental economics in the future is an open question, but already it has changed how economists estimate willingness to pay for environmental services as well as how they have evaluated the effects of pricing policies.[1]

3 Measurement and Economic Science

A third theme is the increased pace of quantitative measurement in economics in the twentieth century (and for that matter in environmental science too).[2] Many economists would agree with Lord Kelvin's dictum, inscribed on the Social Science building at the University of Chicago, that "When you can measure what you are speaking about, and express it in numbers, you know something about it; but when you cannot measure it,

[1] Panhans and Singleton (2017) document the impact of the credibility revolution on economic practices from a historical perspective. For just one of many possible examples of using quasi-experimental methods to estimate the value of environmental improvements, see Deschênes, Greenstone, and Shapiro (2017). For an example applying them to the effects of carbon pricing policies, see Andersson (2019).

[2] Klein and Morgan (2001) discuss the twentieth century as *The Age of Economic Measurement*.

when you cannot express it in numbers, your knowledge is of a meager and unsatisfactory kind: it may be the beginning of knowledge, but you have scarcely, in your thoughts, advanced to the stage of *science*." Accordingly, economists created aggregate statistics like GDP and cost-of-living indices and embedded quantitative economic logic into the administrative state, in the form of benefit–cost analysis. They also began to estimate, as a matter of routine, the demand for various goods and services. Pricing the environment was occasioned by such work, but it also helped to further advance it, by providing means to quantify more values, such as existence values for nature.

4 Measurement of Increasingly More Intangible Objects

Even as they began to measure economic objects quantitatively, economists adopted increasingly abstract understandings of those objects, allowing them to measure the intangible, or to quantify the qualitative. These abstractions were often tied to consumer theory. The interpretation of price indices, for example, evolved from the more concrete notion of an average of market prices to the more abstract notion of consumers' cost of maintaining a given standard of living. As the quality of goods also affects the standard of living, the indices evolved to account for quality changes, such as the options available in automobiles. With such intellectual trends in the background, measuring the value of environmental quality began to appear less far-fetched than it had been. Furthermore, the permissible types of environmental quality open to quantification could be pushed ever farther. Thus, measures of environmental values also proceeded outward from the tangible to the intangible, from the markets for natural resources studied by Pinchot's National Conservation Commission or by early RFF reports, to lands used for nonmarket activities like recreation, to *non*uses like the sheer existence of a unique ecosystem or species.

5 Theories of Surplus Value

Since the late eighteenth century, a common goal in political economy has been the identification of surplus value. François Quesnay and the physiocrats located it in the productive powers of Nature, especially in agriculture. John Stuart Mill similarly spoke of the free gifts of nature, but noted that, while they make us wealthier, natural assets, precisely because they are free, are not themselves wealth in any accounting sense. Said Mill,

> Things for which nothing could be obtained in exchange, however useful or necessary they may be, are not wealth in the sense in which the term is used in Political Economy. Air, for example, though the most absolute of necessaries, bears no price in the market, because it can be obtained gratuitously: to accumulate a stock of it would yield no profit .... But though air is not wealth, mankind are much richer by obtaining it gratis, since the time and labour which would otherwise be required for supplying the most pressing of all wants, can be devoted to other purposes. It is possible to imagine circumstances in which air would be a part of wealth. If it became customary to sojourn long in places where the air does not naturally penetrate, as in diving-bells sunk in the sea, a supply of air artificially furnished would, like water conveyed into houses, bear a price: and if from any revolution in nature the atmosphere became too scanty for the consumption ... air might acquire a very high marketable value.

In the early twentieth century, popular textbooks like Richard Ely's maintained the view that nonmarket natural assets – precisely because they have no market value – provide surplus but do not represent wealth.[3] Fifty years later, with the shift to thinking in terms of quality as much as quantity, it was indeed very easy to imagine the atmosphere being too scanty for (healthy) consumption. Yet it still had no marketable value.

Why not? Mid-century economists explained the problem by its publicness, namely the inability to exclude consumers from breathing clean air without paying for it, giving rise to a free rider problem that undermines the incentives to supply it. Yet households would still be willing to pay for improvements. In this sense, air quality does have (potential) marketable value, and so it could be thought of as wealth even on Mill's own terms. Differences in environmental quality, following Ricardo's earlier analysis of differences in soil fertility among farms, then give rise to economic rents in high-quality areas. The leap from Ricardian rent for differences in the quality of farmland to rents for differences in water or air quality was facilitated by the insistence of Ely and other resource economists that "land" means much more than soil.[4]

Of course, people are rarely charged for environmental quality when it is provided as a public good, so they receive a surplus value for it. Accordingly, in connection with the themes of measurement and the

[3] Mill [1848] (1987) pp. 6–7; Ely (1908) pp. 454–6.

[4] One strand of environmental pricing that has been neglected in this book is the theory of so-called hedonic property values, which looks at how real estate in areas with better air quality or other environment amenities commands a premium over other areas (e.g., Ridker 1967). The literature on hedonic pricing is often tied to Tiebout's (1956) model of people voting with their feet for their preferred level of public goods and attending property taxes. It could equally be tied to Ricardo's early logic. Indeed, when Frederick Waugh defended his dissertation regressing vegetable prices on quality characteristics, Eveline Burns suggested to him a connection to Ricardian rent (Waugh 1929 p. 99).

focus on the consumer, postwar economists began to measure this "consumer's surplus." Thus, even as they were valuing ever more intangible, qualitative objects, economists also measured their value with increasingly abstract constructs. While the theory of these constructs was well established by the 1930s, environmental economics was one leading area where they were brought into practice in the late 1950s and early 1960s. By the same token, by the 1980s, differences in measured environmental values between subtle variants of consumer surplus brought environmental economics into the crossfire between neoclassical and behavioral economics.

6 The Relationship between Theory and Application

In their essay on applied economics, Backhouse and Cherrier (2017) consider the important role of the various sites where economic knowledge is produced, from academia to think tanks to government agencies, in shaping relevant "applications" and judging their success. The postwar history of environmental valuation repeatedly goes through Harvard University; agricultural economics departments; two Ford-supported think tanks, the RAND Corporation and RFF; and government agencies. In this case, the diversity of nodes in the intellectual network of environmental economics and policy allowed different schools of economic thought and different emphases to mesh together. For example, the compulsion in government agencies to find a creative way to estimate numbers that could be used in a bureaucratic procedure encountered the insistence found in neoclassical economics that empirical measures be tied to an economic theory.

These interactions raise questions about the relationship between "theoretical" and "applied" work in economics. The language of "application" suggests the prior existence of a theory that can be taken and applied to a situation at hand. But economists pressed to measure the value for, say, outdoor recreation, had no theory to turn to. They had no precedent for thinking about recreation in those terms, nor, once they adopted Harold Hotelling's suggestion to construct a demand curve, any solid precedent for thinking through how to derive a value from that demand.[5] Measurement had to come first; interpreting what the numbers meant through an economic framework could come later.

[5] Hands and Mirowski (1998) and Mirowski and Hands (1998) have suggested that Hotelling is an underappreciated figure in the history of economic thought, lying behind numerous important strands. The same may be said of his role in environmental economics. He influenced important leaders like Kenneth Arrow and Robert Dorfman, provided

7 Common Property and the Comparative Analysis of Institutional Arrangements

The work across these various research sites also brought neoclassical and institutional economists together. A standard narrative in the history of economic thought is that institutional economics thrived in the inter-war period of economic pluralism, then rapidly declined in the postwar period of neoclassical orthodoxy.[6] While those broad trends are indisputable, institutionalists didn't suddenly disappear; they continued to work and thrive in government agencies and think tanks like RFF well into the 1960s. Moreover, when "new institutional economics" arrived on the scene with, say, Ronald Coase's "Problem of Social Cost" (1960), it was not immediately recognized as new. For all its efforts to extend neoclassical economics to transactions costs and property rights, it initially was received, discussed, and interpreted as just one more theory about comparative institutional arrangements for addressing externalities and common property, of which there had been many. Thus, when they addressed new questions about how to internalize the costs of water and air pollution, economists like Allen Kneese, Thomas Crocker, and John Dales could draw on a rich institutionalist tradition analyzing common property.

8 Engagement with Political Controversies

The economists measuring the values for outdoor recreation, sensing the weak foundation for their enterprise in economic theory, tried to avoid the problem altogether, suggesting it just could not be done. Unfortunately for them, they were not allowed that option. Having come into government to bring their expertise to practical problems, they had at least partially lost control of their research agenda and were forced by their government agencies to perform such valuations. Thus, bureaucratic necessity became the mother to economic invention. Similar forces were at work in measuring the value of lives, when analysts at RAND were forced to evaluate the lives of airplane crews.

In both cases, resistance or denial of the problem was followed by pragmatic but intellectually unsatisfying compromises and, eventually, over a

a central model for the economics of natural resources (Hotelling 1931), a model for optimal pricing with nonrivalry (Hotelling 1938), and the travel cost method for measuring the consumer surplus for outdoor recreation opportunities.

[6] See, for example, Morgan and Rutherford (1998) and Rutherford (2001). To be clear, these authors are perfectly aware of the subtleties involved.

period of 15–20 years, stabilization of measurement procedures, which subsequently became routine. However, new political forces may be beginning to stretch them again in new directions.

Three Possible Futures for the History of Environmental Pricing

Environmental economics naturally will continue to evolve as it faces new policy challenges and operates in new political climates. Nobody can predict the future, but three policy challenges appear likely to engage the attention of environmental economists in the foreseeable future. These challenges seem destined to continue to sound the above themes, albeit with variations.

1 Carbon Pricing

Climate change is obviously the mother of all environmental policy issues facing the world today. Over the next century, the earth's surface is expected to warm 2–4 °C (4–7 °F), which is sure to cause major economic damage and disruption on an unprecedented scale. But, likewise, government policies to avoid, forestall, or mitigate those damages entail unprecedented interventions with the economy, with massive effects on material production, jobs, asset values, and international trade. Consequently, policies that can achieve targeted reductions in greenhouse gasses at the least cost are highly desirable.

Not surprisingly, pollution pricing, either through taxes (like Kneese's effluent fees) or through cap-and-trade (like the schemes proposed by Crocker and Dales), are the leading suggestions from economists. Today, nearly seventy carbon pricing policies have been adopted around the world, covering 23 percent of global greenhouse gas emissions. Most are cap-and-trade schemes, with the most prominent being those of the European Union, California, and China.[7]

The relative merits of carbon taxes and cap-and-trade are subtle, and consequently they depend on subtle variations in their designs, such as whether permits are auctioned or given away for free, whether annual permits can be banked for future use, and whether the cap-and-trade market is paired with a price floor and ceiling. They also depend

[7] Statistics from World Bank (2022). Finch and van den Bergh (2022), Narassimhan et al. (2018), and World Bank (2022) survey cap-and-trade and other carbon pricing schemes around the world.

on various interactions with the economic and political environment, including the need for tax revenue, interactions with preexisting tax distortions, interactions with any preexisting environmental policies, the degree of market power in the fossil fuels industry, the need to distribute offsetting economic rents to labor or to capital in the dirty industries, and the potential for environmentalists to "buy down" the pollution cap and retire permits. The complexity of these issues invites a comparative analysis of institutions for closing the climate commons, not unlike Allen Kneese's approach.[8]

In his proposals to price effluent discharged into a water basin, Kneese had argued that, ideally, the fee would be set equal to the marginal social damages of the effluent. Such a fee would internalize the effect of upstream discharges on downstream uses such as drinking water and water-based recreation into the decisions of the upstream firm, just as if the upstream and downstream interests were jointly owned. Kneese was optimistic that ongoing work on measuring recreation and existence values would one day permit the calculation of such damages. But, meanwhile, recognizing the difficulty of calculating them with contemporary methods, Kneese suggested that fees set at other levels could still achieve pollution-reduction targets, however determined, by the most economically efficient means.

Kneese's optimism about nonmarket valuation was well founded, for today environmental economists do routinely calculate the benefits of outdoor recreation or the damages from conventional air pollution like smog, and they even measure existence values. Nevertheless, the complexity of environmental policy challenges such as global climate change has arguably outrun economists' ability to price them. Not that they have not attempted to rise to the challenge. In particular, economists have attempted to compute the so-called "social cost of carbon" (SCC) using integrated assessment models. Integrated assessment models attempt to compute the economic damages of greenhouse gas emissions through a series of linkages, including the effects of policy options on emissions, of emissions on the global climate, and of climate change on human welfare. William Nordhaus, an economist at Yale University, won the 2018 Nobel Prize in economics in part for his work with such models. In

[8] For a discussion of the comparative advantages of fees, cap-and-trade, and other policies in different contexts, see Goulder and Schein (2013). Interestingly, Thomas Schelling (1992) wrote a fairly early piece on the economics of global warming, comparing the workability of these schemes in the context of international bargaining.

1992, he introduced the Dynamic Integrated model of Climate and the Economy (DICE) to find the optimal path of reductions on greenhouse gas emissions.[9]

Although widely used by economists and planners, such models have sometimes been criticized for their simplistic treatment of the complex linkages involved. The original models used a "loss function" that translated temperature changes into a percentage deduction to GDP through an arbitrary, *ad hoc* relationship. Essentially, the logic was that climate change would reduce agricultural productivity and flood coastal lands, thereby reducing total output and, hence, income. In tension with this book's theme of the rise of the consumer, this focus on production was something of a throwback to the economic logic of one hundred years ago. It ignored impacts on human health, or the values people have for unique places such as, say, a particular arctic ecosystems supporting polar bears, the kinds of values which Krutilla had emphasized in "Conservation Reconsidered." Nor were the estimated impacts rigorously tied to empirical estimates. Highly aggregated, they also missed much of the variability in climate impacts between regions. Finally, given the long time horizon considered, they inevitably were (and are) highly sensitive to discount rates.[10] In 2006, Nordhaus estimated the SCC to be $14 per ton of CO_2, whereas the UK's *Stern Review*, using a lower discount rate, estimated it to be ten times that figure, at $145 (all values here converted to 2022 dollars). In 2010, the official SCC used by US agencies was $30, whereas a recent revision put it at $191. Preliminary endeavors are always subject to revision and improvement, but this wide range of estimates suggests more time may be needed before the estimates stabilize and policies can

[9] Nordhaus's prize was officially awarded "for integrating climate change into long-run macroeconomic analysis" (www.nobelprize.org/prizes/economic-sciences/2018/nordhaus/facts). See Nordhaus (1992) for his original DICE model, Nordhaus (2017) for an update, and Nordhaus (2018) for a summary of changes to the model over time. Other prominent integrated assessment models introduced around the same time include the FUND model (Tol 1997, 2002) and the PAGE model (Hope, Anderson, and Wenman 1993; Hope 2006), which was used by the UK's prominent *Stern Review* (Stern 2007).

[10] Pindyck (2013) provides one trenchant critique. He asks, "What do the models tell us [about climate change policy]?" answering, "very little." Greenstone, Kopits, and Wolverton (2013) review the first official US estimates of the SCC. The NAS (2017) and Carleton and Greenstone (2022) provide recommendations for updating and improving them. More recent estimates have responded to such advice, beginning to incorporate the latest empirical research into the impacts of climate on agriculture, mortality, energy consumption, and sea-level rise (e.g., Rennert et al. 2022). On the sensitivity to discount rates, see the critiques of the *Stern Review* (Stern 2006) from Nordhaus (2007) and Weitzman (2007).

be credibly tied to the estimates. Perhaps illustrating this reality, actual carbon prices in the EU, California, and China are currently about $78, $28, and $8, respectively.[11]

2 Distributional Concerns

An equally difficult challenge for economic analyses of climate change is to account for inequities in its impacts. These inequities stem from three sources. First, temperature and precipitation patterns are expected to change unevenly. Second, even if there were only a uniform level of warming across the globe, the associated damages would still be uneven, with cold regions becoming more temperate and hot regions even hotter, and of course coastal regions more subject to flooding. This heterogeneity appears at both an international scale and a regional one, and overall likely poses greater burdens on the world's poor. Third, the costs of reducing greenhouse gasses from fossil fuels, agriculture, and deforestation also are sure to be borne differentially by different groups.[12]

Today's debates about climate change are not the first time that distributional concerns have become a point of contention in US environmental policy. As discussed in Chapter 8, around 1970 proposed revisions to benefit–cost analyses of water projects, led by disciples of the Harvard Water Program, would include distributional effects across regions as one of several objectives to be considered, alongside economic efficiency, whereas economists like Myrick Freeman and Robert Haveman proposed adjusting benefit–cost analysis with distributional weights at an individual level, with the poor receiving more weight. For neither the first time nor the last, these suggestions embroiled environmental economists in political controversy.

In the United States, debates about equity took a new turn in the 1980s, with the birth of the environmental justice movement. In 1978, 31,000 gallons of polychlorinated biphenyl (PCB), a potent toxin, were illegally dumped along 210 miles of roads in North Carolina. The state identified two sites for disposing the contaminated soil, a publicly owned landfill in Chatham County and a recently foreclosed property in Warren County. It selected the Warren County site, even though its physical characteristics

[11] SCC figures for Nordhaus and the *Stern Review* from Nordhaus (2007); US figures from Greenstone, Kopits, and Wolverton (2013) and Rennert et al. (2022); current cap-and-trade prices from World Bank (2022) as of September 2022.

[12] Burke, Hsiang, and Miguel (2015) and Sager (2019) document global inequities in damages and in abatement costs passed through to households, respectively.

were less suitable, with a shallow water table and with nearby residents reliant on well water. Given that 60 percent of Warren County's residents were Black and 25 percent were below the poverty line, whereas the corresponding figures for Chatham County were only 27 percent and 6 percent, many deduced that the selection procedure was biased by systemic racism. Residents began protesting the siting of the PCB landfill in 1982. These protests drew widespread support from civil rights groups and gained national media attention, raising awareness about the disproportionate pollution burden borne by minorities and the poor.

Since that episode, the academic environmental justice literature has grown alongside the movement.[13] Many activist scholars working in this area view economics as a threat, as a rival mode of thinking. In their mind, economic logic inevitably privileges efficiency over equity and justice, just as, one hundred years ago, it privileged material welfare over wilderness. Of course, most economists disagree. Many have advocated extending benefit–cost analysis of environmental regulations to account for distributional effects of policies, not only on the distribution of pollution but of costs and benefits as well. They argue that this fuller accounting is important because policies to clean up pollution may also burden local citizens with costs, if, for example, they trigger gentrification in local housing markets, harming renters who tend to be poorer than landlords. Some advocate simply documenting these effects in regulatory reviews and allowing the policy process to react, not unlike the Harvard Water Program's proposals. Others have advocated using social welfare functions or other methods of conducting weighted benefit–cost analysis, not unlike the proposals of Freeman and Haveman.[14]

In line with these proposals, US agencies are allowed and even encouraged to document distributional effects and incorporate them into their benefit–cost analyses. Nevertheless, while paying lip service to these ideals, they are yet to meaningfully incorporate distributional effects. The UK has gone somewhat farther than the US, explicitly recommending

[13] Bullard (1994) and UCC (1987) represent two prominent early studies. Mohai, Pellow, and Roberts (2009) and Banzhaf, Ma, and Timmins (2019) provide overviews of the environmental justice literature, the latter focusing on economic aspects. Hampson (2010) describes the Warren Co. episode.

[14] Multi-objective approaches such as documenting distributional impacts alongside conventional benefit–cost analysis have been suggested by many, including most prominently Stiglitz, Sen, and Fitoussi (2010). I also have suggested such an approach (Banzhaf 2011b). Adler (2016) and Fleurbaey and Abi-Rafeh (2016) discuss distributional weights in environmental policy analysis. Anthoff and Emmering (2019) propose a method for incorporating inequality aversion into the SCC.

distributional analyses in its "Green Book" guide, but, again, in practice such analyses continue to be rare.[15]

The United States may be slowly moving to make distributional effects an integral part of the analysis of regulations. Soon after his inauguration, President Biden issued an executive order on "modernizing regulatory review." In that order, he requested the Office of Information and Regulatory Affairs (OIRA), the administrative gatekeeper in charge of such reviews, to "propose procedures that take into account the distributional consequences of regulations ... so as to ensure that regulatory initiatives appropriately benefit and do not inappropriately burden disadvantaged, vulnerable, or marginalized communities." More recently, as of this writing, President Biden has nominated Richard Revesz as administrator of the OIRA. Revesz is a prominent advocate of considering distributional effects when evaluating environmental, health, and safety regulations, and he is likely to make them a priority in his efforts to modernize benefit–cost analysis.[16]

3 Environmental Accounting

A third area where pricing the environment is rapidly developing is augmented or "green" national income accounting. National income accounts like GDP are a gauge of a nation's economic health, and by extension economists and others sometimes interpret them as an indicator of welfare. Pigou referred to the concept as the "national dividend," and he explicitly interpreted it that way. Such welfare interpretations arise from the fact that GDP measures aggregate changes in production by adding together goods and services after first converting them to dollars using constant prices. Furthermore, according to neoclassical economic theory, these prices are equal to consumers' marginal willingness to pay, or value, for a good. By this logic, if GDP increases, consumers are better off because they value the new outputs more, on net.[17]

[15] For the US guidance, see OMB circulars A-94 and A-4 (OMB 1992, 1933). For UK guidance, see H.M. Treasury (2003). For an assessment of UK impact analyses in practice, see Zimmerman and Pye (2018). Germany has included distributional weights in its social costs (*Umweltbudesamt* 2020).

[16] The executive order can be found at www.whitehouse.gov/briefing-room/presidential-actions/2021/01/20/modernizing-regulatory-review/. For Revesz's previous recommendations, see, for example, Revesz (2018).

[17] Mathematically, GDP is a first order approximation to a change in welfare. See Pigou [1932] (1962) for his views on the national dividend.

Of course, such interpretations invite a cavalcade of criticisms. GDP does not include household work or other unpaid work, so, as Pigou admitted many years ago, "if a man marries his housekeeper or his cook, the national dividend is diminished."[18] GDP looks only at flows of expenditures and incomes, so if a natural disaster destroys a stock of assets, GDP could actually increase from the activity of rebuilding. And, similarly, GDP would increase from growth in economic output, even if it is accompanied by pollution that does damage greater than the value of the output it accompanies.

For these and other reasons, Simon Kuznets, a leading architect of GDP accounting in the 1930s, disavowed any welfare interpretation of GDP, viewing it only as an indicator of economic activity, though still a useful gauge of the health of the economy. But other economists have doubled down, trying to reform GDP to account for these deficiencies. John Hicks (1946) suggested an alternative account, now known as *Net* Domestic Product (NDP), which accounts for the depreciation of assets in such a way as to signal the sustainability of national income. That is, NDP accounts for *stocks* of wealth as well as for *flows* of outputs. Thus, for example, if output increased but only by running down factories in such a way as to diminish future output, NDP would essentially penalize GDP so as not to signal the unsustainable gain. Later, economists like Nordhaus and James Tobin (1973) began to suggest other ways to adjust even GDP in its measure of the flows, for such factors as household work and negative externalities like pollution.[19]

Triangulating on these two types of adjustments, the concept of "inclusive wealth" focuses on changes in assets, as in the NDP adjustments, but it includes among these assets "natural capital" such as the stocks of marketed natural resources, stocks of greenhouse gasses, and more intangible assets like ecosystem health. To integrate it into NDP, this natural capital would have to be monetized, a task that grows in complexity as we move from marketable assets like agricultural lands, forests, and mines, to nonmarket assets directly yielding marketed outputs, like fisheries, to nonmarket assets producing nonmarket ecosystem services.

18 Pigou [1932] (1962, p. 33). As noted in Ch. 7, there are intriguing parallels between feminist economics and environmental economics, one sometimes emphasizing the way national accounts privilege market work (traditional a man's domain) over nonmarket work (traditionally a woman's), the other emphasizing the way they privilege market good over nonmarket environmental goods. See, for example, Abraham and Mackie (2005) and Suh and Folbre (2017).

19 Kuznets (1948); Hicks (1946, Ch. 14). Nordhaus and Tobin (1973) provided a seminal example of household and externality adjustments.

Representing one early attempt to measure natural capital, in 1994 the US produced a satellite account that included depreciation of natural resources. Shortly afterward, however, Congress ordered such work suspended pending external review. In fact, a subsequent review by the National Academy of Sciences exonerated such accounts and recommended their expansion. Despite that recommendation – repeated by a second NAS review as well as by Nobel prize winners and other prominent economists – official work in the US on such accounts has stagnated. However, the logjam may now be broken, with the White House and Department of Commerce just releasing a new blueprint for constructing extensive natural capital accounts.[20]

Meanwhile, many other countries and international organizations have pursued a line of work leading to measures of green GDP and/or inclusive wealth. The United Nations' Millennium Ecosystem Assessment documented the tremendous changes humans have made to the earth, the resulting gains in human well-being, and the resulting degradation of ecosystem services and, hence, threats to future well-being. Since that assessment, the UN has adopted the System of Environmental Economic Accounting, an international standard for integrating natural capital and environmental services into national income accounts. Individual nations also have begun their own national ecosystem assessments leading to green accounts, with the UK's moves especially noteworthy.[21]

Each of these efforts entails a new leap in quantification and abstraction. First, although it inherently tries to make money and the environment commensurable, to date, environmental pricing has limited its sphere to the willingness to pay for environmental improvements or the cost of providing them, to make environmental policy more efficient. But if distributional analysis is incorporated, even efficiency and equity will be made commensurate in a common coin. Second, environmental pricing has largely taken place within the limited confines of particular resources in a particular place. In contrast, global climate change is just that – global, so optimal policies require global reach. In theory, the SCC is the same

[20] The initial effort can be found in US BEA (1994). NAS reports include Nordhaus and Kokkelenberg (1999) and Abraham and Mackie (2005). Other prominent calls include Arrow et al. (2004) and Stiglitz, Sen, and Fitoussi (2010). The new proposal can be found in OSTP et al. (2022).

[21] See Millennium Ecosystem Assessment (2005) and UN (2014, 2021), the latter representing two waves of accounting systems, one focused on traditional resources and a second expanded to ecosystems. For an international overview, see Schröter et al. (2016). On developments in the UK, see UK National Ecosystem Assessment (2011), Natural Capital Committee (2015), Bright, Connors, and Grice (2019), and Dasgupta (2021).

everywhere. By the same token, economically efficient abatement requires equating marginal abatement costs throughout the world, otherwise gains from international arbitrage would be left on the table. Finally, incorporating natural capital into national accounts would require tracking an entire inventory of all natural and environmental resources and pricing them, not just particular resources relevant to one particular policy question.

Scientists have dubbed our current geological epoch the Anthropocene, in recognition of humanity's impact on the globe. Alongside that accelerating impact, the extension of environmental markets and administrative pricing appears to be moving apace, in ways that neither Gifford Pinchot nor John Muir could have imagined at the turn of the twentieth century. Just as when the God Committee hearings decided the fate of the snail darter, the answers economists are devising for environmental questions may continue to surprise.

References

Abraham, C., and J. Thedié. 1960. "*Le prix d'une vie humaine dans les decisions economiques.*" *Revue Francaise de Recherche Operationnelle* 4: 157–68.

Abraham, Katharine G., and Christopher Mackie, eds. 2005. *Beyond the Market: Designing Nonmarket Accounts for the United States*. National Research Council, Committee on National Statistics. Washington, DC: National Academies Press.

Adelman, Irma, and Zvi Griliches. 1961. "On an Index of Quality Change." *Journal of the American Statistical Association* 56: 535–48.

Adler, Matthew D. 2016. "Benefit-Cost Analysis and Distributional Weights: An Overview." *Review of Environmental Economics and Policy* 10(2): 264–85.

Alacevich, Michele. 2020. "Paul Rosenstein-Rodan and the Birth of Development Economics." CHOPE Working Paper 2020-04.

Alchian, A.A., G.D. Bodenhorn, S. Enke, C.H. Hitch, J. Hirshleifer, and A.W. Marshall. 1951. "What is the Best System?" Jan. 4. RA D-860.

Allin, Bushrod W. 1953. "Is Group Choice Part of Economics?" *The Quarterly Journal of Economics* 67(3): 362–79.

Amadae, S.M. 2003. *Rationalizing Capitalist Democracy: The Cold War Origins of Rational Choice Liberalism*. Chicago: University of Chicago Press.

American Association of State Highway Officials. 1951. *A Policy on Road User Benefit Analyses for Highway Improvements*. Part I. Passenger Cars in Rural Areas.

Anderson, Terry L., and Peter J. Hill. 2004. *The Not So Wild, Wild West: Property Rights on the Frontier*. Stanford: Stanford University Press.

Andersson, Julius J. 2019. "Carbon Taxes and CO_2 Emissions: Sweden as a Case Study." *American Economic Journal: Economic Policy* 11(4): 1–30.

Anthoff, David, and Johannes Emmerling. 2019. "Inequality and the Social Cost of Carbon." *Journal of the Association of Environmental and Resource Economists* 6(2): 243–73.

Arrow, Kenneth J. 1969. "The Organization of Economic Activity: Issues Pertinent to the Choice of Market versus Non-Market Allocation." In *The Analysis and Evaluation of Public Expenditures: The PPB System*, 47–64. US Congress, Joint Economic Committee. Washington, DC: US Government Printing Office.

Arrow, Kenneth J., and Anthony C. Fisher. 1974. "Environmental Preservation, Uncertainty, and Irreversibility." *Quarterly Journal of Economics* 88(2): 312–19.

Arrow, Kenneth J., Maureen L. Cropper, George C. Eads, Robert W. Hahn, et al. 1996. "Is There a Role for Benefit-Cost Analysis in Environmental, Health, and Safety Regulation?" *Science* 272(5259): 221–22.

Arrow, Kenneth, Partha Dasgupta, Lawrence Goulder, Gretchen Daily, et al. 2004. "Are We Consuming Too Much?" *Journal of Economic Perspectives* 18(3): 147–72.

Arrow, Kenneth, Robert Solow, Paul R. Portney, Edward E. Leamer, Roy Radner, and Howard Schuman. 1993. "NOAA Panel on Contingent Valuation." 15 CFR Chapter IX, *Federal Register* 58: 4601–14.

Ashenfelter, Orley. 2006. "Measuring the Value of a Statistical Life: Problems and Prospects." *Economic Journal* 116: C10–C23.

Ashton, Peter M., Leonard A. Shabman, and Catherine Cooper-Ruska. 1976. "A Legal-Historical Analysis of Navigation User Charges." *Journal of the Water Resources Planning and Management Division* 102(1): 89–100.

Aslanbeigui, Nahid, and Guy Oakes. 2015. *Arthur Cecil Pigou*. London: Palgrave Macmillan.

Association of Environmental and Resource Economists (AERE). 1995. *Membership Handbook*. https://aere.memberclicks.net/assets/docs/handbook2016_000.pdf

Ayres, Robert U., and Allen V. Kneese. 1969. "Production, Consumption, and Externalities." *American Economic Review* 59(3): 282–97.

Ayres, Robert U., Jeroen Van den Berrgh, and John Gowdy. 2001. "Strong Versus Weak Sustainability: Economics, Natural Sciences, and Consilience." *Environmental Ethics* 23(2): 155–68.

Azzi, Cory F., and James C. Cox. 1973. "Equity and Efficiency in Evaluation of Public Programs." *Quarterly Journal of Economics* 87: 495–502.

Backhouse, Roger E. 2017. "From Business Cycle Theory to the Theory of Employment: Alvin Hansen and Paul Samuelson." *Journal of the History of Economic Thought* 39(1): 89–99.

Backhouse, Roger E., and Jeff Biddle. 2000. "The Concept of Applied Economics: A History of Ambiguity and Multiple Meanings." In *Toward a History of Applied Economics*, ed. by Roger E. Backhouse and Jeff Biddle. *History of Political Economy* 32(S): 1–24. Durham: Duke University Press.

Backhouse, Roger E., and Béatrice Cherrier. 2017. "The Age of the Applied Economist: The Transformation of Economics since the 1970s." In *The Age of the Applied Economist: The Transformation of Economics since the 1970s*, ed. by Roger E. Backhouse and Béatrice Cherrier. *History of Political Economy* 49(S): 1–33. Durham: Duke University Press.

Backhouse, Roger E., and Steve G. Medema. 2009a. "Defining Economics: The Long Road to Acceptance of the Robbins Definition." *Economica* 76: 805–20.

Backhouse, Roger E., and Steven G. Medema. 2009b. "Retrospectives: On the Definition of Economics." *Journal of Economic Perspectives* 23(1): 221–33.

Backhouse, Roger E., Bradley Bateman, and Steven Medema. 2010. "The Reception of Marshall in the United States." In *The Impact of Alfred Marshall's Ideas*, ed. by Tiziano Raffaelli, Giacomo Becattini, Katia Caldari, and Marco Dardi, 59–80. Cheltenham, UK: Edward Elgar.

Bailey, Martin J. 1956. "The Welfare Cost of Inflationary Finance." *Journal of Political Economy* 64(2): 93–110.

Bailey, Martin J. 1968. "Comments." In *Problems in Public Expenditure Analysis*, ed. by Samuel B. Chase, Jr., 162–66. Washington, DC: Brookings.

Balisciano, Márcia L. 1998. "Hope for America: American Notions of Economic Planning between Pluralism and Neoclassicism, 1930–1950." In *From Interwar Pluralism to Postwar Neoclassicism*, ed. by Mary S. Morgan and Malcolm Rutherford. *History of Political Economy* 30(S): 153–78. Durham: Duke University Press.

Balogh, Brian. 2002. "Scientific Forestry and the Roots of the Modern American State: Gifford Pinchot's Path to Progressive Reform." *Environmental History* 7(2): 198–225.

Banzhaf, H. Spencer. 2000. "Productive Nature and the Net Product: Quesnay's Economies Animal and Political." *History of Political Economy* 32(3): 517–51.

Banzhaf, H. Spencer. 2001. "Quantifying the Qualitative: Quality-Adjusted Price Indexes, 1915–1961." In *The Age of Economic Measurement*, ed. by Judy L. Klein and Mary S. Morgan. *History of Political Economy* 33(S): 345–70. Durham: Duke University Press.

Banzhaf, H. Spencer. 2004. "The Form and Function of Price Indexes: An Historical Accounting." *History of Political Economy* 36(4): 589–616.

Banzhaf, H. Spencer. 2005. "Green Price Indices." *Journal of Environmental Economics and Management* 49(2): 262–80.

Banzhaf, H. Spencer. 2006. "The Other Economics Department: Demand and Value Theory in Early Agricultural Economics." In *Agreement on Demand: The History of 20th Century Demand Theory*, ed. by Philip Mirowski and D. Wade Hands. *History of Political Economy* 38(S): 9–31. Durham: Duke University Press.

Banzhaf, H. Spencer. 2010a. "The Chicago School of Welfare Economics." In *The Elgar Companion to the Chicago School*, ed. by Ross Emmett, 59–69. Cheltenham, UK: Edward Elgar.

Banzhaf, H. Spencer. 2010b. "The Free Market Environmentalist Case for Cap and Trade." Working Paper, Property and Environment Research Center.

Banzhaf, H. Spencer. 2011a. "Consumer Sovereignty in the History of Environmental Economics." *History of Political Economy* 43(2): 339–45.

Banzhaf, H. Spencer. 2011b. "Regulatory Impact Analyses of Environmental Justice Effects." *Journal of Land Use and Environmental Law* 27(1): 1–30.

Banzhaf, H. Spencer. 2020. "The Conservative Roots of Carbon Pricing." *National Affairs*.

Banzhaf, H. Spencer. 2022. "Financing Outdoor Recreation: An Introduction." *Land Economics* 98(3): 421–27.

Banzhaf, H. Spencer, Timothy Fitzgerald, and Kurt Schnier. 2013. "Nonregulatory Approaches to the Environment: Coasean and Pigouvian Perspectives." *Review of Environmental Economics and Policy* 7(2): 238–58.

Banzhaf, Spencer, Lala Ma, and Christopher Timmins. 2019. "Environmental Justice: The Economics of Race, Place, and Pollution." *Journal of Economic Perspectives* 33(1): 185–208.

Barber, William J. 1985. *From New Era to New Deal: Herbert Hoover, the Economists, and American Economic Policy, 1921–1933*. Cambridge: Cambridge University Press.

Barbier, Edward B. 2011. *Capitalizing on Nature: Ecosystems as Natural Assets*. Cambridge: Cambridge University Press.

Barbier, Edward B. 2021. "The Evolution of Economic Views on Natural Resource Scarcity." *Review of Environmental Economics and Policy* 15(1): 24–44.

Barlow, E.J. 1950. "Preliminary Proposal for Air Defense Study." October. RA D(L)-816-2.

Barnett, Harold J., and Chandler Morse. 1963. *Scarcity and Growth: The Economics of Natural Resource Availability*. Baltimore: The Johns Hopkins Press for Resources for the Future.

Bateman, Bradley W. 1998. "Clearing the Ground: The Demise of the Social Gospel Movement and the Rise of Neoclassicism in American Economics." In *From Interwar Pluralism to Postwar Neoclassicism*, ed. by Mary S. Morgan and Malcolm Rutherford. *History of Political Economy* 30(S): 29–52. Durham: Duke University Press.

Bateman, Bradley W., and Ethan B. Kapstein. 1999. "Retrospectives: Between God and the Market: The Religious Roots of the American Economic Association." *Journal of Economic Perspectives* 13(4): 249–58.

Bateman, Ian J., Amii R. Harwood, Georgina M. Mace, Robert T. Watson, et al. 2013. "Bringing Ecosystem Services into Economic Decision-Making: Land Use in the United Kingdom." *Science* 341(6141): 45–50.

Bator, Francis M. 1957. "The Simple Analytics of Welfare Maximization." *American Economic Review* 47(1): 22–59.

Bator, Francis M. 1958. "The Anatomy of Market Failure." *Quarterly Journal of Economics* 71(3): 351–79.

Baumol, William J. [1952] 1965. *Welfare Economics and the Theory of the State*. Cambridge, MA: Harvard University Press.

Baumol, William J. 1970. "Review of *Cost and Choice*, by James M. Buchanan." *Journal of Economic Literature* 8(4): 1210–11.

Baumol, William J., and Wallace E. Oates. 1971. "The Use of Standards and Prices for Protection of the Environment." *Scandinavian Journal of Economics* 73(1): 42–54.

Baumol, William J., and Wallace E. Oates. 1975. *The Theory of Environmental Policy*. Englewood Cliffs: Prentice-Hall.

Becker, Gary S. 1965. "A Theory of the Allocation of Time." *Economic Journal* 75: 493–517.

Becker, Gary S. 1976. *The Economic Approach to Human Behavior*. Chicago: University of Chicago Press.

Beckmann, Martin J., and Thomas Marschak. 1955. "An Economic Approach to Location Theory." *Kyklos* 8(2): 109–22.

Beckmann, Martin J., C. B. McGuire, and Christopher B. Winsten. 1956. *Studies in the Economics of Transportation*. New Haven: Yale University Press.

Bennett, Brett. 2015. *Plantations and Protected Areas: A Global History of Forest Management*. Cambridge, MA: MIT Press.

Berkman, Richard L., and W. Kip Viscusi. 1973. *Damming the West*. Ralph Nader's Study Group Report on the Bureau of Reclamation. New York: Grossman Publishers.

Berman, Elizabeth Popp. 2017. "From Economic to Social Regulation: How the Deregulatory Moment Strengthened Economists' Policy Position." In *The Age of the Applied Economist: The Transformation of Economics since the 1970s*, ed. by Roger E. Backhouse and Béatrice Cherrier. *History of Political Economy* 49(S): 187–212. Durham: Duke University Press.

Berman, Elizabeth Popp. 2022. *Thinking Like an Economist: How Efficiency Replaced Equality in US Public Policy*. Princeton: Princeton University Press.

Berta, Nathalie. 2017. "On the Definition of Externality as a Missing Market." *European Journal of the History of Economic Thought* 24(2): 287–318.

Berta, Nathalie. 2019. "The History of Incentives in Environmental Economics." In *Incentives and Environmental Policies: From Theory to Empirical Novelties*, ed. by Benjamin Ouvrard and Anne Stenger, 31–54. London: ISTE.

Berta, Nathalie. 2020. "Efficiency without Optimality: A Pragmatic Compromise for Environmental Policies in the Late 1960s." *Journal of the History of Economic Thought* 42(4): 539–62.

Berta, Nathalie. 2021. "A Note on John Dales and the Early History of Emissions Trading: Mixing Standards and Markets for Rights." *Cahiers d'économie politique* 79(1): 61–84.

Berta, Nathalie, and Elodie Bertrand. 2014. "Market Internalization of Externalities: What is Failing?" *Journal of the History of Economic Thought* 36(3): 331–57.

Bertrand, Elodie. 2015. "From the Firm to Economic Policy: The Problem of Coase's Cost." *History of Political Economy* 47(3): 481–510.

Bianchi, Marina. 1998. "Tastes for Novelty and Novel Tastes: The Role of Human Agency in Consumption." In *The Active Consumer: Novelty and Surprise in Consumer Choice*, ed. by Marina Bianchi, 64–86. London: Routledge.

Bianchi, Marina, and Neil De Marchi. 1997. "The Taste-Less Theory of Consumer Choice Meets Novelty." In *Pluralism in Economics*, ed. by Andrea Salanti and Ernesto Screpanti, 177–90. Cheltenham, UK: Edward Elgar.

Biddle, Jeff. 2021. "Statistical Inference in Economics in the 1920s and 1930s: The Crop and Livestock Forecasts of the U.S. Department of Agriculture." In *Exploring the History of Statistical Inference in Economics*, ed. by Jeff Biddle and Marcel Boumans. *History of Political Economy* 53(S): 53–80. Durham: Duke University Press.

Bilmes, Linda, and Joseph Stiglitz. 2006. "The Economic Costs of the Iraq War: An Appraisal Three Years after the Beginning of the Conflict." NBER Working Paper 12054.

Bishop, Richard C., and Thomas Heberlein. 1979. "Measuring Values of Extra-Market Goods: Are Indirect Measures Biased?" *American Journal of Agricultural Economics* 61(5): 926–30.

Bishop, Richard C., Kevin J. Boyle, Richard T. Carson, David Chapman, et al. 2017. "Putting a Value on Injuries to Natural Assets: The BP Oil Spill." *Science* 356(6335): 253–54.

Blomquist, Glenn C. 2015. "Value of Life, Economics of." In *International Encyclopedia of Social and Behavioral Sciences*, ed. by James D. Wright, 2nd ed., 16133–39. Oxford: Elsevier.

Bohm, Peter. 1972. "Estimating Demand for Public Goods: An Experiment." *European Economic Review* 3(2): 111–30.

Boianovsky, Mauro, and Kevin D. Hoover. 2009. "The Neoclassical Growth Model and Twentieth-Century Economics." In *Robert Solow and the Development of Growth Economics*, ed. by Mauro Boianovsky and Kevin D. Hoover. *History of Political Economy* 41(S): 1–23. Durham: Duke University Press.

Bouk, Dan. 2015. *How Our Days Became Numbered: Risk and the Rise of the Statistical Individual.* Chicago: University of Chicago Press.

Boulding, Kenneth E. 1945. "The Consumption Concept in Economic Theory." *American Economic Review* 35(2): 1–14.

Boulding, Kenneth E. 1955. *Economic Analysis*, 3rd ed. New York: Harper Brothers.

Boulding, Kenneth E. 1966. "The Economics of the Coming Spaceship Earth." In *Environmental Quality in a Growing Economy*, ed. by Henry Jarrett, 3–14. Baltimore: The Johns Hopkins Press for Resources for the Future.

Boulier, Bryan L., and Robert S. Goldfarb. 1998. "On the Use and Nonuse of Surveys in Economics." *Journal of Economic Methodology* 5(1): 1–21.

Boumans, Marcel J. 2005. *How Economists Model the World into Numbers*. New York: Routledge.

Boumans, Marcel J. 2009. "Observations of an Expert." History of Observation in Economics Working Paper Series, Working Paper #4.

Bowers, Edward A. 1891. "The Present Condition of the Forests on Public Lands." *Publications of the American Economic Association* 6(3): 57–74.

Bowes, Michael D., and John V. Krutilla. 1985. "Multiple Use Management of Public Forestland." In *Handbook of Natural Resource and Energy Economics*, Vol. 2, ed. by Allen V. Kneese and James L. Sweeney, 531–69. Amsterdam: Elsevier.

Bowley, Arthur L. 1920. "Cost of Living and Wage Determination." *Economic Journal* 30(117): 114–17.

Boyd, James, and H. Spencer Banzhaf. 2007. "What are Ecosystem Services? The Need for Standardized Environmental Accounting Units." *Ecological Economics* 63(2–3): 616–26.

Breit, William, and Barry T. Hirsch, eds. 2009. "Thomas C. Schelling." In *The Lives of the Laureates*, 5th ed., 393–420. Cambridge, MA: MIT Press.

Bright, Geoff, Emily Connors, and Joe Grice. 2019. "Measuring Natural Capital: Towards Accounts for the UK and a Basis for Improved Decision-Making." *Oxford Review of Economic Policy* 35(1): 88–108.

Bromley, Daniel W., and Bruce R. Beattie. 1973. "On the Incongruity of Program Objectives and Project Evaluation: An Example from the Reclamation Program." *American Journal of Agricultural Economics* 55: 472–76.

Bromley, Daniel W., A. Allan Schmid, and William B. Lord. 1971. "Public Water Resource Project Planning and Evaluation." Center for Resource Policy Studies and Programs, The University of Wisconsin.

Brooks, David. 2000. *Bobos in Paradise: The New Upper Class and How They Got There*. New York: Simon and Schuster.

Brooks, Karl Boyd. 2006. *Public Power, Private Dams: The Hells Canyon High Dam Controversy*. Seattle: University of Washington Press.

Brookshire, David S., Alan Randall, and John R. Stoll. 1980. "Valuing Increments and Decrements in Natural Resource Service Flows." *American Journal of Agricultural Economics* 62(3): 478–88.

Broome, John. 1978. "Trying to Value a Life." *Journal of Public Economics* 9: 91–100.

Brown, William G., Ajmer Singh, and Emery N. Castle. 1962. "An Economic Evaluation of the Oregon Salmon and Steelhead Sport Fishery." Agricultural Experiment Station, Corvallis, OR.

Bruni, Luigino, and Robert Sugden. 2007. "The Road Not Taken: How Psychology Was Removed from Economics, and How It Might Be Brought Back." *Economic Journal* 117: 146–73.

Buchanan, James M., and W.M. Craig Stubblebine. 1962. "Externality." *Economica* 29: 371–84.

Bullard, Robert D. 1994. *Dumping in Dixie: Race, Class, and Environmental Quality*, 2nd ed. Boulder: Westview Press.

Burke, Marshall, Solomon M. Hsiang, and Edward Miguel. 2015. "Global Non-Linear Effect of Temperature on Economic Production." *Nature* 527: 235–39.

Burt, Oscar R., and Durward Brewer. 1971. "Estimation of Net Social Benefits from Outdoor Recreation." *Econometrica* 39: 813–27.

Callicott, J. Baird. 1989. *In Defense of the Land Ethic*. Albany: State University of New York Press.

Callicott, J. Baird. 1994. "A Brief History of American Conservation Philosophy." In *Sustainable Ecological Systems*, ed. by W. Wallace Covington and Leonard F. Debano, 10–14. Fort Collins: Rocky Mountain Forest & Range Experiment Station.

Callicott, J. Baird. 1999. *Beyond the Land Ethic*. Albany: State University of New York Press.

Callon, Michel. 1998. "Introduction: The Embeddedness of Economic Markets in Economics." In *The Laws of Markets*, ed. by Michel Callon, 1–57. Oxford: Blackwell.

Cameron, Trudy Ann. 2010. "Euthanizing the Value of a Statistical Life." *Review of Environmental Economics and Policy* 4: 161–78.

Cannan, Edwin. 1922. *Wealth: A Brief Explanation of the Causes of Economic Welfare*, 2nd ed. London: P.S. King & Son.

Carleton, Tamma, and Michael Greenstone. 2022. "A Guide to Updating the US Government's Social Cost of Carbon." *Review of Environmental Economics and Policy* 16(2): 196–218.

Carlson, Jack. 1963. *Valuation of Life Saving*. Dissertation, Harvard University.

Carson, Richard T. 2011. *Contingent Valuation: A Comprehensive Bibliography and History*. Cheltenham, UK: Edward Elgar.

Carson, Richard T., and W. Michael Hanemann. 2005. "Contingent Valuation." In *Handbook of Environmental Economics*, ed. by Karl-Göran Mäler and Jeffrey Vincent, 821–936. Amsterdam: Elsevier.

Carson, Richard T., Robert C. Mitchell, Michael Hanemann, Raymond J. Kopp, Stanley Presser, and Paul A. Ruud. 2003. "Contingent Valuation and Lost Passive Use: Damages from the Exxon Valdez Oil Spill." *Environmental and Resource Economics* 25(3): 257–86.

Carvalho, Jean-Paul. 2007. "An Interview with Thomas Schelling." *Oxonomics* 2: 1–8.

Cason, Timothy N., and Charles R. Plott. 2014. "Misconceptions and Game Form Recognition: Challenges to Theories of Revealed Preference and Framing." *Journal of Political Economy* 122(6): 1235–70.

Castle, Emery N. 1965. "The Market Mechanism, Externalities, and Land Economics." *Journal of Farm Economics* 47(3): 542–56.

Castle, Emery N. 1969. "Testimony Presented to the Water Resources Council Hearing in Portland, Oregon." Aug. 11. AMP 79.

Castle, Emery N., and Russell C. Youmans. 1968. "Economics in Regional Water Research and Policy." *American Journal of Agricultural Economics* 50: 1655–70.

Castle, Emery N., and Russell C. Youmans. 1970. "Economics in Regional Water Research and Policy: Reply." *American Journal of Agricultural Economics* 52: 145–46.

Castle, Emery N., Maurice M. Kelso, and Delworth Gardner. 1963. "Water Resources Development: A Review of New Federal Evaluation Procedures." *Journal of Farm Economics* 45: 693–704.

Castle, Emery N., Maurice M. Kelso, Joe B. Stevens, and Herbert H. Stoevener. 1981. "Natural Resource Economics, 1946–75." In *A Survey of Agricultural Economics Literature*, vol. 3, ed. by Lee R. Martin, 393–500. Minneapolis: University of Minnesota Press.

Cherrier, Beatrice, and Jean-Baptiste Fleury. 2017. "Economists' Interest in Collective Decision after World War II: A History." *Public Choice* 172(1): 23–44.

Christensen, Paul P. 1989. "Historical Roots for Ecological Economics: Biophysical vs. Allocative Approaches." *Ecological Economics* 1: 17–36.

Cicchetti, Charles J., and V. Kerry Smith. 1970. "A Noted on Jointly Supplied Mixed Goods." *Quarterly Review of Economics and Business* 10(3): 90–94.

Cicchetti, Charles J., and V. Kerry Smith. 1973. "Congestion, Quality Deterioration, and Optimal Use: Wilderness Recreation in the Spanish Peaks Primitive Area." *Social Science Research* 2: 15–30.

Cicchetti, Charles J., Robert K. Davis, Steve H. Hanke, and Robert H. Haveman. 1973. "Evaluating Federal Water Projects: A Critique of Proposed Standards." *Science* 181(4101): 723–28.

Cicchetti, Charles J., Anthony C. Fisher, and V. Kerry Smith. 1976. "An Econometric Evaluation of a Generalized Consumer Surplus Measure: The Mineral King Controversy." *Econometrica* 44(6): 1259–76.

Ciriacy-Wantrup, S.V. 1947. "Capital Returns from Soil Conservation Practices." *Journal of Farm Economics* 29: 1181–96.

Ciriacy-Wantrup, S.V. 1956. "Concepts Used as Economic Criteria for a System of Water Rights." *Land Economics* 32(4): 295–312.

Ciriacy-Wantrup, S.V., and Richard C. Bishop. 1975. "'Common Property' as a Concept in Natural Resource Policy." *Natural Resources Journal* 15(4): 713–27.

Clark, John Maurice. 1936. *Preface to Social Economics.* Ed. by Moses Abramovitz and Eli Ginzberg. New York: Farrar and Rinehart.

Clark, John Maurice, Eugene L. Grant, and Maurice M. Kelso. 1952. *Report of Panel of Consultants on Secondary or Indirect Benefits of Water Use Projects.* Submitted to the Bureau of Reclamation.

Clawson, Marion. 1951. *Uncle Sam's Acres.* New York: Dodd, Mead & Company.

Clawson, Marion. 1958. *Statistics on Outdoor Recreation.* Washington, DC: Resources for the Future.

Clawson, Marion. 1959a. "The Crisis in Outdoor Recreation." *American Forests*, March-April. Reproduced as RFF Reprint #13.

Clawson, Marion. 1959b. "Methods of Measuring the Demand for and Value of Outdoor Recreation." Paper presented at a meeting of the Taylor-Hibbard Club, University of Wisconsin, Jan. 13. Reproduced as RFF Reprint #10.

Clawson, Marion. 1981. *New Deal Planning: The NRPB.* Baltimore: The Johns Hopkins Press for Resources for the Future.

Clawson, Marion. 1987. *From Sagebrush to Sage: The Making of a Natural Resource Economist.* Washington, DC: Ana Publications.

Clawson, Marion, and Jack L. Knetsch. 1963. "Outdoor Recreation Research: Some Concepts and Suggested Areas of Study." Paper presented to the National Conference on Outdoor Recreation Research, Ann Arbor, MI. Reproduced as RFF Reprint #43.

Clawson, Marion, and Jack L. Knetsch. 1966. *Economics of Outdoor Recreation.* Baltimore: The Johns Hopkins Press for Resources for the Future.

Coase, R.H. 1937. "The Nature of the Firm." *Economica* 4: 386–405.

Coase, R.H. 1959. "The Federal Communications Commission." *Journal of Law and Economics* 2: 1–40.

Coase, R.H. 1960. "The Problem of Social Cost." *Journal of Law and Economics* 3: 1–44.

Coates, Peter. 1998. *Nature: Western Attitudes since Ancient Times*. Berkeley: University of California Press.
Cobb, Gary D. 1973. "Evolving Water Policies in the United States." *American Journal of Agricultural Economics* 55: 1003–7.
Coffin, William G. 1863. Document No. 32. *Report of the Commissioner of Indian Affairs for 1862*. Washington, DC: Government Printing Office.
Cohen, Jon S., and Martin L. Weitzman. 1975. "A Marxian Model of Enclosures." *Journal of Development Economics* 1(4): 287–336.
Cohen, Lizabeth. 2003. *A Consumers' Republic: The Politics of Mass Consumption in Postwar America*. New York: Alfred A. Knopf.
Collard, David. 1996. "Pigou and Future Generations: A Cambridge Tradition." *Cambridge Journal of Economics* 20(5): 585–97.
Collins, Robert M. 1990. "The Emergence of Economic Growthmanship in the United States: Federal Policy and Economic Knowledge in the Truman Years." In *The State and Economic Knowledge*, ed. Mary O. Furner and Barry Supple, 138–70. Cambridge: Cambridge University Press.
Coman, Katharine. [1911] 2011. "Some Unsettled Problems of Irrigation." *American Economic Review* 1(1): 1–19. Republished in vol. 101(1): 36–48.
Costanza, Robert, Ralph d'Arge, Rudolf De Groot, Stephen Farber, et al. 1997. "The Value of The World's Ecosystem Services and Natural Capital." *Nature* 387(6630): 253–60.
Costanza, Robert, Stephen C. Farber, and Judith Maxwell. 1989. "Valuation and Management of Wetlands Ecosystems." *Ecological Economics* 1: 335–61.
Costanza, Robert, Rudolf de Groot, Paul Sutton, Sander Van der Ploeg, et al. 2014. "Changes in the Global Value of Ecosystem Services." *Global Environmental Change* 26: 152–58.
Coy, Peter. 1997. "The In Your Face Economist." *Businessweek*. Accessed at www.bloomberg.com/news/articles/1997-06-29/the-in-your-face-economist.
Crabbé, Philippe J. 1983. "The Contribution of L.C. Gray to the Economic Theory of Exhaustible Natural Resources and Its Roots in the History of Economic Thought." *Journal of Environmental Economics and Management* 10: 195–220.
Craver, Earlene. 1986. "Patronage and the Directions of Research in Economics: The Rockefeller Foundation in Europe, 1924–38." *Minerva* 24: 205–22.
Crocker, Thomas D. 1966. "The Structuring of Atmospheric Pollution Control Systems." In *The Economics of Air Pollution*, ed. by Harold Wolozin, 61–86. New York: W.W. Norton & Co.
Crocker, Thomas D. 1967. *Some Economics of Air Pollution Control*. Dissertation, University of Missouri.
Crocker, Thomas D. 1968. "Some Economics of Air Pollution Control." *Natural Resources Journal* 8(2): 236–58.
Crocker, Thomas D. 1972. "On Air Pollution Control Instruments," *Loyola of Los Angeles Law Review* 5: 280–97.
Crocker, Thomas D. 2011. "Trading Access to and Use of the Natural Environment: The Multiple Origins of 'Cap and Trade'." Working paper, University of Wyoming.
Cronon, William. 1995. "The Trouble with Wilderness; or, Getting Back to the Wrong Nature." In *Uncommon Ground: Toward Reinventing Nature*, ed. by William Cronon, 69–90. New York: W.W. Norton.

Cropper, Maureen, James K. Hammitt, and Lisa A. Robinson. 2011. "Valuing Mortality Risk Reductions: Progress and Challenges." *Annual Review of Resource Economics* 3: 313–36.

Crutchfield, James A. 1962. "Valuation of Fishery Resources." *Land Economics* 38: 145–54.

Cummings, Ronald G., David S. Brookshire, and William D. Schulze, eds. 1986. *Valuing Environmental Goods: An Assessment of the Contingent Valuation Method*. Totowa, NJ: Rowman & Allanheld.

Currie, John Martin, John A. Murphy, and Andrew Schmitz. 1971. "The Concept of Economic Surplus and Its Use in Economic Analysis." *Economic Journal* 81: 741–99.

Currie, Lauchlin, and Roger Sandilands. 1997. "Implications of an Endogenous Theory of Growth in Allyn Young's Macroeconomic Concept of Increasing Returns." *History of Political Economy* 29(3): 413–43.

Daily, Gretchen C., ed. 1997. *Nature's Services: Society's Dependence on Natural Ecosystems*. Washington, DC: Island Press.

Dales, J.H. 1968a. "Land, Water, and Ownership." *Canadian Journal of Economics* 1(4): 791–804.

Dales, J.H. 1968b. *Pollution, Property, and Prices*. Toronto: University of Toronto Press.

Darmstadter, Joel. 2003. "Hans H. Landsberg and Sam H. Schurr: Reflections and Appreciation." *Energy Journal* 24(4): 1–16.

Dasgupta, Partha. 2021. *The Economics of Biodiversity: The Dasgupta Review*. London: HM Treasury.

Dasgupta, Partha, Stephen Marglin, and Amartya Sen. 1972. *Guidelines for Project Evaluation*. New York: United Nations.

Daston, Lorraine. 1998. "The Nature of Nature in Early Modern Europe." *Configurations* 6: 149–72.

Davidson, Paul, F. Gerard Adams, and Joseph Seneca. 1966. "The Social Value of Water Recreational Facilities Resulting from an Improvement in Water Quality: The Delaware Estuary." In *Water Research*, ed. by Allen V. Kneese, 175–211. Baltimore: The Johns Hopkins Press for Resources for the Future.

Davis, Otto A., and Andrew Whinston. 1962. "Externalities, Welfare, and the Theory of Games." *Journal of Political Economy* 70(3): 241–62.

Davis, Robert K. 1963a. *The Value of Outdoor Recreation: An Economic Study of the Maine Woods*. Dissertation, Harvard University.

Davis, Robert K. 1963b. "Recreation Planning as an Economic Problem." *Natural Resources Journal* 3: 239–49.

Davis, Robert K. 1968. *The Range of Choice in Water Management: A Study of Dissolved Oxygen in the Potomac Estuary*. Baltimore: The Johns Hopkins Press for Resources for the Future.

Dawson, John A. 1957. *The Demand for Irrigation Water in the Ainsworth Area of Nebraska*. PhD Dissertation, University of Chicago.

De Haven, James C., and Jack Hirshleifer. 1957. "Feather River Water for Southern California." *Land Economics* 33: 198–209.

Debates in the Massachusetts Constitutional Convention 1917–1918. 1919. Boston: Wright and Potter.

Demsetz, Harold. 1969. "Information and Efficiency: Another Viewpoint." *Journal of Law and Economics* 12(1): 1–22.

Deschênes, Olivier, Michael Greenstone, and Joseph S. Shapiro. 2017. "Defensive Investments and the Demand for Air Quality: Evidence from the NOx Budget program." *American Economic Review* 107(10): 2958–89.

Desmarais-Tremblay, Maxime. 2017a. "Musgrave, Samuelson, and the Crystallization of the Standard Rationale for Public Goods." *History of Political Economy* 49(1): 59–92.

Desmarais-Tremblay, Maxime. 2017b. "A Genealogy of the Concept of Merit Wants." *European Journal of the History of Economic Thought* 24(3): 409–40.

Desmarais-Tremblay, Maxime. 2020. "W.H. Hutt and the Conceptualization of Consumer Sovereignty." *Oxford Economic Papers* 72(4): 1050–71.

DesRoches, C. Tyler. 2015. *The World as a Garden: A Philosophical Analysis of Natural Capital in Economics*. PhD Dissertation, University of British Columbia

DesRoches, C. Tyler. 2018a. "On the Historical Roots of Natural Capital in the Writings of Carl Linnaeus." *Research in the History of Economic Thought and Methodology* 36C: 103–17.

DesRoches, C. Tyler. 2018b. "What is *Natural* about Natural Capital during the Anthropocene?" *Sustainability* 10. https://doi.org/10.3390/su10030806.

Desrosières, Alain. 1998. *The Politics of Large Numbers: A History of Statistical Reasoning*. Cambridge, MA: Harvard University Press.

Desvousges, William H., F. Reed Johnson, Richard W. Dunford, Kevin J. Boyle, Sara P. Hudson, and K. Nicole Wilson. 1993. "Measuring Natural Resource Damages with Contingent Valuation: Tests of Validity and Responsibility." In *Contingent Valuation: A Critical Assessment*, ed. by Jerry A. Hausman, 91–164. Amsterdam: North Holland.

Devons, Ely. 1961. *Essays in Economics*. London: Allen & Unwin.

Diamond, Peter A., and Jerry A. Hausman. 1994. "Contingent Valuation: Is Some Number Better than No Number?" *Journal of Economic Perspectives* 8(4): 45–64.

Diamond, Peter A., Jerry A. Hausman, Gregory K. Leonard, and Mike A. Denning. 1993. "Does Contingent Valuation Measure Preferences? Experimental Evidence." In *Contingent Valuation: A Critical Assessment*, ed. by Jerry A. Hausman, 41–90. Amsterdam: North Holland.

Dorfman, Robert, ed. 1965. *Measuring Benefits of Government Investments*. Washington, DC: Brookings Institution.

Dorfman, Robert. 1953. "Mathematical, or 'Linear,' Programming: A Nonmathematical Exposition." *American Economic Review* 43: 797–825.

Dorfman, Robert. 1960. "Operations Research." *American Economic Review* 50: 575–86.

Dorfman, Robert. 1963. "An Economic Strategy for West Pakistan." *Asian Survey* 3: 217–23.

Dorfman, Robert. 1974. "The Technical Basis for Decision-Making." In *The Governance of Common Property Resources*, ed. by Edwin T. Haefele, 5–25. Baltimore: The Johns Hopkins Press for Resources for the Future.

Dorfman, Robert. 1978. "Forty Years of Cost-Benefit Analysis." In *Econometric Contributions to Public Policy*, ed. by Richard Stone and William Peterson, 268–84. New York: Macmillan.

Dorfman, Robert. 1996. "Why Benefit-Cost Analysis Is Widely Disregarded and What to Do about It." *Interfaces* 16: 1–6. Reprinted in *Economic Theory and Public Decisions*, ed. by Robert Dorfman. Cheltenham, UK: Elgar, 1997.

Dorfman, Robert. 1997. "Introduction." In *Economic Theory and Public Decisions*, ed. by Robert Dorfman, xiii–xxxiii. Cheltenham, UK: Edward Elgar.

Dorfman, Robert, Paul Samuelson, and Robert M. Solow. 1958. *Linear Programming and Economic Analysis*. New York: McGraw-Hill.

Drèze, J. 1962. *"L'utilité sociale d'une vie humaine." Revue Française de Recherche Opérationnelle* 22: 139–55.

Dublin, Louis, and Alfred Lotka. 1930. *The Money Value of a Man*. New York: Ronald Press.

Dufwenberg, Martin, and Glenn W. Harrison. 2008. "Peter Bohm: Father of Field Experiments." *Experimental Economics* 11(3): 213–20.

Eckstein, Otto. 1957. "Investment Criteria for Economic Development and the Theory of Intertemporal Welfare Economics." *Quarterly Journal of Economics* 71: 56–85.

Eckstein, Otto. 1958. *Water-Resource Development: The Economics of Project Evaluation*. Cambridge, MA: Harvard University Press.

Eckstein, Otto. 1961. "A Survey of the Theory of Public Expenditure Criteria." In *Public Finances: Needs, Sources and Utilization*, ed. by James M. Buchanan, 439–504. Princeton: Princeton University Press.

Edwards, José M. 2010. *Joyful Economists: Remarks on the History of Economics and Psychology from the Happiness Studies Perspective*. PhD Dissertation, Université Paris I Panthéon-Sorbonne.

Ehrlich, Paul R., and Anne Ehrlich. 1968. *The Population Bomb*. New York: Ballentine Books.

Ekelund, Robert B. Jr., and Robert F. Hébert. 1978. "French Engineers, Welfare Economics, and Public Finance in the Nineteenth Century." *History of Political Economy* 10(4): 636–68.

Ekelund, Robert B., Jr., and Robert F. Hébert. 1985. "Consumer Surplus: The First Hundred Years." *History of Political Economy* 17: 419–54.

Ekelund, Robert B., Jr., and Robert F. Hébert. 1999. *The Secret Origins of Modern Microeconomics: Dupuit and the Engineers*. Chicago: University of Chicago Press.

Ellis, Howard S. 1950. "The Economic Way of Thinking." *American Economic Review* 40: 1–12.

Ellis, Howard S. 1953. "Is Group Choice a Part of Economics? Further Comment." *Quarterly Journal of Economics* 67(4): 609–13.

Ellis, Howard S., and William Fellner. 1943. "External Economies and Diseconomies." *American Economic Review* 33(3): 493–511.

Ely, Richard T. 1893. *Outlines of Economics*. New York: Meadville Penna.

Ely, Richard T. 1908. *Outlines of Economics*, 2nd ed. With Thomas S. Adams, Max O. Lorenz, and Allyn A. Young. New York: Macmillan.

Ely, Richard T. 1918a. "Conservation and Economic Theory." In *The Foundations of National Prosperity: Studies in the Conservation of Permanent National Resources*, ed. by Richard T. Ely, Ralph H. Hess, Charles K. Leith, and Thomas Nixon Carver, 3–68. New York: Macmillan.

Ely, Richard T. 1918b. "Preface." In *The Foundations of National Prosperity: Studies in the Conservation of Permanent National Resources*, ed. by Richard T. Ely, Ralph H. Hess, Charles K. Leith, and Thomas Nixon Carver, v–vii. New York: Macmillan.

Ely, Richard T. 1938. *Ground Under Our Feet: An Autobiography*. New York: Macmillan.

Ely, Richard T., and Edward W. Morehouse. 1924. *Elements of Land Economics*. New York: Macmillan.

Ely, Richard T., and George S. Wehrwein. 1940. *Land Economics*. New York: Macmillan.

Emmett, Ross B. 2008. "Frank H. Knight's Criticism of Henry George." *American Journal of Economics and Sociology* 67(1): 61–66.

Enthoven, Alain. 2019. "How Systems Analysis, Cost-Effectiveness Analysis, or Benefit-Cost Analysis First Became Influential in Federal Government Program Decision-Making." *Journal of Benefit-Cost Analysis* 10(2): 146–55.

Etner, François. 1987. *Histoire du calcul économique en France*. Paris: Economica.

Ewert, Sara E. Dant. 2001. "Evolution of an Environmentalist: Senator Frank Church and the Hells Canyon Controversy." *Montana: The Magazine of Western History* (Spring): 36–51.

Ezekiel, Mordecai. 1937. "The Broadening Field of Agricultural Economics." *Journal of Farm Economics* 19: 96–101.

Federal Inter-Agency River Basin Committee (FIARBC), Subcommittee on Benefits and Costs. 1950. *Proposed Practices for Economic Analysis of River Basin Projects*. Report of the Subcommittee on Benefits and Costs. Washington, DC.

Federal Inter-Agency River Basin Committee (FIARBC), Subcommittee on Benefits and Costs. 1958. *Proposed Practices for Economic Analysis of River Basin Projects*. Report of the Subcommittee on Evaluation Standards. Washington, DC.

Fein, Rashi. 1958. *Economics of Mental Illness*. New York: Basic Books.

Fenichel, Eli P., and Joshua K. Abbott. 2014. "Natural Capital: From Metaphor to Measurement." *Journal of the Association of Environmental and Resource Economists* 1(1/2): 1–27.

Fernow, Bernard E. 1891. "Practicability of an American Forest Administration." *Publications of the American Economic Association* 6(3): 75–101.

Fernow, Bernard E. 1902. *Economics of Forestry*. New York: Thomas E. Crowell & Co.

Fernow, Bernard E. [1907]. 1913. *A Brief History of Forestry: In Europe, the United States, and Other Countries*. Toronto: University Press.

Finch, Adam, and Jeroen van den Bergh. 2022. "Assessing the Authenticity of National Carbon Prices: A Comparison of 31 Countries." *Global Environmental Change* 74: 102525.

Fischel, William A. 2006. "Footloose at Fifty: An Introduction to the Tiebout Anniversary Essays." In *The Tiebout Model at Fifty: Essays in Public Economics in Honor of Wallace Oates*, ed. by William A. Fischel, 1–20. Cambridge, MA: Lincoln Institute of Land Policy.

Fisher, Anthony C., and John V. Krutilla. 1974. "Valuing Long Run Ecological Consequences and Irreversibilities." *Journal of Environmental Economics and Management* 1(2): 96–108.

Fisher, Anthony C., and Frederick M. Peterson. 1976. "The Environment in Economics: A Survey." *Journal of Economic Literature* 14(1): 1–33.

Fisher, Anthony C., John V. Krutilla, and Charles J. Cicchetti. 1972. "The Economics of Environmental Preservation: A Theoretical and Empirical Analysis." *American Economic Review* 62(4): 605–19.

Fisher, Anthony C., John V. Krutilla, and Charles J. Cicchetti. 1974. "The Economics of Environmental Preservation: Further Discussion." *American Economic Review* 64(6): 1030–39.

Fisher, Franklin M., Zvi Griliches, and Carl Kaysen. 1962. "The Cost of Automobile Model Changes since 1949." *Journal of Political Economy* 70(5): 433–51.

Fleurbaey, Marc, and Rossi Abi-Rafeh. 2016. "The Use of Distributional Weights in Benefit-Cost Analysis: Insights from Welfare Economics." *Review of Environmental Economics and Policy* 10(2): 286–307.

Fleury, Jean-Baptiste. 2010. "Drawing New Lines: Economists and Other Social Scientists on Society in the 1960s." In *The Unsocial Social Science? Economics and Neighboring Disciplines since 1945*, ed. by Roger E. Backhouse and Philippe Fontaine. *History of Political Economy* 42(S): 315–42. Durham: Duke University Press

Fontaine, Philippe. 2014. "Free Riding." *Journal of the History of Economic Thought* 36(3): 359–76.

Fort, D. M., W.A. Niskanen, A.H. Pascal, and W.F. Sharpe. 1959. "Proposal for a 'Smog Tax'." RAND Corporation paper P-1621-RC.

Fourcade, Marion. 2009. "The Political Valuation of Life: A Comment on W. Kip Viscusi's 'The Devaluation of Life'." *Regulation and Governance* 3: 291–97.

Fourcade, Marion. 2011. "Cents and Sensibility: Economic Valuation and the Nature of 'Nature'." *American Journal of Sociology* 116(6): 1721–77.

Fox, Karl A. 1987. "Agricultural Economics." In *New Palgrave: A Dictionary of Economics*, ed. by John Eatwell, Murray Milgate, and Peter Newman, 55–62. London: Macmillan.

Franco, Marco P. Vianna. 2018. "Searching for a Scientific Paradigm in Ecological Economics: The History of Ecological Economic Thought, 1880s–1930s." *Ecological Economics* 153: 195–203.

Franco, Marco P. Vianna, and Antoine Missemer. 2023. *A History of Ecological Economic Thought*. London: Routledge.

Freeman, A. Myrick, III. 1966. "Adjusted Benefit-Cost Ratios for Six Recent Reclamation Projects." *Journal of Farm Economics* 48: 1002–12.

Freeman, A. Myrick, III. 1967a. "Income Distribution and Planning for Public Investment." *American Economic Review* 57: 494–508.

Freeman, A. Myrick, III. 1967b. "Six Federal Reclamation Projects and the Distribution of Income." *Water Resources Research* 3: 319–32.

Freeman, A. Myrick, III. 1968. "The Relevance of Benefit-Cost Analysis: A Comment on an Exchange." Unpublished manuscript, June. AMP 96.

Freeman, A. Myrick, III. 1969a. "Income Redistribution and Social Choice: A Pragmatic Approach." *Public Choice* 7: 3–21.

Freeman, A. Myrick, III. 1969b. "Project Design and Evaluation with Multiple Objectives." In *The Analysis and Evaluation of Public Expenditures: The PPB System*. A Compendium of papers submitted to the Subcommittee on Economy in Government of the Joint Economic Committee. Vol. 1, 565–78. Washington, DC: Government Printing Office.

Freeman, A. Myrick, III, and Robert H. Haveman. 1970. "Benefit-Cost Analysis and Multiple Objectives: Current Issues in Water Resources Planning." *Water Resources Research* 6: 1533–39.

Freeman, A. Myrick, III, and Robert H. Haveman. 1971. "Water Pollution Control, River Basin Authorities and Economic Incentives: Some Current Policy Issues." *Public Policy* 19: 53–74.

Freeman, A. Myrick III, and Robert H. Haveman. 1972. "Residuals Changes for Pollution Control: A Policy Evaluation." *Science* 177: 322–29.

Freeman, A. Myrick III, and Jeffrey C. Norris. 1988. "Quasi-Optimal Pricing for Cost Recovery in Multiple Purpose Water Resource Projects." In *Environmental Resources and Applied Welfare Economics: Essays in Honor of John V. Krutilla*, ed. by V. Kerry Smith, 119–34. Washington, DC: Resources for the Future.

Friedman, Milton. 1953. "The Methodology of Positive Economics." In *Essays in Positive Economics,* ed. by Milton Friedman, 3–43. Chicago: University of Chicago Press.

Friedman, Milton. 1969. "The Optimum Quantity of Money." In *The Optimum Quantity of Money and Other Essays*, 1–50. Chicago: Aldine.

Friedman, Milton, and L.J. Savage. 1948. "The Utility Analysis of Choices Involving Risk." *Journal of Political Economy* 56(4): 270–304.

Friedman, Milton, and L.J. Savage. 1952. "The Expected Utility Hypothesis and the Measurability of Utility." *Journal of Political Economy* 60(6): 463–74.

Frisch, Ragnar. 1946. "Repercussion Studies at Oslo." *American Economic Review* 38(3): 367–72.

Fromm, Gary. 1965. "Civil Aviation Expenditures." In *Measuring Benefits of Government Investments*, ed. by Robert Dorfman, 172–216. Washington, DC: Brookings.

Fromm, Gary. 1968. "Comments." In *Problems in Public Expenditure Analysis*, ed. by Samuel B. Chase, Jr., 166–76. Washington, DC: Brookings.

Furner, Mary O. 1975. *Advocacy and Objectivity: A Crises in the Professionalization of American Social Science, 1865–1905.* Lexington: University Press of Kentucky.

Furner, Mary O., and Barry Supple, eds. 1990. *The State and Economic Knowledge.* Cambridge: Cambridge University Press.

Gaffney, Mason. 1957. "Concepts of Financial Maturity of Timber and Other Assets." Agricultural Economics Information Series paper no. 62, Raleigh, NC.

Gaffney, Mason. 1961. "Diseconomies Inherent in Western Water Laws: A California Case Study." In *Water and Range Resources and Economic Development of the West*, Proceedings of the Western Agricultural Resource Council. www.masongaffney.org/publications/H3-DiseconomiesInherentinWesternWaterLaws21.CV.CV.pdf.

Gaffney, Mason. 2008. "Keeping Land in Capital Theory: Ricardo, Faustmann, Wicksell, and George." *American Journal of Economics and Sociology* 67(1): 119–41.

Georgescu-Roegen, Nicholas. 1971. *The Entropy Law and the Economic Process.* Cambridge, MA: Harvard University Press.

Giocoli, Nicola. 2003. *Modeling Rational Agents: From Interwar Economics to Early Modern Game Theory.* Cheltenham, UK: Edward Elgar.

Giocoli, Nicola. 2011. "When Low is No Good: Predatory Pricing and US Antitrust Law (1950–1980)." *European Journal of the History of Economic Thought* 18(5): 777–806.

Giocoli, Nicola. 2017. "The (Rail)Road to Lochner: Reproduction Cost and the Gilded Age Controversy over Rate Regulation." *History of Political Economy* 49(1): 31–58.

Giocoli, Nicola. 2018. "'Value Is Not a Fact': Reproduction Cost and the Transition from Classical to Neoclassical Regulation in Gilded Age America." *Journal of the History of Economic Thought* 40(4): 445–70.

Glover, W.H. 1952. *Farm and College.* Madison: The University of Wisconsin Press.

Goldstein, J.R. 1961. "RAND: The History, Operations, and Goals of a Nonprofit Corporation." *Mimeo.* Accessed from www.rand.org/content/dam/rand/pubs/papers/2008/P2236-1.pdf.

Goodwin, Craufurd D. 1981. "The Truman Administration: Toward a National Energy Policy." In *Energy Policy in Perspective: Today's Problems, Yesterday's Solutions*, ed. by Craufurd D. Goodwin, 1–62. Washington, DC: Brookings Institution.

Goodwin, Craufurd D. 1983. "The Value Authority Idea – The Fading of a National Vision." In *TVA: Fifty Years of Grass-Roots Democracy*, ed. by Erwin C. Hargrove and Paul K. Conkin, 263–96. Urbana: University of Illinois Press.

Goodwin, Craufurd D. 2008. "Ecologist Meets Economics: Aldo Leopold, 1887–1948." *Journal of the History of Economic Thought* 30(4): 429–52.

Gordon, H. Scott. 1954. "The Economic Theory of a Common-Property Resource: The Fishery." *Journal of Political Economy* 62(2): 124–42.

Gordon, Irene M., and Jack L. Knetsch. 1979. "Consumer's Surplus Measures and the Evaluation of Resources." *Land Economics* 55(1): 1–10.

Goulder, Lawrence H., and Andrew R. Schein. 2013. "Carbon Taxes Versus Cap and Trade: A Critical Review." *Climate Change Economics* 4(3): 13500103.

Graves, Gregory. 1995. *Pursuing Excellence in Water Planning and Policy Analysis: A History of the Institute for Water Resources*. Report prepared for the US Army Corps of Engineers, Institute for Water Resources.

Gray, L.C. 1913. "The Economic Possibilities of Conservation." *Quarterly Journal of Economics* 27(3): 497–519.

Gray, L.C. 1914. "Rent Under the Assumption of Exhaustibility." *Quarterly Journal of Economics* 28: 466–89.

Gray, L.C., and Mark Regan. 1940. "Needed Points of Development and Reorientation in Land Economic Theory." *Journal of Farm Economics* 22(1): 34–46.

Gray, L.C., Charles L. Stewart, Howard A. Turner, J.T. Sanders, and W.J. Spillman. 1924. "Farm Ownership and Tenancy." In *Yearbook of the Department of Agriculture, 1923*, 507–600. Washington, DC: Government Printing Office.

Greenberg, Kyle, Michael Greenstone, Stephen P. Ryan, and Michael Yankovich. 2022. "The Heterogeneous Value of a Statistical Life: Evidence from US Army Reenlistment Decisions." NBER Working Paper 29104.

Greenstone, Michael, Elizabeth Kopits, and Ann Wolverton. 2013. "Developing a Social Cost of Carbon for US Regulatory Analysis: A Methodology and Interpretation." *Review of Environmental Economics and Policy* 7(1): 23–46.

Griliches, Zvi. 1961. "Hedonic Price Indexes for Automobiles: An Econometric Analysis of Quality Change." In *Price Statistics of the Federal Government*, prepared by the Price Statistics Review Committee of the National Bureau of Economic Research.

Guala, Franceso. 2005. *The Methodology of Experimental Economics*. New York: Cambridge University Press.

Guala, Franceso. 2007. "How to Do Things with Experimental Economics." In *Do Economists Make Markets? On the Performativity of Economics*, ed. by Donald MacKenzie, Fabian Muniesa, and Lucia Siu, 128–62. Princeton: Princeton University Press.

H.M. Treasury. 2003. *The Green Book: Appraisal and Evaluation in Central Government*. www.hm-treasury.gov.uk/d/green_book_complete.pdf.

Haab, Timothy C., Matthew G. Interis, Danield Petrolia, and John C. Whitehead. 2013. "From Hopeless to Curious? Thoughts on Hausman's 'Dubious to Hopeless' Critique of Contingent Valuation." *Applied Economic Perspectives and Policy* 35(4): 593–612.

Hammack, Judd, and Gardner M. Brown. 1974. *Waterfowl and Wetlands: Toward Bioeconomic Analysis*. Baltimore: The Johns Hopkins Press for Resources for the Future.

Hammitt, James K., and Nicolas Treich. 2007. "Statistical vs. Identified Lives in Benefit-Cost Analysis." *Journal of Risk and Uncertainty* 35(1): 45–65.

Hammond, Richard J. 1960. *Benefit-Cost Analysis and Water Pollution Control*. Food Research Institute, Stanford University.

Hammond, Richard J. 1966. "Convention and Limitation in Benefit-Cost Analysis." *Natural Resources Journal* 6 (April): 195–222.

Hampson, Chris. 2010. "Warren County and Environmental Justice: A Community Fighting Back." Senior Thesis, University of North Carolina at Asheville.

Hands, D. Wade, and Philip Mirowski. 1998. "Harold Hotelling and the Neoclassical Dream." In *Economics and Methodology: Crossing Boundaries*, ed. by Roger. E. Backhouse, Daniel M. Hausman, Uskali Mäki, and Andrea Salanti, 322–97. London: Macmillan.

Hanemann, W. Michael. Undated. "Economic Valuation." *Mimeo*. Berkeley: University of California.

Hanemann, W. Michael. 1991. "Willingness-to-Pay vs. Willingness-to-Accept: How Much Can They Differ?" *American Economic Review* 81(3): 635–47.

Hanemann, W. Michael. 1992. "Preface." In *Pricing the European Environment*, ed. by Ståle Navrud, 9–35. New York: Oxford University Press.

Hanemann, W. Michael. 1994. "Valuing the Environment through Contingent Valuation." *Journal of Economic Perspectives* 8(4): 19–43.

Hanemann, W. Michael. 2006. "The Economic Conception of Water." In *Water Crisis: Myth or Reality?* ed. by Peter P. Rogers, M. Ramón Llamas, and Louis Martínez-Cortina, 61–92. London: Taylor & Francis.

Harberger, Arnold C. 1954. "Monopoly and Resource Allocation." *American Economic Review Papers and Proceedings* 44(2): 77–87.

Harberger, Arnold C. [1955] 1974. "The Taxation of Mineral Industries." In *Taxation and Welfare*, 208–17. Chicago: The University of Chicago Press.

Harberger, Arnold C. 1959a. "Using the Resources at Hand More Effectively." *American Economic Review Papers and Proceedings* 49(2): 134–46.

Harberger, Arnold C. 1959b. "The Corporation Income Tax: An Empirical Appraisal." In *Tax Revision Compendium*, Vol. I, submitted to the Committee on Ways and Means. 231–50. Washington, DC: Government Printing Office.

Harberger, Arnold C. [1961] 1974. "The Tax Treatment of Oil Exploration." Paper presented at the Second Energy Institute. In *Taxation and Welfare*, ed. by Arnold C. Harberger, 218–26. Chicago: The University of Chicago Press.

Harberger, Arnold C. 1964a. "The Measurement of Waste." *American Economic Review Papers and Proceedings* 54(3): 58–76.

Harberger, Arnold C. [1964b] 1974. "Taxation, Resource Allocation, and Welfare." In *Taxation and Welfare*, ed. by Arnold C. Harberger, 25–62. Chicago: The University of Chicago Press.

Harberger, Arnold C. 1971. "Three Basic Postulates for Applied Welfare Economics: An Interpretive Essay." *Journal of Economic Literature* 9(3): 785–97.

Hardin, Garrett. 1968. "The Tragedy of the Commons." *Science* 162: 1243–48.

Harrod, R.F. 1938. "Scope and Method in Economics." *The Economic Journal* 48: 383–412.

Harvey, Mark W.T. 1994. *A Symbol of Wilderness: Echo Park and the American Conservation Movement*. Albuquerque: University of New Mexico Press.

Hausman, Jerry A., ed. 1993. *Contingent Valuation: A Critical Assessment*. Amsterdam: North Holland.

Haveman, Robert H. 1965. *Water Resources Investment and the Public Interest*. Nashville: Vanderbilt University Press.

Haveman, Robert H. 1966. "Comment" [on Weisbrod 1966]. In *Problems in Public Expenditure Analysis*, ed. by Samuel B. Chase, Jr., 209–13. Washington, DC: The Brookings Institution.

Haveman, Robert H. 1967. "Benefit-Cost Analysis: Its Relevance to Public Investment Decisions: Comment." *Quarterly Journal of Economics* 81: 695–99.

Haveman, Robert H. 1973. "Efficiency and Equity in Natural Resource and Environmental Policy." *American Journal of Agricultural Economics* 55: 868–78.

Hawley, Ellis W. 1990. "Economic Inquiry and the State in New Era America: Antistatist Corporatism and Positive Statism in Uneasy Coexistence." In *The State and Economic Knowledge*, ed. Mary O. Furner and Barry Supple, 287–324. Cambridge: Cambridge University Press.

Hays, Samuel P. 1959. *Conservation and the Gospel of Efficiency: The Progressive Conservation Movement, 1890–1920*. Cambridge, MA: Harvard University Press.

Hays, Samuel P. 1982. "From Conservation to Environment: Environmental Politics in the United States since World War Two." *Environmental Review* 6(2): 14–41.

Hays, Samuel P. 1987. *Beauty, Health, and Permanence: Environmental Politics in the United States, 1955–1985*. Cambridge: Cambridge University Press.

Heinzerling, Lisa. 2000. "The Rights of Statistical People." *Harvard Environmental Law Review* 24: 189–207.

Henry, John F. 1995. *John Bates Clark: The Making of a Neoclassical Economist*. New York: St. Martin's Press.

Heukelom, Floris. 2012. "Three Explanations for the Kahneman-Tversky Programme of the 1970s." *The European Journal of the History of Economic Thought* 19(5): 797–828.

Hicks, J.R. 1939. "Foundations of Welfare Economics." *Economic Journal* 49: 696–712.

Hicks, J.R. 1941. "The Rehabilitation of Consumers' Surplus." *Review of Economic Studies* 8(2): 108–16.

Hicks, J.R. 1943. "The Four Consumer's Surpluses." *Review of Economic Studies* 11(1): 31–41.

Hicks, J.R. 1946. *Value and Capital*, 2nd ed. Oxford: Clarendon Press.

Hines, Lawrence G. 1958. "Measurement of Recreation Benefits: A Reply." *Land Economics* 34(4): 365–67.

Hirshleifer, Jack. 1950. "Remarks on Bombing Systems Analysis." Memorandum to C.J. Hitch, 15 June. RA D-893-PR.

Hirshleifer, Jack. 1970. *Investment, Interest and Capital*. Englewood Cliffs: Prentice-Hall.

Hirshleifer, Jack, James C. De Haven, and Jerome W. Milliman. 1960. *Water Supply: Economics, Technology, and Policy*. Chicago: University of Chicago Press.

Hitch, Charles. 1953. "Sub-Optimization in Operations Problems." *Journal of the Operations Research Society of America* 1: 87–99.

Hitch, Charles. 1955. "An Appreciation of Systems Analysis." *Journal of the Operations Research Society of America* 3: 466–81.

Hitch, Charles J., and Roland N. McKean. 1960. *Economics of Defense in the Nuclear Age*. Cambridge, MA: Harvard University Press.

Hood, Katherine. 2017. "The Science of Value: Economic Expertise and the Valuation of Human Life in US Federal Regulatory Agencies." *Social Studies of Science* 47(4): 441–65.

Hope, Chris. 2006. "The Marginal Impact of CO_2 from PAGE 2002: An Integrated Assessment Model Incorporating the IPCC's Five Reasons for Concern." *Integrated Assessment Journal* 6(1): 19–56.

Hope, Chris, John Anderson, and Paul Wenman. 1993. "Policy Analysis of the Greenhouse Effect: An Application of the PAGE Model." *Energy Policy* 21(3): 327–38.

Hotelling, Harold. 1931. "The Economics of Exhaustible Resources." *Journal of Political Economy* 39(2): 137–75.

Hotelling, Harold. 1932. "Edgeworth's Taxation Paradox and the Nature of Demand and Supply Functions." *Journal of Political Economy* 40(5): 577–616.

Hotelling, Harold. 1938. "The General Welfare in Relation to Problems of Taxation and of Railway and Utility Rates." *Econometrica* 6(3): 242–69.

Hounshell, David. 1997. "The Cold War, RAND, and the Generation of Knowledge, 1946–1962." *Historical Studies in the Physical and Biological Sciences* 27: 237–67.

Hufschmidt, Maynard A. 1967. "The Harvard Water Program: A Summing Up." In *Water Research*, ed. by Allen V. Kneese and Stephen C. Smith, 441–55. Baltimore: The Johns Hopkins Press for Resources for the Future.

Hufschmidt, Maynard A. 2000. "Benefit-Cost Analysis: 1933–1985." *Water Resources Updates* 116: 42–49.

Jardini, David R. 1996. *Out of the Blue Yonder: The Rand Corporation's Diversification into Social Welfare Research, 1946–1968*. Dissertation, Carnegie-Mellon University.

Jarrett, Henry, ed. 1966a. *Environmental Quality in a Growing Economy*. Baltimore: The Johns Hopkins Press for Resources for the Future.

Jarrett, Henry. 1966b. "Editor's Introduction." In *Environmental Quality in a Growing Economy*, ed. by Henry Jarrett, vii–xv. Baltimore: The Johns Hopkins Press for Resources for the Future.

Johnson, Edwin L. 1967. "A Study in the Economics of Water Quality Management." *Water Resources Research* 3(2): 291–305.

Johnson, Marianne. 2015. "Public Goods, Market Failure, and Voluntary Exchange." In *Market Failure in Context*, ed. by Alain Marciano and Steven G. Medema. *History of Political Economy* 47(S): 174–98. Durham: Duke University Press.

Johnston, Robert J., Kevin J. Boyle, Wiktor Adamowicz, Jeff Bennett, et al. 2017. "Contemporary Guidance for Stated Preference Studies." *Journal of the Association of Environmental and Resource Economists* 4(2): 319–405.

Joint Committee on Conservation. 1909. *Report of the National Conservation Commission*. 3 vols. Washington, DC: Government Printing Office.

Jones-Lee, M.W. 1976. *The Value of Life: An Economic Analysis*. Chicago: The University of Chicago Press.

Jones-Lee, M.W, ed. 1982. *The Value of Life and Safety*. Amsterdam: North-Holland.

Jonsson, Fredrik Albritton. 2013. *Enlightenment's Frontier: The Scottish Highlands and the Origins of Environmentalism*. New Haven: Yale University Press.

Journal of Farm Economics. 1966. "News Notes." 48(1): 177.

Kahneman, Daniel. 1986. "Comments by Professor Daniel Kahneman." In *Valuing Environmental Goods: An Assessment of the Contingent Valuation Method*, ed. by Ronald G. Cummings, David S. Brookshire, and William D. Schulze, 185–94. Totowa, NJ: Rowman & Allanheld.

Kahneman, Daniel, and Jack Knetsch. 1992. "Valuing Public Goods: The Purchase of Moral Satisfaction." *Journal of Environmental Economics and Management* 22: 57–70.

Kahneman, Daniel, and Amos Tversky. 1979. "Prospect Theory: An Analysis of Decision under Risk." *Econometrica* 47(2): 263–91.

Kahneman, Daniel, Jack Knetsch, and Richard H. Thaler. 1990. "Experimental Tests of the Endowment Effect and the Coase Theorem." *Journal of Political Economy* 98(6): 1325–48.

Kahneman, Daniel, Jack Knetsch, and Richard H. Thaler. 1991. "Anomalies: The Endowment Effect, Loss Aversion, and Status Quo Bias." *Journal of Economic Perspectives* 5(1): 193–206.

Kaldor, N. 1939. "Welfare Propositions of Economics and Interpersonal Comparisons of Utility." *The Economic Journal* 49: 549–52.

Kalter, Robert J., and Thomas H. Stevens. 1971. "Resource Investments, Impact Distribution, and Evaluation Concepts." *American Journal of Agricultural Economics* 53: 206–215.

Kalter, Robert J., W.B. Lord, D.J. Allee, E.N. Castle, et al. 1969. *Criteria for Federal Evaluation of Resource Investments*. Water Resource and Marine Science Center, Cornell University.

Kaplan, Fred. 1983. *The Wizards of Armageddon*. New York: Simon and Schuster.

Kaufman, Bruce E. 2017. "The Origins and Theoretical Foundation of Original Institutional Economics Reconsidered." *Journal of the History of Economic Thought* 39(3): 293–322.

Kaufman, Gordon D. 1972. "A Problem for Theology: The Concept of Nature." *Harvard Theological Review* 65(3): 337–66.

Kern, William S. 2003. "McCulloch, Scrope, and Hodgskin: Nineteenth-Century Versions of Julian Simon." *Journal of the History of Economic Thought* 25(3): 289–301.

Kingsland, Sharon E. 1994. "Economics and Evolution: Alfred James Lotka and the Economy of Nature." In *Natural Images in Economic Thought: Markets Read in Tooth and Claw*, ed. by Philip Mirowski, 231–46. Cambridge, UK: Cambridge University Press.

Kirkendall, Richard S. 1963. "L.C. Gray and the Supply of Agricultural Land." *Agricultural History* 37(4): 206–14.

Klarman, Herbert E. 1965. *The Economics of Health*. New York: Columbia University Press.

Klein, Judy L., and Mary S. Morgan. 2001. *The Age of Economic Measurement*. Supplement to vol. 33 of *History of Political Economy*. Durham: Duke University Press.

Kneese, Allen V. 1956. *An Industry Study Approach to the Problem of Exclusive Dealing*. Dissertation, Indiana University.

Kneese, Allen V. 1960. "Normative Problems in the Evaluation of Water-Resources Development Projects." *Southwestern Social Sciences Quarterly* 40(4): 301–13.

Kneese, Allen V. 1962. *Water Pollution – Economic Aspects and Research Needs*. Washington, DC: Resources for the Future.

Kneese, Allen V. 1964. *The Economics of Regional Water Quality Management.* Baltimore: The Johns Hopkins Press for Resources for the Future.

Kneese, Allen V. 1968. "The 'Problem Shed' as a Unit for Environmental Control." *Archives of Environmental Health* 16: 124–27.

Kneese, Allen V. 1969. "Statement of Allen V. Kneese, Director, The Quality of the Environment Program for Resources for the Future, Inc." In *Economic Analysis and the Efficiency of Government: Hearings before the Subcommittee on Efficiency of Government of the Joint Economic Committee,* 91st Cong., 342–9.

Kneese, Allen V. 1971a. "Background for the Economic Analysis of Environmental Pollution." *Swedish Journal of Economics* 73(1): 1–24.

Kneese, Allen V. 1971b. "Environmental Pollution: Economics and Policy." *American Economic Review* 61(2): 153–66.

Kneese, Allen V. 1988. "Three Decades of Water Resources Research: A Personal Perspective." In *Environmental Resources and Applied Welfare Economics: Essays in Honor of John V. Krutilla,* ed. by V. Kerry Smith, 45–55. Washington, DC: Resources for the Future.

Kneese, Allen V., and Blair T. Bower. 1968. *Managing Water Quality: Economics, Technology, Institutions.* Baltimore: The Johns Hopkins Press for Resources for the Future.

Kneese, Allen V., and Karl-Göran Mäler. 1973. "Bribes and Charges in Pollution Control: An Aspect of the Coase Controversy." *Natural Resources Journal* 13: 705–15.

Kneese, Allen V., and Kenneth C. Nobe. 1962. "The Role of Economic Evaluation in Planning for Water Resource Development." *Natural Resources Journal* 2: 445–82.

Kneese, Allen V., and Charles L. Schultze. 1975. *Pollution, Prices, and Public Policy.* Washington, DC: The Brookings Institution.

Kneese, Allen V., Robert U. Ayres, and Ralph C. d'Arge. 1970. *Economics and the Environment: A Materials Balance Approach.* Baltimore: Johnsons Hopkins University Press for Resources for the Future.

Knetsch, Jack L. 1963. "Outdoor Recreation Demands and Benefits." *Land Economics,* November: 387–396.

Knetsch, Jack L. 1964. "Economics of Including Recreation as a Purpose of Eastern Water Projects." *Journal of Farm Economics* 46(5): 1148–57.

Knetsch, Jack L. 1989. "The Endowment Effect and Evidence of Nonreversible Indifference Curves." *American Economic Review* 79(5): 1277–84.

Knetsch, Jack L. 2003. Personal telephone conversation. May 15th.

Knetsch, Jack L., and Robert K. Davis. 1966. "Comparisons of Methods for Recreation Evaluation." In *Water Research,* ed. by Allen V. Kneese and Stephen C. Smith, 125–42. Baltimore: The Johns Hopkins Press for Resources for the Future.

Knetsch, Jack L., and J.A. Sinden. 1984. "Willingness to Pay and Compensation Demanded: Experimental Evidence of an Unexpected Disparity in Measures of Value." *Quarterly Journal of Economics* 99(3): 507–21.

Knetsch, Jack L., Robert H. Haveman, Charles W. Howe, John V. Krutilla, and Michael F. Brewer. 1969. *Federal Natural Resources Development: Basic Issues in Benefit and Cost Measurement.* Natural Resources Policy Center. Washington, DC: George Washington University.

Knight, Frank H. 1924. "Some Fallacies in the Interpretation of Social Cost." *Quarterly Journal of Economics* 38(4): 582–606.

Knight, Frank H. 1944. "Realism and Relevance in the Theory of Demand." *Journal of Political Economy* 52(4): 289–318.

Knight, Frank H. 1953. "Is Group Choice a Part of Economics? Comment." *Quarterly Journal of Economics* 67(4): 605–9.

Krutilla, John V. 1955. "Criteria for Evaluating Regional Development Programs." *American Economic Review Papers & Proceedings* 45(2): 120–32.

Krutilla, John V. 1962. "Welfare Aspects of Benefit-Cost Analysis." *Journal of Political Economy* 69(3): 226–35.

Krutilla, John V. 1967a. "Conservation Reconsidered." *American Economic Review* 57(4): 777–86.

Krutilla, John V. 1967b. "Some Environmental Effects of Economic Development." *Daedalus* 96(4): 1058–70.

Krutilla, John V. 1981. "Reflections of an Applied Welfare Economist." *Journal of Environmental Economics and Management* 8: 1–10.

Krutilla, John V., and Charles J. Cicchetti. 1972. "Evaluating Benefits of Environmental Resources with Special Application to the Hells Canyon." *Natural Resource Journal* 12: 1–28.

Krutilla, John V., and Otto Eckstein. 1958. *Multiple Purpose River Development: Studies in Economic Analysis*. Baltimore: The Johns Hopkins Press for Resources for the Future.

Krutilla, John V., and Anthony C. Fisher. 1975. *The Economics of Natural Environments: Studies in the Valuation of Commodity and Amenity Resources*. Baltimore: The Johns Hopkins Press for Resources for the Future.

Kula, E. 1998. *History of Environmental Economic Thought*. London: Routledge.

Kumekawa, Ian. 2017. *The First Serious Optimist: A.C. Pigou and the Birth of Welfare Economics*. Princeton: Princeton University Press.

Kuznets, Simon. 1948. "On the Valuation of Social Income: Reflections on Professor Hicks' Article." *Economica* 15 (February, May): 1–16, 116–31.

Lagueux, Maurice. 2010. "The Residual Character of Externalities." *European Journal of the History of Economic Thought* 17(4): 957–73.

Lancaster, Kelvin J. 1966. "A New Approach to Consumer Theory." *Journal of Political Economy* 74(2): 132–57.

Landsberg, Hans H. 1964. *Natural Resources for US Growth: A Look Ahead to the Year 2000*. Baltimore: The Johns Hopkins Press for Resources for the Future.

Landsberg, Hans H. 1987. "Resources for Freedom – In Retrospect." In *Resources for Freedom: Summary of Volume I of a Report to the President*, 83–94. Washington, DC: Resources for the Future.

Landsberg, Hans H., Leonard L. Fischman, and Joseph L. Fisher. 1963. *Resources in America's Future: Patterns of Requirements and Availabilities, 1960–2000*. Baltimore: The Johns Hopkins Press for Resources for the Future.

Landsberg, Hans H., and Sam H. Schurr. 1968. *Energy in the United States: Sources, Uses, and Policy Issues*. New York: Random House for Resources for the Future.

Lane, Richard. 2014. *The Nature of Growth: The Postwar History of the Economy, Energy, and the Environment*. Dissertation, University of Sussex.

Lave, Lester B. 1968. "Safety in Transportation: The Role of Government." *Law and Contemporary Problems* 33(3): 512–35.

Leonard, Bryan, and Gary D. Libecap. 2019. "Collective Action by Contract: Prior Appropriation and the Development of Irrigation in the Western United States." *Journal of Law and Economics* 62(1): 67–115.

Leonard, Robert J. 1991. "War as a 'Simple Economic Problem:' The Rise of an Economics of Defense." In *Economics and National Security*, ed. by Craufurd D. Goodwin. *History of Political Economy* 23(S): 261–83. Durham: Duke University Press.

Leonard, Robert J. 2010. *Von Neumann, Morgenstern, and the Creation of Game Theory: From Chess to Social Science, 1900–1960*. Cambridge: Cambridge University Press.

Leonard, Robert. 2019. "E.F. Schumacher and the Making of 'Buddhist Economics,' 1950–1973." *Journal of the History of Economic Thought* 41(2): 159–86.

Leonard, Thomas C. 2016. *Illiberal Reformers*. Princeton: Princeton University Press.

Leopold, Aldo. [1933] 1991. "The Conservation Ethic." Reprinted in *The River of the Mother of God and Other Essays*, ed. by Susan L. Flader and J. Baird Callicott, 181–92. Madison: University of Wisconsin Press.

Leopold, Aldo. 1934. "Conservation Economics." *Journal of Forestry* 32(5): 537–44.

Leopold, Aldo. 1939. "A Biotic View of Land." *Journal of Forestry* 37(9): 727–30.

Leopold, Aldo. [1949] 1987. *A Sand County Almanac and Sketches Here and There*. New York: Oxford University Press.

Levy, David M. 1999. Interview with Arnold Harberger. www.minneapolisfed.org/pubs/region/99-03/harberger.cfm. Accessed July 17, 2007.

Lin, Qi Feng. 2014. "Aldo Leopold's Unrealized Proposals to Rethink Economics." *Ecological Economics* 108: 104–14.

Linnerooth, Joanne. 1982. "Murdering Statistical Lives…?" In *The Value of Life and Safety*, ed. by M.W. Jones-Lee, 229–61. Amsterdam: North-Holland.

List, John A. 2003. "Does Market Experience Eliminate Market Anomalies?" *Quarterly Journal of Economics* 118(1): 41–71.

Little, I.M.D. 1950. *A Critique of Welfare Economics*. Oxford: Oxford University Press.

Loehman, Edna, and Andrew Whinston. 1974. "An Axiomatic Approach to Cost Allocation for Public Investment." *Public Finance Quarterly* 2(2): 236–50.

Lynd, Robert S. 1939. *Knowledge for What? The Place for Social Science in American Culture*. Princeton: Princeton University Press.

Lyons, Barrow. 1955. *Tomorrow's Birthright: A Political and Economic Interpretation of our Natural Resources*. New York: Funk and Wagnalls.

Maas, Harro. 2021. "Politicizing the Environment: (In)direct Inference, Rationality, and the Credibility of the Contingent Valuation Method." In *Exploring the History of Statistical Inference in Economics*, ed. by Jeff Biddle and Marcel Boumans. *History of Political Economy* 53(S): 293–323. Durham: Duke University Press.

Maas, Harro, and Mary S. Morgan, eds. 2012. *Observing the Economy*. Durham: Duke University Press.

Maas, Harro, and Andrej Svorenčík. 2017. "Fraught with Controversy: Organizing Expertise on Contingent Valuation." *History of Political Economy* 49(2): 315–45.

Maass, Arthur. 1951. *Muddy Waters: The Army Engineers and the Nation's Rivers*. Cambridge, MA: Harvard University Press.

Maass, Arthur. 1966. "Benefit-Cost Analysis: Its Relevance to Public Investment Decisions." *Quarterly Journal of Economics* 80: 208–26.

Maass, Arthur. 1967. "Reply." *Quarterly Journal of Economics* 81: 700–2.

Maass, Arthur. 1970. "Public Investment Planning in the United States: Analysis and Critique." *Public Policy* 18: 211–43.

Maass, Arthur. 1989. "Interview with Professor Arthur Maass." *Water Resources People and Issues*. www.usace.army.mil/inet/usace-docs/eng-pamphlets/ep870-1-35/basic.pdf.

Maass, Arthur, and David C. Major. 1970. "Economics in Regional Water Research and Policy: Comment." *American Journal of Agricultural Economics* 52: 144–45.

Maass, Arthur, Maynard M. Hufschmidt, Robert Dorfman, Harold A. Thomas, Jr., Stephen A. Marglin, and Gordon Maskew Fair. 1962. *Design of Water-Resource Systems: New Techniques for Relating Economic Objectives, Engineering Analysis, and Governmental Planning*. Cambridge, MA: Harvard University Press.

MacDonald, Dwight. 1956. *The Ford Foundation: The Men and the Millions*. New York: Reynal.

MacKenzie, Donald, Fabian Muniesa, and Lucia Siu, eds. 2007. *Do Economists Make Markets? On the Performativity of Economics*. Princeton: Princeton University Press.

Major, David C. 1969. "Benefit-Cost Ratios for Projects in Multiple Objective Investment Programs." *Water Resources Research* 5(6): 1174–78.

Major, David C. 1975. "Appraising Proposed Federal Standards for Water Resources Investment." *Science* 187: 79–80.

Major, David C. 1977. *Multiobjective Water Resource Planning*. Washington, DC: American Geophysical Union.

Marciano, Alain. 2013. "Why Market Failures are Not a Problem: James Buchanan on Market Imperfections, Voluntary Cooperation, and Externalities." *History of Political Economy* 45(2): 223–54.

Marglin, Stephen A. 1963a. "The Social Rate of Discount and the Optimal Rate of Investment." *Quarterly Journal of Economics* 77: 95–111.

Marglin, Stephen A. 1963b. "The Opportunity Costs of Public Investment." *Quarterly Journal of Economics* 77: 274–89.

Marglin, Stephen A. 1967. *Public Investment Criteria: Benefit-Cost Analysis for Planned Economic Growth*. Cambridge, MA: MIT Press.

Margolis, Julius. 1969. "Secondary Benefits, External Economies, and Justification of the Public Interest." In *The Analysis and Evaluation of Public Expenditures: The PPB System*. A Compendium of papers submitted to the Subcommittee on Economy in Government of the Joint Economic Committee. Vol. 1, 284–91. Washington, DC: Government Printing Office.

Marschak, Jacob. 1950. "Rational Behavior, Uncertainty Prospects, and Measurable Utility." *Econometrica* 18: 111–41.

Marshall, Alfred. [1920] 1946. *The Principles of Economics*, 8th ed. New York: Macmillan.

McCauley, Douglas J. 2006. "Selling Out on Nature." *Nature* 443(7): 27–28.

McCloskey, Deirdre. 1983. "The Rhetoric of Economics." *Journal of Economic Literature* 21(2): 481–517.

McDean, Harry C. 1983. "Professionalism, Policy, and Farm Economists in the early Bureau of Agricultural Economics." *Agricultural History* 57: 64–82.

McDonald, John F. 2013. "Pigou, Knight, Diminishing Returns, and Optimal Pigouvian Congestion Tolls." *Journal of the History of Economics Thought* 35(3): 353–72.

McFadden, Daniel. 1999. "Rationality for Economists?" *Journal of Risk and Uncertainty* 19: 73–105.

McFadden, Daniel. 2013. "The *New* Science of Pleasure: Consumer Choice Behavior and the Measurement of Well-Being." In *Handbook of Choice Modelling*, ed. by S. Hess and A.J. Daly, 7–48. Cheltenham, UK: Edward Elgar.

McFadden, Daniel, and Gregory K. Leonard. 1993. "Issues in the Contingent Valuation of Environmental Goods." In *Contingent Valuation: A Critical Assessment*, ed. by Jerry A. Hausman, 165–216. Amsterdam: North Holland.

McGee, W.J. 1909. "Water Resources." *Report of the National Conservation Commission*, vol. I, 39–49. Washington, DC: Government Printing Office.

McKean, Roland N. 1958. *Efficiency in Government through Systems Analysis: With Emphasis on Water Resources Development*. New York: John Wiley & Sons.

McKean, Roland N. 1963. "Cost-Benefit Analysis and British Defence Expenditure." *Scottish Journal of Political Economy* 10: 17–35.

Meade, J.E. 1952. "External Economies and Diseconomies in a Competitive Situation." *Economic Journal* 62: 54–67.

Meadows, Donella H., Dennis L. Meadows, Jorgen Randers, and William W. Behrens. 1972. *The Limits to Growth: A Report for the Club of Rome's Project on the Predicament of Mankind*. New York: Universe Books.

Medema, Steven G. 2009. *The Hesitant Hand: Taming Self-Interest in the History of Economic Ideas*. Princeton: Princeton University Press.

Medema, Steven G. 2014a. "The Curious Treatment of the Coase Theorem in the Environmental Economics Literature, 1960–1979." *Review of Environmental Economics and Policy* 8(1): 39–57.

Medema, Steven G. 2014b. "1966 and All That: Codification, Consolidation, Creep, and Controversy in the Early History of the Coase Theorem." *Journal of the History of Economic Thought* 36(3): 271–303.

Medema, Steven G. 2020a. "'Exceptional and Unimportant'? Externalities, Competitive Equilibrium, and the Myth of a Pigovian Tradition." *History of Political Economy* 52(1): 135–70.

Medema, Steven G. 2020b. "The Coase Theorem at Sixty." *Journal of Economic Literature* 58(4): 1045–128.

Medema, Steven G. 2020c. "Embracing at Arm's Length: Ronald Coase's Uneasy Relationship with the Chicago School." *Oxford Economic Papers* 72(4): 1072–90.

Medema, Steven G. 2021. "Taking Root: The Early Reception of Coase's Argument." *Mimeo*. Durham, NC: Duke University.

Meine, Curt. 2010. *Aldo Leopold: His Life and Work*. Madison: University of Wisconsin Press.

Merewitz, Leonard. 1966. "Recreational Benefits of Water Resource Development." *Water Resources Research* 2: 625–40.

Merewitz, Leonard. 1968. "Estimation of Recreational Benefits at Selected Water Development Sites in California." *Annals of Regional Science* 2: 249–73.

Meyer, John M. 1997. "Gifford Pinchot, John Muir, and the Boundaries of Politics in American Thought." *Polity* 30(2): 267–84.

Mill, John Stuart. [1848] 1987. *Principles of Political Economy with some of Their Applications to Social Philosophy*, ed. by William Ashley. Fairfield: Augustus M. Kelley.

Mill, John Stuart. 1874. *Nature, the Utility of Religion, and Theism*. London: Longmans, Green, Reader, and Dyer.

Millennium Ecosystem Assessment. 2005. *Ecosystems and Human Well-Being: Synthesis*. Washington, DC: Island Press.

Miller, Char. 1992. "The Greening of Gifford Pinchot." *Environmental History Review* 16(3): 1–20.

Miller, Char. 2001. *Gifford Pinchot and the Making of Modern Environmentalism*. Washington, DC: Island Press.

Milliman, Jerome W. 1956. "Commonality, the Price System, and Use of Water Supplies." *Southern Economic Journal* 22(4): 426–37.

Mills, Edwin S. 1966. "Economic Incentives in Air Pollution Control." In *The Economics of Air Pollution*, ed. by Harold Wolozin, 40–50. New York: W.W. Norton & Co.

Mirowski, Philip. 2002. *Machine Dreams: Economics Becomes a Cyborg Science*. Cambridge: Cambridge University Press.

Mirowski, Philip, and D. Wade Hands. 1998. "A Paradox of Budgets: The Postwar Stabilization of American Neoclassical Demand Theory." In *From Interwar Pluralism to Postwar Neoclassicism*, edited by Mary S. Morgan and Malcolm Rutherford. *History of Political Economy* 30(S): 260–92. Durham: Duke University Press.

Mishan, E.J. 1971. "Evaluation of Life and Limb: A Theoretical Approach." *Journal of Political Economy* 79(4): 687–705.

Missemer, Antoine. 2017. "Nicholas Georgescu-Roegen and Degrowth." *European Journal of the History of Economic Thought* 24(3): 493–506.

Missemer, Antoine. 2018. "Natural Capital as an Economic Concept: History and Contemporary Issues." *Ecological Economics* 143: 90–96.

Missemer, Antoine, Marion Gaspard, and Roberto Ferreira da Cunha. 2022. "From Depreciation to Exhaustible Resources: On Harold Hotelling's First Steps in Economics." *History of Political Economy* 54(1): 109–35.

Mitchell, Robert Cameron, and Richard T. Carson. 1989. *Using Surveys to Value Public Goods: The Contingent Valuation Method*. Washington, DC: Resources for the Future.

Mitchell, Wesley C., Simon Kuznets, and Margaret G. Reid. 1944. *Prices and the Cost of Living in Wartime – An Appraisal of the Bureau of Labor Statistics Index of the Cost of Living in 1941–1944*. Report of the President's Committee on the Cost of Living. Washington, DC: Government Printing Office.

Mohai, Paul, David Pellow, and J. Timmons Roberts. 2009. "Environmental Justice." *Annual Review of Environment and Resources* 34: 405–30.

Mohring, Herbert, and Mitchell Harwitz. 1962. *Highway Benefits: An Analytical Framework*. Evanston: Northwestern University Press.

Montgomery, W. David. 1972. "Markets in Licenses and Efficient Pollution Control Programs." *Journal of Economic Theory* 5: 395–418.

Moore, Jamie, and Dorothy Moore. 1989. *The Army Corps of Engineers and the Evolution of Federal Flood Plain Management Policy*. Boulder: Institute of Behavioral Sciences.

Morey, Edward R. 1984. "Confuser Surplus." *American Economic Review* 74(1): 163–73.

Morgan, Mary S. 1990. *The History of Econometric Ideas*. Cambridge: Cambridge University Press.

Morgan, Mary S., and Malcolm Rutherford, eds. 1998. *From Interwar Pluralism to Postwar Neoclassicism*. *History of Political Economy* 30(S). Durham: Duke University Press.

Moscati, Ivan. 2007. "Early Experiments in Consumer Demand Theory: 1930–1970." *History of Political Economy* 39(3): 359–401.

Moulin, Hervé. 2002. "Axiomatic Cost and Surplus Sharing." In *Handbook of Social Choice and Welfare, Vol. 1*, ed. by Kenneth J. Arrow, Amartya K. Sen, and Kotaro Suzumura, 289–357. Amsterdam: North-Holland.

Muir, John. [1875] 1980. "Wild Wool." In *Wilderness Essays*, ed. by Frank Buske, 227–42. Salt Lake City: Peregrine Smith.

Muir, John. [1901] 1980. "The Yellowstone National Park." In *Wilderness Essays*, ed. by Frank Buske, 178–219. Salt Lake City: Peregrine Smith.

Muir, John. [1912] 1989. *The Yosemite*. San Francisco: Sierra Club Books.

Muller, Nicholas Z., Robert Mendelsohn, and William Nordhaus. 2011. "Environmental Accounting for Pollution in the United States Economy." *American Economic Review* 101(5): 1649–75.

Muniesa, Fabian, and Michel Callon. 2007. "Economic Experiments and the Construction of Markets." In *Do Economists Make Markets? On the Performativity of Economics*, ed. by Donald MacKenzie, Fabian Muniesa, and Lucia Siu, 163–89. Princeton: Princeton University Press.

Musgrave, Richard A. 1957. "A Multiple Theory of Budget Determination." *Finanzarchiv* 17(3): 333–43.

Mushkin, Selma J. 1962. "Health as an Investment." *Journal of Political Economy* 70(5): 129–57.

Narassimhan, Easwaran, Kelly S. Gallagher, Stefan Koester, and Julio Rivera Alejo. 2018. "Carbon Pricing in Practice: A Review of Existing Emissions Trading Systems." *Climate Policy* 18(8): 967–91.

Nash, Roderick. 1982. *Wilderness and the American Mind*, 3rd ed. New Haven: Yale University Press.

National Academies of Science, Engineering, and Medicine (NAS). 2017. *Valuing Climate Damages: Updating Estimation of the Social Cost of Carbon Dioxide*. https://nap.nationalacademies.org/catalog/24651/valuing-climate-damages-updating-estimation-of-the-social-cost-of.

National Park Service (NPS), Land and Recreational Planning Division. 1949. *The Economics of Public Recreation: An Economic Study of the Monetary Evaluation of Recreation in the National Parks*. Washington, DC: National Park Service.

Natural Capital Committee. 2015. The State of Natural Capital: Protecting and Improving Natural Capital for Prosperity and Wellbeing London: Natural Capital Committee. https://assets.publishing.service.gov.uk/government/uploads/system/uploads/attachment_data/file/516725/ncc-state-natural-capital-third-report.pdf.

Naylor, D. Keith. 2005. "Pinchot, Gifford." In *The Encyclopedia of Religion and Nature*, ed. by Bron R. Taylor and Jeffrey Kaplan. New York: Thoemmes Continuum, 1280–81.

Neel, Susan Rhoades. 1994. "Newton Drury and the Echo Park Dam Controversy." *Forest & Conservation History* 38(2): 56–66.

Nelson, Robert H. 2010. *The New Holy Wars: Economic Religion vs. Environmental Religion in Contemporary America*. University Park: Pennsylvania State Press.

Nerlove, Marc. 1958. *The Dynamics of Supply: Estimation of Farmers' Response to Price*. Baltimore: The Johns Hopkins Press.

Newton, Julianne Lutz. 2006. *Aldo Leopold's Odyssey*. Washington, DC: Island Press.

Niedercorn, John H., and John F. Kain. 1963. "An Econometric Model of Metropolitan Development." *Papers in Regional Science* 11(1): 123–43.

Nishibayashi, Shogo. 2019. "A.V. Kneese's Water Quality Management Research (1960s), within the History of Environmental Economics." *Journal of the History of Economic Thought* 41(3): 411–31.

Nordhaus, William D. 1992. "An Optimal Transition Path for Controlling Greenhouse Gasses." *Science* 258(5086): 1315–19.

Nordhaus, William D. 2007. "A Review of the Stern Review on the Economics of Climate Change." *Journal of Economic Literature* 45(3): 686–702.

Nordhaus, William D. 2017. "Revisiting the Social Cost of Carbon." *Proceedings of the National Academy of Sciences* 114(7): 1518–23.

Nordhaus, William D. 2018. "Evolution of Modeling of the Economics of Global Warming: Changes in the DICE Model, 1992–2017." *Climatic Change* 148: 623–40.

Nordhaus, William D., and Edward C. Kokkelenberg, eds. 1999. *Nature's Numbers: Expanding the National Economic Accounts to Include the Environment.* Panel on Integrated Environmental and Economic Accounting. National Research Council. Washington, DC: National Academies Press.

Nordhaus, William D., and James Tobin. 1973. "Is Growth Obsolete?" In *The Measurement of Economic and Social Performance*, ed. by Milton Moss, 509–64. New York: National Bureau of Economic Research.

O'Neill, John. 1992. "The Varieties of Intrinsic Value." *The Monist* 75(2): 119–37.

Office of Management and Budget (OMB). 1992. Budget Circular A-94. www.whitehouse.gov/wp-content/uploads/legacy_drupal_files/omb/circulars/A94/a094.pdf.

Office of Management and Budget (OMB). 1993. Budget Circular A-4. www.whitehouse.gov/wp-content/uploads/legacy_drupal_files/omb/circulars/A4/a-4.pdf.

Office of Science Technology and Policy (OSTP), Office of Management and Budget, and Department of Commerce. 2022. *National Strategy to Develop Statistics for Environmental-Economic Decisions.* Public Comment Draft. Washington, DC: The White House. www.whitehouse.gov/wp-content/uploads/2022/08/Natural-Capital-Accounting-Strategy.pdf.

Ostrom, Vincent, and Elinor Ostrom. 1965. "A Behavioral Approach to the Study of Intergovernmental Relations." *Annals of the American Academy of Political and Social Science* 359: 137–46.

Outdoor Recreation Resources Review Commission (ORRRC). 1961. *A Progress Report to the President and to the Congress.*

Panhans, Matthew T., and John D. Singleton. 2017. "The Empirical Economist's Toolkit: From Models to Methods." In *The Age of the Applied Economist: The Transformation of Economics since the 1970s*, ed. by Roger E. Backhouse and Béatrice Cherrier. *History of Political Economy* 49(S): 127–57. Durham: Duke University Press.

Papandreou, Andreas A. 1994. *Externality and Institutions.* Oxford: Oxford University Press.

Parsons, George R. 2017. "Travel Cost Models." In *A Primer on Nonmarket Valuation*, 2nd ed, ed. by Patricia A. Champ, Kevin J. Boyle, and Thomas C. Brown, 187–233. Dordrecht, The Netherlands: Springer.

Payne, John W., James R. Bettman, and David A. Schkade. 1999. "Measuring Constructed Preferences: Toward a Building Code." *Journal of Risk and Uncertainty* 19: 243–70.

Pearce, David. 2002. "An Intellectual History of Environmental Economics." *Annual Review of Energy and the Environment* 27: 57–81.

Persky, Joseph. 1993. "Retrospectives: Consumer Sovereignty." *Journal of Economic Perspectives* 7(1): 183–91.

Phaneuf, Daniel J., and Till Requate. 2017. *A Course in Environmental Economics: Theory, Policy and Practice*. Cambridge: Cambridge University Press.

Pigou, A.C. [1932] 1962. *The Economics of Welfare*, 4th ed. London: Macmillan & Co.

Pinchot, Gifford. 1891. "Government Forestry Abroad." *Publications of the American Economic Association* 6(3): 7–57.

Pinchot, Gifford. 1910. *The Fight for Conservation*. New York: Doubleday, Page, & Co.

Pinchot, Gifford. 1947. *Breaking New Ground*. New York: Harcourt, Brace, & Co.

Pindyck, Robert. 2013. "Climate Change Policy: What Do the Models Tell Us?" *Journal of Economic Literature* 51(3): 860–72.

Pisani, Donald J. 2003. "Federal Reclamation and the American West in the Twentieth Century." *Agricultural History* 77(3): 391–419.

Plassmann, Florenz, and T. Nicolaus Tideman. 2004. "Frank Knight's Proposal to End Distinctions among Factors of Production and His Objection to the Single Tax." *History of Political Economy* 36(3): 505–19.

Plater, Zygmunt J.B. 2013. *The Snail Darter and the Dam: How Pork Barrel Politics Endangered a Little Fish and Killed a River*. New Haven: Yale University Press.

Plott, Charles R. 1993. "Contingent Valuation: A View of the Conference and Associated Research." In *Contingent Valuation: A Critical Assessment*, ed. by Jerry A. Hausman, 467–78. Amsterdam: North Holland.

Plott, Charles R. 1996. "Rational Individual Behaviour in Markets and Social Choice Processes: The Discovered Preference Hypothesis." In *The Rational Foundations of Economic Behaviour*, ed. by Kenneth J. Arrow, Enrico Colombatto, Mark Perlman, and Christian Schmidt, 225–50. New York: St. Martin's Press.

Plott, Charles R., and Kathryn Zeiler. 2005. "The Willingness to Pay-Willingness to Accept Gap, the 'Endowment Effect,' Subject Misconceptions, and Experimental Procedures for Eliciting Valuations." *American Economic Review* 95(3): 530–45.

Plott, Charles R., and Kathryn Zeiler. 2007. "Exchange Asymmetries Incorrectly Interpreted as Evidence of Endowment Effect Theory and Prospect Theory?" *American Economic Review* 97(4): 15–38.

Porter, Theodore M. 1991. "Objectivity and Authority: How French Engineers Reduced Public Utility to Numbers." *Poetics Today* 12(2): 245–65.

Porter, Theodore M. 1995. *Trust in Numbers: The Pursuit of Objectivity in Science and Public Life*. Princeton: Princeton University Press.

Portney, Paul R. 1994. "The Contingent Valuation Debate: Why Economists Should Care." *Journal of Economic Perspectives* 8(4): 3–17.

Potter, Neal, and Francis T. Christy, Jr. 1962. *Trends in Natural Resource Commodities*. Baltimore: The Johns Hopkins Press for Resources for the Future.

Price, Reginald C. 1948. "Review Comments on the Tentative Report and Appendix of the American Society of Civil Engineers' Committee on Cost Allocations for Multiple Purpose Water Projects." Memorandum, April 14. RCP 35.

Proceedings of the Endangered Species Committee, United States Department of the Interior. 1979. http://lawdigitalcommons.bc.edu/darter_materials.

Rader, Benjamin G. 1966. *The Academic Mind and Reform: The Influence of Richard T Ely in American Life*. Lexington: University Press of Kentucky.

Raiffa, Howard. 1969. "Preferences for Multi-Attributed Alternatives." Memorandum RM-5868-DOT/RC. Prepared for U.S. Department of Transportation, Federal Railroad Administration, Office of High Speed Ground Transportation. The RAND Corporation, Santa Monica, California.

Randall, Alan. 1972. "Market Solutions to Externality Problems: Theory and Practice." *American Journal of Agricultural Economics* 54(2): 175–83.

Randall, Alan, and John R. Stoll. 1980. "Consumer's Surplus in Commodity Space." *American Economic Review* 70(3): 449–55.

Randall, Alan, Berry Ives, and Clyde Eastman. 1974. "Bidding Games for Valuation of Aesthetic Environmental Improvements." *Journal of Environmental Economics and Management* 1: 132–49.

Regan, Mark M. 1958. "Sharing Financial Responsibility of River Basin Development." *Journal of Farm Economics* 40(5): 1690–702.

Regan, Mark M., and E.L. Greenshields. 1951. "Benefit-Cost Analysis of Resource Development Programs." *Journal of Farm Economics* 33(4): 866–78.

Regan, Mark M., and E.C. Weitzell. 1947. "Evaluation of Soil and Water Conservation Measures and Programs." *Journal of Farm Economics* 29(4): 1275–94.

Reich, Charles A. 1964. "The New Property." *Yale Law Journal* (April): 733–87.

Rennert, Kevin, Frank Errickson, Brian C. Prest, Lisa Rennels, et al. 2022. "Comprehensive Evidence Implies a Higher Social Cost of CO2." *Nature*. https://doi.org/10.1038/s41586-022-05224-9.

Renshaw, Edward F. 1958 "Economics of Pollution Control." *Sewage and Industrial Wastes* 30(5): 680–88.

Renshaw, Edward F. 1963. "The Management of Ground Water Reserves." *Journal of Farm Economics* 45(2): 285–95.

Resources for the Future (RFF). 1954. *The Nation Looks at Its Resources: Report of the Mid-Century Conference on Resources for the Future*. Washington, DC: Resources for the Future.

Resources for the Future (RFF). 1970. "New Guidelines for Water." *Resources* (Jan.): 15–17.

Resources for the Future (RFF). 1977. *Resources for the Future: The First 25 Years*. Washington, DC: Resources for the Future.

Resources for the Future (RFF). 2001. "In Appreciation of Allen V. Kneese." *Resources* (May). www.resources.org/archives/in-appreciation-dr-allen-v-kneese/.

Revesz, Richard L. 2018. "Regulation and Distribution." *New York University Law Review* 93: 1489–578.

Reynolds, D.J. 1956. "The Cost of Road Accidents." *Journal of the Royal Statistical Society* 119: 393–408.

Rice, Dorothy P., and Barbara S. Cooper. 1967. *American Journal of Public Health* 57(11): 1954–66.

Ridker, Ronald G. 1967. *The Economics of Air Pollution*. New York: Prager.

Robbins, Lionel. 1935. *An Essay on the Nature and Significance of Economic Science*. 2nd ed. London: Macmillan.

Robbins, Lionel. 1938. "Interpersonal Comparisons of Utility: Comment." *Economic Journal* 48: 635–41.

Robertson, Morgan M. 2006. "The Nature that Capital Can See: Science, State, and Market in the Commodification of Ecosystem Services." *Environment and Planning D: Society and Space* 24: 367–87.

Rodgers, Andrew Denny, III. 1951. *Bernhard Eduard Fernow: A Story of North American Forestry*. Princeton: Princeton University Press.

Rolston, Holmes, III. 2002. "Naturalizing Callicott." In *Land, Value, Community: Callicott and Environmental Philosophy*, ed. by Wayne Ouderkirk and Jim Hill, 107–22. Albany: State University of New York Press.

Roosevelt, Theodore. 1908. "Conservation as a National Duty." Speech, May 13th. https://voicesofdemocracy.umd.edu/theodore-roosevelt-conservation-as-a-national-duty-speech-text/.

Røpke, Inge. 2004. "The Early History of Modern Ecological Economics." *Ecological Economics* 50: 293–314.

Rothenberg, Jerome. 1967. *Economic Evaluation of Urban Renewal: Conceptual Foundation of Benefit-Cost Analysis*. Washington, DC: Brookings Institution.

Rowe, Robert D., Ralph C. d'Arge, and David S. Brookshire. 1980. "An Experiment on the Economic Value of Visibility." *Journal of Environmental Economics and Management* 7: 1–19.

Roy, René. 1949. "*De la theorie des choix aux budgets de familles*." *Econometrica* 17(July): 179–86.

Rutherford, Malcolm. 2000. "Understanding Institutional Economics: 1918–1929." *Journal of the History of Economic Thought* 22(3): 277–308.

Rutherford, Malcolm. 2001. "Institutional Economics: Then and Now." *Journal of Economic Perspectives* 15(3): 173–94.

Rutherford, Malcolm. 2011. "The USDA Graduate School: Government Training in Statistics and Economics, 1921–1945." *Journal of the History of Economic Thought* 33(4): 419–47.

Rutherford, Malcolm, and C. Tyler DesRoches. 2008. "The Institutionalist Reaction to Keynesian Economics." *Journal of the History of Economic Thought* 30(1): 29–48.

Sabin, Paul. 2013. *The Bet: Paul Ehrlich, Julian Simon, and Our Gamble over Earth's Future*. New Haven: Yale University Press.

Sager, Lutz. 2019. "The Global Consumer Incidence of Carbon Pricing: Evidence from Trade." GRI Working Paper No. 320. www.cccep.ac.uk/wp-content/uploads/2019/04/working-paper-320-Sager.pdf.

Samuelson, Paul A. 1947. *Foundations of Economic Analysis*. Cambridge, MA: Harvard University Press.

Samuelson, Paul A. 1952. "Spatial Price Equilibrium and Linear Programming." *American Economic Review* 42: 283–303.

Samuelson, Paul A. 1954. "The Pure Theory of Public Expenditure." *Review of Economics and Statistics* 36(4): 387–89.

Sandel, Michael J. 1996. *Democracy's Discontent: America in Search of a Public Philosophy*. Cambridge, MA: Harvard University Press.

Sandmo, Angmar. 2015. "The Early History of Environmental Economics." *Review of Environmental Economics and Policy* 9(1): 43–63.

Sassatelli, Roberta. 2007. *Consumer Culture: History, Theory and Politics*. Los Angeles: Sage Publications.

Sax, Joseph L. 1980. *Mountains without Handrails: Reflections on the Natural Parks*. Ann Arbor: University of Michigan Press.

Schabas, Margaret. 2005. *The Natural Origins of Economics*. Chicago: University of Chicago Press.

Schelling, Thomas C. 1968. "The Life You Save May Be Your Own." In *Problems in Public Expenditure Analysis*, ed. by Samuel B. Chase, Jr., 127–76. Washington, DC: Brookings Institution.

Schelling, Thomas C. 1992. "Some Economics of Global Warming." *American Economic Review* 82(1): 1–14.

Schkade, David A., and John W. Payne. 1994. "How People Respond to Contingent Valuation Questions: A Verbal Protocol Analysis of Willingness to Pay For an Environmental Regulation." *Journal of Environmental Economics and Management* 26(1): 88–109.

Schmid, Allan A. 1967. "Nonmarket Values and Efficiency of Public Investments in Water Resources." *American Economic Review* 57(2): 158–68.

Schmithussen, Franz. 2013. "Three Hundred Years of Applied Sustainability in Forests." *Unasylva* 64: 3–11.

Schröter, Matthias, Christian Albert, Alexandra Marques, Wolke Tobon, et al. 2016. "National Ecosystem Assessments in Europe: A Review." *BioScience* 66(10): 813–28.

Schröter, Matthias, Emma H. Zanden, Alexander P.E. Oudenhoven, Roy P. Remme, et al. 2014. "Ecosystem Services as a Contested Concept: A Synthesis of Critique and Counter-Arguments." *Conservation Letters* 7: 514–23.

Schultz, Theodore W. 1961. "Investment in Human Capital." *American Economic Review* 51(1): 1–17.

Schumacher, Ernest F. 1973. *Small is Beautiful: A Study of Economics as If People Mattered*. New York: Harper and Row.

Scitovsky, Tibor. 1954. "Two Concepts of External Economies." *Journal of Political Economy* 62: 143–51.

Scodari, Paul F., and Ann Fisher. 1988. "How Uncle Sam Values Mortality Risk Reductions." In *Highway Safety: At the Crossroads*, ed. by Robert E. Stammer, 182–98. New York: American Society for Civil Engineers.

Scott, Anthony. 1955. "The Fishery: The Objectives of Sole Ownership." *Journal of Political Economy* 63(2): 116–24.

Sen, Amartya. 1987. *On Ethics and Economics*. Oxford: Basil Blackwell.

Sen, Amartya. 2009. *The Idea of Justice*. Cambridge, MA: Belknap Press.

Sent, Esther-Mirjam. 2007. "Some Like It Cold: Thomas Schelling as a Cold Warrior." *Journal of Economic Methodology* 14: 455–71.

Siehl, George H. 2008. "The Policy Path to the Great Outdoors: A History of the Outdoor Recreation Review Commissions." Discussion Paper 08-44. Washington, DC: Resources for the Future.

Simon, Julian L. 1981. *The Ultimate Resource*. Princeton: Princeton University Press.

Simon, Nathalie B., Chris Dockins, Kelly B. Maguire, Stephen C. Newbold, Alan J. Krupnick, and Laura O. Taylor. 2020. "What's in a Name? A Search for Alternatives to 'VSL'." *Review of Environmental Economics and Policy* 13(1): 155–61.

Simpson, David R., Michael A. Toman, and Robert U. Ayres. 2005. *Scarcity and Growth Revisited*. New York: Routledge.

Singleton, John D. 2015. "Sorting Charles Tiebout." In *Market Failure in Context*, ed. by Alain Marciano and Steven G. Medema. *History of Political Economy* 47(S): 199–226. Durham: Duke University Press.

Smith, Adam. [1776] 1965. *An Inquiry into the Nature and Causes of the Wealth of Nations*, ed. by Edwin Cannan. New York: Modern Library.

Smith, Bruce L.R. 1966. *The RAND Corporation: Case Study of a Nonprofit Advisory Corporation*. Cambridge, MA: Harvard University Press.

Smith, Gerald Alonzo. 1982. "Natural Resource Economic Theory of the First Conservation Movement (1895–1927)." *History of Political Economy* 14(4): 483–95.

Smith, James Allen. 1991. *The Idea Brokers: Think Tanks and the Rise of the New Policy Elite*. New York: Free Press.

Smith, Mark C. 1994. *Social Science in the Crucible: The American Debate over Objectivity and Purpose, 1918–1941*. Durham: Duke University Press.

Smith, V. Kerry, ed. 1979. *Scarcity and Growth Reconsidered*. New York: RFF Press.

Smith, V. Kerry, ed. 1984. *Environmental Policy under Reagan's Executive Order: The Role of Benefit-Cost Analysis*. Chapel Hill: University of North Carolina Press.

Smith, V. Kerry. 1988. "The Influence of Resource and Environmental Problems on Applied Welfare Economics." In *Environmental Resources and Applied Welfare Economics: Essays in Honor of John V. Krutilla*, ed. by V. Kerry Smith, 3–44. Washington, DC: Resources for the Future.

Smith, V. Kerry. 1992. "Arbitrary Values, Good Causes, and Premature Verdicts." *Journal of Environmental Economics and Management* 22(1): 71–89.

Smith, V. Kerry. 2004. "Krutilla's Legacy: Twenty-First-Century Challenges for Environmental Economics." *American Journal of Agricultural Economics* 86(5): 1167–78.

Smith, V. Kerry. 2006. "Fifty Years of Contingent Valuation." In *Handbook of Contingent Valuation*, ed. by Anna Alberini and James R. Kahn, 7–65. Cheltenham, UK: Edward Elgar.

Smith, V. Kerry. 2011. "Inventing Price Systems and Substitutes for Them." *History of Political Economy* 43(2): 347–52.

Smith, V. Kerry. 2015. "Krutilla's Conservation Reconsidered." *Mimeo*.

Smith, V. Kerry, and H. Spencer Banzhaf. 2004. "A Diagrammatic Exposition of Weak Complementarity and the Willig Condition." *American Journal of Agricultural Economics* 86(2): 455–66.

Smith, Vernon L. 1979. "Incentive Compatible Experimental Processes for the Provision of Public Goods." In *Research in Experimental Economics*, ed. by Vernon L. Smith, 59–168. Greenwich: JAI Press.

Smith, Vernon L. 1982. "Markets as Economizers of Information: Experimental Examination of the 'Hayek Hypothesis'." *Economic Inquiry* 20(2): 165–79.

Smout, T.C. 2000. *Nature Contested: Environmental History in Scotland and Northern England since 1600*. Edinburgh: Edinburgh University Press.

Solow, Robert M. 1971. "The Economist's Approach to Pollution and Its Control." *Science* 173: 498–503.

Solow, Robert M. 1993. "Sustainability: An Economist's Perspective." In *Economics of the Environment, Selected Readings*, ed. by Robert Dorfman and Nancy S. Dorfman, 3rd ed., 179–87. New York: Norton.

Spengler, Joseph J. 1968. "The Economics of Safety." *Law and Contemporary Problems* 33(3): 619–38.

Spillman, W.J. 1918. "Work of the Office of Farm Management Relating to Land Classification and Land Tenure." *American Economic Review papers and proceedings* 8(1): 65–71.

Stapleford, Thomas A. 2009. *The Cost of Living in America: A Political History of Economic Statistics, 1880–2000*. Cambridge: Cambridge University Press.

Stapleford, Thomas A. 2011a. "Reconceiving Quality: Political Economy and the Rise of Hedonic Price Indexes." In *Histories on Econometrics*, ed. by Marcel Boumans, Arian Dupont-Kieffer, and Duo Qin. *History of Political Economy* 43(S): 309–28. Durham: Duke University Press.

Stapleford, Thomas A. 2011b. "Aftershocks from a Revolution: Ordinal Utility and Cost-of-Living Indexes." *Journal of the History of Economic Thought* 33(2): 187–222.

Stavins, Robert. 2011. "The Problem of the Commons: Still Unsettled after 100 Years." *American Economic Review* 101: 81–108.

Steiguer, J. Edward de. 2006. *The Origins of Modern Environmental Thought*. Tucson: University of Arizona Press.

Steiner, Peter O. 1969a. "The Public Sector and the Public Interest." In *The Analysis and Evaluation of Public Expenditures: The PPB System*. Vol. 1. A Compendium of papers submitted to the Subcommittee on Economy in Government of the Joint Economic Committee, 13–45. Washington, DC: Government Printing Office.

Steiner, Peter O. 1969b. *Public Expenditure Budgeting*. Washington, DC: Brookings.

Stern, Nicholas. 2007. *The Economics of Climate Change: The Stern Review*. New York: Cambridge University Press.

Stigler, George J. 1946. *Production and Distribution Theories*. New York: Macmillan.

Stigler, George J. 1947. *The Theory of Price*. New York: Macmillan.

Stiglitz, Joseph E., Amartya Sen, and Jean-Paul Fitoussi. 2010. *Mismeasuring Our Lives: Why GDP Doesn't Add Up*. New York: The New Press.

Sturn, Richard. 2010. "'Public Goods' Before Samuelson: Interwar *Finanzwissenschaft* and Musgrave's Synthesis." *European Journal of the History of Economic Thought* 17(2): 279–312.

Suh, Jooyeoun, and Nancy Folbre. 2017. "Time, Money, and Inequality." *Oeconomia* 7(1): 3–24.

Svorenčík, Andrej. 2015. *The Experimental Turn in Economics: A History of Experimental Economics*. Dissertation, University of Utrecht.

Takayama, Takashi, and George G. Judge. 1964. "Equilibrium among Spatially Separated Markets: A Reformulation." *Econometrica* 32(4): 510–24.

Taussig, F.W. 1919. "Price Fixing as Seen by a Price Fixer." *Quarterly Journal of Economics* 33: 205–41.

Taylor, Henry C. 1905. *An Introduction to the Study of Agricultural Economics*. New York: Macmillan.

Taylor, Henry C. 1907. "Economic Problems in Agriculture by Irrigation." *Journal of Political Economy* 15(4): 209–28.

Taylor, Henry C. 1919. *Agricultural Economics*. New York: Macmillan.

Taylor, Henry C. 1922. "The Development of the American Farm Economic Association." *Journal of Farm Economics* 4: 92–99.

Taylor, Henry C., and Anne Dewees Taylor. 1952. *The Story of Agricultural Economics in the United States, 1840–1932*. Ames: Iowa State College Press.
Teele, R.P. 1904. "The Organization of Irrigation Companies." *Journal of Political Economy* 12: 161–78.
Teele, R.P. 1926. "The Financing of Non-Governmental Irrigation Enterprises." *Journal of Land and Public Utility Economics* 2(4): 427–40.
Teele, R.P. 1927. "The Federal Subsidy in Land Reclamation." *Journal of Land & Public Utility Economics* 3(4): 337–42.
Thaler, Richard. 1980. "Toward a Positive Theory of Consumer Choice." *Journal of Economic Behavior and Organization* 1(1): 39–60.
Thaler, Richard, and Sherwin Rosen. 1976. "The Value of Life Saving." In *Household Production and Consumption*, ed. by Nestor E. Terleckyj, 265–98. New York: Columbia University Press for NBER.
The Ford Foundation. 1949. *Report of the Study for the Ford Foundation on Policy and Program*. Detroit: Ford Foundation.
The Ford Foundation. 1953. *The Ford Foundation Annual Report for 1952*. www.fordfoundation.org/about/library/annual-reports/1952-annual-report/.
The Ford Foundation. 1954. *The Ford Foundation Annual Report: 1953*. New York: Ford Foundation.
The President's Materials Policy Commission. 1952. *Resources for Freedom*. A Report to the President. Washington, DC: US Government Printing Office.
Thelen, David P. 1972. *The New Citizenship: Origins of Progressivism in Wisconsin, 1885–1900*. Colombia: University of Missouri Press.
Thurstone, Louis L. 1931. "The Indifference Function." *Journal of Social Psychology* 2(2): 139–67.
Tiebout, Charles M. 1956. "A Pure Theory of Local Expenditures." *Journal of Political Economy* 64(5): 416–24.
Tietenberg, Tom. 2006. *Emissions Trading: Principles and Practice*, 2nd ed. Washington, DC: Resources for the Future.
Tietenberg, Tom. 2010. "Cap-and-Trade: The Evolution of an Economic Idea." *Agricultural and Resource Economics Review* 39(3): 359–67.
Tol, Richard S.J. 1997. "On the Optimal Control of Carbon Dioxide Emissions: An Application of FUND." *Environmental Modeling and Assessment* 2(3): 151–63.
Tol, Richard S.J. 2002. "Estimates of the Damage Costs of Climate Change, Part I: Benchmark Estimates." *Environmental and Resource Economics* 21: 47–73.
Trentmann, Frank. 2016. *Empire of Things: How We Became a World of Consumers, from the Fifteenth Century to the Twenty-First*. New York: HarperCollins.
Trice, Andrew H., and Samuel E. Wood. 1958. "Measurement of Recreation Benefits." *Land Economics* 34(3): 195–207.
Turner, Frederick Jackson. [1893] 1920. "The Significance of the Frontier in American History." In *The Frontier in American History*, ed. by Frederick Jackson Taylor. New York: Henry Holt and Company, 1–38.
Twight, Ben W. 1990. "Bernhard Fernow and Prussian Forestry in America." *Journal of Forestry* 88(2): 21–25.
UK National Ecosystem Assessment. 2011. *UK National Ecosystem Assessment: Synthesis of the Key Findings*. Cambridge: UNEP-WCMC. http://uknea.unep-wcmc.org/Resources/tabid/82/Default.aspx

UmweltBudesamt. 2020. Methodenkonvention 3.1 zur Ermittlung von Umweltkosten. www.umweltbundesamt.de/sites/default/files/medien/1410/publikationen/2020-12-21_methodenkonvention_3_1_kostensaetze.pdf.

United Church of Christ (UCC). 1987. *Toxic Wastes and Race in the United States*. Report of the Commission for Racial Justice. http://uccfiles.com/pdf/ToxicWastes&Race.pdf.

United Nations (UN). 2014. *System of Environmental-Economic Accounting 2012: Central Framework*. New York: United Nations. https://seea.un.org/sites/seea.un.org/files/ seea_cf_final_en.pdf.

United Nations (UN). 2021. *System of Environmental-Economic Accounting: Ecosystem Accounting*. White cover publication, pre-edited text subject to official editing. https://seea.un.org/ecosystem-accounting.

United States Bureau of Economic Analysis (US BEA). 1994. "Integrated Economic and Environmental Satellite Accounts." *Survey of Current Business* 74: 33–49.

United States Department of Agriculture (USDA). 1920. *Annual Report of the Department of Agriculture*. Washington, DC: Government Printing Office.

United States Senate. 1957. Evaluation of Recreation Benefits from Reservoirs. Hearings before a subcommittee of the Committee of Public Works, March 12–14.

Valavanis, Stefan. 1958. "Traffic Safety from an Economist's Point of View." *Quarterly Journal of Economics* 72(4): 477–84.

Van Hise, Charles. 1909. "Address of Dr. Charles Van Hise." *Report of the National Conservation Commission*, vol. I, 178–80. Washington, DC: Government Printing Office.

Viner, Jacob. 1932. "Cost Curves and Supply Curves." *Zeitschrift Für National-ökonomie* 3(1): 23–46.

Viscusi, W. Kip. 1993. "The Value of Risks to Life and Health." *Journal of Economic Literature* 31: 1912–46.

Viscusi, W. Kip. 2009a. "The Devaluation of Life." *Regulation and Governance* 3: 103–27.

Viscusi, W. Kip. 2009b. "Reply to the Comments on 'The Devaluation of Life'." *Regulation and Governance* 3: 306–9.

Viscusi, W. Kip. 2011. "What's to Know? Puzzles in the Literature on the Value of Statistical Life." *Journal of Economic Surveys* 26(5): 763–68.

von Neumann, John, and Oskar Morganstern. 1944. *Theory of Games and Economic Behavior*. Princeton: Princeton University Press.

Wahl, Richard W. 1995. "Redividing the Waters: The Reclamation Act of 1902." *Natural Resources and Environment* (Summer): 31–38.

Wallis, W.A., and Milton Friedman. 1942. "The Empirical Derivation of Indifference Functions." In *Studies in Mathematical Economics and Econometrics in Honor of Henry Schultz*, ed. by Oskar Lange, Francis McIntyre, and Theodore Yntema, 175–89. Chicago: University of Chicago Press.

Walsh, Richard G., Donn M. Johnson, and John R. McKean. 1992. "Benefit Transfer of Outdoor Recreation Demand Studies, 1968–1988." *Water Resources Research* 28(3): 707–13.

Warde, Paul. 2011. "The Invention of Sustainability." *Modern Intellectual History* 8(1): 153–70.

Water Resources Council (WRC). 1962. *Policies, Standards, and Procedures in the Formulation, Evaluation, and Review of Plans for Use and Development of Water and Related Land Resources*. Senate Document 97.

Water Resources Council (WRC). 1964. *Supplement No. 1, Evaluation Standards for Primary Outdoor Recreation Benefits.* (Supplement to *Policies, Standards, and Procedures in the Formulation, Evaluation, and Review of Plans for Use and Development of Water and Related Land Resources.*) Senate Document 97.

Water Resources Council (WRC) Special Task Force. 1969. *Procedures for Evaluation of Water and Related Land Resource Projects.* Report to the Water Resources Council by the Special Task Force. April.

Water Resources Council (WRC) Special Task Force. 1971a. *Proposed Principles and Standards for Planning Water and Land Resources.* Washington, DC: Water Resources Council.

Water Resources Council (WRC) Special Task Force. 1971b. *Procedures for Planning Water and Land Resources: Findings and Recommendations of the Special Task Force.* Washington, DC: US Government Printing Office.

Waugh, Frederick V. 1929. *Quality as a Determinant of Vegetable Prices.* New York: Columbia University Press.

Weintraub, E. Roy. 1991. *Stabilizing Dynamics: Constructing Economic Knowledge.* Cambridge, UK: Cambridge University Press.

Weisbrod, Burton A. 1959. "On the Sovereignty of Consumer, Citizen, and Stockholder." *Southern Economic Journal* 26(2): 156–58.

Weisbrod, Burton A. 1961. *Economics of Public Health: Measuring the Economic Impacts of Diseases.* Philadelphia: University of Pennsylvania Press.

Weisbrod, Burton A. 1964. "Collective-Consumption Services of Individual-Consumption Goods." *Quarterly Journal of Economics* 78(3): 471–77.

Weisbrod, Burton A. 1966. "Income Redistribution Effects and Benefit-Cost Analysis." In *Problems in Public Expenditure Analysis*, ed. by Samuel B. Chase, Jr., 177–209. Washington, DC: The Brookings Institution.

Weitzman, Martin L. 1974a. "Prices vs. Quantities." *Review of Economic Studies* 41(4): 477–91.

Weitzman, Martin L. 1974b. "Free Access vs. Private Ownership as Alternative Systems for Managing Common Property." *Journal of Economic Theory* 8(2): 225–34.

Weitzman, Martin L. 2007. "A Review of the Stern Review on the Economics of Climate Change." *Journal of Economic Literature* 45(3): 703–24.

Wennergren, E. Boyd. 1964. "Valuing Non-Market Priced Recreational Resources." *Land Economics* 43: 303–14.

Whittington, Dale, and V. Kerry Smith. 2020. "The *Ex-Ante* Economic Analysis of Investments in Large Dams: A Brief History." *Water Economics and Policy* 6(4): https://doi.org/10.1142/S2382624X20500101

Willig, Robert D. 1976. "Consumer's Surplus without Apology." *American Economic Review* 66(4): 589–97.

Winch, Donald. 1972. "Marginalism and the Boundaries of Economic Science." *History of Political Economy* 4(2): 325–43.

Winch, Donald. 2006. "The Problematic Theory of the Consumer in Orthodox Economic Thought." In *The Making of the Consumer: Knowledge, Power, and Identity in the Modern World*, ed. by Frank Trentmann, 31–51. Oxford: Berg.

Wohl, Martin. 1968. "A Conceptual Framework for Evaluating Traffic Safety System Measures." RAND report RM-5632-DOT.

Wold, Herman O.A. 1949. "Discussion" [of Roy (1949)]. *Econometrica* 17(July): 187–88.

Wolfe, Linnie Marsh. [1945] 2003. *Son of the Wilderness: The Life of John Muir.* Madison: University of Wisconsin Press.

Wolfe, Roy I. 1964. "Perspective on Outdoor Recreation: A Bibliographical Survey." *Geographical Review* 54(2): 203–39.

Wolloch, Nathaniel. 2017. *Nature in the History of Economic Thought: How Natural Resources Became and Economic Concept.* London: Routledge.

World Bank. 2022. "Carbon Pricing Dashboard." https://carbonpricingdashboard.worldbank.org/.

Worster, Donald. 1994. *Nature's Economy: A History of Ecological Ideas*, 2nd ed. Cambridge: Cambridge University Press.

Worster, Donald. 2008. *A Passion for Nature: The Life of John Muir.* Oxford: Oxford University Press.

Young, Allyn A. 1913. "Review of Pigou's Wealth and Welfare." *Quarterly Journal of Economics* 27(4): 672–86.

Young, Allyn A. 1928. "Increasing Returns and Economic Progress." *Economic Journal* 38: 527–42.

Zeckhauser, Richard. 1989. "Distinguished Fellow: Reflections on Thomas Schelling." *Journal of Economic Perspectives* 3(2): 153–64.

Zimmermann, Michel, and Steve Pye. 2018. "Inequality in Energy and Climate Policies: Assessing Distributional Impact Consideration in UK Policy Appraisal." *Energy Policy* 123: 594–601.

Index

OTHER BOOKS IN THE SERIES

(Continued from Page ii)

JERRY EVENSKY, *Adam Smith's Moral Philosophy: A Historical and Contemporary Perspective on Markets, Law, Ethics, and Culture (2005)*

HARRO MAAS, *William Stanley Jevons and the Making of Modern Economics (2005)*

ANTHONY M. ENDRES, GRANT A. FLEMING, *International Organizations and the Analysis of Economic Policy, 1919–1950 (2002)*

DAVID LAIDLER, *Fabricating the Keynesian Revolution: Studies of the Inter-War Literature on Money, the Cycle, and Unemployment (1999)*

ESTHER-MIRJAM SENT, *The Evolving Rationality of Rational Expectations: An Assessment of Thomas Sargent's Achievements (1998)*

HEATH PEARSON, *Origins of Law and Economics: The Economists' New Science of Law, 1830–1930 (1997)*

ODD LANGHOLM, *The Legacy of Scholasticism in Economic Thought: Antecedents of Choice and Power (1998)*

YUICHI SHIONOYA, *Schumpeter and the Idea of Social Science (1997)*

J. DANIEL HAMMOND, *Theory and Measurement: Causality Issues in Milton Friedman's Monetary Economics (1996)*

WILLIAM J. BARBER, *Designs within Disorder: Franklin D. Roosevelt, the Economists, and the Shaping of American Economic Policy, 1933–1945 (1996)*

JUAN GABRIEL VALDES, *Pinochet's Economists: The Chicago School of Economics in Chile (1995)*

PHILIP MIROWSKI (ed.), *Natural Images in Economic Thought: "Markets Read in Tooth and Claw" (1994)*

MALCOLM RUTHERFORD, *Institutions in Economics: The Old and the New Institutionalism (1994)*

KAREN I. VAUGHN, *Austrian Economics in America: The Migration of a Tradition (1994)*

LARS JONUNG (ed.), *The Stockholm School of Economics Revisited (1991)*

E. ROY WEINTRAUB, *Stabilizing Dynamics: Constructing Economic Knowledge (1991)*

M. JUNE FLANDERS, *International Monetary Economics, 1870–1960: Between the Classical and the New Classical (1990)*

PHILIP MIROWSKI, *More Heat Than Light: Economics as Social Physics, Physics as Nature's Economics (1990)*

MARY S. MORGAN, *The History of Econometric Ideas (1990)*

GERALD M. KOOT, *English Historical Economics, 1870–1926: The Rise of Economic History and Mercantilism (1988)*

KIM KYUN, *Equilibrium Business Cycle Theory in Historical Perspective (1988)*

WILLIAM J. BARBER, *From New Era to New Deal: Herbert Hoover, the Economists, and American Economic Policy, 1921–1933 (1985)*

TAKASHI NEGISHI, *Economic Theories in a Non-Walrasian Tradition (1985)*

Printed in the United States
by Baker & Taylor Publisher Services